Biosafety Measures, Technology Risks and the World Trade Organization

This book examines the work of the World Trade Organization (WTO), with a focus on the capacity of its judiciary to strike a reasoned balance between free trade in biotechnology and biosafety as to promote the 2030 Agenda for Sustainable Development and its Sustainable Development Goals. By adopting an innovative interpretation of the precautionary principle and proportionality analysis, the work offers normative suggestions to develop what the author terms "a constructive bridge of knowledge" between decision-makers, scientists, social experts and expert witnesses, which can support a judicial balance by design rather than by chance.

Biotechnology is sometimes regarded as a panacea for modern-day challenges, such as feeding a growing world population and counteracting climate-change problems, and a means of offering significant economic opportunities. However, biotechnology can present uncertain, though serious, risks to human health and the environment (i.e., biosafety). Trading biotech products magnifies these risks and benefits globally. This book explores the topical, though still underexplored, question of how to find a point of equilibrium between the revolutionary advancement offered by technology and the need to safeguard biosafety from uncertain, though potentially irreversible, technology risks. It offers a thorough analysis of normative, judicial and epistemic issues hindering a reasoned balance between trade and non-trade interests under the WTO. The work offers practical relevance for the resolution of legal disputes in contexts of uncertainty, as well as innovative theoretical contributions.

It will be a valuable resource for policymakers working on precautionary governance and management, scholars in the areas of trade law, human rights law and environmental law, law students and practitioners, as well as NGOs working in the field of new technologies, biosafety, sustainability and food safety.

Alessandra Guida is Lecturer in Climate, Justice & Human Rights | Law and the Challenges of Technology | Corporate Environmental Law | Clinical Law in the School of Law at Queen's University Belfast.

Biosafety Measures, Technology Risks and the World Trade Organization

Thriving and Surviving in the Age of Biotech

Alessandra Guida

Routledge
Taylor & Francis Group
LONDON AND NEW YORK

First published 2023
by Routledge
4 Park Square, Milton Park, Abingdon, Oxon OX14 4RN

and by Routledge
605 Third Avenue, New York, NY 10158

Routledge is an imprint of the Taylor & Francis Group, an informa business

British Library Cataloguing-in-Publication Data
A catalogue record for this book is available from the British Library

ISBN: 978-1-032-35186-5 (hbk)
ISBN: 978-1-032-35187-2 (pbk)
ISBN: 978-1-003-32574-1 (ebk)

DOI: 10.4324/9781003325741

Typeset in Galliard
by Apex CoVantage, LLC

For Stella who enlightened me
and Antonio who completed me

Contents

Acknowledgements xvi
List of treaties and declarations xvii
List of cases xxv
List of figures and tables xxxii
Glossary xxxiv

PART I
Context – international trade in biotechnology 1

1 International trade in biotechnology and protection of biosafety: an uneasy combination 3

PART II
Addressing normative, judicial and epistemic challenges in trading biotechnology under the WTO 39

2 Normative, judicial and epistemic challenges for the WTO: free trade and biosafety 41

3 Proportionality analysis to address WTO normative and judicial challenges in the context of biotechnology 96

4 The precautionary principle to address WTO epistemic challenges in the context of biotechnology 136

PART III
Analysis of WTO biotechnology legal disputes 179

5 Introduction to and key reasons for a critical analysis of WTO biotechnology legal disputes 181

6 Allocation of the burden of proof to establish a prima facie case and standard of review to examine biotechnology matters: preliminary issues in the WTO jurisprudence on biotechnology 200

7 Adopting precautionary measures on biosafety in contexts of sufficient scientific evidence 228

8 Adopting precautionary measures on biosafety in contexts of insufficient scientific evidence 263

PART IV
Final insights 289

9 Conclusion 291

Index 309

Detailed Contents

Acknowledgements xvi
List of treaties and declarations xvii
List of cases xxv
List of figures and tables xxxii
Glossary xxxiv

PART I
Context – international trade in biotechnology 1

1 International trade in biotechnology and protection of biosafety: an uneasy combination 3
1.1 Introduction 3
1.2 Discovering biotechnology: benefits, risks and social issues in trading biotech products 9
1.2.1 Benefits in trading biotech products 9
1.2.1.1 Biotechnology and the reduction of hunger 9
1.2.1.2 Biotechnology and economic development 11
1.2.2 Risks in trading biotech products 12
1.2.2.1 Risks to human health 12
1.2.2.2 Risks to the environment 16
1.2.3 Social issues in trading biotech products 18
1.3 Challenges in international trade in biotechnology 23
1.4 Legal loopholes: the need for proportionality analysis and a precautionary approach 28
1.5 Objectives of the study 31
1.6 Methodology of the study 32
1.7 Scope of the study 34
1.8 Structure of the study 35

PART II
Addressing normative, judicial and epistemic challenges in trading biotechnology under the WTO 39

2 **Normative, judicial and epistemic challenges for the WTO: free trade and biosafety** 41
2.1 Introduction 41
2.2 The WTO: role, mandate and dispute settlement body 42
2.3 Protection of human health and the environment as WTO goals 44
2.4 Requirements to protect human health and the environment under the WTO 46
2.4.1 Ensuring human health and the environment in the context of the GATT Agreement *47*
2.4.1.1 Chapeau of Article XX: general requirements to prevent unjustifiable trade limitations 47
2.4.1.2 Article XX(b) and (g): general exceptions to ensure the protection of health and the environment 48
2.4.2 Ensuring human health and the environment in the context of the SPS *and* TBT Agreements *57*
2.5 Difficulties ensuring human health and the environment under the WTO: an implicit prima facie pre-eminence of free trade 59
2.6 WTO law and other international law regimes: normative antinomies 64
2.6.1 WTO law and international human rights law 65
2.6.1.1 WTO law and the right to health 69
2.6.1.2 WTO law and the right to a healthy environment 76
2.6.2 WTO law and international environmental law 79
2.6.2.1 Responsibility and obligations to address loss of biological diversity 80
2.6.2.2 Responsibility and obligations to address the use of pesticides 84
2.7 WTO judicial and epistemic challenges 88
2.8 Conclusion 94

3 **Proportionality analysis to address WTO normative and judicial challenges in the context of biotechnology** 96
3.1 Introduction 96
3.2 Proportionality: meaning, structure and use of a migrant legal criterion 98

3.2.1 The concept of proportionality 98
3.2.2 The structure of proportionality 99
3.2.3 Migration of proportionality across jurisdictions 101
3.3 Justification to use proportionality analysis in WTO biotechnology cases 103
3.3.1 Proportionality under the WTO 104
3.3.2 Balancing test (or proportionality stricto sensu*) under the WTO 107*
3.3.3 Reasons to apply proportionality analysis to biotechnology cases 111
3.4 The structure of balancing according to Robert Alexy 113
3.5 Proportionality analysis applied to biotechnology scenarios 118
3.6 Refining proportionality analysis: new factors for the balancing process in the context of biotechnology 122
3.6.1 Pro Homine *(or* pro personae*)* principle *as a new factor to establish the abstract weight of the competing interests in the balancing process 123*
3.6.2 Reliability of evidence *as a new factor to determine the reliability of empirical premises in the balancing process 125*
3.6.3 The precautionary principle *as a new criterion to break stalemates and reduce judicial epistemic discretion 131*
3.7 Conclusion 134

4 The precautionary principle to address WTO epistemic challenges in the context of biotechnology 136
4.1 Introduction 136
4.2 Precaution: main features, migration across jurisdictions and implementing dimensions 138
4.2.1 Concept, formulation(s) and elements of precaution 138
4.2.2 Migration of precaution across jurisdictions and its current status 143
4.2.3 Implementation of precaution through three dimensions 146
4.3 Applicability of precaution under the WTO 149
4.3.1 Gateway provisions to precaution in WTO law 149
4.3.1.1 Gateway to precaution in the SPS Agreement *149*
4.3.1.2 Gateway to precaution in the GATT Agreement *154*

4.3.2 Precaution as a key means to achieve the WTO goal of sustainable development 160
4.3.3 Multilateral environmental agreements and the WTO: further implications for precaution in WTO law 163
4.4 Implementing precaution in the context of biotechnology under the WTO 164
4.4.1 Precaution as a balancing and dynamic criterion to address the epistemic issues in the context of biotechnology 165
4.4.1.1 Effectiveness 166
4.4.1.2 Proportionality 166
4.4.1.3 Non-discrimination and consistency 167
4.4.1.4 Costs and benefits 168
4.4.1.5 Re-examination in light of scientific development 168
4.4.2 Precaution and the reversal of the burden of proof to break stalemate cases 171
4.5 Conclusion 176

PART III
Analysis of WTO biotechnology legal disputes 179

5 Introduction to and key reasons for a critical analysis of WTO biotechnology legal disputes 181
5.1 Introduction 181
5.2 1998 EC – Hormones *182*
5.2.1 Case background 182
5.2.2 Key findings 184
5.3 2008 US/Canada – Hormones Continued Suspension *186*
5.3.1 Case background 186
5.3.2 Key findings 188
5.4 2006 EC – Biotech *190*
5.4.1 Case background 190
5.4.2 Key findings 192
5.5 Analytical focus of the case studies 194
5.6 Conclusion 198

6 Allocation of the burden of proof to establish a prima facie case and standard of review to examine biotechnology matters: preliminary issues in the WTO jurisprudence on biotechnology 200
6.1 Introduction 200

6.2 Prima facie case and allocation of the burden of proof in WTO jurisprudence on biotechnology 201
6.2.1 Establishing a prima facie case under the WTO 201
6.2.2 Allocation of the burden of proof to establish a prima facie case and adopt biosafety measures 204
6.2.3 Suggestions for improvements 209
6.3 Standard of review to examine WTO biotechnology cases 212
6.3.1 Standard of review and WTO law 213
6.3.2 (Un)suitability of the standard of review adopted by panels to examine biotechnology legal disputes 214
6.3.3 Suggestions for improvements 220
6.4 Conclusion 226

7 Adopting precautionary measures on biosafety in contexts of sufficient scientific evidence 228
7.1 Introduction 228
7.2 Appropriate risk assessment in the context of sufficient evidence: critical analysis of the criteria under Articles 2.2 and 5.1 of the SPS Agreement *230*
7.2.1 'Scientific principles' under Article 2.2 230
7.2.2 'Sufficiency of scientific evidence' under Article 2.2 231
7.2.3 'Appropriateness of risk assessments' in the sense of Article 5.1 and Annex A(4) 232
7.3 Judicial interpretation of sufficiency of scientific evidence and appropriateness of risk assessment in WTO biotechnology cases 236
7.3.1 Judicial interpretations of appropriateness of risk assessments and sufficiency of scientific evidence do not fit the uncertain nature of biotech disputes 236
7.3.2 Panels' quantitative interpretation of biotechnology risks 239
7.3.3 Panel's arbitrary selection of evidence 243
7.3.4 WTO judicial bodies and their role as gatekeeper in examining scientific evidence and risk assessments 245
7.4 Suggestions for improvements 249
7.4.1 What should make appropriate *a risk assessment in the scientifically uncertain context of biotechnology? 249*
7.4.1.1 Inferences *along with* multiple and positive correlations *to supplement uncertain scientific evidence and to shape risk assessments appropriate to biotechnology circumstances 250*

7.4.1.2 Holistic data *to supplement uncertain scientific evidence and to shape risk assessments appropriate to biotechnology circumstances 254*
7.4.2 Who should advise panels on the reliability of opposing and uncertain risk assessments concerning biotechnology? 257
7.5 Conclusion 261

8 Adopting precautionary measures on biosafety in contexts of insufficient scientific evidence 263
8.1 Introduction 263
8.2 Adopting biosafety measures in cases of insufficient evidence: critical reflections on Article 5.7 of the SPS Agreement *264*
8.3 Judicial interpretation of the role of insufficient evidence in adopting biosafety measures 265
8.4 Suggestions for improvements 271
8.4.1 Standards of proof and the case of biotechnology 272
8.4.2 Evidentiary threshold and the precautionary principle in biotechnology cases 276
8.4.3 Suggestions for an appropriate standard of proof to apply precautionary measures in biotechnology cases: the Bayesian scale of legal evidence and scientific (un)certainties *278*
8.4.3.1 Meaning and purposes of a scale of legal evidence and scientific (un)certainties 278
8.4.3.2 Practical relevance of a scale of legal evidence and scientific (un)certainties *to apply precautionary measures in the context of biotechnology 280*
8.4.4 Complementing the Bayesian scale with frequentist statistics 286
8.5 Conclusion 287

PART IV
Final insights 289

9 Conclusion 291
9.1 Introduction 291
9.2 The complexities surrounding the international trade i n biotechnology 292

9.2.1 *Epistemic, normative and judicial challenges in ensuring biosafety and balancing trade with non-trade interests under the WTO* 292
9.2.2 *Controversial aspects in the judicial examination of biotechnology legal disputes* 293
9.3 *Where to from here: suggestions for a way forward* 296
9.3.1 *Striking a reasoned balance between trade and non-trade interests: proportionality as a solution for* judicial *issues in the context of biotechnology* 296
9.3.2 *Overcoming the normative antinomies between WTO law and other international law regimes: proportionality as a solution for* normative *issues in the context of biotechnology* 296
9.3.3 *Adopting a proportionality analysis in the context of biotechnology* 297
9.3.4 *Handling scientific uncertainties: precaution as a solution for the* epistemic *issues in the context of biotechnology* 298
9.3.5 *Implementing precaution in the context of biotechnology* 300
9.3.6 *Allocating the burden of proof to establish a prima facie case and adopt biosafety measures in the context of biotechnology* 302
9.3.7 *Creating a* bridge of knowledge *between WTO decision-makers and experts of biotechnology* 303
9.3.8 *Refining the concept of appropriateness of risk assessments in the context of biotechnology* 304
9.3.9 *Adopting a* multilevel degree of deference *as a new standard of review to examine biotechnology cases* 304
9.4 *Future research* 305
9.5 *Final observations* 306

Index 309

Acknowledgements

This book arose out of a PhD and would not exist without the support of a number of people that I would like to thank sincerely. In particular, I am indebted to my supervisors Carlos Bernal Pulido, Aline Jaeckel and Kirsten Davies for the extraordinary supervision received, their generous comments on my drafts and their patience in challenging me to produce my best work. My gratitude also goes to George Tomossy, who has been the principal supervisor of my PhD project for almost one year. I am very grateful to have had the chance to work with him.

I would also like to thank Eleanor McGhee and Debbie Loo for making the lives of PhD candidates easier through their tireless work and incredible attitude towards problem solving. Also, I cannot thank enough my dearest colleagues and friends Christina Simmig and Khaled Khwaileh. Our trio gave to me the strength to overcome hurdles that seemed unbearable.

I gratefully acknowledge the financial support for this study provided by Macquarie University for both my master of research and PhD.

A special thanks to my mum, dad, sister and best friend Imma, who always trusted my choices and helped me to go through many storms. You showed me that there are no distances or hard paths, such as the PhD, that can make our bond weak.

Dulcis in fundo, heartfelt thanks to my husband, Antonio, for his incredible capacity of understanding my needs, supporting my ambition and tolerating my long working hours. I could not do what I did without his invaluable support every step of the way. Last but not least, I have to thank my little baby, Stella, who went through the last months of my PhD inside me. Baby, thanks for tolerating the high intake of caffeine, and please always remember that you proved to be able to achieve major breakthroughs. After all, you already handled a PhD in law.

Of course, all errors remain my own. This study is current as of 14 July 2021.

Treaties and declarations

Treaties

1946	*Constitution of the World Health Organization*, signed 22 July 1946, 14 UNTS 185 (entered into force 7 April 1948)
1948	*General Agreement on Tariffs and Trade* (adopted 30 October 1947, entered into force provisionally 1 January 1948) 55 UNTS 187
1952	*International Plant Protection Convention*, opened for signature 1 May 1952 (entered into force 3 April 1952)
1953	*Convention for the Protection of Human Rights and Fundamental Freedoms*, opened for signature 4 November 1950, 213 UNTS 222 (entered into force 3 September 1953), as amended by *Protocol No 14bis to the Convention for the Protection of Human Rights and Fundamental Freedoms*, opened for signature 27 May 2009, CETS No 204 (entered into force 1 September 2009)
1965	*International Convention on the Elimination of All Forms of Racial Discrimination (CERD)*, opened for signature 21 December 1965, 660 UNTS 195 (entered into force 4 January 1969)
1966	*International Convention for the Conservation of Atlantic Tunas (ICCAT)*, opened for signature 14 May 1966, 673 UNTS 63 (entered into force 21 March 1969)
1966	*International Covenant on Economic, Social and Cultural Rights*, opened for signature 16 December 1966, 993 UNTS 3 (entered into force 3 January 1976)
1969	*Vienna Convention on the Law of Treaties*, opened for signature 23 May 1969, 1155 UNTS 331 (entered into force 27 January 1980)
1975	*Convention on International Trade in Endangered Species of Wild Fauna and Flora*, signed 3 March 1973, 993 UNTS 243 (entered into force 1 July 1975)
1979	*Convention on the Elimination of All Forms of Discrimination Against Women* (CEDAW), opened for signature 18 December 1979, 1249 UNTS 13 (entered into force 3 September 1981)

1980	*Convention for the Conservation of Antarctic Marine Living Resources (CCAMLR)*, opened for signature 1 August 1980, UNTS 1329 47 (entered into force 7 April 1982)
1980	*Convention on the Conservation of Antarctic Marine Living Resources*, opened for signature 1 August 1980, 1329 UNTS 47 (entered into force 7 April 1981)
1982	*United Nations Convention on the Law of the Sea*, opened for signature 10 December 1982, 1833 UNTS 3 (entered into force 16 November 1994)
1985	*Vienna Convention for the Protection of the Ozone Layer*, opened for signature 22 March 1985, 1513 UNTS 293 (entered into force 22 September 1988)
1986	*African Charter on Human and Peoples' Rights*, opened for signature 1981, 21 ILM 58 (entered into force 21 October 1986)
1987	*Montreal Protocol on Substances that Deplete the Ozone Layer*, opened for signature 16 September 1987, 1522 UNTS 3 (entered into force 1 January 1989)
1987	*Report of the World Commission on Environment and Development: Our Common Future, UNGA, UN Doc A/42/427 (4 August 1987) ('Brundtland Report')*
1988	*Additional Protocol to the American Convention on Human Rights in the Area of Economic, Social, and Cultural Rights*, opened for signature 17 November 1988, OAS No 69 (entered into force 16 November 1999)
1989	*Basel Convention on the Control of Transboundary Movements of Hazardous Wastes and their Disposal*, opened for signature 23 March 1989, 1673 UNTS 57 (entered into force 5 May 1992)
1989	*Convention on the Rights of the Child* (CRC), opened for signature 20 November 1989, 1577 UNTS 3 (entered into force 2 September 1990)
1990	*International Convention on Oil Pollution Preparedness, Response, and Co-operation*, opened for signature 30 November 1990, 1891 UNTS 51 (entered into force 13 May 1995)
1990	*International Convention on the Protection of the Rights of All Migrant Workers and Members of Their Families*, opened for signature 18 December 1990, 2220 UNTS 3 (entered into force 1 July 2003)
1991	*Convention on the Ban of the Import of Hazardous Wastes into Africa and on the Control of their Transboundary Movements within Africa*, opened for signature 30 January 1991, 30 ILM 773 (entered into force 22 April 1998)
1992	*Convention for the Protection of the Marine Environment of the North East Atlantic*, opened for signature 22 September 1992, 32 ILM 1069 (entered into force 25 March 1998)

1992	*Convention on Biological Diversity Convention on Biological Diversity*, opened for signature 5 June 1992, 1760 UNTS 79 (entered into force 29 December 1993)
1992	*Convention on the Protection of the Marine Environment of the Baltic Sea Area*, opened for signature 9 April 1992, 1507 UNTS 167 (entered into force 17 January 2000)
1992	*North American Free Trade Agreement*, opened for signature 17 December 1992, 32 ILM 605 (1993) (entered into force 1 January 1999)
1992	*United Nations Convention on the Protection and Use of Transboundary Watercourses and International Lakes*, opened for signature 17 March 1992, 31 ILM 1316 (1992) (entered into force 6 October 1996)
1992	*United Nations Framework Convention on Climate Change,* opened for signature 4 June 1992, 1771 UNTS 107 (entered into force 21 March 1994)
1994	*Agreement on Safeguards*, *Marrakesh Agreement Establishing the World Trade Organization*, opened for signature 15 April 1994, 1867 UNTS 3 (entered into force 1 January 1995) Annex 1A
1994	*Agreement on Subsidies and Countervailing Measures (SCM), Marrakesh Agreement Establishing the World Trade Organization*, opened for signature 15 April 1994, 1869 UNTS 14 (entered into force 1 January 1995) Annex 1A
1994	*Agreement on Technical Barriers to Trade, Marrakesh Agreement Establishing the World Trade Organization*, opened for signature 15 April 1994, 1867 UNTS 3 (entered into force 1 January 1995) Annex 1A
1994	*Agreement on the Application of Sanitary and Phytosanitary Measures, Marrakesh Agreement Establishing the World Trade Organization*, opened for signature 15 April 1994, 1867 UNTS 3 (entered into force 1 January 1995) Annex 1A
1994	*Agreement on Implementation of Article VI of the General Agreement on Tariffs and Trade 1994* (Anti-Dumping Agreement)*, Marrakesh Agreement Establishing the World Trade Organization*, opened for signature 15 April 1994, 1867 UNTS 3 (entered into force 1 January 1995) Annex 1A
1994	*Agreement on the Protection of the River Scheldt*, opened for signature 26 April 1994, 34 ILM 851 (1995)
1994	*Agreement on Trade-Related Aspects of Intellectual Property Rights, Marrakesh Agreement Establishing the World Trade Organization*, opened for signature 15 April 1994, 1867 UNTS 3 (entered into force 1 January 1995) Annex 1C
1994	*Agreement on Trade-Related Aspects of Investment Measures, Marrakesh Agreement Establishing the World Trade Organization*, opened for signature 15 April 1994, 1867 UNTS 3 (entered into force 1 January 1995) Annex 1A

1994	*Convention on Cooperation for the Protection and Sustainable Use of the River Danube*, opened for signature 29 June 1994 EMuT 994:49 (entered into force 22 October 1998)
1994	*Dispute Settlement Understanding, Marrakesh Agreement Establishing the World Trade Organization*, opened for signature 15 April 1994, 1867 UNTS 3 (entered into force 1 January 1995) Annex 2
1994	*Energy Charter Treaty*, opened for signature 17 December 1994, 33 ILM 360 (entered into force 16 April 1998)
1994	*General Agreement on Tariffs and Trade 1994, Marrakesh Agreement Establishing the World Trade Organization*, opened for signature 15 April 1994, 1867 UNTS 3 (entered into force 1 January 1995) Annex 1A
1994	*General Agreement on Tariffs and Trade Agreement, Marrakesh Agreement Establishing the World Trade Organization*, opened for signature 15 April 1994, 1867 UNTS 3 (entered into force 1 January 1995) Annex 1A
1994	*General Agreement on Trade in Services, Marrakesh Agreement Establishing the World Trade Organization*, opened for signature 15 April 1994, 1867 UNTS 3 (entered into force 1 January 1995) Annex 1B
1994	*Protocol to the 1979 Convention on Long-Range Transboundary Air Pollution on Further Reduction of Sulphur Emissions*, opened for signature 14 June 1994, UN Doc EB.AIR/R. 84 (entered into force 5 August 1998)
1994	*The WTO Agreement, Marrakesh Agreement Establishing the World Trade Organization*, opened for signature 15 April 1994, 1867 UNTS 3 (entered into force 1 January 1995)
1995	*Agreement for the Implementation of the Provisions of the United Nations Convention on the Law of the Sea of 10 December 1982 relating to the Conservation and Management of Straddling Fish Stocks and Highly Migratory Fish Stocks*, opened for signature 4 August 1995, UN Doc A/CONF.164/38 (entered into force 11 December 2001)
1995	*Agreement on Agriculture, Marrakesh Agreement Establishing the World Trade Organization,* opened for signature 15 April 1994, 1867 UNTS 3 (entered into force 1 January 1995) annex 1A
1995	*Convention to Ban the Importation into Forum Island Countries of Hazardous and Radioactive Wastes and to Control the Transboundary Movement and Management of Hazardous Wastes within the South Pacific Region*, opened for signature 16 September 1995, 2001 ATS 17 (entered into force 21 October 2001)
1996	*Agreement on the Conservation of Cetaceans of the Black Sea, Mediterranean Sea and Contiguous Atlantic Area*, opened for signature 24 November 1996, 36 ILM 777 (entered into force 1 June 2001)

1998	*Convention on Access to Information, Public Participation in Decision-Making and Access to Justice in Environmental Matters*, opened for signature 25 June 1998, 2161 UNTS 447 (entered into force 30 October 2001) ('*Aarhus Convention*')
1998	*Kyoto Protocol to the United Nations Framework Convention on Climate Change*, opened for signature from 16 March 1998 to 15 March 1999, 2303 UNTS 162 (entered into force 16 February 2005)
1998	*Rotterdam Convention on the Prior Informed Consent Procedure for Certain Hazardous Chemicals and Pesticides in International Trade*, opened for signature 11 September 1998, 2244 UNTS 337 (entered into force 24 February 2004)
1999	*Convention on the Protection of the Rhine*, opened for signature 12 April 1999 (2000), *Official Journal of the European Communities* L.289/31
2000	*Cartagena Protocol on Biosafety to the Convention on Biological Diversity*, opened for signature 15 May 2000, 2226 UNTS 208 (entered into force 22 September 2003)
2000	*Cartagena Protocol on Biosafety to the Convention on Biological Diversity*, opened for signature 15 May 2000, 2226 UNTS 208 (entered into force 22 September 2003)
2000	*Communication from the Commission on the precautionary principle*, COM/2000/0001 final
2000	*Convention on the Conservation and Management of Highly Migratory Fish Stocks in the Western and Central Pacific Ocean*, opened for signature 5 September 2000, ATNIF 11 (entered into force on 19 June 2004)
2001	*International Treaty on Plant Genetic Resources for Food and Agriculture*, opened for signature 3 November 2001 (entered into force 29 June 2004)
2001	*Stockholm Convention on Persistent Organic Pollutants*, opened for signature 23 May 2001, 2256 UNTS 119 (entered into force 17 May 2004)
2002	*Resolution 2 Plan of Implementation of the World Summit on Sustainable Development, A/CONF.199/20 (4 September 2002)*
2005	*World Summit Outcome, GA Res 60/1, UN GAOR, 60th sess, 8th plen mtg, Agenda Items 46 and 120, Supp No 49, UN Doc A/RES/60/1 (24 October 2005)*
2006	*International Tropical Timber Agreement*, opened for signature 3 April 2006, 2797 UNTS 75 (entered into force 7 December 2011)
2007	*Convention on the Rights of Persons with Disabilities*, opened for signature 30 March 2007, 2515 UNTS 3 (entered into force 3 May 2008)

2007	*Treaty of Lisbon amending the Treaty on European Union and the Treaty establishing the European Community*, opened for signature 13 December 2007 [2007] OJ C 306/01 (entered into force 1 December 2009)
2009	*Agreement on Port State Measures to Prevent, Deter and Eliminate Illegal, Unreported and Unregulated Fishing*, opened for signature 22 November 2009, 129 STAT 664 (entered into force June 5, 2016)
2011	*Nagoya Protocol on Access to Genetic Resources and the fair and equitable sharing of benefits arising from their utilization to the convention on biological diversity*, opened for signature 2 February 2011, Doc. UNEP/CBD/COP/DEC/X/1 (entered into force 12 October 2014)
2013	*Minamata Convention on Mercury*, opened for signature 10–11 October 2013 (entered into force 16 August 2017)
2016	*Comprehensive Economic and Trade Agreement (CETA) between Canada, of the one part, and the European Union and its Member States, of the other part*, opened for signature 30/10/2016, [2016] OJ L 11/23 (Provisional application 21 September 2017)
2019	*Agreement between the United States of America, the United Mexican States, and Canada* [2019] https://ustr.gov/trade-agreements/free-trade-agreements/united-states-mexico-canada-agreement/agreement-between

Declarations

1948	*Universal Declaration of Human Rights, GA Res 217A (III), UN GAOR, UN Doc A/810 (10 December 1948)*
1972	*Stockholm Declaration* (Report of the United Nations Conference on the Human Environment, Stockholm, 5–16 June 1972, A/Conf.48/14/Corr. 1, 11 ILM 1416 (1972))
1984	*Ministerial Declaration of the First International Conference on the Protection of the North Sea* (Bremen, 31 October–1 November 1984)
1986	*Declaration on the Right to Development, GA Res 41/128* (4 December 1986)
1986	*Vienna Declaration on Human Rights and Programme of Action, GA Res 41/128* (4 December 1986)
1987	*Ministerial Declaration of the Second International Conference on the Protection of the North Sea* (London, 24–25 November 1987)
1990	*Baltic Sea Declaration* (Ronneby, 3 September 1990)
1990	*Bergen Ministerial Declaration on Sustainable Development in the European Commission for Europe (ECE) Region*, UN Doc A/CONF.151/PC/10 (1990)

1990	*Declaration on Environmentally Sound and Sustainable Development in Asia and the Pacific*, UN Doc A/CONF.151/PC38 (16 October 1990)
1990	*Ministerial Declaration of the Third International Conference on Protection of the North Sea* (The Hague, 8 March 1990)
1992	*Rio Declaration on Environment and Development* (adopted 14 June 1992) 31 ILM 874
1993	*Ministerial Declaration on the Protection of the Black Sea*, 7 April 1993
1993	*Vienna Declaration and Programme of Action Adopted by the World Conference on Human Rights in Vienna* (25 June 1993), *GA Res 36/133* (14 December 1981)
1994	*Ministerial Declaration of the Seventh Trilateral Government Conference on the Protection of the Wadden Sea*, 30 November 1994
1995	*Ministerial Declaration of the Fourth International Conference on Protection of the North Sea* (Esbjerg, 8–9 June 1995)
1998	*Declaration on the Protection of the Marine Environment of the Baltic Sea, adopted on 15 February 1988 in Helsinki by the Ministers Responsible for the Environmental Protection of the Baltic Sea States*
2000	*Malmo Ministerial Declaration, First Global Ministerial Environment Forum – Sixth Special Session of the Governing Council of the United Nations Environment Programme*, 5th plen mtg (29–21 May 2000)
2001	*Ministerial Declaration*, WTO Doc WT/MIN(01)/DEC/1 (20 November 2001, adopted on 14 November 2001)
2002	*International Law Association New Delhi Declaration of Principles of International Law Relating to Sustainable Development*, UN Doc. A/CONF.199/8 (9 August 2002)
2002	*Ministerial Declaration of the Fifth International Conference on the Protection of the North Sea* (Bergen, 20 and 21 March 2002)
2002	*Report of the World Summit on Sustainable Development, CONF, 17th plen mtg, UN Doc A/CONF 199L 1 (4 September 2002) Resolution 1 Political Declaration, annex ('Johannesburg Declaration on Sustainable Development')*
2009	*Implementation of Agenda 21, the Programme for the Further Implementation of Agenda 21 and the outcomes of the World Summit on Sustainable Development*, GA Res A/RES/64/236, UN GAOR, 64th session, 68th plen mtg, Agenda item 53 (a), Un Doc 64/236 (24 December 2009)
2010	*Berne Declaration, Canadian Council for International Co-operation & Misereor, Human Rights Impact Assessment for Trade and Investment Agreements* (Report of the Expert Seminar, 23–24 June 2010)
2010	*World People's Conference on Climate Change and the Rights of Mother Earth* (2010); *Universal Declaration of the Rights of Mother Earth*

2012	*The Future We Want,* GA Res 66/288, UN GAOR, 66th sess, 123rd plen mtg, Agenda Item 19, UN Doc A/Res/66/288 (27 July 2012)
2015	*Declaration of the 3rd National Congress of Physicians in the Crop-Sprayed Towns* (Presidents Medardo Avila-Vazquez and Miryam Gorban) 2016 IJHNFM: International Journal of Human Nutrition and Functional Medicine (26 November 2015)

Cases

International Court of Justice

Case Concerning the Pulp Mills on the River Uruguay (Argentina v. Uruguay) (Judgment) [2010] ICJ Rep 71

Gabčíkovo-Nagymaros Project (Hungary-Slovakia) (Judgment) [1997] ICJ Rep 7

Military and Paramilitary Activities in and against Nicaragua (Nicaragua v United States of America) (Judgment) [1986] ICJ Rep 14

North Sea Continental Shelf Cases (Federal Republic of Germany/Denmark; Federal Republic of Germany/Netherlands) (Judgment) [1969] ICJ Rep 3

Nuclear Tests (New Zealand v. France) (Judgment) [1995] ICJ Rep 288

Pulp Mills on the River Uruguay (Argentina v. Uruguay) (Judgment) [2010] ICJ Rep 14

World Trade Organization

Appellate Body Report, *Australia – Measures Affecting Importation of Salmon*, WTO Doc WT/DS18/AB/R (20 October 1998) ('*Australia – Salmon*')

Appellate Body Report, *Australia – Measures Affecting the Importation of Apples from New Zealand*, WTO Doc WT/DS367/AB/R (29 November 2010) ('*Australia – Apples*')

Appellate Body Report, *Brazil Measures Affecting Imports of Retreaded Tyres*, WTO Doc WT/DS332/AB/R (3 December 2007) ('*Brazil – Retreaded Tyres*')

Appellate Body Report, *Canada – Certain Measures Affecting the Automotive Industry*, WTO Doc WT/DS139/AB/R, WT/DS142/AB/R (31 May 2000) ('*Canada – Autos*')

Appellate Body Report, *Canada – Continued Suspension of Obligations in the EC – Hormones Dispute*, WTO Doc WT/DS321/AB/R (16 October 2008) ('*Canada – Continued Suspension*')

Appellate Body Report, *Canada – Dairy (Article 21.5-New Zealand and US II)*, WTO Doc WT/DS103/AB/RW2 WT/DS113/AB/RW2 (20 December 2002) ('*Canada – Dairy*')

Appellate Body Report, *Canada – Measures Affecting the Export of Civilian Aircraft*, WTO Doc WT/DS70/AB/R (2 August 1999) ('*Canada – Aircraft*')

Appellate Body Report, *Canada – Measures Relating to Exports of Wheat and Treatment of Imported Grain*, WTO Doc WT/DS276/AB/R (30 August 2004) ('*Canada – Wheat Exports and Grain Imports*')

Appellate Body Report, *Chile – Price Band System and Safeguard Measures Relating to Certain Agricultural Products (Article 21.5-Argentina)*, WTO Doc WT/DS207/AB/RW (7 May 2007) ('*Chile – Price Band System (Article 21.5-Argentina)*')

Appellate Body Report, *China – Measures Related to the Exportation of Various Raw*, WTO Doc WT/DS394, 395, and 398/AB/R (22 February 2012) ('*China – Raw Materials*')

Appellate Body Report, *China – Measures Related to the Exportation of Rare Earths, Tungsten, and Molybdenum*, WTO Doc WT/DS431/AB/R WT/DS432/AB/R WT/DS433/AB/R (7 August 2014) ('*China – Rare Earths*')

Appellate Body Report, *Dominican Republic – Measures Affecting the Importation and Internal Sale of Cigarettes*, WTO Doc WT/DS302/AB/R (25 April 2005) ('*Dominican Republic – Import and Sale of Cigarettes*')

Appellate Body Report, *European Communities – Conditions for the Granting of Tariff Preferences to Developing Countries*, WTO Doc WT/DS246/AB/R (7 April 2004) ('*EC – Tariff Preferences*')

Appellate Body Report, *European Communities – Measures Affecting Asbestos and Asbestos-Containing Products*, WTO Doc WT/DS135/AB/R (5 April 2001) ('*EC – Asbestos*')

Appellate Body Report, *European Communities – Measures Concerning Meat and Meat Products (Hormones)*, WTO Doc WT/DS26/AB/R-WT/DS48/AB/R (16 January 1998) ('*EC – Hormones*')

Appellate Body Report, *Japan – Measures Affecting Agricultural Products*, WTO Doc WT/DS76/AB/R, AB-1998–8 (22 February 1999) ('*Japan – Agricultural Products II*')

Appellate Body Report, *Japan – Measures Affecting Importation of Apples*, WTO Doc WT/DS245/AB/R (26 November 2003) ('*Japan – Apples*')

Appellate Body Report, *Japan – Taxes on Alcoholic Beverages*, WTO Doc WT/DS8/AB/R, WT/DS10/AB/R, WT/DS11/AB/R (4 October 1996) ('*Japan – Alcoholic Beverages II*').

Appellate Body Report, *Korea – Import Bans, and Testing and Certification Requirements for Radionuclides*, WTO Doc WT/DS495/AB/R (11 April 2019) [5.106] ('*Korea – Radionuclides*')

Appellate Body Report, *Korea – Taxes on Alcoholic Beverages*, WTO Doc WT/DS75/AB/R WT/DS84/AB/R (18 January 1999) ('*Korea – Alcoholic Beverages*')

Appellate Body Report, *Korea – Measures Affecting Imports of Fresh, Chilled and Frozen Beef*, WTO Doc WT/DS161/AB/R, WT/DS169/AB/R (11 December 2000) ('*Korea – Various Measures on Beef*')

Appellate Body Report, *United States – Anti-Dumping Measures on Certain Hot-Rolled Steel Products from Japan*, WTO Doc WT/DS184/AB/R (24 July 2001) ('*US – Hot Rolled Steel*')

Appellate Body Report, *United States – Import Prohibition of Certain Shrimp and Shrimp Products*, WTO Doc WT/DS58/AB/R (6 November 1998) ('*US – Shrimp*')

Appellate Body Report, *United States – Investigation of the International Trade Commission in Softwood Lumber from Canada – Recourse to Article 21.5 of the DSU by Canada*, WTO Doc WT/DS277/AB/RW (13 April 2006) ('*US – Softwood Lumber VI (Article 21.5-Canada*')

Appellate Body Report, *United States – Standards for Reformulated and Conventional Gasoline*, WTO Doc WT/DS2/AB/R (29 April 1996) ('*US – Gasoline*')

Appellate Body Report, *United States – Certain Measures Relating to Shrimp From Thailand*, WTO Doc WT/DS343/AB/R (16 July 2008) ('*US – Shrimp (Thailand)*')

Appellate Body Report, *United States – Continued Suspension of Obligations in the EC-Hormones Dispute*, WTO Doc WT/DS320/AB/R (21 March 2008) ('*US/Canada – Hormones Continued Suspension*')

Appellate Body Report, *United States – Countervailing Duties on Certain Corrosion-Resistant Carbon Steel Flat Products from Germany*, WTO Doc WT/DS213/AB/R (28 November 2002) ('*US – Carbon Steel*')

Appellate Body Report, *United States – Customs Bond Directive for Merchandise Subject to Anti-Dumping/Countervailing Duties*, WTO Doc WT/DS345/AB/R (16 July 2008) ('*US – Customs Bond Directive*')

Appellate Body Report, *United States – Definitive Safeguard Measures on Imports of Circular Welded Carbon Quality Line Pipe from Korea*, WTO Doc WT/DS202/AB/R (15 February 2002) ('*US – Line Pipe*')

Appellate Body Report, *United States – Import Prohibition of Certain Shrimp and Shrimp Products, Recourse to Article 21.5 of the DSU by Malaysia*, WTO Doc WT/DS58/AB/RW, AB-1998–4 (22 October 2001) ('*US – Shrimp (Article 21.5-Malaysia)*')

Appellate Body Report, *United States – Measures Affecting Imports of Woven Wool Shirts and Blouses from India*, WTO Doc WT/DS33/AB/R (25 April 1997) ('*US – Wool Shirts and Blouses*')

Appellate Body Report, *United States – Measures Affecting the Cross-Border Supply of Gambling and Betting Services*, WTO Doc WT/DS285/AB/R (7 April 2005) ('*US – Gambling*')

Appellate Body Report, *United States – Oil Country Tubular Goods Sunset Reviews*, WTO Doc WT/DS268/AB/R (29 November 2004) ('*US – Oil Country Tubular Goods Sunset Reviews*')

Appellate Body Report, *United States – Section 211 Omnibus Appropriations Act of 1998*, WTO Doc WT/DS176/AB/R (1 February 2002) ('*US – Section 211 Appropriations Act*')

Appellate Body Report, *United States – Standards for Reformulated and Conventional Gasoline*, WTO Doc WT/DS2/AB/R (29 April 1996) ('*US – Gasoline*')

Appellate Body Report, *United States – Transitional Safeguard Measure on Combed Cotton Yarn from Pakistan*, WTO Doc WT/DS192/AB/R (8 October 2001) ('*US – Cotton from Pakistan*')

Panel Report, *Australia – Certain Measures Concerning Trademarks, Geographical Indications and Other Plain Packaging Requirements Applicable to Tobacco Products and Packaging*, WTO Doc WT/DS435/R, WT/DS441/R WT/DS458/R, WT/DS467/R (28 June 2018) ('*Australia – Tobacco Plain Packaging (Indonesia)*')

Panel Report, *Australia – Measures Affecting Importation of Salmon*, WTO Doc WT/DS18/R (12 June 1998) ('*Australia – Salmon*')

Panel Report, *Brazil Measures Affecting Imports of Retreaded Tyres*, WTO Doc WT/DS332/R (12 June 2007) ('*Brazil – Retreaded Tyres*')

Panel Report, *Brazil – Certain Measures Concerning Taxation and Charges*, WTO Doc WT/DS472/R WT/DS497/R (30 August 2017) ('*Brazil – Taxation*')

Panel Report, *Canada/Japan – Tariff on Imports of Spruce, Pine, Fir (SPF) Dimension Lumber*, WTO Doc L/6470–36S/167 (19 July 1989) ('*Canada/Japan – Tariff on Imports*')

Panel Report, *Canada – Continued Suspension of Obligations in the EC-Hormone Dispute*, WTO Doc WT/DS321/R (31 March 2008) ('*Canada – Continued Suspension*')

Panel Report, *China – Measures Related to the Exportation of Various Raw Materials*, WTO Doc WT/DS394/R, WT/DS395/R, WT/398/R (5 July 2011) ('*China – Raw Materials*')

Panel Report, *European Communities – Conditions for the Granting of Tariff Preferences to Developing Countries*, WTO Doc WT/DS246/R (1 December 2003) ('*EC – Tariff Preferences*')

Panel Report, *European Communities – Measures Concerning Meat and Meat Products (Hormones) Complaint by the United States*, WTO Doc WT/DS26/R/USA (18 August 1997) ('*EC – Hormones*')

Panel Report, *European Communities – Measures Affecting the Approval and Marketing of Biotech Products*, WTO Doc WT/DS291/R-WT/DS292/R-WT/DS293/R (29 September 2006) ('*EC – Biotech*')

Panel Report, *Indonesia – Measures Concerning the Importation of Chicken Meat and Chicken Products*, WTO Doc WTO Doc WT/DS484/R (17 October 2017) ('*Indonesia – Chicken*')

Panel Report, *Japan – Measures Affecting Importation of Apples*, WTO Doc WT/DS245/R (15 July 2003) ('*Japan – Apples*')

Panel Report, *Japan-Measures Affecting the Importation of Apples-Recourse to Article 21.5 of the DSU by the United States*, WTO Doc WT/DS245/RW (23 June 2005) ('*Japan – Apples (Article 21.5)*')

Panel Report, *Korea – Import Bans, and Testing and Certification Requirements for Radionuclides*, WTO Doc WT/DS495/R (22 February 2018) ('*Korea – Radionuclides*')

Panel Report, *Russian Federation – Measures on the Importation of Live Pigs, Pork and Other Pig Products from the European Union*, WTO Doc WT/DS475/R (19 August 2016) ('*Russia – Pigs (EU)*')

Panel Report, *Spain – Tariff Treatment of Unroasted Coffee*, WTO Doc L/5135–28S/102 (11 June 1981) ('*Spain – Coffee*')

Panel Report, *Thailand – Restrictions on Importation of and Internal Taxes on Cigarettes*, WTO Doc WT/DS10/R – 37S/200 (7 November 1990) ('*Thai – Cigarettes*')

Panel Report, *United States – Measures Affecting the Production and Sale of Clove Cigarettes*, WTO Doc WT/DS406/R (2 September 2011) ('*US – Clove Cigarettes*')

Panel Report, *United States – Measures Concerning the Importation, Marketing and Sale of Tuna and Tuna Products*, WTO Doc WT/DS381/R (15 September 2011) ('*US – Tuna II*')

Panel Report, *United States – Restrictions on Imports of Tuna*, WTO Doc WT/DS29/R (16 June 1994) ('*Tuna – Dolphin II*')

Panel Report, *United States – Continued Suspension of Obligations in the EC-Hormones Dispute*, WTO Doc WT/DS320/R (31 March 2008) ('*US/Canada – Hormones Continued Suspension*')

Panel Report, *United States – Measures Affecting the Importation of Animals, Meat and Other Animal Products from Argentina*, WTO Doc WT/DS447/R (24 July 2015) ('*US – Animals*')

Panel Report, *United States – Restrictions on Imports of Tuna*, WTO Doc DS21/R – 39S/155 (3 September 1991) ('*Tuna – Dolphin*')

Panel Report, *United States – Taxes on Automobile*, WTO Doc WT/DS31/R (11 October 1994) ('*US – Taxes*')

European Court of Justice

Artegodan and Others v Commission (T-74/00, T-76/00, T-83/00 to T-85/00, T-132/00, T-137/00 and T-141/00) [2002] ECR II-4948

Commission v Denmark (C-192/01) [2003] ECR I-9724

Commission v Denmark (Danish Bottles) (C-302/86) [1988] ECR 4607

Commission v Germany (Beer Purity) (C-178/84) [1987] ECR 1227

Dow AgroSciences v European Commission (T-475/07) [2008] ECR 214

Giorgio Fidenato and Others (Case C-111/16) [2017] ECR 431

Gowan Comércio Internacional e Serviços Lda v Ministero della Salute (C-77/09) [2010] ECR I–13555

Greenpeace France and Others (Case C-6/99) [2000] ECR148

Land Oberösterreich and Republic of Austria v Commission of the European Communities (439/05 P – 454/05 P) [2007] ECR 510 ('*Austrian case*')

Monsanto Agricoltura Italia SpA and Others v Presidenza del Consiglio dei Ministri and Others (Case C-236/01) [2003] ECR 431 ('*Monsanto Italy*')
Monsanto SAS et al. v Ministre de l'Agriculture et de la Pêche (Case 58/10 – Case 68/10) ECR [2011] 553 ('*France Monsanto*')
Opinion of Advocate General Bot, *Giovanni Pesce and Others* (Joined Cases C-78/16 and C-79/16) [2016] ECR 340
Pfizer Animal Health SA v Council (Case T-13/99) [2002] ECR 209 *Rewe-Zentral AG v Bundesmonopolverwaltung für Branntwein* (C-120/78) [1979] ECR 649 ('*Cassis de Dijon*')

European Court of Human Rights

Lithgow and Others v United Kingdom (1986) 8 Eur Court HR (Ser A) 329
Fayed v United Kingdom (1994) 18 Eur Court HR (Ser A) 393
Open Door and Dublin Well Woman v Ireland [1992] Eur Court HR 1
Handyside v United Kingdom (1976) 24 Eur Court HR 523
Hirst v United Kingdom (2005) 2, 42 Eur Court HR 849
James and Others v United Kingdom (1986) 8 Eur Court HR 123
Lithgow and Others v United Kingdom (1986) 8 Eur Court HR (Ser A) 329
Tătar v Romania [2009] 67021 Eur Court HR
Vilnes and Others v Norway [2013] Eur Court HR 1

Inter-American Court of Human Rights

Environment and Human Rights (Advisory Opinion) (Inter-Am Ct HR OC-23/17, 15 November 2017)
Kawas Fernandez v Honduras, Inter-Am Ct HR, C-196 (3 April 2009)
Mayagna Community (Sumo) Awas Tingni, Inter-Am Ct HR, C-79 (31 August 2001)
Medio Ambiente y Derecho Humanos (Opinión Consultiva) (Corte Interamericana de Derechos Humanos, OC-23/17, 15 Noviembre 2017)
Yakye Axa Indigenous Community v Paraguay, Inter-Am Ct HR, C-125 (17 June 2005)

International Crimes Tribunal

Chief Prosecutor v Md. Liakat Ali (absconding) and Aminul Islam @ Rajab Ali @ K.M Aminul Haque @ Md. Aminul Haque Talukder (absconding), ICT-BD No. 05 of 2016, judgment of November 5, 2018 ('*Liakat and Aminul judgment*')
Chief Prosecutor v Md. Sakhawat Hossain, Md. Billal Hossain Biswas, Md. Lutfor Morol (died during trial), Md. Ibrahim Hossain alias Ghungur Ibrahim (absconded), Sheikh Mohammad Mujibur Rahman alias Mujibur Rahman (absconded), Md. A. Aziz Sardar son of late Ful Miah Sardar (absconded), Abdul Aziz Sardar son of late Ahmmad Sardar (absconded), Kazi Ohidul Islam alias Kazi Ohidus Salam (absconded), and Md. Abdul Khaleque

Morol (absconded), ICT-BD No. 04 of 2015, judgment of 10 August 2016 (*'Sakhawat and others judgment'*)

International Tribunal for the Law of the Sea

Case concerning Land Reclamation by Singapore in and around the Straits of Johor (Malaysia v. Singapore) (Provisional Measures), verbatim record of 25 September 2003, ITLOS/PV.03/02/Corr.1

M/V 'Louisa' Case (Saint Vincent and the Grenadines v. Kingdom of Spain) (Provisional Measures) (ITLOS Case No. 18, 23 December 2010

Southern Bluefin Tuna Cases (New Zealand v. Japan; Australia v. Japan) (Provisional Measures) (ITLOS Cases No. 3 & 4, 27 August 1999)

The MOX Plant Case (Ireland v UK) (Provisional Measures) (ITLOS Case No. 10, 3 December 2001)

Seabed Disputes Chamber

Seabed Disputes Chamber Responsibilities and Obligations of States Sponsoring Persons and Entities with Respect to Activities in the Area (Advisory Opinion) (Seabed Disputes Chamber, Case No. 17, 1 February 2011)

Domestic tribunals

Canadian International Trade Tribunal, *Dry Wheat Pasta*, Inquiry No. NQ-2017–005 (Reasons issued 10 August 2018)

Arbitration

Decision by the Arbitrators, *Brazil – Export Financing Programme for Aircraft – Recourse to Arbitration by Brazil under Article 22.6 of the Dispute Settlement Understanding (DSU) and Article 4.11 of the Agreement on Subsidies and Countervailing Measures (SCM)*, WTO Doc WT/DS46/ARB (28 August 2000)

Decision by the Arbitrators, *European Communities – Measures Concerning Meat and Meat Products (Hormones) – Recourse to arbitration by the European Communities under Article 22.6 of the DSU*, WTO Doc WT/DS26/ARB (12 July 1999)

Decision by the Arbitrators, *European Communities – Regime for the Importation, Sale and Distribution of Bananas – Recourse to Arbitration by the European Communities under Article 22.6 of the DSU*, WTO Doc WT/DS27/ARB/ECU (24 March 2000)

Decision by the Arbitrators, *United States – Anti-Dumping Act of 1916 (Original Complaint by the European Communities)*, WTO Doc WT/DS136/ARB (24 February 2004)

Trail Smelter Case (US v Canada) (Arbitration Award, 16 April 1938 and 11 March 1941) 3 RIAA 1905

Figures and tables

Chapter 1

Table 1.1	Summary of benefits and risks in trading biotech products	22
Table 1.2	Summary of normative, judicial and epistemic issues in trading biotechnology	27

Chapter 2

Table 2.1	Historical summary of judicial interpretations of the 'necessary' parameter	53
Table 2.2	Summary of judicial interpretations of the 'relating to' parameter	56
Table 2.3	Summary of possible normative antinomies between international human rights law and WTO law	77
Table 2.4	Summary of possible normative antinomies between international environmental law and WTO law	89

Chapter 3

Figure 3.1	Reliability and uncertainty in relation	116

Chapter 6

Table 6.1	Summary of WTO judicial bodies' degrees of requirements concerning evidence to establish a prima facie case	203
Table 6.2	*Multilevel degree of deference* as new standard of review to be applied by panels when examining biotechnology cases	225

Chapter 7

Figure 7.1 Scientific principles, sufficient scientific evidence and appropriateness of risk assessments under WTO law 235
Figure 7.2 'Appropriateness' of risk assessment in the WTO jurisprudence on biotechnology 248

Chapter 8

Figure 8.1 Scale of legal evidence and scientific (un)certainties 281

Glossary

Abstract Weight The abstract weight is the first factor of Alexy's law of balancing and considers the relevance of a right or principle which is assessed without any link to a concrete case.

Biosafety Measure Measures aiming at the *safety* of human health and the environment from the adverse impacts of *bio*technology.

Biotech Products Products resulting from the application of biotechnology techniques to food, animals, and plants.

Burden of Argumentation The burden of argumentation is the third element of Alexy's theory of balancing. It operates when the application of the 'weight formula' results in a stalemate.

Expert Witnesses Experts of biotechnology through their experience and personal history

Free Trade or Trade Liberalisation It is a WTO goal aiming at enhancing commercial values.

Holistic Data Data considering physical and social impacts of the examined products.

Inferences Inferences constitute a demonstration of probability, which is not based on deduction but on experience or statistical correlation.

Intensity of Interference The intensity of interference is the second factor of Alexy's law of balancing and stands for the intensity of interference by non-satisfaction of, or detriment to, the principles, rights, values, or interests at stake.

IPCC scale It is a quantitative scale ranging from 'virtually certain' to 'very unlikely'.

Law(s) of Balancing The *law of balancing* is the first element of Alexy's theory of balancing. It comprises and puts in relation the abstract weight, the intensity of interference and reliability of empirical premises of the principles, rights, or interests at stake. Decision-makers should consider these three factors in any balancing process.

The *first law of balancing* is part of Alexy's theory of balancing and reads as follows:

> *The greater the degree of non-satisfaction of, or detriment to, one principle [right], the greater must be the importance of satisfying the other.*

The *second law of balancing* is part of Alexy's theory of balancing and reads as follows:

> *The more heavily an interference in a constitutional right [or legal principle] weighs, the greater must be the certainty of its underlying premises.*

Legal scale It is a qualitative scale taking account of the standards of proof in civil and criminal cases.

Multiple and Positive Correlations Correlations showing that two or more variables are positively correlated as their values tend to go up or down together.

Normative Antinomies Normative conflicts between norms of the same or different legal regimes.

Precautionary Measures They are protective measures adopted to address, anticipate, prevent or minimise any adverse impact on human health and/or the environment by means of the precautionary principle.

Protective Measures Measures adopted to protect human health and/or the environment from any source, biotechnology included. Protective measures include biosafety measures.

Reasoned and Structured (or true) Judicial Balance A judicial balance is reasoned and structured when decision-makers, first, provide reasons for why they strike the balance the way they do, and then, adopt a criterion, such as proportionality analysis, supporting the balance through an analytical structure.

Reliability of Premises (or Assumptions) Reliability of empirical premises (or assumptions) refers to the certainty of the underlying empirical assumptions in question.

Scale of Legal Evidence and Scientific (Un)certainties A scale combining the quantitative IPCC scale and a qualitative legal scale taking account of standards of proof in civil and criminal cases.

SPS measures Sanitary (human and animal health) and phytosanitary (plant health) measures adopted in the context of the SPS Agreement. They include, but are not limited to, biosafety and precautionary measures.

Stalemate cases Stalemates are cases where there is no one right or interest considered more important than (an) other(s) because the weight of the rights or interests at stake is identical.

Uncertain Scientific Evidence A body of scientific evidence is uncertain when reputable experts of the scientific community agree that further research needs to be carried out on the examined products.

Weight Formula The weight formula is the second element of Alexy's theory of balancing. It encompasses the three factors of the law of balancing (ie, abstract weight, intensity of interference, and reliability of empirical premises) with the purpose of obtaining the 'concrete weight' of the competing principles, rights, or interests at stake, meaning their relevance under the circumstances of a case.

WTO Biotechnology Cases The WTO biotechnology cases (or legal disputes) are *EC-Hormones*, *EC-Biotech*, and *US/Canada-Hormones Continued Suspension*.

Part I

Context – international trade in biotechnology

1 International trade in biotechnology and protection of biosafety

An uneasy combination

1.1 Introduction

Biotechnology, which 'literally is technology based on biology',[1] is revolutionising our life. It is a broad concept that refers to a group of technologies that produce a large variety of products (biotech products), which comprise genetically engineered products, commonly known as genetically modified organisms (GMOs).[2] It enables us to modify the biological system of humans, animals and plants with the purposes of:

- improving health and suitability of animals for their cloning or industrial applications,
- strengthening plants and their products through the selection and breeding of desirable characteristics, and
- managing food production in labs.

Since biotechnology enhances our capacity to increase food production and design *super* animals, plants and crops, this technology might play a key role in 'alleviat[ing] hunger and poverty, assist[ing] in adaptation to climate change and maintain[ing] the natural resource base'.[3] Biotechnology, which is used in agriculture and considered part of agricultural technologies (AgTech), is often portrayed as a suitable means to achieve *Goal 2: Zero Hunger* of the sustainable development agenda aiming to feed the millions of people who are undernourished today.[4] Simultaneously, the potential contribution of biotechnology

1 National Research Council, *Animal Biotechnology Science-Based Concerns* (The National Academies Press, 2002), 18.

2 Australian Government – Department of Agriculture, Water, and the Environment, 'Biotechnology' (Web Page), www.agriculture.gov.au/ag-farm-food/biotechnology. The United States Department of Agriculture (ASDA), 'Agricultural Biotechnology Glossary' *ASDA* (Web Page), www.usda.gov.

3 Food and Agriculture Organization of the United Nations (FAO), 'FAO's Role in Biotechnology' *FAO* (Web Page), www.fao.org/biotechnology/en/.

4 See 'Sustainable Development Goals, Goal 2: Zero Hunger', *United Nations* (Web Page), www.un.org/sustainabledevelopment/hunger/.

DOI: 10.4324/9781003325741-2

to address climate change challenges in the agricultural sectors explains the numerous references to climate-resilient GMOs in international climate-change adaptation law frameworks.[5] Further, biotech products can present significant economic opportunities for both developed and developing countries: 'A total of US$186.1 billion economic benefits were gained by countries planting biotech crops from 1996 to 2016'.[6]

Because of its benefits, international trade in biotech products is flourishing. For example, during the first 22 years of commercialisation of biotech products, the United States (US), India, Brazil, China and Canada have gained the most economically from trading biotech crops, totalling US$172.5 billion.[7]

Nevertheless, biotechnology and trade have also been described as 'the elements from which modern nightmares are made'.[8] This is because trading biotech products simultaneously magnifies the spread of the risks posed by these products, mainly to human health and the environment.[9] Examples of such risks include allergenicity to a novel gene product, antibiotic resistance and the increasing use of pesticides on genetically modified (GM) crops.[10] Trading biotech products can also cause loss of biodiversity and, more generally, damage the environment in which biotech products are cultivated for trade.[11] This is because:

> Agricultural biotechnology is closely associated with modern intensive farming and, as part of that, with the massive use of synthetic agrochemicals

5 Anne Saab, *Narratives of Hunger in International Law Feeding the World in Times of Climate Change* (Cambridge University Press, 2019); Anne Saab, 'Climate-Resilient Crops and International Climate Change Adaptation Law' (2016) 29(2) *Leiden Journal of International Law* 503; Giulia Claudia Leonelli, 'GMO Risks, Food Security, Climate Change and the Entrenchment of Neo-Liberal Legal Narratives' (2018) 9(3–4) *Transnational Legal Theory* 302.

6 'Brief 53: Global Status of Commercialized Biotech/GM Crops in 2017: Biotech Crop Adoption Surges as Economic Benefits Accumulate in 22 Years', *ISAAA* (Web Page) 8, www.isaaa.org/resources/publications/briefs/53/download/isaaa-brief-53-2017.pdf.

7 Ibid.

8 Cinnamon Carlarne, 'From the USA with Love: Sharing Home-Grown Hormones, GMOs, and Clones with a Reluctant Europe' (2007) 37 *Environmental Law* 301, 302.

9 Any benefit or risk posed by biotech products is magnified through the international trade of such products, not least because placing those products on the international market means reaching many people.

10 Maria Weimer, *Risk Regulation in the Internal Market: Lessons from Agricultural Biotechnology* (Oxford University Press, 2019) 5–6; Aaron Smith and Colin A Carter, 'Estimating the Market Effect of a Food Scare: The Case of Genetically Modified StarLink Corn' (2007) 89(3) *Review of Economics and Statistics* 522; T. Netherwood, et al., 'Assessing the Survival of Transgenic Plant DNA in the Human Gastrointestinal Tract' (2004) 22 *Nature Biotechnology* 204.

11 See, e.g., Andreas Lang et al., 'Laboratory Tests with Lepidoptera to Assess Non-Target Effects of Bt Maize Pollen: Analysis of Current Studies and Recommendations for a Standardised Design' (2019) 31(39) *Environmental Sciences Europe* 1; Al Agi et al., 'Efficacy of Seed Mixes of Transgenic Bt and Nontransgenic Cotton against Bollworm, Helicoverpa Zea

(pesticides), [which can] lead to the destruction of the very foundation of agricultural production – the earth that feeds us and that provides for a number of ecological services vital for life on earth.[12]

Accordingly, trading biotech products can threaten *biosafety*, which is defined by the *Cartagena Protocol on Biosafety to the Convention on Biological Diversity* ('*Cartagena Protocol on Biosafety*') as the protection of 'human health and the environment from the possible adverse effects of the products of modern biotechnology'.[13] Nevertheless, the risks posed by trading biotechnology to human health and the environment are still highly debated in the scientific community, in which a high level of scientific uncertainty remains on the benefits and risks of biotechnology.[14] International trade in biotech products lies at the nexus between human health, environmental degradation and, as discussed in Section 1.2.3, global social justice; thus, the regulation of biotechnology is described as a 'wicked problem'.[15]

Against this background, the international trade in biotechnology is regulated by the WTO, representing 'the only global international organization dealing with the rules of trade between nations' that includes within it a dispute-settlement mechanism.[16] The *Agreement Establishing the World Trade Organization* (*WTO Agreement*), as a whole, reflects 'the balance struck by WTO members between trade and non-trade-related concerns'.[17] Within the WTO framework, international trade in biotechnology raises the question as to how decision-makers ought to balance trade with non-trade values, such as biosafety, under conditions of uncertainty.

WTO law, as does any other legal system, aims to prevent cases in which parties hold conflicting rights or legal interests.[18] Nonetheless, such cases may arise, especially when WTO states involved in a legal dispute adopt different levels of protection for ensuring biosafety. This creates particularly challenging cases for

---

Boddie' (2001) 5 *Journal of Cotton Science* 74. See also Andreas Schäffer et al., 'The Silent Spring – On the Need for Sustainable Plant Protection' (Deutsche Akademie der Naturforscher Leopoldina e V, Discussion No 16/2018) 61, www.leopoldina.org/uploads/tx_leopublication/2018_Diskussionspapier_Pflanzenschutzmittel_EN_02.pdf.

12 Weimer (n 10) 5; Caire Robinson, Michael Antoniou and John Fagan, *GMO Myths and Truths: A Citizen's Guide to the Evidence on the Safety and Efficacy of Genetically Modified Crops and Foods* (Earth Open Source, 3rd ed, 2015) 88–96. See also Jennifer Hsaio, 'GMOs and Pesticides: Helpful or Harmful?' *SITN, Harvard University Science in the News: Special Edition on GMOs* (Web Page, 10 August 2015), http://sitn.hms.harvard.edu/flash/2015/gmos-and-pesticides/.

13 *Cartagena Protocol on Biosafety*, 1.

14 See Section 1.2.

15 Weimer (n 10) 5.

16 'What Is the WTO?' *World Trade Organization* (Web Page), www.wto.org/english/thewto_e/whatis_e/whatis_e.htm.

17 AB Report, *China – Raw Materials*, [306]; *WTO Agreement*.

18 Lorenzo Zucca, *Constitutional Dilemmas – Conflicts of Fundamental Legal Rights in Europe and the USA* (Oxford University Press, 2007) 3.

the WTO dispute settlement bodies. The question becomes even more intricate when both parties have a 'trump card',[19] meaning that they pursue legitimate and worthwhile requests under the WTO (i.e., free trade of goods and protection of biosafety) and all claims are surrounded by uncertain scientific evidence. How are the scales of justice tipped in this circumstance?

Such a case may be submitted to *WTO judicial bodies*, which are composed of panels and the Appellate Body (AB).[20] WTO judicial bodies 'have an important and unique role [as they] can offer a longer term and independent perspective, seeking balance [between trade and non-trade values] and coherence in the interest of justice'.[21] In accomplishing this task, WTO judicial bodies ought to make decisions reflecting the *goals set out in the preamble of the WTO Agreement*:

> [R]elations in the field of trade and economic endeavour should be conducted with a view to [1] raising standards of living, [2] ensuring full employment and a large and steadily growing volume of real income and effective demand, and [3] expanding the production of and trade in goods and services, while [4] allowing for the optimal use of the world's resources in accordance with [5] the objective of sustainable development, [6] seeking both to protect and preserve the environment and [7] to enhance the means for doing so in a manner consistent with their respective needs and concerns at different levels of economic development.[22]

Nevertheless, striking a reasoned balance between trade and non-trade values under the WTO has never been more difficult than now. Besides the challenges raised by the COVID-19 pandemic, the WTO judiciary is called to balance trade and non-trade interests while it is undergoing a profound crisis ignited by both Trump and Biden administrations, which have paralysed the WTO's ability to resolve trade disputes between countries by blocking new appointments to the Appellate Body.

This study aims to illuminate how WTO judicial bodies ought to balance trade and non-trade interests when deciding scientifically uncertain matters

19 Ibid.

20 Although panels are quasi-judicial bodies and the AB is the only judicial body of the WTO, both are generally referred to as 'the judicial bodies of the WTO': Caroline Henckels, 'GMOs in the WTO: A Critique of the Panel's Legal Reasoning in EC-Biotech' (2006) 7 *Melbourne Journal of International Law* 278, 281 citing Joseph Weiler, 'The Rule of Lawyers and the Ethos of Diplomats: Reflections on the Internal and External Legitimacy of WTO Dispute Settlement' (2002) 13 *American Review of International Arbitration* 177, 189. Donald McRae, 'What Is the Future of WTO Dispute Settlement?' (2004) 7(1) *Journal of International Economic Law* 3; Andrew D Mitchell and David Heaton, 'The Inherent Jurisdiction of WTO Tribunals: The Select Application of Public International Law Required by the Judicial Function' (2010) 31(3) *SSRN Electronic Journal* 559.

21 Cairo Robb, Marie-Claire Cordonier Segger and Caroline Jo, 'Sustainable Development Challenges in International Dispute Settlement' in Marie-Claire Cordonier, HE Judge and CG Weeramantry (eds), *Sustainable Development Principles in the Decisions of International Courts and Tribunals* (Routledge, 2017) 147, 170.

22 *WTO Agreement* preamble.

concerning the international trade in biotechnology. This issue relates to the more general question of how to find a point of equilibrium between the revolutionary advancement offered by technology and the need to safeguard human health and the environment from uncertain, though potentially irreversible, technology risks.

The significance of this study arises first and foremost from the factual urgency to ensure that the moribund WTO judiciary steps up and assumes its '*central role*'[23] in achieving the 2030 Agenda for Sustainable Development, which 'seeks balance, and does not favour one or another international regime'.[24] As noted by the Director-General of the WTO, Ngozi Okonjo-Iweala, 'failure to revive [the WTO] will undermine governments' efforts to pull the global economy out of the recession caused by the COVID-19 pandemic'.[25] The WTO Director-General adds that in a world economy already imperilled by COVID-19, understanding how the WTO judiciary can strike a reasoned balance between trade and non-trade values, especially the protection of human health and environmental safeguarding in trade contexts, can be the antidote to revive this fundamental organization.[26] As a result, there is a sharply increased demand for recent scholarly work in this field but little supply at the moment.[27]

Moreover, given the rate of technological advances, international trade in biotechnology products will likely continue to flourish in the future. This is especially true considering that, despite its collateral effects to biosafety, biotechnology is viewed as the means to counteract climate-change problems, mitigate food hunger and secure food for a growing population. Also, the international trade in biotechnology products and its potential adverse effects on biosafety is rapidly drawing public attention, not least because the biotechnology industry has recently started exploring new techniques, such as clustered, regularly interspaced short palindromic repeats (CRISPR), aimed at not only *altering* the location of genetic materials, but '[*r*]*ewriting* the code of life'.[28] Given the potentially serious and irreversible negative effects caused by this innovative biotechnology

23 WTO, 'The WTO and the Sustainable Development Goals' *WTO* (Web Page) (emphasis added), www.wto.org/english/thewto_e/coher_e/sdgs_e/sdgs_e.htm.

24 Robb, Segger and Jo (n 21) 170.

25 Ngozi Okonjo-Iweala, 'Reviving the WTO' (22 June 2020, Brookings), www.brookings.edu/opinions/reviving-the-wto/.

26 Ibid.

27 See, e.g., RDM Kumala, 'Legal Analysis of Government Policy on Large Scale Social Restrictions in Handling Covid-19' (2020) 2(2) *The Indonesian Journal of International Clinical Legal Education* 181; E James, 'The BMA COVID-19 Ethical Guidance: A Legal Analysis' (2020) 26(2) *The New Bioethics* 176; Zhiqiong June Wang, 'Law in Crisis: A Critical Analysis of the Role of Law in China's Fight Against COVID-19' (2020) 29(2) *Griffith Law Review* 253.

28 UNEP, *Frontiers 2018/19 Emerging Issues of Environmental Concern* (United Nations Environment Programme-UNEP, 2019) 12 https://wedocs.unep.org/bitstream/handle/20.500.11822/27538/Frontiers1819.pdf?sequence=1&isAllowed=y. See also Gregory E Kaebnick and Bruce Jennings, 'De-Extinction and Conservation' (2017) 47 *The Hastings Center Report* 2 (emphasis added).

technique on human health and the environment,[29] the 2018/2019 United Nations Environment Programme's (UNEP) 2019 report encourages a valid debate on how biotechnology can support, coexist with, or undermine the goals of sustainable development.[30] This makes inquiries, such as this study, timely and significant.

Finally, the COVID-19 pandemic clearly demonstrates the importance of taking precautionary actions to reduce further risk to humans, even when uncertainties remain about the transmission and precise effects of the virus. The same argument applies to the risks of trading biotechnology. Nevertheless, what remains unclear is the minimum level of evidence allowing precautionary measures to apply, which leaves decision-makers with little guidance as to how to balance trade interests with biosafety concerns. The significance of this study also lies in suggesting a *scale of legal evidence and scientific (un)certainties* showing appropriate standard(s) of proof (or level of legal evidence) and level of uncertainty that might/should allow precautionary measures to apply, even in cases of scientific uncertainty and qualitatively insufficient scientific evidence.[31]

This chapter establishes the context of this investigation. This section outlines the parameters of the biotechnology trade debate. Section 1.2 outlines the main benefits, risks and social concerns, along with the remaining uncertainties in trading this technology. Section 1.3 discusses whether the WTO framework enables WTO judicial bodies to achieve a fair balance between trade and non-trade interests and, in doing so, sheds light on the main challenges in achieving such judicial balance. Then, Section 1.4 considers whether the principles of proportionality and precaution are suitable criteria through which WTO judicial bodies can overcome the identified challenges. Section 1.5 sets out the objectives of this study, which chiefly aims to investigate how WTO judicial bodies ought to balance free trade in biotech products and biosafety and to what extent proportionality analysis and the precautionary principle can assist WTO judicial bodies in achieving such a balance. Section 1.6 provides information on the theoretical and practical contributions offered by this study to, respectively, the literature and judicial decision-makers required to balance competing interests in contexts of uncertainty. Section 1.7 explains in greater detail the methodology adopted in this book, which involves conceptual, analytical and normative – but not empirical – methods, while the scope and structure of the study are provided in Sections 1.8 and 1.9, respectively.

29 See e.g., Magnus Lundgren, Emmanuelle Charpentier and Peter C Fineran, *CRISPR: Methods and Protocols* (Springer, 2015); Brad Plumer et al., 'A Simple Guide to CRISPR, One of the Biggest Science Stories of the Decade' *Vox* (27 December 2018), www.vox.com/2018/7/23/17594864/crispr-cas9-gene-editing.

30 UNEP (n 28) 16 https://wedocs.unep.org/bitstream/handle/20.500.11822/27538/Frontiers1819.pdf?sequence=1&isAllowed=y. See also Kaebnick and Jennings (n 28).

31 See Section 1.6.

1.2 Discovering biotechnology: benefits, risks and social issues in trading biotech products

New technologies, such as biotech products, are characterised by high levels of uncertainty as to their risks and benefits.[32] This emerges clearly from the following discussion of benefits (see Section 1.2.1), risks (see Section 1.2.2) and social concerns (see Section 1.2.3) surrounding the international trade in biotech products, the analysis of which is not extended to the large variety of all these products. Rather, it focuses on products stemming from the agricultural and animal biotechnology industry, such as GM crops, food and animals.[33]

1.2.1 Benefits in trading biotech products

1.2.1.1 Biotechnology and the reduction of hunger

Biotechnology can help to improve the production of food, especially through GM crops.[34] This might be a solution to 'explosive population growth':[35]

> The Food and Agricultural Organisation projects the global population to grow to approximately 9.7 billion by 2050. . . . Current agricultural practices alone cannot sustain the world population and eradicate malnutrition and hunger on a global scale in the future.[36]

However, it is not appropriate to overstate this benefit. According to the Food and Agricultural Organization (FAO), hunger is not the outcome of a lack of food,[37]

32 For instance, CRISPR can inadvertently trigger cancer.
33 Section 1.8 explains the reasons behind this choice.
34 This is especially true considering that biotech products are designed in laboratories.
35 Ruchir Raman, 'The Impact of Genetically Modified (GM) Crops in Modern Agriculture: A Review' (2017) 8(4) *GM Crops and Food* 195, 197.
36 Ibid. See also Christopher Gerry, 'Feeding the World One Genetically Modified Tomato at a Time: A Scientific Perspective' *SITN – Science in the News* (9 August 2015).
37 Food and Agriculture Organization, 'The Future of Food and Agriculture Trends and Challenges' *FAO* (Web Page 2017), www.fao.org/3/a-i6583e.pdf; Food and Agriculture Organization, 'How Close Are We to Achieve #ZeroHunger? The State of Food Security and Nutrition in the World 2017' *FAO* (Web Page, 2017), www.fao.org/state-of-food-security-nutrition/en/; Food and Agriculture Organization, 'Unlocking the Water Potential of Agriculture' *FAO* (Web Page, 2003), www.fao.org/3/y4525e/y4525e00.htm; Jomo Kwame Sundaram, 'The World Produces Enough Food to Feed Everyone. So Why do People Go Hungry?' *World Economic Forum* (Web Page, 11 July 2016), www.weforum.org/agenda/2016/07/the-world-produces-enough-food-to-feed-everyone-so-why-do-people-go-hungry; Jeremy Erdman, 'We Produce Enough Food to Feed 10 Billion People. So Why Does Hunger Still Exist?' *Medium* (2 February 2018) https://medium.com/@jeremyerdman/we-produce-enough-food-to-feed-10-billion-people-so-why-does-hunger-still-exist-8086d2657539; World Hunger, '2018 World Hunger and Poverty Facts and Statistics (Fight Hunger with Knowledge – Hunger Notes)' *World Hunger* (Web Page, 2018), www.worldhunger.org/world-hunger-and-poverty-facts-and-statistics/.

but of unfair distribution and a lack of universal access.[38] If we accept that there is more than enough food produced in the world to feed its current population,[39] biotechnology does not represent a *solution* to sustain a growing world population.

Nevertheless, the capacity of biotechnology to enhance food production can potentially reduce world hunger[40] by reducing the cost of food.[41] This, in turn, might help to realise the *right to food* for everyone,[42] though some remain sceptical.[43]

A further benefit of biotechnology lies in the fact that GM food is climate-change resilient.[44] Indeed, the genetic modification of crops aims to, among other goals, achieve environmental resistance to drought or flooding.[45] This explains why *United Nations Framework Convention on Climate Change* (*UNFCCC*)

38 Committee on Economic, Social and Cultural Rights, *General Comment No. 12: The Right to Adequate Food* (*ICESCR*, Article 11) [5].

39 Food and Agriculture Organization, 'The Future of Food and Agriculture' (n 37); Food and Agriculture Organization, *How Close Are We to Achieve #ZeroHunger?* (n 37); Food and Agriculture Organization, 'Unlocking the Water Potential of Agriculture' (n 37); Sundaram (n 37); Erdman (n 37).

40 Colestous Juma, 'Preventing Hunger: Biotechnology Is Key Preventing Hunger: Change Economic Policy' (2012) 479 *Nature* 1; Frank Tenente, 'Feeding the World One Seed at a Time: A Practical Alternative for Solving World Hunger' (2007) 5(2) *Northwestern Journal of Human Rights* 298; Peter M Rosset, 'Preventing Hunger: Change Economic Policy' (2011) 479 *Nature* 472; Judit Berman et al., 'Can the World Afford to Ignore Biotechnology Solutions That Address Food Insecurity?' (2013) 83(1–2) *Plant Molecular Biology* 5. See also Ronald Cantrell as quoted in CS Prakash, 'Benefits of Biotechnology for Developing Countries' *AgBioWorld* (Web Page), www.agbioworld.org/biotech-info/topics/dev-world/benefits.html.

41 GJ Persley, 'Agricultural Biotechnology and the Poor: Promethean Science' (2000) *Biotechnology* 3, 5, 9. See also Michael Stebbins, '3 Ways GMOs Keep the Cost of Food Down' *Forbes* (Online, 29 April 2016), www.forbes.com/sites/gmoanswers/2016/04/29/3-ways-gmos-keep-cost-of-food-down/#77e3e92b1261. The increasing cost of food is the main obstacle to universal access and a main reason for the increasing rate of global poverty. The 2017 global poverty update from the World Bank outlines that '[c]ompared to the estimates produced in October 2016, the total number of poor increased by 2.5 million (from 766.0 to 768.5 million)': Francisco Ferreira, Christoph Lakner and Carolina Sanchez, 'The 2017 Global Poverty Update from the World Bank' *World Bank* (Blog Post, 16 October 2017) http://blogs.worldbank.org/developmenttalk/2017-global-poverty-update-world-bank. See also Mandi Woodruff, 'These Foods Will Be More Expensive in 2018' *US News & World Report* (Online, 2 November 2017), https://money.usnews.com/money/blogs/my-money/articles/2017-11-02/these-foods-will-be-more-expensive-in-2018.

42 The right to food is an internationally recognised human right, which is enshrined, for instance, in the *Universal Declaration of Human Rights* (Article 25) and in the ICESCR (Article 11).

43 See Kung-Chung Liu and Uday S Racherla, *Innovation, Economic Development, and Intellectual Property in India and China* (Springer, 2019); John A Glaser, 'White Biotechnology' (2005) 7(4) *Clean Technologies and Environmental Policy* 233, 835.

44 Saab, 'Climate-Resilient Crops and International Climate Change Adaptation Law' (n 5); Leonelli (n 5). See also Jeff McMahon, 'What If GMOs Can Fight Climate Change?' *Forbes* (Online, 7 May 2019), www.forbes.com/sites/jeffmcmahon/2019/05/07/what-about-gmos-that-fight-climate-change/#5f6fbb033e1b.

45 Leonelli (n 5).

technical papers mention drought-resistant seeds and/or gene technologies as practical and attractive means to contribute to climate-change adaptation.[46] Consequently, biotech food can also be a solution for communities in which hunger levels have been raised because of extreme weather conditions affecting local cultivations.[47] However, some commentators note that 'the effectiveness of climate resilient GM crops is yet to be established'[48] and that applying conventional breeding techniques can achieve the same objectives.[49]

1.2.1.2 Biotechnology and economic development

International trade in biotech products can present significant economic opportunities, especially for developing countries.[50] From 1996 to 2016, with the commercialisation of biotech crops, Argentina gained US$23.7 billion, India earned US$21.1 billion and Brazil gained US$19.8 billion.[51] There are also significant economic advantages in trading biotech products for developed countries. In the same 1996–2016 time frame, the United States gained US$80.3 billion, and Canada US$8 billion, from trading biotech products.[52] Naturally, the economic benefits created by biotechnology strongly depend upon the possibility to *trade*

46 RJT Klein et al., 'Application of Environmentally Sound Technologies for Adaptation to Climate Change, FCCC/TP/2006/2' *FCCC Technical Papers* (2006); Saab, 'Climate-Resilient Crops and International Climate Change Adaptation Law' (n 5); Leonelli (n 5) 305.

47 See United Nations Climate Change, 'UN Warns Climate Change Is Driving Global Hunger' *UNFCC* (Web Page, 12 September 2018) https://unfccc.int/news/un-warns-climate-change-is-driving-global-hunger; Fiona Harvey and Karen McVeigh, 'Global Hunger Levels Rising Due to Extreme Weather, UN Warns' *The Guardian* (Online, 1 September 2018), www.theguardian.com/environment/2018/sep/11/global-hunger-levels-rising-due-to-extreme-weather-un-warns; Jessica Eise and Kenneth Foster, 'World Hunger Has Risen for Three Straight Years, and Climate Change Is a Cause' *The Conversation* (Online, 22 October 2018) https://theconversation.com/world-hunger-has-risen-for-three-straight-years-and-climate-change-is-a-cause-103818.

48 Leonelli (n 5).

49 Saab, 'Climate-Resilient Crops and International Climate Change Adaptation Law' (n 5).

50 See Silja Baller et al., 'The Networked Readiness Index 2016' in Silja Baller, Soumitra Dutta and Bruno Lanvin (eds), *The Global Information Technology Report 2016 – Innovating in the Digital Economy* (The World Economic Forum and INSEAD, 2016) 3, 4; Joseph Cortright and Heike Mayer, *Signs of Life: The Growth of Biotechnology Centers in the US* (The Brookings Institution Center on Urban and Metropolitan Policy, 2002) 6; Zion Market Research, 'Agricultural Biotechnology Market by Type (Molecular Diagnostics, Molecular Markers, Tissue Culture, Vaccines, Genetic Engineering, and Others) and by Application (Transgenic Crops, Synthetic Biology-Enables Products, and Others): Global Industry Perspective, Comprehensive Analysis, and Forecast, 2018–2025' *Zion Market Research* (Web Page, 8 July 2019), www.zionmarketresearch.com/report/agricultural-biotechnology-market; IBISWorld, 'Where Knowledge Is Power, Global Biotechnology Industry – Market Research Report' *IBISWorld* (Web Page, February 2019), www.ibisworld.com/global/market-research-reports/global-biotechnology-industry/.

51 Brief 53 (n 6) 8.

52 Ibid.

biotech products with no restrictions.[53] That is because biotech products are commercial products.[54] Trading biotech products can, as such, support the *right to development* of states trading these products.[55]

1.2.2 Risks in trading biotech products

International trade in biotech products can carry a range of *collateral effects* on human health and the environment.[56] Nevertheless, science is not definitive, as will be demonstrated in the following discussion of the most debated human health and environmental risks caused by the international trade of goods produced from the agricultural and animal biotechnology industry.

1.2.2.1 Risks to human health

Scientific studies have identified potential risks of biotechnology to human health, the most significant of which are allergenicity to a novel gene product, antibiotic resistance and health issues caused by the increased use of pesticides. International trade in biotech products can arguably magnify these risks, if only because trade is a means to reach a large number of consumers around the world.[57]

The first risk is that people with food allergies may have an anomalous immune reaction to allergens (i.e., specific proteins that biotechnology introduces to food).[58] Some studies underline non-target health effects caused by biotech products.[59] However, others claim that 'there is no proof that the introduced novel

53 European Parliament, Directorate-General for External Policies of the Union, 'Briefing – The Impact of Biotechnology on Developing Countries' (Web Page, 14 February 2013) EXPO/B/DEVE/FWC/2009–01/Lot5/32, 11. See also Kym Anderson and LA Jackson, 'Standards, Trade and Protection: The Case of GMOs' (2005) *World Bank* 1.

54 Paul Diehl, 'An Overview of Biotechnology and the Biotech Industry' *The Balance* (Online, 30 November 2019), www.thebalance.com/what-is-biotechnology-375612.

55 See Section 2.6.1.

56 See Elisa Pellegrino et al., 'Impact of Genetically Engineered Maize on Agronomic, Environmental and Toxicological Traits: A Meta-Analysis of 21 Years of Field Data' (2018) 8(1) *Scientific Reports* 1.

57 Cultivation of biotech products can affect only local communities.

58 Ania Wieczorek, 'Use of Biotechnology in Agriculture – Benefits and Risks' (2003) 3 *Biotechnology* 1. See also Raman (n 35) 202; Smith and Carter (n 10). World Health Organization, *Strategies for Assessing the Safety of Foods Produced by Biotechnology*, Report of the Joint WHO/FAO Consultation, Geneva (Web Page, 1991) http://apps.who.int/iris/bitstream/10665/41465/1/9241561459-eng.pdf; OECD, *Safety Evaluation of Foods Derived by Modern Biotechnology – Concepts and Principles* (1993), www.oecd.org/science/biotrack/41036698.pdf; FDA Federal Register, 'FDA Statement of Policy, "Foods Derived from New Plant Varieties"' (1992) 57 *Department of Health and Human Services*, www.fda.gov/food/guidanceregulation/guidancedocumentsregulatoryinformation/biotechnology/ucm096095.htm.

59 Sean A Weaver and Michael C Morris, 'Risks Associated with Genetic Modification: An Annotated Bibliography of Peer Reviewed Natural Science Publications' (2005) 18(2) *Journal of Agricultural and Environmental Ethics* 157, 184.

protein(s) in any commercialized G[enetic] E[ngineered] food crop has caused food allergy'.[60] Further, a 2018 meta-analysis claims that genetically engineered products can not only improve the quality of food production, but also reduce health risks.[61]

Second, genetically engineering crops can involve adding genes to the crop to make them resistant to certain antibiotics. Such resistance can lead to serious human health problems.[62] This is, however, contested by other scientific studies.[63]

Third, the alleged increased use of pesticides on biotech products can give rise to human diseases.[64] Most biotech products are engineered to produce their own pesticides, or pesticides-resistant.[65] An example is glyphosate, which is a widely used herbicide, especially on biotech crops. The best-known and the most-used glyphosate herbicide is Roundup.[66] This herbicide kills all plants in GM fields apart from GM crops that, for this feature, are known as ***glyphosate-tolerant*** or ***Roundup Ready (RR) crops***.[67] 'Approximately 80 percent of the total area devoted

60 Gregory S Ladics, 'Assessment of the Potential Allergenicity of Genetically-Engineered Food Crops' (2019) 16(1) *Journal of Immunotoxicology* 43; Intan Ria Neliana et al., 'Development of Allergenicity and Toxicity Assessment Methods for Evaluating Transgenic Sugarcane Overexpressing Sucrose–Phosphate Synthase' (2019) 9(23) *Agronomy* 1, 11.

61 Pellegrino et al. (n 56).

62 Netherwood et al. (n 10); SM Martin-Orue et al., 'Degradation of Transgenic DNA from Genetically Modified Soya and Maize in Human Intestinal Simulations' (2002) 87 *British Journal of Nutrition* 533; Paula S Duggan et al., 'Survival of Free DNA Encoding Antibiotic Resistance from Transgenic Maize and the Transformation Activity of DNA in Ovine Saliva Ovine Rumen Fluid and Silage Effluent' (2000) 191 *FEMS Microbiology Letters* 71 cited in; Weaver and Morris (n 59) 171–172. See also Government of the Netherlands, 'Antibiotic-Resistant Genes' *Government of the Netherlands* (Web Page), www.government.nl/topics/biotechnology/antibiotic-resistant-genes.

63 Robert EW Hancock, 'The Role of Fundamental Research and Biotechnology in Finding Solutions to the Global Problem of Antibiotic Resistance' (1997) 24(Supplement_1) *Clinical Infectious Diseases* S148; DA Goldstein et al., 'Human Safety and Genetically Modified Plants: A Review of Antibiotic Resistance Markers and Future Transformation Selection Technologies' (2005) 99(1) *Journal of Applied Microbiology* 7.

64 Charles M Benbrook, 'Impacts of Genetically Engineered Crops on Pesticides Use in the US – The First Sixteen Years' (2012) 24(24) *Environmental Sciences Europe* 1; Raman (n 35) 202. See also USDA, 'Recent Trends in GE Adoption' *United States Department of Agriculture Economic Research Service* (Web Page, 18 September 2019), *www.ers.usda.gov/data-products/adoption-of-genetically-engineered-crops-in-the-us/recent-trends-in-ge-adoption.aspx#.UdGtl8u9KSM; Food & Water Watch, 'Superweeds – How Biotech Crops Bolster the Pesticide Industry' Food & Water Watch* (Web Page, July 2013), 6, www.foodandwaterwatch.org/sites/default/files/Superweeds%20Report%20July%202013.pdf.

65 Md Wasim Aktar, Dwaipayan Sengupta and Ashim Chowdhury, 'Impact of Pesticides Use in Agriculture: Their Benefits and Hazards' (2009) 2(1) *Interdisciplinary Toxicology* 1.

66 Clive James, 'Brief 44 – Global Status of Commercialized Biotech/GM Crops: 2012' *The International Service for the Acquisition of Agri-biotech Applications* (Web Page, 2012) No 44, www.isaaa.org/resources/publications/briefs/44/download/isaaa-brief-44-2012.pdf.

67 Sylwester Świątkiewicz et al., 'Nutritional Efficiency of Genetically-Modified Insect Resistant Corn (MON 810) and Glyphosate-Tolerant Soybean Meal (Roundup Ready) for Broilers' (2010) 54(1) *Bulletin of the Veterinary Institute in Pulawy* 43. See also Jordan Wilkerson,

to these [biotechnology] crops have been planted with herbicide-resistant crops, virtually all being glyphosate-resistant (GR) crops'.[68] Notably, although RR crops were supposed to control weeds and pests, it has been asserted that GE crops 'have led to the emergence of superweeds and super pests'.[69] These superweeds then developed a resistance to glyphosate herbicides. Farmers are consequently forced to use greater quantities of herbicides to eradicate weeds.[70]

Thus, '[c]ontrary to often-repeated claims that today's genetically engineered crops have, and are reducing pesticide use',[71] and despite the fact that GM crops do not necessarily imply the use of pesticides, scientific studies underline that GM cultivations require increasing use of pesticides,[72] especially glyphosate.[73] However, scientific debate is polarised, even in relation to this consideration. Indeed, according to some in the scientific community, 'while increasing global yield by 22%, GM crops reduced pesticide (active ingredient) usage by 37% and environmental impact (insecticide and herbicide use) by 18%'.[74]

Regardless of whether there is increasing or decreasing use of pesticides on biotech products, researchers have warned about the dangerous effects of herbicides on human health,[75] including on human intelligence quotients.[76] Particularly,

---

'Why Roundup Ready Crops Have Lost their Allure' *SITN – Science in the News* (Online, 10 August 2015) http://sitn.hms.harvard.edu/flash/2015/roundup-ready-crops/.

68 Stephen O Duke and Stephen B Powles, 'Glyphosate-Resistant Crops and Weeds: Now and in the Future' (2009) 12(3&4) *AgBioForum* 346.

69 Vandana Shiva, 'Introduction' in Vandana Shiva, Debbie Barker and Caroline Lockhart (eds), *The GMO Emperor Has No Clothes: A Global Citizens Report on the State of GMOs – False Promises, Failed Technologies* (Navdanya, 2010) 11, 12.

70 John Fagan, Michael Antoniou and Claire Robinson, *GMO Myths and Truths – An Evidence-Based Examination of the Claims Made for the Safety and Efficacy of Genetically Modified Crops and Foods* (Earth Open Source, 2nd ed, 2014) 237; Stefaan Blancke et al., 'Fatal Attraction: The Intuitive Appeal of GMO Opposition' (2015) 20(7) *Trends in Plant Science* 414, 415. See also Shiva (n 69) 14.

71 Charles M Benbrook, 'Impacts of Genetically Engineered Crops on Pesticides Use in the U.S. – The First Sixteen Years' (2012) 24(24) *Environmental Sciences Europe* 1.

72 Robinson, Antoniou and Fagan (n 12) 79–86. See also Hsaio (n 12).

73 Charles M Benbrook, 'Trends in Glyphosate Herbicide Use in the United States and Globally' (2016) 28(3) *Benbrook Environ Sci Eur* 1, 10.

74 Raman (n 35) 198; Wilhelm Klümper and Matin Qaim, 'A Meta-Analysis of the Impacts of Genetically Modified Crops' (2014) 9(11) *PlosOne* 1; Andy Coghlan, 'Genetically Modified Crops: A Decade of Disagreement' (2006) 189(2535) *New Scientist* 10; Wieczorek (n 58) 3. On the contrary, according to some, GM crops do not increase yield potential; Robinson, Antoniou and Fagan (n 12) 72–78.

75 Ki-Hyun Kima, Ehsanul Kabirb and Shamin Ara Jahanc, 'Exposure to Pesticides and the Associated Human Health Effects' (2017) 575 *Science of The Total Environment* 525; Antonio F Hernándeza et al., 'Toxic Effects of Pesticide Mixtures at a Molecular Level: Their Relevance to Human Health' (2013) 307 *Toxicology* 136; Virginie Rizzatia et al., 'Effects of Pesticide Mixtures in Human and Animal Models: An Update of the Recent Literature' (2016) 254 *Chemico-Biological Interactions* 231.

76 David C Bellinger, 'A Strategy for Comparing the Contributions of Environmental Chemicals and Other Risk Factors to Neurodevelopment of Children' (2012) 120(4) *Environmental Health Perspectives* 501.

several scientific studies shed light on 'the documented effects of glyphosate and its ability to induce disease'.[77] In 2015 the International Agency for Research on Cancer (IARC) assessed glyphosate as 'probably carcinogenic to humans'.[78] Over the following years, this outcome has been confirmed by other studies claiming a direct link between glyphosate and numerous human diseases, such as asthma, Parkinson's disease, lupus and non-Hodgkin's lymphoma, to mention only a few.[79] However, there remains scientific uncertainty about the effects of glyphosate on human health.[80] Indeed, the 2016 the US FAO Panel of Experts on Pesticide Residues in Food and the Environment and the World Health Organization (WHO) Core Assessment Group on Pesticide Residues (JMPR) concluded that 'glyphosate is unlikely to pose a carcinogenic risk to humans from exposure through the diet'.[81]

In short, some scientific studies warn that trading biotech products entails exporting goods that are poisoning food supplies and, consequently, humans.[82]

77 Anthony Samsel and Stephanie Seneff, 'Glyphosate's Suppression of Cytochrome P450 Enzymes and Amino Acid Biosynthesis by the Gut Microbiome: Pathways to Modern Diseases' (2013) 15(4) *Entropy* 1416; Céline Gasniera et al., 'Glyphosate-Based Herbicides Are Toxic and Endocrine Disruptors in Human Cell Lines' (2009) 262(3) *Toxicology* 184.

78 IARC and WHO, *Evaluation of Five Organophosphate Insecticides and Herbicides* (20 March 2015) vol 112, www.iarc.fr/en/media-centre/iarcnews/pdf/MonographVolume112.pdf. See also Danny Hakim, 'Doubts About the Promised Bounty of Genetically Modified Crops' *The New York Times* (Online, 29 October 2016), https://nyti.ms/2dR9DRr.

79 Anthony Samsel and Stephanie Seneff, 'Glyphosate Pathways to Modern Diseases V: Amino Acid Analogue of Glycine in Diverse Proteins' (2016) 16 *Journal of Biological Physics and Chemistry* 9; Philip J Landrigan and Fiorella Belpoggi, 'The Need for Independent Research on the Health Effects of Glyphosate-Based Herbicides' (2018) 17(1) *Environmental Health: A Global Access Science Source* 1.

80 For the current controversial discussion on the effects posed by glyphosate to human health, see European Food Safety Authority (EFSA), 'Conclusion on the Peer Review of the Pesticide Risk Assessment of the Active Substance Glyphosate' (2015) 1(11) *EFSA Journal* 1, www.efsa.europa.eu/en/efsajournal/pub/4302; Kathryn Z Guyton et al., 'Carcinogenicity of Tetrachlorvinphos, Parathion, Malathion, Diazinon, and Glyphosate' (2015) 16 *Lancet Oncology* 490; John Peterson Myers et al., 'Concerns over Use of Glyphosate-Based Herbicides and Risks Associated with Exposures: A Consensus Statement' (2016) *Environmental Health* 15; Lars Niemann et al., 'A Critical Review of Glyphosate Findings in Human Urine Samples and Comparison with the Exposure of Operators and Consumers' (2015) 10 *Journal für Verbraucherschutz und Lebensmittelsicherheit* 3, cited in André Conrad et al., 'Glyphosate in German Adults – Time Trend (2001 to 2015) of Human Exposure to a Widely Used Herbicide' (2017) 220(1) *International Journal of Hygiene and Environmental Health* 8. See also Daniel Cressey, 'Widely Used Herbicide Linked to Cancer' *Nature News* (Online, 24 March 2015), www.nature.com/news/widely-used-herbicide-linked-to-cancer-1.17181#:~:text=Glyphosate%2C%20a%20chemical%20found%20in,is%20probably%20carcinogenic%20to%20humans.

81 Biotech Gallery – IARC (International Agency for Research on Cancer), 'Glyphosate Cancer Determination Challenged by World Consensus' *Genetic Literacy Project* (Web Page, 22 October 2017), https://geneticliteracyproject.org/glp-facts/iarc-international-agency-research-cancer-glyphosate-determination-world-consensus/.

82 See, e.g., Kai Zhao et al., 'Edible Safety Assessment of Genetically Modified Rice T1C-1 for Sprague Dawley Rats through Horizontal Gene Transfer, Allergenicity and Intestinal Microbiota' (2016) 11(10) *PLoS One* 1; Norman C Ellstrand, 'When Transgenes Wander, Should

Viewed through this lens, international trade in biotech products undermines the enjoyment of the ***right to health*** of people living in states importing and exporting such products.[83] On the contrary, other studies claim no significant risks in this regard. In sum, any discussion on the effects posed by the international trade in biotech products to human health is currently ridden with uncertainty.

1.2.2.2 Risks to the environment

International trade in biotech products can cause environmental degradation through the use of pesticides that, in the view of some scientists, seems to increase with GM crops.[84] It has been noted that '[h]erbicide-tolerant GM crops accumulate herbicide and herbicide residues highly toxic to humans and animals as well as plants'.[85] Pesticides can contaminate soil, water, turf and other vegetation. Further, they can kill insects or weeds and be toxic to a host of other organisms and non-target plants.[86] Scientific studies underline an interaction between climate change, global warming and distribution of pesticides in nature, though 'the magnitude of interference remains unclear'.[87]

Nevertheless, the relationship between biotechnology and the use of pesticides, climate change and global warming, is also viewed through a different lens. For example, according to Leonelli, 'GMOs are held to play a key role to achieve climate-change adaptation and food security simply *because* GMO development, patenting and trade responds to the profit-making goals of market actors'.[88] There are also scientific studies emphasising the possibility of biotechnology to 'save energy and significantly reduce CO_2 [carbon dioxide] emissions'[89] and the use of pesticides.[90] The question of whether the interna-

We Worry?' (2001) 125(4) *Plant Physiology* 1543; Allison A Snow, 'Transgenic Crops – Why Gene Flow Matters' (2002) 20(6) *Nature Biotechnology* 542. See also Genetic Literacy Project, 'Thierry Vrain; Molecular Biologist Claims GMOs "Poison Food Supply"' *Genetic Literacy Project* (Web Page, 1 January 2019), https://geneticliteracyproject.org/glp-facts/thierry-vrain-molecular-biologist-claims-gmos-poison-food-supply/.

83 See Section 2.6.1.1.

84 See Robinson, Antoniou and Fagan (n 12) and Hsaio (n 73).

85 Krishna Dronamraju, *Impact of GM Crops on Biodiversity and the Environment* (World Scientific Publishing, 2008) 4. See also Shobha Sondhia, 'Herbicide Residue Hazards and Their Mitigation Modalities' in *Biennial Conference of the Indian Society of Weed Science on 'Doubling Farmers' Income by 2022: The Role of Weed Science'* (Indian Society of Weed Science, 2017) 21; Robinson, Antoniou and Fagan (n 12) 111–113.

86 Aktar, Sengupta and Chowdhury (n 65) 5. See also Jamie Benidickson, 'Pesticides and Precaution' in AM. Herzberg and RW Oldford (eds), *Statistics, Science and Public Policy VII: Environment, Health and Globalization* (Queen's University, School of Policy Studies, 2003).

87 Heinz-R Köhler and Rita Triebskorn, 'Wildlife Ecotoxicology of Pesticides: Can We Track Effects to the Population Level and Beyond?' (2013) 341 *Science* 759, 764.

88 Leonelli (n 5) 309 (emphasis in original).

89 See Organisation for Economic Co-operation and Development (OECD), 'Industrial Biotechnology and Climate Change – Opportunities and Challenges' *OECD* (Web Page, 2011), www.oecd.org/sti/biotech/49024032.pdf.

90 Gesine Schütte et al., 'Herbicide Resistance and Biodiversity: Agronomic and Environmental Aspects of Genetically Modified Herbicide-Resistant Plants' (2017) 29(5) *Environmental*

tional trade in biotech products negatively affects the environment through the increased use of pesticides on such products is, accordingly, still uncertain.[91] The proliferation of invasive alien species (IAS) is a prominent cause of damage to biodiversity.[92] New and more dominant species might overrun existing species.[93] For example, marine scientists have warned that if GM fish escape from fish farms, 'they could further upset the oceans' delicate ecology, causing ecological disruption or species extinction'.[94] Conversely, proponents of GE animals sustain that GM animals are highly domesticated and will not endanger local species.[95]

Genetically novel organisms can also have unforeseen impacts on non-target species.[96] For instance, pollen from biotech corn might accidentally kill or harm monarch butterflies[97] and bees.[98] There is, however, uncertainty concerning the

---

Sciences Europe 1. See also Graham Brookes and Peter Barfoot, 'Environmental Impacts of Genetically Modified (GM) Crop Use 1996–2014: Impacts on Pesticide Use and Carbon Emissions' (2016)7(2) *GM Crops Food* 84; ISAAA, 'International Service for the Acquisition of Agri-Biotech Applications, Biotechnology and Climate Change Climate Change and Its Effect in Agriculture' *ISAAA* (Web Page, April 2013) No 43, www.isaaa.org/resources/publications/pocketk/43/default.asp.

91 Loss of biodiversity can also be caused by cross-pollination between transgenic and traditional crops, which happens when genes from biotech varieties are transferred to wild or weedy plants.

92 *Convention on Biological Diversity, Agricultural Biodiversity Genetic Use Restriction Technologies* (GURTs) (2006), www.biodiv.org/programmes/areas/agro/gurts.asp; IUCN, 'Impacts of GMOs on Biodiversity and Human Health (The World Conservation Union, Information Paper, August 2007)' 26, https://cmsdata.iucn.org/downloads/ip_gmo_09_2007_1_.pdf.

93 Lillian LaReesa Wolfenbarger and PR Phifer, 'The Ecological Risks and Benefits of Genetically Engineered Plants' (2000) 290 *Science* 2088; Byong H Lee, *Fundamentals of Food Biotechnology* (John Wiley & Sons, 2014) 452–453. See also Government of the Netherlands, 'Biotechnology – Consequences of GMOs for biodiversity' *Government of the Netherlands* (Web Page), www.government.nl/topics/biotechnology/consequences-of-gmos-for-biodiversity.

94 William M Muir, 'The Threats and Benefits of GM Fish' (2004) 5(7) *European Molecular Biology Organization* 654, 655. See also William M Muir and Richard D Howard, 'Assessment of Possible Ecological Risks and Hazards of Transgenic Fish with Implications for Other Sexually Reproducing Organisms' (2002) 11 *Transgenic Research* 101; EM Hallerman and AR Kapuscinski, 'Ecological and Regulatory Uncertainties Associated with Transgenic Fish' in CL Hew and GL Fletcher (eds), *Transgenic Fish* (World Science Publishing Company, 1992) 209; James M Tiedje et al., 'The Planned Introduction of Genetically Engineered Organisms: Ecological Considerations and Recommendations' (1989) 70 *Ecology* 289; Anne R Kapuscinski and Eric M Hallerman, 'Transgenic Fish and Public Policy: Anticipating Environmental Impacts of Transgenic Fish' (1990) 15 *Fisheries* 2.

95 FAO, 'GMOs and the Environment' *FAO* (Web Page), www.fao.org/3/x9602e/x9602e07.htm.

96 Lang et al. (n 11); Jenny Lazebnik et al., 'Effects of a Genetically Modified Potato on a Non-Target Aphid Are Outweighed by Cultivar Differences' (2017) 90(3) *Journal of Pest Science* 855; Agi et al. (n 11); Wieczorek (n 58).

97 Karen S Oberhauser et al., 'Temporal and Spatial Overlap Between Monarch Larvae and Corn Pollen' (2001) 98 *Proceedings of the National Academy of Sciences* 11913; Jerome Tschenn et al., 'Effects of Corn Plants and Corn Pollen on Monarch Butterfly Oviposition Behaviour' (2001) 30 *Environmental Entomology* 495; Anthony M Shelton and Mark K Sears, 'The Monarch Butterfly Controversy: Scientific Interpretations of a Phenomenon' (2001) 6 *The Plant Journal* 483; Wieczorek (n 58) 4.

98 Rosa Binimelis and Fern Wickson, 'The Troubled Relationship between GMOs and Beekeeping: An Exploration of Socioeconomic Impacts in Spain and Uruguay' (2019) 43(5)

domain of non-target species. Qualitative and quantitative data claim 'modest or no effect on the abundance of non-target insects, suggesting no substantial effect on insect community diversity'.[99] Thus, as for the risks to human health, environmental damages and loss of biodiversity caused by trading biotech products remain both potentially serious yet also uncertain.

1.2.3 Social issues in trading biotech products

Besides health and environmental risks, international trade in biotech products also provokes concerns about the social impact on farmers, consumers and, more generally, the global community. Some commentators assert that trading biotech products raises problems of socio-economic justice:

> For example, in contrast to claims that agricultural biotechnology will 'feed the poor', it is argued that the use of genetically engineered crops contributes to global inequality, disregarding the interests of small farmers, especially in developing countries.[100]

Because this study does not focus on the analysis of social issues surrounding the international trade in biotech products,[101] this section discusses only those relevant to the present study. One relates to the fact that, traditionally, farmers save seeds for the next season, but GM seeds and crops are protected by patents and intellectual property rights (IPRs).[102] This 'pathway for corporations to "own"

Agroecology and Sustainable Food Systems 546; Peng Han et al., 'Quantification of Toxins in a Cry1Ac + CpTI Cotton Cultivar and Its Potential Effects on the Honey Bee Apis Mellifera L.' (2010) 19(8) *Ecotoxicology* 1452; Alison J Haughton et al., 'Invertebrate Responses to the Management of Genetically Modified Herbicide-Tolerant and Conventional Spring Crops. II. Within-Field Epigeal and Aerial Arthropods' (2003) 358(1439) *Philosophical Transactions of the Royal Society B: Biological Sciences* 1863; Cathy Hawes et al., 'Responses of Plants and Invertebrate Trophic Groups to Contrasting Herbicide Regimes in the Farm Scale Evaluations of Genetically Modified Herbicide-Tolerant Crops' (2003) 358(1439) *Philosophical Transactions of the Royal Society B: Biological Sciences* 1899; Matthias Schindler et al., 'Monitoring Agricultural Ecosystems by Using Wild Bees as Environmental Indicators' (2013) 71(8) *BioRisk* 53.

99 Pellegrino et al. (n 56) 9. See also Steven E Naranjo, 'Effects of GM Crops on Non-Target Organisms' in Agnès Ricroch, Surinder Chopra and Shelby J Fleischer (eds), *Plant Biotechnology – Experience and Future Prospects* (Springer, 2014) 129; Lora A Morandin and Mark L Winston, 'Wild Bee Abundance and Seed Production in Conventional, Organic, and Genetically Modified Canola' (2005) 15(3) *Ecological Applications* 871; Yagya Prasad Paudel et al., 'Honey Bees (Apis Mellifera L.) and Pollination Issues: Current Status, Impacts and Potential Drivers of Decline' (2015) 7(6) *Journal of Agricultural Science* 93.

100 John Vidal, 'Why Is the Gates Foundation Investing in GM Giant Monsanto?' *The Guardian* (Online 29 September 2010), www.theguardian.com/global-development/poverty-matters/2010/sep/29/gates-foundation-gm-monsanto, cited in Weimer (n 10) 6.

101 See Section 1.8.

102 See IPR, 'European IPR Helpdesk Fact Sheet Intellectual Property in Biotechnology' *IPR* (June 2014), www.iprhelpdesk.eu/sites/default/files/newsdocuments/IP_in_Biotechnology.pdf.

seeds'[103] prohibits seed saving by farmers.[104] Thus, farmers are forced to buy new seeds for every planting season,[105] which creates economic dependencies and financial challenges for farmers, while of course enhancing trade for biotechnology companies. Studies attribute the estimated 300,000 Indian farmer-suicides over the past two decades to the cultivation and commercialisation of GMOs in India.[106] Every year, Indian peasants pay more than US$200 million to Monsanto, which is a leading international biotech corporation.[107] Thomas and De Tavernier point out that during the Uruguay Round of the GATT, which lays the foundations for establishing the WTO, biotech multinational Monsanto 'pushed intellectual property rights over seeds and life forms into TRADE treaties'.[108] More specifically, the WTO *Trade-Related Aspects of Intellectual Property Rights* (TRIPs) *Agreement* prevents farmers from seed saving and exchange, thereby threatening their livelihood, through Article 27.3.[109] 'It is beyond any reasonable doubt that the *TRIPs Agreement* serves the purpose of protecting the profit-making prospects of transnational corporations and market actors'.[110]

103 Shiva (n 69) 21.

104 See, e.g., M Rafiqul Islam, *International Trade Law of the WTO* (Oxford University Press, 2006) 419.

105 This aspect is particularly relevant considering that the analysis in Section 2.6.1.1 highlights that Article 9 of the *Treaty on Plant Genetic Resources* enshrines the rights of farmers to 'save, use, exchange and sell farm-saved seed/propagating material'.

106 Gigesh Thomas and Johan De Tavernier, 'Farmer-Suicide in India: Debating the Role of Biotechnology' (2017) 13(8) *Life Sciences, Society and Policy* 1. See also Srijit Mishra, 'Farmers' Suicides in India, 1995–2012: Measurement and Interpretation' (Working Paper 2014/62) *Asia Research Centre, LSE* (Web Page), www.lse.ac.uk/asiaResearchCentre/_files/ARCWP62-Mishra.pdf; Vandana Shiva, 'From Seeds of Suicide to Seeds of Hope: Why Are Indian Farmers Committing Suicide and How Can We Stop This Tragedy?' *Huffington Post* (Online, 25 May 2011), www.huffpost.com/entry/from-seeds-of-suicide-to_b_192419; Glenn Davis Stone, 'Constructing Facts: Bt. Cotton Narratives in India' (2012) 47(38) *Economic and Political Weekly* 62; Glenn Davis Stone, 'Contradictions in the Last Mile: Suicide, Culture and E-Agriculture in India' (2011) 36(6) *Science, Technology, & Human Values* 759; Vandana Shiva, 'Monsanto in India – A Story of Corruption, Biopiracy, Seed Monopoly and Farmers Suicides' in Vandana Shiva, Debbie Barker and Caroline Lockhart (eds), *The GMO Emperor Has No Clothes: A Global Citizens Report on the State of GMOs – False Promises, Failed Technologies* (Navdanya, 2010) 143; Ramin Jahanbegloo and Vandana Shiva, *Talking Environment: Vandana Shiva in Conversation with Ramin Jahanbegloo* (Oxford University Press, 2013).

107 Thomas and De Tavernier (n 106) 5. See also Vandana Shiva, 'Seed Monopolies, GMOs and Farmer Suicides in India: A Response to Nature' *GMWatch* (Blog Post, 2013), www.navdanya.org/blog/?p=744.

108 Thomas and De Tavernier (n 106); see also Shiva (n 106).

109 Thomas and De Tavernier (n 106).

110 Leonelli (n 5). See also Thomas and De Tavernier (n 106) 5, citing Vandana Shiva, 'Earth Democracy: Beyond Death Democracy and Killing Economies' (2010) 21(1) *Capitalism Nat Socialism* 83. See also Holger Hestermeyer, 'Reality or Aspiration? Solidarity in International Environmental and World Trade Law' in Holger Hestermeyer (ed), *Coexistence, Cooperation and Solidarity: Liber Amicorum Rüdiger Wolfrum* (Martinus Nijhoff, 2012) 45; Holger Hestermeyer, *Human Rights and the WTO: The Case of Patents and Access to Medicines* (Oxford University Press, 2007).

As has become clear, social questions surrounding the international trade in biotech products are 'deeply interrelated with questions of corporate power and global monopolies seeking profit over people'.[111] Only a handful of biotech multinationals dominate the global market,[112] but nonetheless, their business can 'lock farmers into a cycle of dependency on products produced by the same compan[ies]',[113] companies that, in the view of some commentators, attempt to also monopolise research on biotech products.[114] This undoubtedly affects the well-being, especially the mental health, of such farmers.

Given the seriousness of social problems posed by the international trade in biotech products, WTO judicial bodies will likely face disputes concerning biotechnology and, arguably, Article 27.3 of the *TRIPs Agreement*. In that case, the judicial balance between the competing requests at stake must also consider these social problems.

A further social issue stemming from the international trade in biotech products relates to the fact that foods derived from GE crops do not always carry a specific label.[115] For example, the United States, Canada and Argentina, the major producers of GM food, do not enact GM food-labelling regulations.[116] This becomes an issue when such food is imported and exported internationally, not least because without labels, identification of GM food becomes impossible. Consequently, consumers cannot make an informed choice and the purpose of labelling 'to verify whether people have been harmed over the years by consuming G[enetically] M[odified] F[ood]' becomes vain.[117]

As a final point, it must be recognised that international trade in biotechnology encompasses an ethical dimension, which is broadly discussed in the

111 Noam Chomsky, *Profit over People: Neoliberalism and the Global Order* (Seven Stories Press, 1998), cited in Weimer (n 10) 7.

112 Raman identifies Monsanto, Bayer CropScience, Dupont, Syngenta and Groupe Limagrain as the current 'big five' biotech companies; Raman (n 35) 203.

113 Weimer (n 10) 6. See also David Barboza, 'The Power of Roundup; A Weed Killer Is a Block for Monsanto to Build On' *The New York Times* (Online, 2 August 2001), www.nytimes.com/2001/08/02/business/the-power- of-roundup-a-weed-killer-is-a-block-for-monsanto-to-build-on.html; Ronald Evens and Kenneth Kaitin, 'The Evolution of Biotechnology and Its Impact on Health Care' (2015) 34(2) *Health Affairs* 210, 211; Lucía Goldfarb and Annelies Zoomers, 'The Drivers behind the Rapid Expansion of Genetically Modified Soya Production into the Chaco Region of Argentina' (2013) *Biofuels – Economy, Environment and Sustainability* 73, 74.

114 Robinson, Antoniou and Fagan (n 12) 32–39; Raman (n 35) 203. See also Roger A McEowen, 'Legal Issues Related to the Use and Ownership of Genetically Modified Organisms' (2004) 43 *Washburn Law Journal* 611, 625.

115 The use of GM feed represents a potential way to circumvent traceability of genetic foods. Meat labelling does not provide indications of whether the meat was produced with animals raised with GM feed.

116 Behrokh Mohajer Maghari and Ali M Ardekani, 'Genetically Modified Foods and Social Concerns' (2011) 3(3) *Journal of Medical Biotechnology* 109, 113. See also P Byrne, D Pendell and G Graff, 'Labeling of Genetically Engineered Foods' *Colorado State University Extension 2010 Fact sheet No. 9.371*, http://extension.colostate.edu/docs/pubs/foodnut/09371.pdf.

117 Maghari and Ardekani (n 116) 113.

literature and generally considered part of the social issues raised by biotechnology.[118] These ethical and moral discussions are beyond the scope of this study.[119] Nonetheless, it is important to acknowledge that the current fragmentation of international law reflects the general ethical dilemma of what is preferable and for whom. Is it preferable to support economic development of states and, accordingly, accept related risks surrounding technological innovation? Or is it preferable to adopt a precautionary policy and consider the well-being of people and the environment as a priority despite remaining uncertainties? As 'judgments must also pay due regard to . . . ethical considerations',[120] WTO judicial bodies have to consider ethical concerns surrounding international trade in biotech products.[121]

To conclude, international trade in biotech products might be a means to relieve world hunger and support the right to food, even though there is no agreement on this. On the contrary, the economic advantage for both developed and developing countries in trading biotech products and, accordingly, the capacity of biotechnology to enhance the right to development – at least from an economic perspective – of states importing and exporting such products, are broadly supported in the literature. Simultaneously, according to some in the scientific community, trading biotechnology bears serious, and sometimes irreversible, risks to human health and the environment that could have short- and long-term impacts.[122] Trading biotech products might, in turn, undermine the right to health and contribute to environmental degradation, loss of biodiversity, climate change and global warming.[123] Still, a high level of uncertainty on all these risks remains.

The benefits, risks and social issues discussed in this chapter are magnified by the international trade in biotech products. Indeed, while cultivating these products circumscribes their positive and negative effects to a specific area (e.g., area

118 See especially Richard Twine, *Animals as Biotechnology – Ethics, Sustainability and Critical Animal Studies* (Routledge, 2010); Paul B Thompson, *Food Biotechnology in Ethical Perspective* (Springer 2007); Richard Sherlock and John D Morrey (eds), *Ethical Issues in Biotechnology* (Rowman & Littlefield Publishers, 2002); Anjana Munshiand and Vandana Sharma, 'Safety and Ethics in Biotechnology and Bioengineering: What to Follow and What Not To' in Debmalya Barh and Vasco Azevedo (eds), *Omics Technologies and Bio-Engineering: Towards Improving Quality of Life, Volume 1* (Academic Press, 2017) 577.

119 Section 1.8.

120 Weimer (n 10) 13.

121 Any judicial balance is a special kind of reflection of the ethical domain relating to the analysed dispute(s). The judicial balance between competing rights, legal principles or interests should aim to achieve a middle ground between moral dilemmas. On this point, see especially Zucca (n 18).

122 It is estimated that an accurate assessment of the effects stemming from the alteration of biological processes of living beings requires a decade or more. See José L Domingo, 'Safety Assessment of GM Plants: An Updated Review of the Scientific Literature' (2016) 95 *Food and Chemical Toxicology* 12, 17. See also LP Gianessi and JE Carpenter, *Agricultural Biotechnology: Insect Central Benefits* (Unpublished report, National Center for Food and Agricultural Policy, July 1999).

123 See Section 2.6.1.2.

Table 1.1 Summary of benefits and risks in trading biotech products

Benefits in trading biotech products		*Risks in trading biotech products*	
According to part of the scientific community . . .	*In the view of another part of the scientific community . . .*	*According to some scientific and/or sociological studies . . .*	*In the view of another part of the scientific community . . .*
Biotech products can reduce world hunger and help to realise the right to food for everyone	Biotechnology does not represent a solution to sustain a growing world population, not least because there is more than enough food produced in the world to feed everyone	Biotech products can cause allergenicity to a novel gene product and non-target health effects	The introduced novel proteins in commercialised biotech products do not cause food allergy Biotech products can improve the quality of food production Their use can reduce health risks
Biotech products are climate-change resilient	The effectiveness of climate-resilient biotech products is yet to be established, and applying conventional breeding techniques can achieve the same objectives	Biotech products can cause antibiotic resistance that can lead to serious human health problems	Resistance to antibiotics does not cause serious issues to human health
Biotech products can present significant economic opportunities and support the right to development of states	The economic benefits generated by biotechnology strongly depend upon the possibility to trade biotech products with no restrictions. Nonetheless, trade restrictions might be necessary to ensure biosafety	Biotech products can cause health issues due to increasing use of pesticides	Biotech products reduce pesticide usage
		Biotech products can cause environmental degradation due to the increased use of pesticides	Biotech products save energy and reduce CO_2 emissions and the use of pesticides

Benefits in trading biotech products		*Risks in trading biotech products*	
According to part of the scientific community . . .	*In the view of another part of the scientific community . . .*	*According to some scientific and/or sociological studies . . .*	*In the view of another part of the scientific community . . .*
		Biotech products can reduce biodiversity because of the proliferation of invasive alien species (IAS) and the impacts to non-target species	GM animals are very domesticated and will not endanger local species Biotech products have only a modest or no effect on the abundance of non-target insects
		Biotech products can adversely affect farmers, consumers, and, more generally, the global community	

surrounding fields where biotech products are grown), international trade places both the benefits and risks of biotech products on the global market.

Against this background, WTO judicial bodies are at the centre of an intricate and polarised debate, in which balancing requests for trading biotech products and ensuring biosafety is particularly challenging, as Section 1.3 analyses.

1.3 Challenges in international trade in biotechnology

Competing requests of member states require WTO judicial bodies to establish whether the risks in trading biotech products justify trade restrictions aimed at ensuring biosafety. This is, indeed, the focus of the judicial analysis in *EC – Hormones*,[124] *EC – Biotech*[125] and *US/Canada – Hormones Continued Suspension*,[126] which are, to date, the only WTO legal disputes on biotechnology.[127] As discussed in detail in Chapter 2, adopting biosafety measures and striking a judicial balance between trade and non-trade interests becomes an arduous task because of the normative, judicial and epistemic issues occurring within the WTO.

124 AB Report, *EC – Hormones*.
125 Panel Report, *EC – Biotech*.
126 AB Report, *US/Canada – Hormones Continued Suspension*.
127 Part III of this study conducts an in-depth analysis of WTO biotechnology cases.

Normative issues: In balancing the competing requests concerning the international trade in biotech products, WTO judicial bodies refer to a normative framework (i.e., WTO law), which 'was not drafted with the full complexity of biotechnology issues in mind'.[128] This can be inferred from the fact that WTO law requires member states to align their biosafety measures with the WTO's stringent and science-centric requirements that do not accommodate the complex uncertainties associated with biotechnology.[129] Predictably, the biosafety measures adopted in all WTO biotechnology cases were assessed as not in line with WTO law.[130]

Further, WTO law makes the implementation of biosafety measures difficult for member states, beyond the WTO normative framework. This is because there is a 'priority given to trade values within the WTO, [which underlines a bias for trade interests and] undermines the ability of States to respect international obligations in the non-trade arena'.[131] Nevertheless, the special pre-eminence of trade interests in the WTO does not echo the preamble of the *WTO Agreement* that does not set a hierarchy between WTO goals. Rather, the preamble lists several paramount objectives.[132] '[F]ree trade is neither the only nor the overriding purpose' to pursue under the WTO.[133]

Because of this implicit priority given to trade values under the WTO, taking a measure to protect health or the environment can be both required by human rights law or international environmental law, and forbidden (or at least not supported) by WTO norms. This underlines a normative tension between WTO law and other international law regimes, which is further fuelled by the fragmentation of international law.[134]

128 Arthur E Appleton, 'The Labeling of GMO Products Pursuant To International' (2000) 8(1994) *New York University Environmental Law Journal* 566, 570.

129 See Rim Lassoued et al., 'Risk and Safety Considerations of Genome Edited Crops: Expert Opinion' (2019) 1 *Current Research in Biotechnology* 11, 15; Jack Stilgoe, Richard Owen and Phil Macnaghten, 'Developing a Framework for Responsible Innovation' (2013) 42(9) *Research Policy* 1568.

130 See Chapters 5–8.

131 Sarah Joseph, *Blame It on the WTO? A Human Rights Critique* (Oxford University Press, 2011) 59. See also Caroline Dommen, 'Raising Human Rights Concerns in the World Trade Organization: Actors, Processes and Possible Strategies' (2002) 24 *Human Rights Quarterly* 1.

132 Peter-Tobias Stoll and Frank Schorkopf, *WTO – World Economic Order, World Trade Law* (Martinus Nijhoff, 2006) 33 (emphasis altered). See also Franz Xaver Perrez, 'The Mutual Supportiveness of Trade and Environment International Law Stable' (2006) 100 *Cambridge University Press on behalf of the American Society of International Law* 65.

133 Stoll and Schorkopf (n 132) 33 (emphasis altered). See also Xaver Perrez (n 132)..

134 For further insights on the fragmentation of international law, see Tamar Megiddo, 'Beyond Fragmentation: On International Law's Integrationist Forces' (2019) 44(1) *Yale Journal of International Law* 4; Anne Peters, 'Fragmentation and Constitutionalism' in Anne Orford, Florian Hoffmann and Martin Clark (eds), *The Oxford Handbook of the Theory of International Law* (Oxford University Press, 2016) 1011; Andrew Lang, 'Twenty Years of the WTO Appellate Body's "Fragmentation Jurisprudence"' (2015) 14(3) *Journal of International Trade Law & Policy* 116.

Against this background, neither WTO law nor WTO jurisprudence entrenches criteria to resolve these normative issues. Nevertheless, WTO judicial bodies cannot escape all international commitments to harmonise international law regimes.[135] Even more, their judicial balance should echo the *WTO Agreement*, reflecting the national need for equilibrium between trade and non-trade-related values, rather than a special priority given to the former.

These normative issues make it difficult for member states to adopt biosafety measures within and beyond the WTO. Simultaneously, they also have implications for the WTO judiciary, as discussed in the following paragraphs.

Judicial issues: The creation of an international trade system with its own dispute-settlement mechanism causes an imbalance between the responsibilities and duties of states under the WTO and their international obligations to ensure the protection of human health and the environment, which are not supported by an equally strong dispute settlement system.[136] Indeed, when trade and non-trade requests stand in opposition to one another, WTO judicial bodies do not provide for a reasoned balance between both.[137] This is because non-trade interests 'only become relevant when States choose to invoke them as justifications to restrict trade (and thus risk non-compliance with the WTO), rather than when States might threaten non-trade interests by removing barriers to trade in, for example, a harmful product'.[138] This might be viewed as a consequence stemming from the mentioned bias towards trade values within the WTO.

A further central hurdle in striking a balance in the context of biotechnology lies in the fact that 'the WTO is institutionally not ready for such a fundamental balancing of values and interests (mainly economic versus non-economic), and that such balancing is at the core of the proportionality analysis'.[139] The WTO

135 Julia Ya Qin, 'Managing Conflicts Between Rulings of the World Trade Organization and Regional Trade Tribunals: Reflections on the Brazil – Tyres Case' (2010) *Making Transnational Law Work in the Global Economy* 601, 624–627. See also J Pauwelyn, *Conflict of Norms in Public International Law: How WTO Law Relates to Other Rules of International Law* (Oxford University Press, 2003) 240–241.

136 Joseph (n 131) 59. See also Anne Orford, 'Beyond Harmonization: Trade, Human Rights and the Economy of Sacrifice' (2005) 18(2) *Leiden Journal of International Law* 179.

137 Joseph (n 131) 59; Orford (n 136).

138 Ibid. For an in-depth analysis of normative and judicial issues preventing a reasoned balance between free trade and biosafety, see Carlos Bernal Pulido and Alessandra Guida, 'Introduction to the Special Issue on Biotechnology in International Economic Law and Human Rights: Reconciling Biotechnology with Human Rights and the Protection of the Environment under International Law' (2021) 12(3) *European Journal of Risk Regulation* 543.

139 Mads Andenas and Stefan Zleptnig, 'Proportionality: WTO Law: In Comparative Perspective' (2007) 42 *Texas International Law Journal* 371, 373, citing Jan Neumann and Elizabeth Türk, 'Necessity Revisited: Proportionality in World Trade Organization Law After Korea – Beef, EC – Asbestos and EC – Sardines' (2003) 37(1) *Journal of World Trade* 199. See also Center for International Environmental Law, 'Second Guessing National Level Policy Choices: Necessity, Proportionality and Balance in the WTO Services

lacks an analytical structure for balancing competing rights, interests or values, as detailed in Chapter 2.

Such structure is embodied by the *proportionality analysis*, also known as *proportionality balancing*, the appeal of which lies in its accommodating character in the face of conflicting interests,[140] such as in the context of biotechnology. WTO law does not enshrine proportionality *expressis verbis*, which supports the argument that WTO judicial bodies are not required to balance competing interests by means of the analytical structure provided by proportionality analysis.

Epistemic issues: Uncertainties of risks and contested scientific opinions surrounding the assessment of biotech products make the judicial balance between free trade and biosafety even more difficult.[141] There is, therefore, an epistemic problem: Risks posed by biotech products to biosafety entail uncertainty. This uncertainty lowers the reliability of empirical premises, in the sense of the certainty of the underlying assumptions. In other words, can we answer the question of how reliable the empirical assumption is that trading biotech products causes *serious* risks to human health? So far, we cannot. Indeed, the current high level of scientific uncertainty does not allow us to consider this, or any other, premise as reliable. Thus, the reliability of empirical premises concerning the adverse effects of trading biotechnology to human health and the environment is uncertain. Given that, the epistemic problem of uncertainties surrounding the international trade in biotech products makes it difficult for WTO judicial bodies to establish the reliability of empirical premises concerning the adverse effects posed by trading these products to biosafety.

Further epistemic problems are raised by circumstances in which, in the view of the decision-maker, there is no right, principle or interest prevailing over others. These cases, which are generally termed *stalemates*, entail numerous unknowns. How to solve such unknowns is confined to the almost total discretion of decision-makers. This, however, can undermine the objectivity of final judicial decisions in stalemate cases.

The *precautionary principle*, which is an international environmental law principle, can be helpful in this regard, not least because it is considered one of the two main approaches to regulating new technologies.[142] Although there is still some debate on the formulation and interpretation of this principle, scholars agree on its proactive rationale, which calls for actions at an early stage, even when there is still uncertainty as to the harmfulness of a given product or procedure.[143]

Negotiations' *CIEL* (Web Page, 2003) 4, www.ciel.org/wp-content/uploads/2015/03/Necessity_3Sep03.pdf.

140 Ming Sung Kuo, 'Resolving the Question of Inter-Scalar Legitimacy into Law? A Hard Look at Proportionality Balancing in Global Governance' (2018) 31(4) *Leiden Journal of International Law* 793, 799.

141 This emerges clearly from the analysis in Section 1.2.

142 Lassoued et al. (n 129) 12.

143 Aline L Jaeckel, *The International Seabed Authority and the Precautionary Principle – Balancing Deep Seabed Mineral Mining and Marine Environmental Protection* (Brill Nijhoff,

Table 1.2 Summary of normative, judicial and epistemic issues in trading biotechnology

Normative Issues	*Judicial Issues*	*Epistemic Issues*
WTO law was drafted without considering the complexity of trading biotechnology	As non-trade interests become relevant when WTO states choose to invoke them as justifications to restrict trade, the WTO judicial bodies do not provide for a reasoned balance between trade and non-trade interests	Epistemic issues stem from the fact that risks posed by trading biotechnology to biosafety entail uncertainty
The priority given to trade values under the WTO normative framework makes the implementation of biosafety measures difficult for member states in trade contexts and beyond. Indeed, WTO states might find difficult to accomplish their international obligations to ensure biosafety	The WTO is considered as institutionally not ready for balancing economic and non-economic interests	The reliability of empirical premises concerning the effects of trading biotech products to human health and the environment is uncertain
The priority given to trade interests under the WTO creates normative antinomies between WTO law and international human rights law as well as international environmental law	The WTO lacks an analytical structure for balancing competing rights, interests or values	Epistemic problems are raised by circumstances where, in the view of the decision-maker, there is no right, principle, or interest prevailing over the other(s) (i.e., stalemate cases)

Nevertheless, the former secretary to the Committee on Trade and Environment (CTE) notes that under the WTO, 'countries are permitted to take precautionary measures in certain circumstances, but that they face real challenges when defending a precautionary action before the WTO Dispute Settlement Body'.[144] As for proportionality, WTO law does not explicitly refer to the precautionary

2017) 30; David Freestone and Ellen Hey, 'Implementing the Precautionary Principle: Challenges and Opportunities' in David Freestone and Ellen Hey (eds), *The Precautionary Principle and International Law: The Challenge of Implementation* (Kluwer Law International, 1996) 249, 264; Jacqueline Peel, *The Precautionary Principle in Practice: Environmental Decision-Making and Scientific Uncertainty* (Federation Press, 2005) 219.

144 Sabrina Shaw and Risa Schwartz, *UNU-IAS Report Trading Precaution: The Precautionary Principle and the WTO United* (November 2005) 11, http://collections.unu.edu/eserv/UNU:3103/Precautionary_Principle_and_WTO.pdf.

principle. This is arguably the catalyst feeding the ongoing debate on whether precaution can be interpreted and applied in the context of the WTO.

In the light of the foregoing, the question is how these normative, judicial and epistemic issues can be overcome to enable WTO judicial bodies to balance the competing interests in trading biotech products. Can the mentioned proportionality analysis and precautionary principle offer a valid solution to these challenges? Section 1.4 casts further light in this regard.

1.4 Legal loopholes: the need for proportionality analysis and a precautionary approach

The competing nature of requests for trading biotech products and ensuring biosafety makes the judicial balance between trade and non-trade values the fulcrum of biotech legal disputes. Performing such a balance requires overcoming the normative, judicial and epistemic issues illustrated in Section 1.3. The judicial performance of proportionality analysis and the adoption of the precautionary principle can be helpful to decision-makers in this regard. Proportionality analysis, which Kumm described as one of 'the most successful legal transplants in the second half of the twentieth century',[145] represents a valuable tool to address both normative and judicial issues for the following reasons.

Proportionality analysis can foster a solution to the normative issues under the WTO because of its capacity to solve normative antinomies and its function of creating a framework of analysis. Proportionality is broadly conceived as a valid approach to 'defragmentation' of international law.[146] This is even more relevant considering that according to some commentators, WTO judicial bodies in general, and the AB in particular, have a key role in fostering a solution, or at least a constructive approach, to the fragmentation of international law.[147] Also, in guiding WTO judicial bodies' balance between competing requests, proportionality analysis can mitigate the difficulty of member states to adopt biosafety measures

145 Mattias Kumm, 'Constitutional Rights as Principles: On the Structure and Domain of Constitutional Justice. A Review Essay on *A Theory of Constitutional Rights*' (2004) 2(3) *International Journal of Constitutional Law* 574, 595.

146 See, e.g., Adamantia Rachovitsa, 'Fragmentation of International Law Revisited: Insights, Good Practices, and Lessons to Be Learned from the Case Law of the European Court of Human Rights' (2015) 28(4) *Leiden Journal of International Law* 863; Martti Koskenniemi and Päivi Leino, 'Fragmentation of International Law? Postmodern Anxieties' (2002) 15(3) *Leiden Journal of International Law* 553; Alec Stone Sweet and Jud Mathews, 'Proportionality Balancing and Global Constitutionalism' (2008) 1 *Faculty Scholarship Series* 1; Stephan W Schill, 'Cross-Regime Harmonization through Proportionality Analysis: The Case of International Investment Law, the Law of State Immunity Proposal' (2009) 16 *Indiana Journal of Global Studies* 483; Anne van Aaken, 'Defragmentation of Public International Law Through Interpretation: A Methodological Proposal' (2009) 16(2) *Indiana Journal of Global Studies* 483; Thomas Kleinlein, 'Judicial Lawmaking by Judicial Restraint? The Potential of Balancing in International Economic Law' (2011) 12(5) *German Law Journal* 1141.

147 Megiddo (n 134) 131.

under the WTO. This is because in performing a judicial balance by means of proportionality analysis, WTO decision-makers would consider all relevant factors, including the degree of necessity for adopting biosafety measures, and states' difficulty to bear the burden of proof in a context perforated with uncertainties.

Proportionality analysis is also a means to address the outlined *judicial issues* because it provides WTO judicial bodies with an analytical structure guiding the balance between competing rights, interests or values. Accordingly, its adoption would fill the WTO deficit relating to the lack of an analytical structure supporting the judicial balance of competing interests. Adopting proportionality analysis can, as such, enable WTO judicial bodies to perform a *structured* or *reasoned* balance.

Moreover, performing a structured judicial balance by means of *proportionality analysis would support the achievement of the WTO goal of sustainable development*, which 'seeks balance, and does not favour one or another international regime'.[148] The concept of sustainable development, coined in the *Brundtland Report*, captures '[the] need to reconcile economic development with protection of the environment'.[149] If pursued in the context of biotechnology, sustainable development would support the development carried by biotechnology without curtailing the interest to safeguard human health and the environment.[150] However, by ascribing a special priority to trade interests, the WTO normative framework makes the attainment of the WTO goal of sustainable development unlikely because it establishes a hierarchy between economic and non-economic values, which does not favour an integration between trade and non-trade interests:

> [A] large part of the attractiveness of the concept of sustainable development rests on an understanding of integration as balancing different, and often conflicting needs, without any hierarchy between the three pillars (economic growth, environmental protection and social development).[151]

A reasoned judicial balance between economic and non-economic (i.e., human health or environmental) values would, accordingly, overcome such a hierarchy, thereby allowing the achievement of sustainable development.

Importantly, although the WTO does not *require* WTO judicial bodies to balance competing interests through proportionality analysis, this does not mean

148 Robb, Segger and Jo (n 21) 170.

149 *Gabčíkovo-Nagymaros Project (Hungary-Slovakia)* [140]. The concept of sustainable development is, however, broader than this. See especially Nico Schrijver, 'Advancements in the Principles of International Law on Sustainable Development' in Marie-Claire Cordonier Segger and CG Weeramantry (eds), *Sustainable Development Principles in the Decisions of International Courts and Tribunals 1992–2012* (Routledge, 2017) 99, 104–108.

150 See the *Brundtland Report*.

151 Federico Ortino, 'Investment Treaties, Sustainable Development and Reasonableness Review: A Case Against Strict Proportionality Balancing' (2017) 30(1) *Leiden Journal of International Law* 71, 85.

that WTO law does not *enable* decision-makers to adopt proportionality. As numerous commentators note, there is capacity to interpret proportionality into WTO law, despite the lack of explicit reference to it.[152]

This study argues that performing a structured balance through proportionality analysis is the key to addressing both normative and judicial issues. Nevertheless, proportionality analysis is not a criterion that decision-makers can use to solve the epistemic issues posed by the high level of uncertainty about the adverse effects of international trade in biotechnology on biosafety. Effective judicial employment of the precautionary principle can foster a solution in this regard.[153]

The precautionary principle calls for actions at an early stage, even when uncertainties remain. The premise of the precautionary principle is that uncertainties *shall not* be used as a reason for postponing protecting measures. *The precautionary principle is*, as such, *a suitable legal tool to handle uncertainties surrounding international trade in biotech, thereby fostering a solution to the epistemic issues* caused by such uncertainties. Unsurprisingly, the precautionary principle was invoked to support biosafety requests in all WTO biotechnology legal disputes. This principle finds room under WTO law, despite the lack of its explicit reference in the text of the WTO agreements and the judicial reluctance in operationalising precaution.[154]

The precautionary principle is also a substantial condition for achieving the WTO goal of sustainable development:

> The application of the precautionary principle, with its aim of protecting the environment now and in the future, is widely regarded as a necessary condition for the attainment of sustainable development.[155]

What is more, the risks of biotechnology may be mitigated to some degree if this technology is assessed in the context of sustainable development. As Kurlsson

152 See, e.g., Andrew D Mitchell, 'Proportionality and Remedies in WTO Disputes' (2007) 17(5) *European Journal of International Law* 985; Jan Neumann and Elisabeth Turk, 'Necessity Revisited: Proportionality in World Trade Organization Law after Korea-Beef EC-Asbestos and EC-Sardines' (2003) 37(1) *World Trade Journal* 199; Alan Sykest, 'The Least Restrictive Means' (2003) 70(1) *The University of Chicago Law Review* 403; Valentina Vadi, 'The Migration of Constitutional Ideas to Regional and International Economic Law: The Case of Proportionality' (2015) 35(3) *Northwestern Journal of International Law & Business* 557; Megiddo (n 134); Stone Sweet and Mathews (n 146); Alec Stone Sweet and Jud Mathews, 'Global Constitutionalism and Transnational Governance' in Alec Stone Sweet and Jud Mathews (eds), *Proportionality Balancing and Constitutional Governance: A Comparative and Global Approach* (Oxford University Press, 2019) 162; Thomas Cottier et al., 'The Principle of Proportionality in International Law: Foundations and Variations' (2017) 18(4) *The Journal of World Investment & Trade* 628.

153 See Philippe Sands and Jacqueline Peel, *Principles of International Environmental Law* (Cambridge University Press, 2012) 187.

154 See Chapter 4.

155 Arie Trouwborst, *Precautionary Rights and Duties of States* (Martinus Nijhoff, 2006) 34.

notes, '[i]f genetically modified organisms are to contribute to welfare they must be considered in the context of sustainable development . . . These dimensions can be interpreted through the principl[e] of [inter alia] precaution'.[156]

Moreover, ***the precautionary principle can be a valuable means to break judicial stalemates***, which are cases in which the scales of justice are in equipoise because, in the view of the decision-maker, there is no right, principle or interest that prevails over the others.[157] This stems from the capacity of the principle to reverse, in some circumstances, the burden of proof and place it on the proponent of biotech products, leading to a more equitable outcome. Further, the precautionary approach does affect the standard of proof by lowering the evidentiary threshold.[158] Thus, by reversing the burden of proof, or simply by affecting the standard of proof, precaution might allow decision-makers to break a stalemate.

Therefore, there is a need to perform proportionality analysis and adopt a precautionary approach to regulate international trade in biotech products. After all, both proportionality analysis and the precautionary principle support the WTO goal of sustainable development, the attainment of which would be unlikely without employing these criteria. To emphasise such a need, this book pursues the objectives outlined in Section 1.5.

1.5 Objectives of the study

The overarching research questions of this study are:

1. How ought WTO judicial bodies to balance free trade in biotechnology and biosafety?
2. To what extent can proportionality analysis and the precautionary principle assist WTO judicial bodies in achieving such a balance?

In answering these questions, the study analyses the normative, judicial and epistemic issues (outlined in Section 1.3) surrounding international trade in biotechnology. In exploring the judicial analysis of WTO biotechnology cases, this book shows how those issues are addressed in WTO courtrooms. In so doing, it seeks to demonstrate that proportionality analysis can enable WTO judicial bodies to conduct a reasoned balance between trade, human rights law and/or environmental law, while the precautionary principle can address the epistemic uncertainties on the adverse effects of international trade in biotechnology on biosafety.

156 Mikael Kurlsson, 'Biosafety Principles for GMOs in the Context of Sustainable Development' (2003) 10(1) *International Journal of Sustainable Development and World Ecology* 15.

157 For a detailed discussion on stalemate cases, see Chapter 3.

158 Arie Trouwborst, 'The Precautionary Principle in General International Law: Combating the Babylonian Confusion' (2007) 16 *Review of European Community & International Environmental Law* 185, 192; Freestone and Hey (n 143); Peel (n 143) 6; Jaeckel (n 143) 55.

This study intends to demonstrate that the judicial performance of proportionality analysis under the WTO does not represent an intrusion into national normative sovereignty. Rather, asking WTO judicial bodies to justify their rulings in light of a structured balancing process, which is offered by proportionality analysis, would only enhance transparency and objectivity of final decisions, decisions that would inevitably interfere with national policies about either the commercialisation of products or biosafety.

Additionally, this study will emphasise that the precautionary principle is compatible with technological innovation and, by extension, free trade in biotech products. Although commonly depicted as a legal tool standing primarily on the side of environmental protection, this study will highlight that the precautionary principle is a dynamic, rather than a static, tool supporting the adoption of biosafety measures. It requires the consideration of all interests at stake (i.e., free trade in biotech products) and for decision-makers to keep pace with the development of scientific knowledge on the effects caused by biotechnology.

1.6 Methodology of the study

Legal doctrine, which 'sets the terms for future resolution of cases in an area',[159] can raise three kinds of research problems: conceptual or analytical, empirical, and normative.[160]

'Conceptual and analytical clarity is an elementary prerequisite for the rationality of any field of knowledge'.[161] An *analytical* methodology allows a systematic and conceptual elucidation of the law.[162] It is also known as *conceptual* methodology because it 'purports to grasp the reality of law by understanding the concept of law''[163] Adopting such a methodology aids, in turn, to shed light on how to untangle conceptual and analytical problems.

The *empirical* dimension of a legal doctrine is concerned with describing enacted law and judicial practice.[164] It is commonly agreed that if we want to arrive at statements of valid law on the basis of empirical facts, such facts must be interpreted in light of certain assumptions that will then be developed into legislative facts.[165] This can be done through the adoption of an empirical methodol-

159 Emerson H Tiller and Frank B Cross, 'What Is Legal Doctrine?' (2006) 100(1) *Northwestern University Law Review* 517.

160 See especially Robert Alexy, *A Theory of Constitutional Rights* (Oxford University Press, 2002) 6–10.

161 Ibid 14.

162 Ibid 7.

163 Carlos Bernal Pulido, 'In Search of the Ontological Structure of Law' (2012) *Analisi e Diritto* 59, 64. Bernal Pulido further asserts: 'Concepts are common elements in distinct thought contents which help to determine what those thoughts are about or involve': Ibid.

164 Alexy (n 160) 7.

165 Ibid 8. See also Neil MacCormick, 'Law as Institutional Fact' (1974) 90 *LQR* 102.

ogy, which can aid examination of how a legal doctrine is understood in reality to address related empirical problems.

A *normative* dimension of a legal doctrine goes, instead, beyond the understanding and the establishment of validity of the law.[166] A normative methodology addresses the question of how the law *should* address legal problems to explore the justification and critique of the law and legal practice.[167]

The present study conducts an analysis that addresses conceptual and analytical as well as normative, but not empirical, dimensions of the two research questions listed in Section 1.5.[168] It carries a *conceptual* analysis because this study drafts a notion of proportionality, which is useful for the judicial settlement of WTO biotechnology legal disputes. In so doing, it contributes to (re)defining the concept of proportionality under the WTO.

In discussing and developing the concept of proportionality, Chapter 3 adopts a conceptual methodology. The same methodology is also adopted in Chapter 4, which contributes to clarifying how the concept of precaution can be interpreted under the WTO to allow effective operationalisation of the precautionary principle in the context of biotechnology. To some extent, a conceptual methodology is also adopted in Chapter 7, which refines the concept of appropriateness of risk assessment under WTO law. The study and refinement of the three concepts of proportionality, precaution and appropriateness are mainly based on a critical analysis of primary and secondary legal sources.

This study is also *analytical* because it aspires to describe the relationship between several WTO sources[169] and the relationship between different international law sources[170] to enhance the protection of biosafety and guarantee interest in trading biotechnology. This analysis is conducted against the acknowledged fragmentation of international law. This study makes some suggestions about how to achieve its defragmentation or, at least, to mitigate the fragmentation of international law that, according to some predictions, 'is inevitably destined to increase'.[171]

In this light, the discussion of the normative tension between WTO law and international law in Chapter 2 relies on an analytical methodology. This investigation is mainly based on the examination of relevant WTO agreements, judicial interpretations of relevant WTO provisions and responsibilities and obligations

166 Alexy (n 160) 8.

167 Ibid.

168 For further insights on the empirical methodology, see B Leiter, *Naturalizing Jurisprudence. Essays on American Legal Realism and Naturalism in Legal Philosophy* (Oxford University Press, 2007); B Leiter, 'Naturalism in Legal Philosophy' *Stanford Encyclopedia of Philosophy* (2007), http://plato.stanford.edu/entries/lawphil-naturalism/. See also Pasquale Pasquino, 'Major Rules in Constitutional Democracies – Some Remarks about Theory and Practice' in Stéphanie Novak and Jon Elster (eds), *Majority Decisions: Principles and Practices* (Cambridge University Press, 2014) 219.

169 Section 2.4.

170 Section 2.6.

171 Megiddo (n 134) 125.

stemming from international human rights law and international environmental law, which require most WTO states to address or prevent human health and environmental risks posed by international trade in biotechnology.

Further, this study tackles ***normative*** questions because it discusses how the WTO judicial balance can (and should) solve the normative tension between WTO provisions and WTO law and international law. Therefore, the analysis of *EC – Hormones*, *EC – Biotech* and *US/Canada – Hormones Continued Suspension* in Chapters 6, 7 and 8 is conducted by adopting a normative methodology. The case analysis of WTO jurisprudence on biotechnology, which is confined to these three cases, is mainly based on a detailed discussion of the judicial reasoning and related observations in the literature.

Through the employment of a normative methodology, this study also suggests a normative theory that provides reasons for actions to WTO adjudicators. In doing so, this study adopts the general framework of the theory of proportionality to guide adjudicators in solving normative tensions. It also adopts the general framework of the precautionary principle to guide WTO judicial bodies in addressing the epistemic uncertainties surrounding international trade in biotech products and, simultaneously, to refine the theory of proportionality.[172] The framework for assessing the extent to which proportionality analysis and the precautionary principle can assist WTO adjudicators is chiefly based on a critical analysis of academic literature and primary legal sources.

1.7 Scope of the study

In delineating the scope and limitations of this study, this book does not engage with ethical issues and moral dilemmas surrounding the international trade in biotech products.[173] Social issues concerning biotechnology are, instead, addressed only in relation to the discussion of the right to health and the right to a healthy environment of people living in countries importing and exporting biotech products.

Also, in providing a constructive answer to the research questions, this study analyses only the WTO agreements and legal disputes that might help in this regard. Accordingly, this book does not engage with the current debate on the interpretation and application in trade contexts of safeguarding measures, which are regulated under the *Agreement of Safeguards*[174] and Article XIX of the *GATT Agreement*.[175] Similarly, the *Agreement on Agriculture* (*AoA*) does not encompass

172 Chapters 3 and 4.

173 Nevertheless, this study acknowledges the importance of WTO judicial bodies considering the ethical and moral debates surrounding the international trade in biotech products, especially given that what is happening in international law, including its fragmentation, reflects general ethical issues and moral dilemmas that, as such, cannot be overlooked in courtrooms. Further insights on legal implications caused by moral dilemmas are explored in Zucca (n 18).

174 Agreement on Safeguards, art 2 referring to Article XIX of the *GATT Agreement*.

175 In this respect, see Alan O Sykes, *The WTO Agreement on Safeguards: A Commentary* (Oxford University Press, 2006); Sheela Rai, *Recognition and Regulation of Safeguard*

provisions that might help answer the aforementioned research questions and, as such, its examination falls outside the scope of this study.

Moreover, as this study focuses on the judicial balance between the interests in trading biotech products and ensuring biosafety, it does not aim to investigate the aspects of trade in services or features of intellectual property concerning biotechnology.

Although biotechnology can be examined from legal, economic, societal, political and scientific perspectives, this book focuses on legal analysis. As such, the research does not claim to deepen the other domains. Where reference is made to the scientific debate, it is only for the purpose of providing a non-scientific audience with sufficient knowledge about the current debate on the effects of trading biotech products on human health and the environment.

Further, as already anticipated, the only biotech products discussed are those stemming from the agricultural and animal biotechnology industry. This is because the three WTO biotechnology legal disputes concern only such products. Specifically, *EC – Biotech* refers to GM food, while *EC – Hormones* and *US/ Canada – Hormones Continued Suspension* relate to one of the most contentious uses of biotechnology in animal agriculture: meat and meat products injected with synthetic hormones for growth purposes. Other biotech products fall outside the scope of this research.

Finally, as the analysis in this study focuses on international law, with an emphasis on WTO law, national provisions on the regulation of biotechnology are referred to only when they provide useful insights or illustrative examples. Additionally, this study cannot provide an in-depth examination of *all* fields of international law that relate to the discussed topic. For example, the *right to food* and the *right to development* are only briefly discussed to provide the reader with necessary foundations to navigate the complexity surrounding the international trade of biotech products. Considering that WTO law and the WTO judicial system prioritise the interest in trading goods, including biotech products, over other interests, such as biosafety,[176] a general, in-depth discussion of the right to food and the right to development, which are supported by trading biotechnology, would not be particularly illuminating for the purposes of the present study. Instead, this research focuses on whether biosafety is ensured in trade contexts. As such, it discusses the right to health and the right to a healthy environment under the WTO and only in relation to the discussed topic.

1.8 Structure of the study

Part I of this study establishes the scene by providing, in the present chapter, a summary of benefits, risks, social issues and uncertainties surrounding the

---

Measures Under GATT/WTO (Routledge, 2011); Alan O Sykes, 'The Safeguards Mess: A Critique of WTO Jurisprudence' (2003) 2(3) *World Trade Review* 261.

176 Section 2.5.

international trade in biotech products along with a brief explanation of the normative, judicial and epistemic issues in the context of biotechnology. It then makes the case for a judicial performance of proportionality analysis and a precautionary approach to the regulation of international trade in biotechnology. This chapter also outlines the objective of the study, its theoretical and practical relevance, methodology and scope.

Part II establishes the context and analytical framework of this study by discussing in detail the normative, judicial and epistemic challenges surrounding the international trade in biotechnology. Chapter 2 introduces the role, mandate and dispute-settlement mechanism of the WTO. It then addresses the normative issues concerning the international trade in biotechnology by exploring how the protection of human health and the environment is reflected in the WTO framework. This investigation lays the normative foundation for examining the regulation of international trade in biotechnology under the WTO and simultaneously sheds light on whether WTO law supplements, or is in tension with, international human rights law and international environmental law. It also demonstrates how normative issues and gaps in the context of the WTO exacerbate judicial and epistemic problems in trading biotechnology.

Chapter 3 explores the key role that proportionality analysis might have in solving the judicial issues in balancing free trade and biosafety. It discusses the justification to use proportionality analysis to address WTO biotechnology cases and, in doing so, illustrates the theory of the rationality of balancing developed by Robert Alexy. This theory is then applied to biotechnology scenarios and refined by suggesting the consideration of three new factors to the balancing process – the *pro homine* principle, reliability of evidence, and the precautionary principle – to strike a reasoned balance and reduce the epistemic discretion of decision-makers.

Chapter 4 delves into the role of the precautionary principle in addressing the epistemic issues stemming from the scientific uncertainty and contested scientific opinions on the risks posed by international trade in biotech products to biosafety. Here, emphasis is placed on the judicial dimension in implementing precaution, which is the only one relevant for the purposes of the present study. WTO states face real challenges when defending a precautionary action before WTO judicial bodies. Chapter 4 identifies the grounds allowing precaution to be interpreted into WTO law and emphasises the dynamic nature of such a tool along with its capacity to lower the evidentiary threshold and reverse, in some circumstance, the burden of proof.

Part III analyses three WTO cases: *EC – Hormone*, *US/Canada – Hormones Continued Suspension* and *EC – Biotech*. Chapter 5 sets out the background to the cases, the legal issues addressed and conclusions drawn by WTO judicial bodies in each case. The chapter then narrows the analytical focus to four key challenges discussed in the following three chapters. Specifically, Chapter 6 explores how WTO judicial bodies allocate the burden of proof to establish a prima facie case in the three biotechnology cases. It also examines the suitability of the standard of review requiring panels to conduct an objective assessment of the matter.

A refined idea of a prima facie case and the proposal of a new standard of review provide a solution to address, respectively, the criticised judicial concept of prima facie case and the limits of the current standard of review adopted by panels to examine biotechnology matters.

Chapters 7 and 8 discuss the judicial examination of precautionary measures on biosafety in contexts of, respectively, sufficient and insufficient scientific evidence. In doing so, Chapter 7 suggests what should be considered an appropriate risk assessment in the scientifically uncertain context of biotechnology and who should advise panels on the reliability of opposing and uncertain risk assessments concerning biotechnology. Chapter 8 explores the reasons and reasoning underlying the judicial reluctance to allow member states to adopt precautionary measures on biosafety in contexts of qualitatively insufficient scientific evidence. In doing so, the chapter suggests how WTO judicial bodies should assess the state of scientific knowledge concerning biotechnology and, simultaneously, establishes the evidentiary threshold allowing precaution to apply.

Part IV concludes with final reflections by revisiting, in Chapter 9, the complexities of balancing free trade and biosafety and the support that proportionality analysis and the precautionary principle might give in achieving such a balance. This final chapter emphasises the remaining challenges hindering a reasoned judicial balance between trade and non-trade interests in contexts involving scientific uncertainties. In doing so, it recounts the key findings and suggestions developed in this study to address the discussed normative, judicial and epistemic issues surrounding the international trade in biotech products.

Part II

Addressing normative, judicial and epistemic challenges in trading biotechnology under the WTO

2 Normative, judicial and epistemic challenges for the WTO

Free trade and biosafety

2.1 Introduction

The WTO is tasked with addressing the challenges identified in Chapter 1: Trading biotech products carries benefits and risks, both surrounded by scientific uncertainty.[1] Under the WTO, member states have obligations to facilitate trade with a view to, inter alia, raising standards of living and protecting the environment. In line with this, there are WTO provisions permitting member states to limit international trade of goods to safeguard human health and the environment from harmful effects posed by such a trade. However, these limitations ought to be justifiable.[2]

This chapter outlines the main challenges that WTO states encounter when justifying trade limitations. To achieve this aim, Section 2.2 accounts for the mandate of the WTO and, in particular, the dispute settlement system. Section 2.3 illustrates how the WTO normative framework purports to consider biosafety by entrenching the safeguards of human health and the environment as goals. Section 2.4 investigates requirements to protect human health and the environment under the WTO, while Section 2.5 identifies critical normative issues and gaps that underline the existence of an implicit prima facie pre-eminence of free trade under the WTO. Section 2.6 demonstrates how normative issues under the WTO can make it difficult for member states to fulfil international human rights law and international environmental law obligations with regard to human health and environmental protection. Such challenges underlie the existence of normative antinomies between WTO law and other international law regimes.[3] Section 2.7 shows how the normative issues and WTO gaps discussed in the previous sections exacerbate judicial and epistemic problems in trading biotechnology. Finally, Section 2.8 provides a conclusion.

1 Section 1.2.
2 Section 1.8.
3 See Norberto Bobbio, *Teoria dell'ordinamento giuridico* (Giappichelli, 1960).

DOI: 10.4324/9781003325741-4

2.2 The WTO: role, mandate and dispute settlement body

The WTO was created after World War II during the wave of a growing international awareness of how freer trade can advance national economies. Before its establishment, the International Bank for Reconstruction and Development (IBRD), the International Monetary Fund (IMF) and the International Trade Organization (ITO) were empowered with regulating a stable, stronger and freer global economy. The latter, however, was not supported by the United States and never came into being.

The failure to establish an institution specifically focused on the protection of international trade, along with a growing need to promote economic prosperity, led to the *1947 General Agreement on Tariffs and Trade* (*GATT 1947*).[4] The agreement incorporates rules for non-discriminatory trade and principles of tariff negotiations. The *1994 GATT Agreement* (*GATT Agreement*) enhanced the 1947 rules with the purpose of reducing or eliminating trade barriers, such as tariffs and quotas.[5]

Nonetheless, the *GATT Agreement* was conceived of only as 'a stopgap measure until a permanent arrangement was found'.[6] This explains why during the Uruguay Round, the international community favourably received the proposal to establish the WTO as a permanent trade organisation. Thus, in 1995 the *Marrakesh Agreement* established the WTO, a Geneva-based international organisation that currently has 164 member states. Its mandate is to address '[t]he desire of WTO member countries for greater coherence in global economic policy-making through closer cooperation between the WTO, World Bank and IMF [which] is expressed in several agreements, ministerial declarations and decisions'.[7]

The mandate of the WTO is significantly expanded from that of its predecessor (i.e., GATT 1947), which had focused only on promoting international trade.[8] The broader WTO's mandate is reflected in the number of agreements,[9] which cover trade in goods,[10] services,[11] IPRs[12] and, to some extent, foreign

4 *GATT 1947.*

5 *GATT Agreement.* See Eun Sup Lee, *World Trade Regulation – International Trade under the WTO Mechanism* (Springer, 2012) 32.

6 M Rafiqul Islam, *International Trade Law of the WTO* (Oxford University Press, 2006) 3.

7 World Trade Organization, 'The WTO and Other Organizations' *WTO* (Web Page), www.wto.org/english/thewto_e/coher_e/coher_e.htm.

8 *GATT 1947* focused solely on reducing trade barriers and quotas and thereby promoting international trade.

9 The WTO agreements have been ratified by most of the world's trading nations: World Trade Organization, 'What is the WTO?' *WTO* (Web Page, 2018), www.wto.org/english/thewto_e/whatis_e/ whatis_e.htm.

10 See, for instance, the *AoA*.

11 The trade in services is covered by the *GATS Agreement.*

12 The *TRIPs Agreement* covers trade in intellectual property rights.

investments.[13] Moreover, there are agreements regulating trade barriers[14] and the implementation of sanitary and phytosanitary measures.[15] At the 2001 Doha Ministerial Conference, WTO members agreed also to negotiate on the relationship between WTO rules and multilateral environmental agreements (MEAs), the most relevant of which are discussed in Section 2.6.2.

Recently, a few WTO states began bilateral negotiations aimed at adopting free trade agreements (FTAs). The most significant, though incomplete, are the Transatlantic Trade and Investment Partnership (TTIP) between the European Union and the United States,[16] and the *Comprehensive Economic and Trade Agreement* (*CETA*) between the European Union and Canada.[17] These FTAs strengthen a science-based approach that is further discussed in Chapter 7. In so doing, these FTAs do not adequately include the precautionary principle. For example, the *CETA* advocates for science-based judicial decisions[18] and requires science-based approval processes for biotechnology.[19] The reference to the precautionary principle is marginal, and the implementation of precautionary measures must be provisional.[20] This may be regarded as an undermining of the precautionary principle and the protection of human health and the environment this principle supports, although it affects only a very small number of WTO states to date.[21] Future implementation of FTA agreements will shed further light on the role of precaution in the context of those agreements. Further, these agreements can also cast light on the key role of proportionality in trade contexts. Indeed, the text of *CETA* emphasises 'the need for proportionality between the seriousness of the infringement, the interests of third parties, and the applicable measures, remedies and penalties'.[22]

While the agreements are at the heart of the WTO, its dispute-settlement mechanism is 'the most far-reaching consequenc[e]' of the international trade

13 The WTO regulates foreign investment through the *TRIMs Agreement*.

14 *TBT Agreement*.

15 *SPS Agreement*.

16 TTIP negotiations began in 2013 and are frozen as of this writing. See Ferdi De Ville and Gabriel Siles-Brügge, *TTIP: The Truth about the Transatlantic Trade and Investment Partnership* (John Wiley & Sons, 2015). See also Patrick Messerlin, *The TransAtlantic Trade and Investment Partnership: The Services Dimension Patrick* (Special Report No 106/2015), http://ase.tufts.edu/gdae.

17 *CETA* negotiations began in 2009, and it was provisionally applied from 2017 but awaits ratification by several EU member states. It removes all tariffs on industrial products traded between the EU and Canada within seven years. See Nazife Ozge Kilic, Omer Sanlioglu and Ilhan Gullu, 'Evaluation of the EU-Canada Comprehensive Economic and Trade Agreement (CETA) in Terms of Turkish Foreign Trade' (2017) 4(3) *Pressacademia* 275.

18 *CETA* art 24.11 [2].

19 *CETA* art 25.2 [2].

20 *CETA* art 20.37.

21 George Thurley, 'Protecting Public Health in EU and Post-Brexit Trade Agreements' *European Public Health Alliance* (Web Page, 27 September 2018), https://epha.org/protecting-public-health-in-eu-and-post-brexit-trade-agreements/.

22 *CETA* art 20.32 para 2.

system.[23] The WTO dispute-settlement system is open only to states and has been described as 'probably the most powerful international dispute system in the world'.[24] This system requires WTO states to attempt to solve any dispute through consultations between parties. If consultations do not lead to a settlement, the dispute settlement body (DSB), which comprises all member states, has the authority to establish, refer matters to and adopt reports issued by panels and the AB.[25] Panels are composed of three, and exceptionally five, experts selected on an ad hoc basis; as such, there is no institutional continuity of personnel between the different ad hoc panels. The AB's seven members are appointed by the DSB to serve for four-year terms, though each person may be reappointed for another four-year term.

The crucial question is whether the structure of the dispute-settlement mechanism of the WTO, and in particular WTO judicial bodies (i.e., panels and the AB), achieves an equilibrium between the promotion of trade and the protection of human health and the environment. This question is legitimate considering that WTO dispute settlement decisions are made by trade experts 'who may not be particularly conversant with non-trade issues such as human rights, which can again lead to an undue dominance of trade values over potentially competing values'.[26] The case analysis in Part III of this study sheds light on the judicial balance between trade and non-trade values in WTO biotechnology cases to explore whether WTO dispute settlement decisions pursue, and then achieve, such equilibrium.

For the purposes of the present study, it is important only to emphasise that biotechnology legal disputes require WTO judicial bodies to establish whether requests for ensuring non-trade interests justify trade limitations. This requires a judicial balance between competing interests. In performing this balance, WTO judicial bodies refer to the WTO normative framework, which enshrines several goals, as discussed in Section 2.3.

2.3 Protection of human health and the environment as WTO goals

While the raison d'être of the WTO is to facilitate free trade, the underlying aim is to alleviate poverty through economic growth and raising standards of living for all. Indeed, the WTO has numerous goals, several of which are relevant to a state's interest in protecting its biosafety. The goals are spelled out in the preamble of the *WTO Agreement*, which, importantly, 'informs not only the GATT 1994, but also the other covered agreements'.[27] It confirms that member states agree on trading:

23 Sarah Joseph, *Blame It on the WTO? A Human Rights Critique* (Oxford University Press, 2011) v.
24 Ibid 65.
25 Ibid.
26 Ibid.
27 AB Report, *US – Shrimp* [129].

> with a view to raising standards of living, ensuring full employment and a large and steadily growing volume of real income and effective demand, and expanding the production of and trade in goods and services, while allowing for the optimal use of the world's resources in accordance with *the objective of sustainable development*, seeking both to *protect and preserve the environment*.[28]

Two formulations stand out as particularly relevant to biosafety: First, the optimal use of resources in accordance with sustainable development and second, protection and preservation of the environment. These considerations are undoubtedly relevant to biosafety.

However, the preamble does not specifically address the human health dimension of biosafety. Nonetheless, protecting human health can be considered an implicit WTO goal for at least two reasons. First, the WTO objective of sustainable development entails the safeguarding of, inter alia, human health. As clarified by the WHO, '[t]he Sustainable Development Goals (SDGs) set a broad agenda to advance health . . . by 2030. Health is [indeed] centrally positioned within the SDGs'.[29] Second, panels and the AB broadly acknowledge that 'few interests are more "vital" and "important" than protecting human beings from health risks'.[30] The question is whether the acknowledged importance of human health protection corresponds to the decisions made by panels and the AB. The case analysis in Part III of this study sheds light on this aspect.

Here, it is important to highlight that free trade, protection of human health and preservation of the environment are competing WTO goals in the context of biotechnology. What is more, they are *equal* WTO objectives. The *2006 Max Planck Commentaries on World Trade Law* leave no doubt in this regard:

> As far as the objectives of the WTO are concerned, it can be asserted that according to the relevant provisions of the WTO Agreement *free trade is neither the only nor the overriding purpose*. Incidentally, this term does not appear at all in the preamble to the WTO Agreement . . . The Preamble . . . lists *several overriding and paramount objectives*.[31]

This was supported by the panel in *EC – Tariff Preferences*, which points out that '[t]he WTO Agreement contains multiple policy objectives and all of these objectives are important'.[32]

28 *WTO Agreement* preamble (emphasis added).

29 Pan American Health Organization (PAHO) and World Health Organization, 'Health, Environment and Sustainable Development: Towards the Future We Want' (2013), *PAHO* (Web Page), www.paho.org/hq/dmdocuments/2013/seminario-rio-20-eng.pdf.

30 Panel Report, *Brazil – Retreaded Tyres* [7.108]; AB Report, *Brazil – Retreaded Tyres* [179]; AB Report, *EC – Asbestos* [172]; Panel Report, *Brazil – Taxation* [7.873].

31 Peter-Tobias Stoll and Frank Schorkopf, *WTO – World Economic Order, World Trade Law* (Martinus Nijhoff, 2006) 33 (emphasis in original). See also Franz Xaver Perrez, 'The Mutual Supportiveness of Trade and Environment International Law Stable' (2006) 100 *Cambridge University Press on behalf of the American Society of International Law* 65.

32 Panel Report, *EC – Tariff Preferences* [7.52].

Moreover, the absence of an overriding and paramount goal also implies a lack of hierarchy between WTO objectives. After all, the lack of hierarchy between economic, environmental and social objectives represents a prerequisite to achieving the WTO goal of sustainable development:

> [A] large part of the attractiveness of the concept of sustainable development rests on an understanding of integration as balancing different, and often conflicting needs, *without any hierarchy between the three pillars* (economic growth, environmental protection and social development).[33]

Therefore, the language of the *WTO Agreement* supports both the claims that free trade must be enhanced under the WTO and that ensuring human health and the environment are key pillars of trade relations.[34] The question, in turn, is how the WTO legal framework ensures the attainment of such non-trade goals. Put differently, what circumstances permit WTO states to limit trade in biotechnology to safeguard human health and the environment in trade contexts? In approaching this investigation, Section 2.4 discusses WTO requirements to adopt biosafety measures in the context of the *GATT*, *SPS* and *TBT Agreements.*

2.4 Requirements to protect human health and the environment under the WTO

WTO law permits member states to adopt protective measures that restrict international trade in biotechnology to ensure the protection of human health and the environment. Protective measures must, however, justify trade restrictions. In this respect, the *GATT*, *SPS* and *TBT Agreements* set the requirements to be met to successfully implement measures ensuring human health and the environment in trade contexts. While the chapeau of Article XX of the *GATT Agreement* enshrines general requirements to implement protective measures in the context of not only the *GATT*, but also the *SPS* and *TBT Agreements*, each of these agreements provides additional conditions that member states willing to implement protective measures must satisfy, as discussed next.[35]

33 Federico Ortino, 'Investment Treaties, Sustainable Development and Reasonableness Review: A Case Against Strict Proportionality Balancing' (2017) 30(1) *Leiden Journal of International Law* 71, 85 (emphasis added).

34 The protection of human health and the preservation of the environment become relevant under the WTO when related to international trade of goods or services.

35 The GATT, SPS and TBT are multilateral trade agreements, thus, binding on *all* WTO states. See Emily Crawford, 'Proportionality' in Rüdiger Wolfrum (ed), *Max Planck Encyclopedia of Public International – Oxford University Press* (Oxford University Press, 2011).

2.4.1 *Ensuring human health and the environment in the context of the* GATT Agreement

2.4.1.1 *Chapeau of Article XX: general requirements to prevent unjustifiable trade limitations*

Under the *GATT Agreement*, WTO states can adopt measures to minimise risks posed by international trade in biotechnology to human health and the environment in light of the *general exceptions* enshrined in Article XX(b) and (g). The *chapeau* (otherwise known as the introductory paragraphs) of such provision highlights that protective measures triggered in the context of the *GATT*,[36] *SPS*[37] and *TBT*[38] *Agreements* do not apply in a way that would constitute:

1. a means of arbitrary or
2. unjustifiable discrimination between countries where the same conditions prevail, or
3. a disguised restriction on international trade.

All these conditions need to be read side-by-side since 'they impart meaning to one another'.[39] The AB explains that the function of the chapeau, which aims to 'prevent abuse of the exceptions', must steer its interpretation.[40]

Three important considerations can be drawn from the AB's reasoning. First, the *cause of discrimination* is the first factor to examine to understand whether a measure results in arbitrary or unjustifiable discrimination.[41] Second, *if* there is *abuse* in adopting the exceptions specified in Article XX, there will be *arbitrary or unjustifiable discriminations.*[42] Third, the adoption of discriminatory measures can be deemed 'arbitrary or unjustifiable' if 'this discrimination bear[s] no rational connection to the objective' pursued by the specific exception under which those measures have been adopted.[43]

In light of this, the requirements set out in the chapeau of Article XX of the *GATT Agreement* underline that WTO states implementing protective measures must focus on reducing trade limitations, rather than on ensuring non-trade values. This aligns with Article XX, the main purpose of which is to set conditions preventing member states from implementing arbitrary, discriminatory and unjustifiable trade restrictions. This seems to entail that trade liberalisation

36 *GATT Agreement* art XX chapeau.
37 *SPS Agreement* art 2 para 3.
38 *TBT Agreement* preamble.
39 AB Report, *US – Gasoline* 25.
40 AB Report, *Brazil – Retreaded Tyres* [226]–[227].
41 Ibid [226]. See also AB Report, *US – Gasoline*; AB Report, *US – Shrimp [Article 21.5 – Malaysia]*.
42 AB Report, *Brazil – Retreaded Tyres* [227].
43 Ibid.

has greater importance than the other WTO objectives. Section 2.5 discusses this further.

2.4.1.2 Article XX(b) and (g): general exceptions to ensure the protection of health and the environment

Aligning protective measures with the chapeau of Article XX of the *GATT Agreement* is only the preliminary step to adopt biosafety measures in the context of this agreement. Article XX(b) and (g) spell out specific exceptions that permit member states to limit international trade, though only if the implemented protective measures are assessed as:

b) '*necessary* to protect human, animal or plant life or health'[44] or
g) '*relating* to the conservation of exhaustible natural resources'.[45]

These two exceptions are the only options to ensure the protection of human health and the environment under the *GATT Agreement.* As such, discussing what falls within their scope and what is considered 'necessary' and 'relating to' is central.

2.4.1.2.1 SCOPE OF ARTICLE XX(B) OF THE *GATT AGREEMENT*

The rather broad scope of Article XX(b) has raised the question of whether this exception encompasses only matters relating to the life or health of humans, animals or plants or, rather, to all environmental interests. In 2011's *China – Raw Materials*, the panel's reasoning suggests a narrow interpretation of the scope of this exception because it argues that a measure falls within the scope of Article XX(b) only if it specifically aims to safeguard health.[46] In 2017 *Brazil – Taxation*, the panel encompasses environmental matters in the scope of this exception.[47] More specifically, in this 2017 case, the EU claimed that the Brazilian measures concerning taxation and charges in the automotive, electronics and technology industries were inconsistent with WTO law.[48] Brazil argued that the contested INOVAR-AUTO program was justified in light of, among others, Article XX(b) of the *GATT Agreement* because it was a measure to safeguard human health by improving vehicle safety and reducing CO_2 emissions.[49] The panel agreed with Brazil. A national policy reducing air pol-

44 *GATT Agreement* art XX(b) (emphasis added).
45 Ibid, art XX(g) (emphasis added).
46 Panel Report, *China – Raw Materials.* See Donald W Zeigler, 'The Alcohol Industry and Trade Agreements: A Preliminary Assessment' (2009) 104 *Addiction* 13.
47 Panel report, *Brazil – Taxation* [7.873].
48 Specifically, the EU referred to the GATT 1994, the *TRIMs Agreement* and the *SCM Agreement.*
49 Panel report, *Brazil – Taxation* [7.864].

lution resulting from the consumption of gasoline fell within the scope of Article XX(b), if only because it has positive effects on both the environment and human health.[50]

Therefore, the 2017 *Brazil – Taxation* case shows that there is significant scope for environmental matters relating to the protection of human, animal or plant health under Article XX(b) of the *GATT Agreement*. However, the interpretation of its scope depends largely on the factual and legal context of each case.[51] This judgment is relevant also because it recognises the profound link between the protection of human health and the environment. This is particularly relevant in the context of biotechnology, in which adverse effects to the environment might have serious negative effects for human, animal and plant health.[52]

To conclude, a broad judicial interpretation of the exceptions under Article XX of the *GATT Agreement* 'reflect[s] the balance that [this provision] seeks to strike between trade liberalisation on the one hand and other important policy objectives and social values on the other'.[53] Further, 'nothing in [the *GATT*] Agreement shall be construed to prevent the adoption or enforcement by any contracting party of measures falling within the scope of Article XX'.[54] A narrow judicial interpretation of this provision would infringe such obligation. For these reasons, a broad interpretation of this exception should be preferred over a narrow approach.[55]

2.4.1.2.2 ARTICLE XX(B) OF THE *GATT AGREEMENT*: WHAT IS 'NECESSARY'?

WTO states can adopt measures to safeguard human, animal or plant life as well as health only if considered *necessary*. Defining *necessary* becomes, accordingly, fundamental to understanding when protective measures can be implemented in the context of such exception. While the GATT does not elucidate the meaning of *necessary* under Article XX(b), WTO jurisprudence provides some insight in this regard.

In the early 1990s, WTO judicial bodies showed a tendency to interpret the term *necessary* restrictively. For example, in 1990 *Thai – Cigarette*, the United States complained about import licensing restrictions and internal taxes on cigarettes imposed by Thailand. The latter argued that those restrictions were *necessary* to safeguard human health. Nevertheless, the panel disagreed, as 'necessity' implies 'the lack of alternative', or it must involve the least degree of inconsistency with the

50 Ibid [7.879].
51 AB Report, *US – Gasoline* 25.
52 See Chapter 1.
53 Glyn Ayres and Andrew D Mitchell, 'General and Security Exceptions Under the GATT 1994 and the GATS' in Indira Carr, Shawkat Alam and Md Jahid Hossain Bhuiyan (eds), *International Trade Law and the WTO* (Federation Press, 2013) 226, 232–233; *US – Gasoline* (n 39) 18.
54 *GATT Agreement* art XX chapeau.
55 Panel Report, *US – Clove Cigarettes* [6.64]–[6.71], [7.299]–[7.304].

GATT.[56] By equating *necessity* to the lack of alternative measures, the panel adopted a strict interpretation of the word *necessary*. A similarly restrictive approach was put forward in 1991 *Tuna – Dolphin*[57] and in 1994 *Tuna – Dolphin II*.[58]

Interestingly, interpretation of the *necessary* concept seems to adopt a different nuance in more recent WTO case law. The AB in 2000 *Korea – Various Measures on Beef* argues that:

> [T]he reach of the word 'necessary' is not limited to that which is 'indispensable' or 'of absolute necessity' or 'inevitable' . . . [T]he term 'necessary' refers . . . to a range of degrees of necessity.[59]

According to the AB, decision-makers should determine whether a measure can be deemed *necessary* by undertaking a test. This test comprises two steps: (1) a *weighing and balancing exercise* and (2) *searching for alternative measures*, which were aptly explained by Ayres and Mitchell:

1. Once it has been determined that a measure is designed to achieve an objective in one of the subparagraphs of Article XX, a panel should undertake the following *weighing and balancing exercise*:
    a. consider the *importance* of the objective that the measure is designed to achieve; then
    b. in the light of the importance of the objective, consider:
        i. the *contribution* that the measure makes to that objective; and
        ii. the degree to which the measure *restricts international trade*.
2. If step 1 leads to a preliminary conclusion that the measure is 'necessary', determine whether there is an *alternative measure* proposed by the complainant that:
    a. is *less trade-restrictive*;
    b. is *consistent* with the *GATT 1994*;
    c. is *reasonably available* to the respondent; and
    d. meets the *level of protection* the respondent seeks to achieve.

    If the respondent can demonstrate that step 1 is satisfied and that there is no reasonably available alternative according to step 2, the measure at issue is 'necessary'.[60]

56 Panel Report, *Thai – Cigarettes* [75]. The panel refers to the necessity limb of a conception of the principle of proportionality, which is discussed in greater detail in Chapter 3.
57 Panel Report, *Tuna – Dolphin* [5.28] (emphasis added).
58 Panel Report, *Tuna – Dolphin II* [3.81].
59 AB Report, *Korea – Various Measures on Beef* [161].
60 Ayres and Mitchell (n 53) 242–243. See also, Federico Ortino, *Basic Legal Instruments for the Liberalisation of Trade – A Comparative Analysis of EC and WTO Law* (Hart Publishing, 2004) 406.

Therefore, in 2000 *Korea – Various Measures on Beef*, the restrictive approach left room for a broader interpretation of the 'necessary' requirement by means of what WTO judicial bodies and commentators defined as a ***necessity test***.[61]

Since then, the necessity test has been adopted in several subsequent cases.[62] For example, in 2001 *EC – Asbestos*, the AB considered the contested measures necessary for the protection of human health and, accordingly, as falling under the scope of Article XX(b) of the *GATT Agreement*, by applying the test developed in 2000 *Korea – Various Measures on Beef*. What is more, in making such a decision, the AB emphasises the vital importance of protecting human health from risks caused by asbestos fibres.[63] Similarly, in 2007 *Brazil – Retreaded Tyres* and 2017 *Brazil – Taxation*, panels and the AB adopted a broad interpretation of the exception under Article XX(b) of the *GATT Agreement* and acknowledged that 'few interests are more "vital" and "important" than protecting human beings from health risks'.[64]

Despite the proclaimed central role ascribed to human health protection, WTO judicial bodies argue that even if the application of the necessity test identifies a risk to human health and the consequent adoption of measures designed to prevent such risk, this is not sufficient to trigger human health measures by pursuing Article XX(b) of the *GATT Agreement*. Protective measures adopted in light of this exception must also be ***the least trade restrictive***. This emerged clearly in 2017 *Brazil – Taxation*, in which the Brazilian measures were deemed designed to pursue a proven risk to human health (and the environment) but, nonetheless, were rejected by the panel as not 'the least trade restrictive'.[65] Similarly, in 2017 *Indonesia – Chicken*, the panel assessed the Indonesian measures as designed to protect human health from proven risks caused by thawing chicken meat at tropical temperatures.[66] But again, such measures were considered 'not provisionally justified under Article XX(b)' because of their trade-restrictiveness.[67] The final outcomes of these two 2017 cases highlight the importance of implementing protective measures that are

61 Despite the term 'necessity test', the AB's reference to ***the contribution of the contested measure to attain the declared objective*** suggests the judicial adoption of also a 'suitability test', which are both components of the proportionality analysis, as Chapter 3 discusses.

62 See, e.g., AB Report, *Dominican Republic – Import and Sale of Cigarettes* 70; AB Report, *US – Shrimp (Thailand)*; AB Report, *US – Customs Bond Directive* [316]. In *China – Raw Materials*, the panel claimed that measures can be deemed necessary for the protection of human health '[if they] are apt to contribute materially to the realization of [the] declared objective': Panel report, *China – Raw Materials* [VII.518].

63 AB Report, *EC – Asbestos* [172].

64 Panel Report, *Brazil – Retreaded Tyres* [7.108], [144], [179]. Panel report, *Brazil – Taxation* [7.873].

65 Panel report, *Brazil – Taxation* [7.4.6.2.2.3]; [8.6(f)].

66 Panel Report, *Indonesia – Chicken* [7.208].

67 Ibid [7.239]–[7.240].

the least trade-restrictive or, put differently, proportional to the trade interest to be successfully adopted in light of Article XX(b).[68]

To conclude, over the years, the *necessary* parameter has undergone different judicial interpretations, as summarised in Table 2.1. The restrictive interpretation of *necessity* arguably does not support member states in adopting measures to protect human, animal or plant life or health:[69]

> [N]arrow interpretations of the plain meaning of the exceptions may ultimately make them high hurdles to those seeking to implement environmentally protective trade measures.[70]

Further, a narrow interpretation of the term *necessary* would not encompass environmental measures in the scope of this exception. This would, in turn, overshadow the intrinsic linkage between human health and environmental protection in the context of biotechnology.[71]

More recent jurisprudence has explicitly addressed the promotion and protection of human, animal and plant life or health as a goal of the highest importance and simultaneously has signalled a greater willingness to adopt a broad interpretation of *necessity* by means of the necessity test, which the AB developed in 2000 *Korea – Various Measures on Beef*. As protective measures must also be proportional to the interest in trading biotechnology, WTO judicial bodies are implicitly required to perform a proportionality analysis in biotechnology legal disputes, as discussed in Chapter 3.

2.4.1.2.3 SCOPE OF ARTICLE XX(G) OF THE *GATT AGREEMENT*: WHAT IS 'RELATING TO'?

The general exception under Article XX(g) allows WTO states to adopt protective measures '*relating* to the conservation of exhaustible natural resources'.[72] Importantly, this exception can include environmental matters, as it did in 1998 *US – Shrimp*, in which the AB finds that wild animals, such as sea turtles, could be deemed an 'exhaustible natural resource'.[73] Also the word *conservation* is broadly interpreted. Indeed, in 2011 *China – Raw Materials*, the AB explains that it

68 As the analysis in Chapter 3 asserts, performing a judicial proportionality analysis, which also comprises suitability and necessity tests, becomes fundamental for establishing whether the contested measures are necessary and proportional to the other interest(s) at stake.

69 AB report, *US – Gasoline* 30.

70 Shawkat Alam, *Sustainable Development and Free Trade – Institutional Approaches* (Routledge, 2008) 74.

71 Environmental damage caused by massive cultivations of biotech products can adversely affect the health of farmers and people living in areas surrounding crops fields. There is, as such, a profound link between human health and environmental protection.

72 *GATT Agreement* art XX(g) (emphasis added).

73 AB report, *US – Shrimp* [152]–[154].

Table 2.1 Historical summary of judicial interpretations of the 'necessary' parameter

Year	*Case*	*'Necessary to' interpreted by the WTO judicial bodies . . .*	*Implications stemming from the judicial interpretation of the 'necessary' parameter*
1990	*Thai – Cigarette*	. . . as lack of alternative . . . as the least degree of inconsistency with the *GATT Agreement*	The WTO judicial bodies show a restrictive judicial interpretation of the 'necessary' parameter that does not permit member states to encompass environmental matters relating to the protection of human, animal or plant life or health under Article XX(b) of the *GATT Agreement*. A narrow interpretation of this parameter is not desirable, especially in the context of biotechnology where health and environmental matters are strictly related to each other.
1991	*Tuna – Dolphin*	. . . as lack of all options reasonably available	
1994	*Tuna – Dolphin II*	. . . as lack of existing alternatives	
2000	*Korea – Various Measures on Beef*	. . . by referring to a range of degrees of necessity: The greater the contribution to achieve the declared objective, the easier a measure might be considered to be necessary	The AB's development of the 'necessity test' broadens the interpretation of the exception under Article XX(b) and, at the same time, underscores the judicial need for performing a proportionality analysis by referring to *suitability* and *necessity*, which are two tests of the proportionality analysis.
2001	*EC – Asbestos*	. . . not in relation to the goal of a measure, but the necessity of the means to that end	The WTO judicial bodies emphasise the importance of assessing the 'necessary' parameter in relation to the means adopted to achieve the protection of human, animal or plant life or health. This, in turn, underlines the importance of adopting the least trade restrictive measures and, consequently, performing the 'necessity test', which assists decision-makers in evaluating whether the contested measures are more trade restrictive than necessary.

(*Continued*)

Table 2.1 (Continued)

Year	*Case*	*'Necessary to' interpreted by the WTO judicial bodies . . .*	*Implications stemming from the judicial interpretation of the 'necessary' parameter*
2007	*Brazil measures Affecting Imports of Retreaded Tyres*	. . . as the result of a judicial reasoning considering (1) the importance of the objective pursued by that measure; (2) the contribution that the measure makes to that objective; (3) the degree to which the measure restricts international trade; (4) alternative measures	More recent jurisprudence has highlighted a judicial trend to opt for a broad interpretation of the exception under Article XX(b). A broad interpretation allows stakeholders to encompass environmental matters relating to the protection of human, animal or plant life or health within the scope of Article XX(b). Adopting a broad interpretation of the 'necessary' parameter facilitates national adoptions of biosafety measures in the context of Article XX(b).
2011	*China–Raw Materials*	. . . as measures apt to contribute materially to the realisation of the declared objective	
2017	*Indonesia–Chicken*	. . . as the result of the 'weighing and balancing' test developed by the AB in *Korea – Various Measures on Beef*	
2017	*Brazil–Taxation*	. . . as measures that are potentially capable of contributing to the pursued objective	

indicates 'preservation of the environment, especially of natural resources'.[74] In 2014 *China – Rare Earths*, the AB adds that conservation could comprise a range of different actions depending on whether the exhaustible natural resource was living or non-living.[75] Thus, WTO judicial bodies' interpretation of this exception

74 AB Report, *China – Raw Materials* [355].

75 AB Report, *China – Rare Earths* [5.89].

enhances its scope beyond its literal meaning to encompass environmental matters. This is particularly relevant in the context of biosafety.[76]

To fall under the scope of this exception, protective measures must also be assessed as *relating to* the conservation of exhaustive resources. Here, too, the *GATT Agreement* does not clarify its meaning, and WTO jurisprudence fills this shortfall.

In 1996 *US – Gasoline*, the AB emphasises that measures adopted under Article XX(g) must demonstrate a 'substantial relationship' with the conservation of exhaustible natural resources.[77] Importantly, the AB adds that a *substantial relationship* does not equate to the higher degree of necessity required to trigger the exception enshrined in Article XX(b).[78] In 1998 *US – Shrimp* and 2017 *Brazil – Taxation*, the AB adds that this 'substantial relationship' must be interpreted as a 'close and genuine relationship between ends and means'.[79] The reference to a 'genuine' relationship between ends and means implies the implementation of *proportional* measures 'relating to' – and not 'necessary for' – the conservation of exhaustive resources. Indeed, the AB underlines that the design of the domestic measure was 'not disproportionately wide in its scope and reach in relation to the policy objective of protection and conservation of sea turtle species'.[80] Similarly, the AB in 2011 *China – Raw Materials* and 2015 *China – Rare Earth* emphasises that design and structure of the measure at stake are key aspects to be examined in establishing whether such a measure 'relates to' the conservation of exhaustible natural resources.[81] Also, the AB clarifies that judicial analysis of this exception must be 'a holistic assessment that considers the factual and legal context in a given dispute through a case-by-case approach'.[82]

The developed judicial interpretation of what is considered *relating to* is highly relevant in the context of biotechnology for two main reasons. First, it underlines that WTO judicial bodies are called to assess whether the contested biosafety measures are *proportional* to the other interest at stake, which is a key judicial step in the context of biotechnology, as discussed extensively in Chapter 3. Second, acknowledging that the judicial analysis of Article XX(g) must be a holistic assessment of the matter at stake has a primary importance, especially because the judicial analysis of biotechnology cases seems to overlook holistic

76 This is because environmental matters concerning the biotechnology legal cases do not refer to the conservation of exhaustible natural resources but, rather, the potentially adverse impacts posed by the international trade in biotech products to the environment.

77 AB report, *US – Gasoline* 19.

78 Ibid. The same interpretation of the term 'relate to' was corroborated by the panel in Panel report, *Tuna – Dolphin II* and Panel Report, *US – Taxes.*

79 AB report, *US – Shrimp* [136]; Panel report, *Brazil – Taxation* [7.987].

80 AB report, *US – Shrimp* [141]. It is also worth noting that the judicial interpretation of Article XX(g) has developed a 'relating to' test, which is less strict than the necessity test, as noted also by the AB in AB report, *US – Gasoline* and AB report, *Korea – Various Measures on Beef*; see Crawford (n 35).

81 AB report, *China – Raw Materials* [355]; AB report, *China – Rare Earths* [355]. See also AB report, *US – Shrimp* [135]–[137].

82 AB report, *China – Raw Materials* [5.95].

Table 2.2 Summary of judicial interpretations of the 'relating to' parameter

Year	*Case*	*'Relating to' interpreted by the WTO judicial bodies . . .*	*Implications stemming from the judicial interpretation of the 'relating to' parameter*
1996	*US – Gasoline*	. . . as a substantial relationship with the conservation of exhaustible natural resources	Over the years, the WTO judicial bodies have showed a broad interpretation of the exception under Article XX(g). A broad interpretation should permit member states to successfully adopt biosafety measures in the context of this exception.
1998	*US – Shrimp*	. . . as a close and genuine relationship between ends and means	
2011	*China – Raw Materials*	. . . in relation to the examination of the design and structure of the measure at stake	
2015	*China – Rare Earth*	. . . by means of a holist assessment that takes account of factual and legal context on a case-by-case approach	
2017	*Brazil – Taxation*		

data that, nonetheless, are highly relevant to grasp the complexity surrounding biotechnology.[83]

To conclude, by adopting a broad judicial interpretation of the exception under Article XX(g), WTO judicial bodies show that a measure can be considered '*relating* to the conservation of exhaustible natural resources' and falling, as such, under the scope of Article XX(g) when there is a meaningful relationship with the conservation of exhaustible natural resources and it is proportional in pursuing the conservation of exhaustive resources. This case-by-case holistic evaluation must consider the design and structure of the measure at stake along with the factual and legal context of a case. As such, the *WTO Agreement* provides biosafety measures that can restrict free trade, at least in principle. As Part III of this book demonstrates, the practical application of such provisions is a different matter.

The GATT does not represent the only agreement that encompasses provisions allowing WTO states to safeguard human health and the environment from risks posed by trading biotechnology. There are similar provisions in the context of the *SPS* and *TBT Agreements*, as discussed in the following section.

83 In this regard, see especially Apolline Roger, 'In the Public Interest? A Comparative Analysis of Norway and EU GMO Regulations' (2015) 24(3) *Review of European, Comparative and International Environmental Law* 264.

2.4.2 Ensuring human health and the environment in the context of the SPS *and* TBT *Agreements*

The *SPS* and *TBT Agreements* form part of WTO law and permit member states to ensure biosafety by encompassing provisions to limit trade to safeguard human health or the environment. The *SPS Agreement* provides general sanitary and phytosanitary standards for food safety and animal and plant health. It sets member states' rights and obligations for triggering food safety and animal or plant health measures with a clear focus on preventing unjustified limitations to trade. In light of Article 2.2, WTO states can apply sanitary and phytosanitary measures, although 'only to the extent *necessary* to protect human, animal or plant life or health'.[84] This agreement adopts a risk management strategy based ostensibly on scientific evidence. Indeed, SPS measures cannot be maintained 'without sufficient scientific evidence'[85] because they must be based on 'scientific principles'[86] and a scientific risk assessment considered 'appropriate to the circumstances'.[87] Nevertheless, Article 5.7 offers member states the possibility of adopting SPS measures in contexts in which there is insufficient scientific evidence provided that a range of conditions are satisfied.[88]

The *SPS Agreement* expresses a preference for harmonised SPS standards. Indeed, Article 3 invites member states to conform their standards to the international ones.[89] If states do this, their SPS measures are presumed to comply with the *SPS Agreement.*[90] However, Article 3.3 recognises the members' right to establish an appropriate level of protection (ALOP) that is higher than international standards.[91] States choosing this option must justify their SPS standards by performing scientific risk assessments that are assessed as aligning with Article 5.[92]

The highly complex and scientifically uncertain nature of biotechnology makes it difficult for member states to justify biosafety measures under the science-centric *SPS Agreement.* However, because this agreement applies only to man-made risks,[93] Macmillan observes that 'measures in relation to GMOs are likely to fall within the SPS Agreement'.[94] Unsurprisingly, WTO judicial bodies considered the biosafety measures triggered in the three biotechnology cases discussed in

84 *SPS Agreement* art 2 [2] (emphasis added).
85 Ibid.
86 Ibid.
87 Ibid, art 5.1.
88 An in-depth analysis of the *SPS Agreement* art 5.7 is conducted in Section 4.3.1.1.
89 *SPS Agreement* art 3.
90 Ibid, art 3.2.
91 The ALOP is the level of protection established at the national level, and it should arguably reflect government policy and community expectations.
92 Chapter 4.3.1.1.
93 AB Report, *EC – Hormones* [32]. In line with the AB's clarification in *EC – Hormones*, the author distinguishes man-made risks, meaning risks stemming from events that are caused by humans, from naturally-occurring risks.
94 Fiona Macmillan, *WTO and the Environment* (Sweet & Maxwell, 2001) 142.

Part III of the present study as falling under the scope of the *SPS Agreement*. Yet, in all three disputes, the triggered biosafety measures were found not to be based on risk assessments complying with the scientific criteria under the *SPS Agreement* and, accordingly, with WTO law.

The *TBT Agreement* aims to ensure non-discriminatory technical regulation, standards and conformity assessment procedures to avoid unnecessary obstacles to trade. Similarly to the *SPS Agreement*, the *TBT Agreement* '[r]ecogni[ses] that no country should be prevented from taking measures *necessary* . . . for the protection of human, animal or plant life or health, of the environment'.[95] Article 2.2 of the *TBT Agreement* pushes further, acknowledging that the protection of human health or safety, animal or plant life or health, or the environment is deemed a 'legitimate objective' allowing restrictions to international trade.[96] However, unlike the *SPS Agreement*, the *TBT Agreement* places less emphasis on the scientific justification of protective measures. Indeed, 'there is no requirement [for states] to base their regulations on scientific evidence' even if they rely on a standard more stringent than the international ones.[97] Rather than focusing on the scientific justification of the contested protective measures, the *TBT Agreement* emphasises the importance of implementing the least trade-restrictive measures and, importantly, it requires member states to consider the risks that non-fulfilment of the desired policy objectives would create.[98]

At this point, an observation is in order. Less emphasis on the scientific justification of the contested measures and greater attention to their necessity and proportionality aligns with the rationale of the precautionary principle that, as Chapter 4 asserts, finds room in the context of both the *SPS* and *TBT Agreements*.[99] Consequently, shifting the science-centric focus of the *SPS Agreement* towards a more holistic approach would coherently align with the *TBT Agreement* and, most importantly, it would not prevent member states from operationalising the precautionary principle in the context of the *SPS Agreement*.

To bring this abstract discussion back to the topic at hand, WTO law enables member states to safeguard the environment and human health *only if* the implemented protective measures:

1. are designed by considering the importance of 'minimiz[ing] negative trade effects'[100] (as expressed in the *SPS Agreement*) or '[avoiding to] create unnecessary obstacles to international trade' (as required by the *TBT Agreement*),[101]

95 *TBT Agreement* preamble.

96 'Legitimate objectives' allow trade limits that 'shall not be more trade-restrictive than necessary to fulfil a legitimate objective': *TBT Agreement* art 2 [2]. Instead, the *SPS Agreement* does not refer to 'legitimate objective'.

97 *TBT Agreement* art 5 [6].

98 Ibid, art 2.2.

99 A heavy reliance on scientific knowledge makes for difficult implementation of the precautionary principle. See case analysis in Chapter 8.

100 *SPS Agreement* art 5 [4].

101 *TBT Agreement* preamble.

2. fall under the scope of Article XX(b) or (g) of the *GATT Agreement*, *SPS Agreement* or *TBT Agreement*,
3. are deemed 'necessary' or 'relating to' the protection of human health and/or the environment,
4. satisfy the conditions settled in the chapeau of Article XX of the *GATT Agreement*,[102] and
5. are maintained with 'sufficient scientific evidence',[103] scientifically justified[104] and based on a 'risk assessment appropriate to the circumstances'[105] if triggered in the context of the *SPS Agreement* – unless they fall under the scope of Article 5.7.[106]

These conditions are jointly sufficient, meaning that satisfying *all* these requirements is a necessary condition to adopt protective measures in the context of the *GATT*, *SPS* and *TBT Agreements*. Nevertheless, fulfilling this range of criteria is so onerous that in almost all WTO cases on human health and environmental protection mentioned in this chapter, states' requests to implement protective measures were rejected.[107]

2.5 Difficulties ensuring human health and the environment under the WTO: an implicit prima facie pre-eminence of free trade

Although WTO law permits member states to adopt measures protecting human health and the environment, economic interests, including free trade in biotechnology, seem to be implicitly more important than non-economic interests, such as biosafety. '[T]he dominant commercial ethos of WTO negotiators . . . led to design rules . . . naturally dominated by free trade and commercial values'.[108] This means that while in principle there is no explicit priority between WTO goals,[109] implicitly trade has pre-eminence. In other words, the WTO is characterised by an implicit prima facie pre-eminence of free trade over other WTO goals. The following shortfalls substantiate the existence of this priority under the WTO.

1. *WTO 'democratic deficit' in relation to non-trade interests*: As argued by a number of commentators, the WTO is characterised by a *democratic deficit*, meaning that WTO rules and dispute settlement 'undermine the ability of

102 *GATT Agreement* art XX chapeau. In this respect, see Alam, *Sustainable Development and Free Trade*.
103 *SPS Agreement* art 2 [2].
104 Ibid, arts 5.1, 5.7.
105 Ibid, art 5.1.
106 Ibid, art 2.2.
107 See, e.g., Panel report, *Thai – Cigarettes*; Panel report, *Tuna – Dolphin*; Panel report, *Tuna – Dolphin II*; AB report, *US – Gasoline*.
108 Joseph (n 23) 58.
109 Stoll and Schorkopf (n 31) 33; see also Perrez (n 31).

> States to enact laws that reflect the democratic will of their people'[110] to ensure the enhancement of non-trade interests, such as human health and environmental protection. This deficit can affect the capacity of states to ensure the protection of human health and the environment in biotechnology cases and, more generally, in health/environment-related disputes. For example, in *EC – Biotech*, the panel decided that the ban by six European member states to prohibit or restrict the marketing of biotech products was a breach of WTO law. In the view of Joseph, '[t]he lifting of the ban would be likely to be against the wishes of the majority of European peoples and consumers, who fear that such hormones could be unsafe for their health'.[111]

The root cause of such deficit might lie in the fact that '[WTO] Negotiating teams have tended to represent a narrow range of interests, and are not necessarily skilled at anticipating or appreciating the "non-trade" impacts of trade deals, for example in the fields of human rights, environment, and health'.[112] Additionally, the analysis in the 2002 *Report of the United Nations Conference on Trade and Development* (UNCTAD) highlights that around two-thirds of world trade was conducted by multinational corporations in the latter half of the 1990s.[113] 'It is arguable', Joseph commented, 'that [the] WTO negotiation process is simply amplifying the lobbying power of actors who already have huge national influence, namely multinational corporations, the major engines of global trade'.[114] After all, the discussion in Chapter 1 highlights that social issues surrounding international trade in biotechnology are deeply interrelated with questions

110 Joseph (n 23) 57; see also Jeffrey L Dunoff, 'The Death of the Trade Regime' (1999) 10 *European Journal of International Law* 733; Thomas Cottier, 'Preparing for Structural Reform of the WTO' (2007) 10 *Journal of International Economic Law* 497; Daniel C Esty, 'The World Trade Organization's Legitimacy Crisis' (2002) 1 *World Trade Review* 7; Karen J Alter and Kal Raustiala, 'The Rise of International Regime Complexity' (2018) 14(1) *Annual Review of Law and Social Science* 329; Kal Raustiala, 'Rethinking the Sovereignty Debate in International Economic Law' (2003) 6 *Journal of International Economic Law* 841.

111 Joseph (n 23) 57. See also, European Commission, 'Several European Countries Move to Rule Out GMOs' *Environment* (Web Page), https://ec.europa.eu/environment/europeangreencapital/countriesruleoutgmos/.

112 Joseph (n 23) 58. See, generally, Joseph Stiglitz, 'Social Justice and Global Trade' (2006) 169 *Far Eastern Economic Review* 18, 22; Sophia Murphy, *Concentrated Market Power and Agricultural Trade, August 2006* (Heinrich Boell Stiftung, Berlin, 2006); Ilan Kapoor, 'Deliberative Democracy and the WTO' (2004) 11 *Review of International Political Economy* 522; Susan K Sell, *Private Power, Public Law: The Globalization of Intellectual Property Rights* (Cambridge University Press, 2003).

113 United Nations Conference on Trade and Development (UNCTAD), World Investment Report 2002, Transnational Corporations and Export Competitiveness, UN Doc UNCTAD/WIR/2002 (2002) 153.

114 Joseph (n 23) 58.

around the power of multinational biotechnology corporations.[115] Nevertheless, it must be acknowledged that the WTO has increased consultation and cooperation with non-governmental organisations (NGOs),[116] and that '[g]reater NGO participation could help make the WTO more effective'.[117] As the WTO restricts the participation of non-trade interest groups, the organisation is deprived of diverse views by stakeholders. This is reflected by WTO judicial bodies that tend to grant pre-eminence to trade. There are no political checks to detect this.

2. *WTO range of criteria undermining the national sovereignty on health and environmental policies*: Under the *GATT*, *SPS* and *TBT Agreements*, biosafety, or more generally, protective measures, will breach WTO law if they do not meet a range of narrow criteria (see Sections 2.4.1 and 2.4.2). These requirements are so stringent that member states' requests for adopting protective measures were rejected in almost all cases referred to above, such as the 1991 *US – Restrictions on Imports of Tuna*, 2017 *Indonesia – Chicken* and 2017 *Brazil – Taxation*.[118] This does not mean, however, that there are no WTO cases in which the contested measures have been found to reflect policies aimed to protect health within the meaning of WTO law.[119] Nevertheless, the lack of adequate attention to non-trade interests under the WTO led to requirements that likely hinder effective employment of human health and environmental measures.[120] This, in turn, might undermine the sovereignty of member states to implement national health and environmental policies, thereby preventing them from enjoying the acknowledged WTO right to establish their own ALOP.
3. *Protective measures as exceptions to substantive obligations established in the GATT Agreement*: Under the *GATT Agreement*, the only provision allowing WTO states to limit international trade to protect human health and the

115 See Section 1.2.3.

116 WTO, *The Future of the WTO: Addressing Institutional Challenges in the New Millennium* (Report by the Consultative Board of the Director-General of the WTO to former Director-General Supachai Panitchpakdi) (2004) 41–43; Steve Charnovitz, 'The WTO and Cosmopolitics' (2004) 7(3) *Journal of International Economic Law* 675, 676–677; Joseph (n 23) 60. Art V2 of the *WTO Agreement* gives authority in consulting and cooperating with NGOs.

117 Charnovitz (n 116) 681.

118 Almost all aforementioned WTO cases highlight that requests for adopting measures safeguarding human health and/or the environment are ultimately rejected by WTO judicial bodies. See, e.g., Panel report, *Thai – Cigarettes*; Panel report, *Tuna – Dolphin*; Panel report, *Tuna – Dolphin II*; AB report; AB report, *US – Gasoline*; Panel report, *Indonesia – Chicken*; Panel report, *Brazil – Taxation*.

119 See generally AB report, *US – Gasoline*; AB report, *EC – Asbestos*; AB report, *Brazil – Retreaded Tyres*.

120 In regard to non-trade concerns under the WTO, see Sara Dillon, 'A Farewell to "Linkage": International Trade Law and Global Sustainability Indicators' (2002) 51 *Rutgers Law Review* 87; Andrew TF Lang, 'Reflecting on "Linkage": Cognitive and Institutional Change in the International Trading System' (2007) 70 *Modern Law Review* 523.

environment (i.e., Article XX) is termed 'general exceptions'.[121] This seems to suggest that protective measures are considered 'exceptions to substantive obligations established in the GATT Agreement [to advance free trade]'.[122] This places the burden of proof and argumentation on those who seek to apply the exceptions. This, in turn, supports the argument that the WTO exhibits an implicit prima facie pre-eminence of trade interests, despite the lack of a hierarchy between WTO goals.

4. *Lack of WTO provisions designed to ensure the protection of human health and the environment*: The dominant commercial ethos of WTO negotiators contributed to the drafting of a legislative framework without provisions designed with the primary purpose of protecting human health and the environment in trade contexts.[123] For example, it might be thought that the *SPS Agreement* was introduced to address states' concerns over (phyto)sanitary issues that were not covered by the WTO until the adoption of this agreement. However, preventing illegitimate trade restrictions was the reason for the introduction of such an agreement.[124] Indeed, WTO law lacks provisions the primary purpose of which is to ensure protection of human health and/or the environment in conducting trade relations:

> [F]ood safety laws, which have a significant impact on the human rights to adequate standards of health care and food, are analysed in terms of their scientific justifiability under the SPS, with a focus on their impact on trade flows rather than human health. Similarly, environmental measures are assessed according to their trade impact, rather than their environmental impact.[125]

It might be possible to overcome this problem through interpretation. In approaching WTO provisions enabling member states to ensure biosafety, WTO judicial bodies might shift the focus from trade to biosafety in trading goods. However, WTO decision-makers also approach protective measures with a focus on trade.[126] For example, in *US – Shrimp*, the AB interpreted the term *relating to* under Article XX(g) by emphasising the need for a 'close and genuine relationship between ends and means'.[127] The reference to 'ends and means' aims to avoid disguised protectionist measures. In other words, WTO judicial bodies interpret measures designed to protect the environment with the primary goal to prevent

121 *GATT Agreement* art XX.
122 AB report, *US – Shrimp* [121].
123 *WTO Agreement* preamble.
124 See WTO, 'Understanding the WTO Agreement on Sanitary and Phytosanitary Measures' *WTO* (Web Page), www.wto.org/english/tratop_e/sps_e/spsund_e.htm.
125 Joseph (n 23) 59. See also David M Driesen, 'What Is Free Trade? The Real Issue Lurking behind the Trade and Environment Debate' (2001) 41 *Virginia Journal of International Law* 279, 295–300; 325–327.
126 Joseph (n 23).
127 AB report, *US – Shrimp* [136].

unjustifiable trade restrictions, rather than ensuring environmental protection in trade contexts.

What is more, effective protection of human health and the environment under the WTO is particularly difficult considering that:

> Obligations in trade agreements *proscribe* certain governmental behaviours that impede trade, while environmental laws *prescribe* affirmative governmental actions to protect public health and ecosystems. In other words, free trade agreements do not contain any affirmative obligations to protect the environment or public health; rather, they establish constraints on the capacity of member states to implement domestic regulatory standards.[128]

5. *Lack of a process to challenge trade measures that negatively affect human health*: The WTO lacks a process to challenge trade measures that turned out to adversely affect human health. For instance, suppose that serious health damages have arisen from GMOs introduced into the European market despite the EU's attempt to ban these products. There are no options under the WTO to enable an affected person to challenge the WTO measures that allowed GMOs into the European marketplace.[129]

These five gaps indicate an evident bias towards the goal of trade liberalisation under the WTO. An implicit prima facie pre-eminence of free trade in the WTO legal framework and at the judicial level has at least two consequences.[130]

First, it makes the *achievement of the WTO goal of sustainable development unattainable*. Indeed, this goal can be pursued by employing a 'process-based approach [that] will include the creation of 'interlocking mechanisms', such as environmental or social units in development-related departments at the national and international levels'.[131] The realisation of an integrative mechanism rests on effective integration and the lack of any hierarchy between economic growth, environmental protection and social development – the three pillars of sustainable development.[132] By ascribing a higher importance to free trade, it is unlikely to perform this integrative process under the WTO. This might also explain why, according to Halle and Meléndez-Ortiz, there is a gap between the proclaimed intention to harmonise trade and environmental policies and reality in which,

128 David A Wirth, 'The International Organization for Standardization: Private Voluntary Standards as Swords and Shields' in Geert Van Calster and Denise Prévost (eds), *Research Handbook on Environment, Health and the WTO* (Edward Elgar, 2013) 139; Douglas J Caldwell and David A Wirth, 'Trade and the Environment: Equilibrium or Imbalance? (Book Review)' (1996) 17 *Michigan Journal of International Law* 563; Islam (n 5) (emphasis added).

129 Joseph (n 23) 59.

130 Section 2.8 highlights further consequences for the WTO judiciary.

131 Ortino (n 33) 85.

132 Ibid.

rather than suggesting practical measures to close the implementation gap, there is only an enhancement of the statement of the intention.[133]

Second, '*the priority given to trade values within the WTO undermines the ability of States to respect international obligations in the non-trade arena*'.[134] WTO states can face challenges in discharging their international obligations to safeguard human health and the environment from risks posed by trading biotechnology. Thus, the implicit prima facie pre-eminence of trade values under the WTO can give rise to normative antinomies between WTO law and international human right law, and international environmental law, as discussed in detail in Section 2.6.

To conclude, this section shows the existence of an implicit prima facie pre-eminence of trade interests, which entails a bias towards requests to enhance free trade in biotechnology:

> WTO procedures and processes are currently biased in favour of commercial trade interests and developed States. This systemic bias is likely to generate outcomes that favour such interests and act to the detriment of other interests, such as those of developing States or non-trade (for example, human rights, environmental) interests, if the respective sets of interests should conflict.[135]

Keeping this implicit pre-eminence of trade interests 'will continue to skew WTO outputs in favour of trade and commercial interests to the potential detriment of social justice and other non-trade interests'.[136] Further, this imbalance renders it unlikely that the WTO goal of sustainable development can be achieved. Lastly, WTO states can be prevented from implementing international law obligations not related to trade interests. Against this background, Section 2.6 explores the relationship between WTO law and international law regimes.

2.6 WTO law and other international law regimes: normative antinomies

As an intergovernmental organisation, the WTO is subject to international law, and its member states are parties to several international human rights treaties and MEAs. As such, most WTO states have responsibilities and obligations to guarantee the right to health and protect the environment from risks posed by

133 Mark Halle and Ricardo Meléndez-Ortiz, 'The Case for a Positive Southern Agenda on Trade and Environment' in Adil Najam, Mark Halle and Ricardo Meléndez-Ortiz (eds), *Envisioning a Sustainable Development Agenda for Trade and Environment* (2007) 9, 12.

134 Joseph (n 23) 59 (emphasis added); see also Caroline Dommen, 'Raising Human Rights Concerns in the World Trade Organization: Actors, Processes and Possible Strategies' (2002) 24 *Human Rights Quarterly* 1.

135 Joseph (n 23) 68.

136 Ibid 71.

trading biotechnology. Nevertheless, analysis of biosafety under the WTO indicates that the implicit pre-eminence of trade interests can undermine the capacity of member states to accomplish their international responsibilities and obligations in relation to the protection of human health and the environment.

This section explores the relevant responsibilities and obligations under international human rights law, which requires member states to guarantee the right to health (and to some degree the right to a healthy environment), not least in the context of biotechnology. Moreover, this section explores the relevant responsibilities and obligations under international environmental law, which prescribes affirmative governmental actions to protect the environment. This analysis demonstrates the extent to which WTO law is supportive of, or in tension with, these two fields of international law.

2.6.1 WTO law and international human rights law

International trade in biotechnology can have positive and negative impacts on human rights. While trading biotechnology can support the *right to development* and, some argue, also the *right to food*, it can undermine the *right to health* and the *right to a healthy environment*. These rights are discussed in turn in the following paragraphs.

Chapter 1 highlights that trading biotech products can support the *right to development* of states importing and exporting these products, at least in so far as the right to development focuses on economic growth.[137] The close relation between technologies and economic development of countries was already underlined in the 1980 *Report of the Independent Commission on International Development Issues* (*'Brandt Report'*), according to which '[s]cientific, technological and economic opportunities should be developed to allow a more humane social and economic order of all people'.[138] This connection between the enjoyment of human rights and the economic development of countries has given rise to the idea of development as a standalone right. In this respect, several UN General Assembly resolutions,[139] the 1986 *UN Declaration on the Right to Development*,[140] and the *Vienna Declaration on Human Rights and Programme of Action*,[141] acknowledge the right to development as an inalienable right.

137 See *UN General Assembly Resolutions on the Right to Development*, GA Res 41/128, (4 December 1986) preamble.

138 Independent Commission on International Development Issues under the Chairmanship of Willy Brandt, Report on *North–South: A Program for Survival* (Pan World Affairs, 1980) (*'The Brandt Report'*) III.9/17.

139 See, e.g., *GA Res 36/133* (14 December 1981); *GA Res 37/199* (18 December 1982) cited in M Rafiqul Islam, *International Law – Current Concepts and Future Directions* (Lexis-Nexis Butterworths, 2014) 647. *Res 4* (XXXIII) 21 February 1977; *62 UN ESCOR Supp (No 6)*, UN Doc E/5927 (1978).

140 *Declaration on the Right to Development*, arts 1(1), 3.

141 *Vienna Declaration and Programme of Action Adopted by the World Conference on Human Rights in Vienna*, art 10.

Nevertheless, a cross-analysis of legal publications addressing the question 'Is there a right to development?' revealed that, even 25 years after the adoption of the 1986 *UN Declaration on the Right to Development*, this question remains unanswered.[142] Whether the right to development is a self-standing right is still debated.[143] However, *sustainable development* has become a buzzword and a generally acknowledged aim of the UN.[144]

Further, trading biotechnology can, arguably, support the achievement of the *right to food*.[145] The human right to food is recognised at international[146] and national levels.[147] By Overby's count, more than 100 documents acknowledge this right.[148] Article 11 of the *International Covenant on Economic, Social and Cultural Rights* (*ICESCR*) underlines three crucial aspects of the right to food. First, everyone has a right 'to an adequate standard of living for himself and his family, including adequate food, clothing and housing and to the continuous improvement of living conditions'.[149] Second, international cooperation among states plays an 'essential importance' in implementing the right to food.[150] Third, everyone has 'the fundamental right . . . to be free from hunger'.[151] Interestingly, some international instruments assert that the enjoyment of the right to food is intrinsically linked to the guarantee of the right to health.[152] This is particularly interesting in the context of biotechnology, not least because trading biotech might enhance the former and simultaneously undermine the latter.

142 Isabella D Bunn, *The Right to Development and International Economic Law – Legal and Moral Dimensions* (Hart Publishing, 2012) 128.
143 Mads Andenas, Jeremy Perelman and Christian Scharling (eds), *The Fight Against Poverty and the Right to Development* (Springer, 2021).
144 *The Future We Want*. See Section 4.3.2 for a thorough analysis of sustainable development under the WTO.
145 See Section 1.2.1.
146 See e.g., *ICESCR* art 11; *Universal Declaration of Human Rights* art 25.
147 See e.g., art 22 of the Haiti Constitution; art 34 of the Republic of the Congo Constitution; art 227 of the Brazil Constitution; art 48 of the Ukraine Constitution; art 16 of the Nigeria Constitution; art 51 of the Guatemala Constitution; art 53 of the Paraguay Constitution; art 281 of the Ecuador Constitution; art 4 of the Mexico Constitution; art 47 of the India Constitution; art 63 of the Nicaragua Constitution; and art 38 of the Pakistan Constitution.
148 Penny Overby, 'The Right to Food' (1990) 54 *Saskatchewan Law Review* 19, cited by; Abadir M Ibrahim, 'International Trade and Human Rights: An Unfinished Debate' (2013) 14(1) *German Law Journal* 321, 326.
149 *ICESCR* art 11 [1]. Moreover, the literature is full of valid contributions addressing the capacity of biotechnology to address world hunger and the implementation of the right to food. See especially Anganile Willie Mwenifumbo, *The Impact of Agro-Biotechnology on the Right to Food in Africa: Silver Bullet or Not?* (Lambert Academic Publishing, 2012); Kerstin Mechlem and Terri Raney, 'Agricultural Biotechnology and the Right to Food' in Francesco Francioni (ed), *Biotechnologies and International Human Rights* (Hart Publishing, 2007) 131.
150 *ICESCR* art 11 [1].
151 Ibid art 11 [2].
152 *Universal Declaration of Human Rights* art 25 [1]; *Nagoya Protocol* annex 2(m).

However, discussing responsibilities and obligations of WTO states parties to treaties recognising the right to development and the right to food is not an objective of this study as these are presumed to be supported by trade in biotechnology anyway.[153] The focus of this study lies in exploring whether WTO law allows the enjoyment of the rights relating to the protection of human health and the environment, which are potentially undermined by trading biotechnology. In so doing, it discusses responsibilities and obligations on most WTO states required to ensure the enjoyment of the *right to health* and the *right to a healthy environment*, though the status as self-standing human right of the latter is still debated. In approaching this analysis, it must be noted that when the WTO was established, 'few human rights lawyers at the time realized the significance of this event for their discipline'.[154] The creation of an international trade system with its own dispute-settlement mechanism caused an imbalance between the responsibilities and duties of states under the WTO and their human rights' obligations:

> [S]hould conflicts emerge between the two sets of obligations, States may be tempted systematically to prioritize their duties under the WTO, because of the sanctions attached to non-compliance, leaving aside the comparatively 'softer' commitments made under human rights treaties.[155]

The question of whether, and if so to what extent, WTO law supports or is in tension with international human rights law is not addressed by WTO judicial bodies, which rarely invoke or refer to human rights in their reports.[156] Nonetheless, the synergy between WTO law and international human rights law can be inferred from the fact that these two fields of international law share the common goals of promoting development and raising standards of living for all[157] (though the perception of these goals differs in trade and human rights contexts).[158] Harrison goes further, stating there is no need to address the question of whether

153 See Section 1.8.

154 Joseph (n 23) v; David P Fidler, 'Implementing Trade Commitments with a Public Health Perspective' in Richard Smith et al. (eds), *Trade and Health: Towards Building a National Strategy* (WHO, 2015) 45, 46.

155 Joseph (n 23) v.

156 A quarter of a century after its establishment, WTO dispute-settlement practices do not allow private parties to invoke human rights, except in rare cases in which amicus curiae briefs are admitted from non-governmental organisations. See Ernst-Ulrich Petersmann, 'How to Reconcile Human Rights, Trade Law, Intellectual Property, Investment and Health Law? WTO Dispute Settlement Panel Upholds Australia's Plain Packaging Regulations of Tobacco Products' (2018) *EUI Working Papers* 1, 3.

157 The underlying reason for the creation of this international organisation was to devise the blueprint for a stronger postwar global economy to facilitate the alleviation of poverty.

158 See Gillian Moon, 'The WTO-Minus Strategy: Development and Human Rights Under WTO Law' (2008) 2(1) *Human Rights & International Legal Discourse* 1; Richard Smith et al., *Trade and Health: Building a National Strategy* (WHO, 2015); Alka Bhatia, 'Capacity Building in Trade and Health' in Richard Smith et al. (eds), *Trade and Health: Towards Building a National Strategy* (WHO, 2015) 19; Joseph (n 23).

international trade affects the protection and promotion of human rights, 'because it is in the very nature of the existing trade regime to enhance human rights protection'.[159] Similarly, some scholars are convinced that the world trade regime has a mutual basis with human rights.[160]

In contrast to this rosy picture of the WTO, numerous scholars claim that human rights and international trade regimes are in a relationship of enmity.[161] Joseph, for example, underlines that one of the first assessments of the human rights impact of the WTO carried out by a Sub-Commission on the Promotion and Protection of Human Rights was 'almost entirely negative'.[162] McBeth adds the following:

> WTO rules and practices have variously been accused of actively preventing the realisation of human rights (such as the difficulties posed for access to patented essential medicines . . .), of failing to provide the means for better realisation of human rights (such as the omission of most human rights from the list of permissible general exceptions to trade rules set out in various WTO agreements), and of interpreting its own rules in a manner that is not conducive to the realisation of human rights (such as the implied ban on discrimination between products on the basis of the manner in which they were produced if those products appear to be physically alike).[163]

Against this background, the following analysis discusses whether WTO law supports or impairs the enjoyment of the right to health and the right to a healthy environment, which are potentially undermined by the international trade in biotechnology.

159 James Harrison, *The Human Rights Impact of the World Trade Organisation* (Hart Publishing, 2007).

160 See, e.g., Ernst-Ulrich Petersmann, 'Human Rights and International Trade Law: Defining and Connecting the Two Fields Human Rights and International Trade' in Thomas Cottier, Joost Pauwelyn and Elisabeth Bürgi Bonanomi (eds), *Human Rights and International Trade* (Oxford University Press, 2005) 29; Gao Pengcheng, 'Rethinking the Relationship between the WTO and International Human Rights' (2009) 8(3) *Richmond Journal of Global Law & Business* 397; Petersmann (n 156); Ernst Ulrich Petersmann, 'Human Rights, International Economic Law and "Constitutional Justice"' (2008) 19(4) *European Journal of International Law* 769.

161 See, e.g., Philip Alston, 'Resisting the Merger and Acquisition of Human Rights by Trade Law: A Reply to Petersmann' (2002) 13(4) *European Journal of International Law* 815; Andrew Lang, 'Re-Thinking Trade and Human Rights' (2007) 15(2) *Tulane Journal of International and Comparative Law* 335; Jagdish Bhagwati, 'Afterword: The Question of Linkage' (2002) 96(1) *The American Journal of International Law* 126; Emily Reid, *Balancing Human Rights, Environmental Protection and International Trade: Lessons from the EU Experience* (Hart Publishing, 2015); Ibrahim (n 148). See also Berne Declaration, *Canadian Council for International Co-operation & Misereor, Human Rights Impact Assessment for Trade and Investment Agreements* (Report of the Expert Seminar, 23–24 June 2010).

162 Harrison (n 159) 128; Joseph (n 23) 1. See Report for the Sub-Commission on the Promotion and Protection of Human Rights by J Oloka-Onyango and U Deepika, *The Realization of Economic, Social and Cultural Rights: Globalization and its Impact on the Full Enjoyment of Human Rights*, UN Doc E/CN.4/Sub.2/2000/13 (15 June 2000).

163 Adam McBeth, *International Economic Actors and Human Rights* (Routledge, 2010) 4.

2.6.1.1 *WTO law and the right to health*

As trading biotech products can have adverse impacts on, inter alia, the health of people, consumers and farmers, the international trade of these products can undermine the right to health, which has primary importance in international law. The *Constitution of the World Health Organization* (*WHO Constitution*) proclaims that '[t]he enjoyment of the highest attainable standard of health is one of the fundamental rights of every human being'.[164] Importantly, most WTO states (all WTO states except the European Union, Hong Kong–China, Liechtenstein, Macao–China, Chinese Taipei, and Tanzania) are party to the *WHO Constitution*. As such, they are bound to guarantee *the enjoyment of the highest attainable standard of health*, even in the context of facilitating free trade.

Moreover, in line with the *1948 Universal Declaration*,[165] Article 12 of the *ICESCR* – deemed 'one of the *core* international human rights treaties'[166] – recognises 'the right of everyone to the enjoyment of the highest attainable standard of physical and mental health'.[167] The 158 WTO states that ratified this Convention are, accordingly, bound to guarantee the enjoyment of the right to health.

More generally, as parties to international human rights treaties, most WTO states have *general* and *specific* obligations to protect the right to health from risks posed by trading biotechnology, including the five sets of obligations discussed in the following pages.

2.6.1.1.1 OBLIGATIONS TO RESPECT, PROTECT AND FULFIL THE RIGHT TO HEALTH

In regard to general obligations, international human rights law developed the triad obligations to *respect*, *protect* and *fulfil*; these are enshrined in, for instance, the *WHO Constitution* and *ICESCR*:

> The obligation to *respect* is a negative obligation, requiring states to refrain from interfering with or curtailing the enjoyment of human rights. The

164 *WHO Constitution*, preamble. See also, *WHO Framework Convention on Tobacco Control (FCTC)* of May 2003. See *UN Treaty Series* Vol 2302, 166.

165 Article 25(1) of the *1948 Universal Declaration on Human Rights* establishes that '[e]veryone has the right to a standard of living adequate for the health and well-being of himself and of his family'.

166 United Nations Human Rights – Office of the High Commissioner, 'International Human Rights Law' *OHCHR* (Web Page), www.ohchr.org/EN/ProfessionalInterest/Pages/InternationalLaw.aspx.

167 *ICESCR* art 12. See also *International Convention on the Elimination of All Forms of Racial Discrimination* (CERD) art 5 (e)(iv); *Convention on the Elimination of All Forms of Discrimination Against Women* (CEDAW) art 12; *Convention on the Rights of the Child* (CRC) art 24; *International Convention on the Protection of the Rights of All Migrant Workers and Members of Their Families* arts 28 and 43(e); *Convention on the Rights of Persons with Disabilities* art 25; *Protocol to the African Charter on Human and Peoples' Rights on the Rights of Women in Africa* art 14.

> obligation to *protect* is a positive obligation, requiring states to protect individuals and groups against human rights abuse by others. The obligation to *fulfil* is also a positive obligation, requiring states to take positive action to facilitate the enjoyment of human rights.[168]

Also, state parties to the Basel Convention on the Control of Transboundary Movements of Hazardous Wastes and their Disposal ('Basel Convention'), 156 of which are WTO member states, are required to fulfil the three general obligations to respect, protect and fulfil the right to health.[169]

This means that if the protection of human health is hampered – or, at least, not facilitated – by WTO law or WTO judicial bodies, state parties to the *WHO Constitution*, *ICESCR* and *Basel Convention* may be in breach of their general (negative) obligation(s) to *respect* and (positive obligations to) *protect and fulfil* the acknowledged right to health.

At this point, it is crucial to recall that WTO law does not provide positive obligations to protect human health from the risks posed by international trade in biotechnology. This does not support, or at least it does not align with, the positive approach taken in international human rights law. In contrast to the explicit foundation of international human rights law – which is centred on the constitutional *rights of citizens* – the focus of WTO law is the *right of states* to protect public health.[170] This might explain why WTO judicial bodies, in discussing cases on the protection of human health, do not refer to international human rights law. In *2018 Australia–Tobacco Plain Packaging (Indonesia)*, for example, the panel established that the complainants (Ukraine, Honduras, the Dominican Republic, Cuba and Indonesia) failed to demonstrate that Australia's tobacco plain packaging (TPP) measures, which require tobacco products to be sold in plain packages in the interest of public health, violated WTO obligations.[171] In so doing, the panel supported the interest in public health, not least because the tobacco plain packages measures under Australian law have proved positive in reducing tobacco usage[172] and, in turn, the number of people dying of smoking-related causes.[173]

168 Dinah Shelton and Ariel Gould, 'Positive and Negative Obligations' in Dinah Shelton (ed), *International Human Rights Law* (Oxford University Press, 2013) 562, 566 (emphasis added). See also Manfred Nowak, *UN Covenant on Civil and Political Rights: CCPR Commentary* (NP Engel Verlag, 2nd ed, 2005) xxi; Viviana Waisman, 'Human Trafficking: State Obligations to Protect Victims' Rights, the Current Framework and a New Due Diligence Standard' (2010) 33 *Hastings International and Comparative Law Review* 385, 406.

169 *Basel Convention* preamble. All WTO states are party to the *Basel Convention* except Fiji, Grenada, Hong Kong–China, Macao–China, Solomon Islands and Chinese Taipei.

170 Petersmann (n 156) 2.

171 Panel report, *Australia – Tobacco Plain Packaging (Indonesia)*.

172 William New, 'Australian Tobacco Plain Packaging Upheld in Decision at WTO' *Intellectual Property Watch* (Web Page, 28 June 2018), www.ip-watch.org/2018/06/28/australian-plain-packaging-upheld-decision-wto/.

173 According to WHO data published in July 2019, tobacco kills more than 8 million people each year. See WHO, 'Tobacco' *WHO* (Web Page, 27 May 2020), www.who.int/news-room/fact-sheets/detail/tobacco.

In taking such a decision, the panel avoided referring to international human rights law. This, according to Petersmann, demonstrates that 'the judicial balancing of economic rights . . . and public health protection can remain consistent with H[uman] R[ights] L[aw] even if the judges focus on governmental rights to protect public health rather than on corresponding human rights'.[174]

However, even if the WTO judicial bodies may not overlook the right to health, they also cannot be said to facilitate national adoptions of human health measures. This is in tension with the general obligation in international human rights law to fulfil and, accordingly, take positive actions to facilitate, the enjoyment of the right to health. For example, the judicial interpretation of the 'necessary' parameter[175] hindered the adoption of measures aimed to ensure the right to health in 1990 *Thai – Cigarettes*,[176] 1998 *EC – Hormones*, 2008 *US – Hormones Continued Suspension*[177] and 2011 *China – Raw Materials*.[178] As mentioned previously, this does not mean that there are no WTO cases in which the contested measures have been found to reflect policies aimed to protect health within the meaning of WTO law.[179] Nevertheless, the lack of positive obligations to ensure the protection of human health under the WTO, and the discussed implicit prima facie pre-eminence of trade values over non-trade values, militate against the proclaimed need for a synergy between human rights law and WTO law.

2.6.1.1.2 OBLIGATIONS TO CONSIDER ADVERSE EFFECTS TO HUMAN HEALTH POSED BY BIOTECHNOLOGY

In addition to the general obligations to respect, protect and fulfil the right to health, the *Cartagena Protocol on Biosafety to the Convention on Biological Diversity* ('*Cartagena Protocol on Biosafety*'),[180] the *Nagoya Protocol on Access to Genetic Resources and the Fair and Equitable Sharing of Benefits Arising from their Utilization to the Convention on Biological Diversity* ('*Nagoya Protocol*')[181] and the *International Health Regulations* (2005) (*IHRs*)[182] are three legally binding international instruments carrying specific obligations for numerous member states.

174 Petersmann (n 156) 4.

175 The necessary parameter is settled in art XX(b) of the *GATT Agreement*, art 2.2 of the *SPS Agreement* and art 2.2 of the *TBT Agreement*.

176 In Panel report, *US – Thai Cigarettes* [81].

177 Part III of this study discusses in detail the two *Hormones*.

178 AB report, *China – Raw Materials* [5].

179 See AB report, *US – Gasoline*; AB report, *EC – Asbestos*; AB report, *Brazil – Retreaded Tyres*.

180 *Cartagena Protocol on Biosafety*.

181 *Nagoya Protocol*.

182 WHO, 'International Health Regulations', entered into force 15 June 2007, art 2 (emphasis added), www.who.int/ihr/publications/9789241580496/en/ ('*IHRs*').

The Cartagena Protocol on Biosafety aims to safeguard biological diversity from adverse effects of biotechnology, considering its risks to both human health and the environment.[183] Article 16.1 of the Protocol requires its parties, 147 of which are WTO states, to 'establish and maintain appropriate mechanisms, measures and strategies to regulate, manage and control risks . . . associated with the use, handling and transboundary movement of living modified organisms'.[184]

Interestingly, while contracting states are obliged to consider the adverse effects of biotechnology on human health and the environment as identified during risk assessments,[185] states do not need to consider socio-economic factors unless they wish to do so.[186] In other words, biosafety is considered key, while socio-economic considerations of living modified organisms, including social (i.e., cultural/traditional/religious/ethical aspects) and financial aspects arising from the sustainable use of biological diversity and the trade in biotechnology,[187] can be freely decided upon by contracting states.

In this regard, WTO law seems to be in tension with the Protocol. The implicit pre-eminence of free trade under the WTO invites the argument that socio-economic considerations of trading biotechnology are the key tenet. In this respect, Macmillan asserted:

> It is arguable that, in general terms, the WTO agreements are in cultural clash with the Biosafety Protocol in two senses. First, because the WTO agreements are essentially concerned with preventing certain limitations on the international movements of goods while the Biosafety Protocol is concerned with imposing limitations on such movements. Secondly, because the trade agreements contain what have been described as 'negative' obligations with respect to environmental and health protection as a result of the fact that they impose no minimum levels for regulation in these areas.[188]

2.6.1.1.3 OBLIGATIONS TO TAKE A PRECAUTIONARY APPROACH TO 'PREVENT, MINIMIZE, CONTAIN, MITIGATE' RISKS TO HUMAN HEALTH IN SCIENTIFICALLY UNCERTAIN SCENARIOS

Importantly, the *Cartagena Protocol on Biosafety* explicitly pursues the aim to ensure an adequate level for biosafety in accordance with the precautionary

183 *Cartagena Protocol on Biosafety* art 4.

184 Ibid art 16. All WTO states are party to the *Cartagena Protocol on Biosafety* except Australia, Brunei Darussalam, Hong Kong–China, Israel, Liechtenstein, Macao-China, Singapore, Chinese Taipei, the Russian Federation, the United States and Vanuatu.

185 Ibid art 16(2).

186 Ibid arts 26(1), 16(2).

187 See *Conference of the Parties to the Convention on Biological Diversity Serving as the Meeting of the Parties to the Cartagena Protocol on Biosafety, Eighth meeting, Cancun, Mexico, 4–17 December 2016 Agenda item 15*, UNEP CBD/CP/MOP/DEC/VIII/13 (14 December 2016).

188 Macmillan (n 94) 139; David A Wirth, 'The Role of Science in the Uruguay Round & NAFTA Trade Disciplines' (1994) 27 *Cornell International Law Journal* 817, 818, 851–852.

approach contained in Principle 15 of the *Rio Declaration*.[189] Further, the *Nagoya Protocol* requires its states parties, 48 of which are also WTO states, to, inter alia, take a precautionary approach in the development and application of modern biotechnology.[190]

More specifically, this supplementary Protocol stresses the importance of taking 'appropriate response measures', which are described as 'reasonable actions to prevent, minimize, contain, mitigate or otherwise avoid damage, as appropriate and restore biological diversity'.[191] The adoption of measures aimed to ensure human health in scientifically uncertain scenarios is also required by the *IHRs*.[192]

As Chapter 8 demonstrates in detail, WTO judicial bodies seem reluctant to allow member states to implement precautionary measures to prevent human health risks. For example, in 1998 *EC – Hormones* and 2008 *US/Canada – Hormones Continued Suspension*, European attempts to adopt precautionary measures to protect human health from risks posed by hormone-injected meat and meat products failed.[193] More recently, in 2018 *Korea – Radionuclides*, Japan complained about Korea's import ban of certain Japanese food products after the Fukushima Dai-ichi Nuclear Power Plant (FDNPP) accident on Japan's northeastern coast in March 2011.[194] Korea argued that scientific uncertainty surrounding the presence of undisclosed amounts of leaks of radionuclides justified the triggering of precautionary measures in light of Article 5.7 of the *SPS Agreement* that, as broadly discussed in Chapter 4, reflects the precautionary principle.[195] The panel acknowledged that 'Korea's import bans and additional testing requirements are applied to protect human health from the risks arising from the presence of contaminants in foods'.[196] Nevertheless, it found that Korea was not allowed to adopt protective measures in light of Article 5.7 of the *SPS Agreement*, since such measures did not fulfil all requirements of this provision.[197] As these two cases demonstrate, there is a clear judicial reticence to implementing precaution to ensure the protection of human health and, as discussed in Section 2.6.2, also the environment.

189 *Cartagena Protocol on Biosafety* art 1, preamble.
190 *Nagoya Protocol* preamble. The 48 WTO states that are also party to the *Nagoya Protocol* are Albania, Bulgaria, Burkina Faso, Cambodia, Central African Republic, Colombia, Congo, Croatia, Cuba, Czech Republic, Democratic Republic of the Congo, Denmark, Estonia, Eswatini, Finland, France, Germany, Guinea, Guinea-Bissau, India, Ireland, Italy, Japan, Korea (Republic of), Latvia, Liberia, Lithuania, Luxembourg, Mali, Mexico, Moldova (Republic of), Mongolia, Netherlands, Norway, Romania, Slovak Republic, Slovenia, Spain, Sweden, Switzerland, Togo, Uganda, United Arab Emirates, United Kingdom, Venezuela (Bolivarian Republic of), Viet Nam, Sri Lanka and Suriname.
191 Ibid art 2.
192 *IHRs* art 43 [1].
193 These two cases are extensively discussed in Part III of this book.
194 Panel report, *Korea–Radionuclides* [1.1].
195 Ibid [7.88].
196 Ibid [7.32].
197 Ibid [7.111].

2.6.1.1.4 OBLIGATIONS TO 'PREVENT, PROTECT AGAINST, CONTROL AND PROVIDE A PUBLIC HEALTH RESPONSE TO' RISKS POSED BY TRADING BIOTECHNOLOGY

The *IHRs* aim to 'prevent, protect against, control and provide a public health response to the international spread of disease in ways that are commensurate with and restricted to public health risks, and which avoid unnecessary interference with international traffic and trade'.[198] This applies to biotechnology because the international trade of potentially dangerous biotech products could *spread* these health issues and/or human diseases.[199] Moreover, human diseases potentially caused by the international trade of these products can be interpreted as falling within the scope of 'public health risk', which is defined by the *IHRs* as:

> [a] likelihood of an event that may affect adversely the health of human populations, with an emphasis on one which may spread internationally or may present a serious and direct danger.[200]

The international trade in biotechnology can be viewed as the *event* spreading health issues and/or human diseases.

Even more interesting, the *IHRs* underline that an event caused by an environmental *contamination* that has the potential to spread across international borders represents a key example of a circumstance that may predispose disease to international virality. As such, it requires the adoption of human health measures by states involved.[201] The concept of 'contamination' is described as 'the presence of . . . a *toxic agent* . . . in or on a product prepared for consumption . . . that may constitute a public health risk'.[202] While the *IHRs* do not clarify the term *toxic agent*, its definition can be found in the *Basel Convention*:

> [Toxic agents (delayed or chronic) are] [s]ubstances or wastes which, if they are inhaled or ingested or if they penetrate the skin, may involve delayed or chronic effects, including carcinogenicity.[203]

It is undeniable that herbicides sprayed on biotech crops, especially glyphosate, which has been classified as 'probably carcinogenic to humans',[204] can be deemed toxic substances. In light of this, by encompassing international trade in biotech

198 *IHRs* art 2 (emphasis added).
199 See Section 1.2.2.
200 *IHRs* art 1.
201 Ibid annex II.
202 Ibid art 1 (emphasis added).
203 *Basel Convention* annex III 9 (H.11).
204 International Agency for Research on Cancer and World Health Organization, *IARC Monographs: Evaluation of Five Organophosphate Insecticides and Herbicides* (vol 112) *IARC* (Web Page, 20 March 2015), www.iarc.fr/en/media-centre/iarcnews/pdf/MonographVolume112.pdf.

into the scope of the *IHRs*, WTO states that are parties to these regulations (i.e., all WTO states except Eswatini, European Union, Hong Kong-China, Macao-China, and Chinese Taipei) are required 'to prevent, protect against, control and provide a public health response to the international spread of disease[s]'.[205] Yet, no committees under the WTO have the task of assessing or monitoring the impact of trade on human health. Introducing WTO mechanisms for gathering and assessing data on the impact of trade on human health might support such obligations.[206]

2.6.1.1.5 RESPONSIBILITY TO INFORM CONSUMERS AND OBLIGATION TO EXCHANGE INFORMATION ON BIOSAFETY

A further aspect to emphasise is that human health protection is not limited to the protection of physical health. Rather, as the *WHO Constitution* stressed, '[h]ealth is a state of complete *physical*, *mental* and *social* well-being and not merely the absence of disease or infirmity'.[207] This is particularly pertinent to this topic, since the analysis in Chapter 1 illustrates that international trade in biotechnology can endanger not only physical health, but also the social well-being of consumers and farmers involved in biotechnology.

In regard to the social well-being of consumers, WTO parties to the *Cartagena Protocol on Biosafety* are required to enable stakeholders to access information on biosafety through 'international biosafety information exchange mechanisms'.[208] By accessing information, consumers can make informed choices. The obligation to share relevant information concerning human health and environmental matters is acknowledged not only in this Protocol, but also in a plethora of other international instruments.[209] For example, the *International Plant Protection Convention* (*IPPC*) requires its parties, of which many are WTO member states, to 'cooperate, to the extent practicable, in providing technical and biological information necessary for pest risk analysis'.[210]

Establishing mechanisms under the WTO to obtain information on the impact of trade to human health might help WTO members meet their obligations to exchange data and cooperate in sharing information on biosafety.[211] This is espe-

205 *IHRs* art 2.

206 Rosie Cooney, *The Precautionary Principle in Biodiversity Conservation and Natural Resource Management: An Issues Paper for Policy-Makers, Researchers and Practitioner* (IUCN, 2004) 24.

207 *WHO Constitution* preamble (emphasis added).

208 *Cartagena Protocol on Biosafety* art 20(2).

209 See, e.g., *ibid* art 23; *CBD* art 17; *UNCLOS* art 244; *Rotterdam Convention* art 14(1); *Vienna Convention for the Protection of the Ozone Layer* annex II.1; *Treaty on Plant Genetic Resources* art 13.2(a).

210 *IPPC* art 8[1](c). All WTO state are party to the IPPC except Angola, Brunei Darussalam, Hong Kong–China, Liechtenstein, Macao–China, Chinese Taipei.

211 There are forms of cooperation and information exchange between the WTO and MEAs secretariats in relation to the impact of trade on the environment. See Section 2.6.2.

cially relevant when considering that access to information on biotech products is particularly difficult because leading states in the production and trade of biotechnology, such as the United States, Argentina and Canada, do not require mandatory labelling of food derived from GE crops. Without labels, the identification of GM food becomes impossible, as is accessing information to allow consumers to make informed choices. Providing more stringent WTO rules on labelling of biotech products might aid in this regard.

Finally, it is important to underline that the international trade in biotechnology also affects the well-being of farmers of biotech products and, accordingly, their right to health. According to Article 9 of the *International Treaty on Plant Genetic Resources for Food and Agriculture* ('*Treaty on Plant Genetic Resources*'), farmers have the right to '*save*, use, exchange and sell farm-saved seed/propagating material'.[212] However, GM seeds and crops are protected by patents and *IPRs* that prohibit seed saving by farmers, as discussed in Chapter 1. This can cause farmers financial distress and create dependency on the relevant biotechnology company.[213] WTO states producing and trading biotechnology, which are also parties to *Treaty on Plant Genetic Resources*, are required to guarantee the enjoyment of this right.[214] The difficulty for states to ensure this farmers' right is further exacerbated by Article 27.3 of the *TRIPs Agreement*, which prevents farmers from seed saving and exchange.[215]

To summarise, the discussion in this section highlights that WTO rules and shortfalls might prevent member states from accomplishing several obligations (summarised in Table 2.3). Yet, the implicit pre-eminence of free trade and a judicial reluctance towards the operationalisation of the precautionary principle under the WTO might hinder effective implementation of precautionary actions for ensuring human health.

2.6.1.2 WTO law and the right to a healthy environment

Trading biotech products can affect not only human health, but also the environment of exporting and importing countries. The existence of *environmental rights* as *human rights* has been acknowledged by some international instruments that, though not legally binding, have received strong political consensus.

212 *Treaty on Plant Genetic Resources* art 9(3) (emphasis added).

213 See Section 1.2.3.

214 *Treaty on Plant Genetic Resources* art 9(1). A total of 127 WTO states are party to *the Treaty on Plant Genetic Resources*, while 30 WTO states are not party (Bahrain (Kingdom of), Barbados, Belize, Plurinational State of Botswana, Brunei Darussalam, China, Dominica, Gambia, Grenada, Hong Kong–China, Israel, Kazakhstan, Liechtenstein, Macao–China, Mexico, Mozambique, New Zealand, Russian Federation, Saint Kitts and Nevis, Saint Vincent and the Grenadines, Singapore, Solomon Islands, South Africa, Suriname, Chinese Taipei, Tajikistan, Tanzania, Ukraine, Vanuatu, Viet Nam), and 7 WTO states are signatory (Cabo Verde, Colombia, Dominican Republic, Haiti, Nigeria, Thailand, the former Yugoslav Republic of Macedonia).

215 See Section 1.2.3.

Table 2.3 Summary of possible normative antinomies between international human rights law and WTO law

International Law		*WTO Law*
WTO states' obligation(s) to . . .		*Possible normative antinomies*
. . . respect, protect, and fulfil	• the right to health[i]	• WTO law does not provide positive obligations to protect human health from the risks posed by the international trade in biotechnology. • Neither WTO law nor the WTO judicial bodies facilitate national adoptions of human health measures. This is in tension with the general obligation to *fulfil* and, accordingly, take positive actions to facilitate, the enjoyment of the right to health. • In contrast to the explicit foundation of international human rights law, which is centred on the constitutional rights of citizens, the focus of WTO law is on the right of states to protect public health.
. . . take a precautionary approach	• to protect the environment and human health from adverse risks in trading biotechnology[ii]: unlike socio-economic and financial considerations of living modified organisms, biosafety is considered key[iii]	• The adoption of precautionary actions preventing or reducing risks to human health is neither explicitly provided under the WTO nor facilitated by the WTO judicial bodies. • Socio-economic and financial considerations on the international trade in biotechnology are key under the WTO.
. . . prevent, protect against, control, and provide a public health response	• 'to the international spread of disease in ways that are commensurate with and restricted to public health risks, and which avoid unnecessary interference with international traffic and trade'[iv]	• No committees under the WTO have the task of assessing or monitoring the impact of trade on human health. Accordingly, preventing, protecting against, controlling and providing a public health response is highly difficult under the WTO.

(*Continued*)

Table 2.3 (Continued)

International Law		*WTO Law*
WTO states' obligation(s) to . . .		*Possible normative antinomies*
. . . exchange information	• on biosafety[v]	• Without strict WTO rules on labelling of biotech products, the identification of biotech food exported by states that do not require mandatory labelling becomes impossible as much as accessing information that would allow consumers to make informed choices.
. . . inform consumers	• about the adverse effects posed by trading biotechnology[vi]	
. . . establish and maintain appropriate mechanisms, measures and strategies to regulate, manage and control	• 'risks [to human health] associated with the use, handling and transboundary movement of living modified organisms'[vii]	
. . . guarantee	• the farmers' rights to 'save, use, exchange and sell farm-saved seed/propagating material'[viii]	• Article 27.3 of the *TRIPs Agreement* prevents farmers from seed saving and exchange.

i *Basel Convention* Preamble; *ICESCR* art 12; *WHO Constitution* Preamble.
ii *Cartagena Protocol on Biosafety* art 1, Preamble; *Nagoya–Kuala Lumpur Supplementary Protocol* Preamble.
iii *Conference of the Parties to the Convention on Biological Diversity Serving as the Meeting of the Parties to the Cartagena Protocol on Biosafety.*
iv *IHRs* art 2.
v *Cartagena Protocol on Biosafety* art 20(2).
vi Ibid.
vii Ibid art 16.
viii *Treaty on Plant Genetic Resources* art 9(1), (3).

Examples are the 2002 *Johannesburg Declaration on Sustainable Development*,[216] the 1972 *Stockholm Declaration*,[217] the *ICESCR*[218] and the *Brundtland Report*.[219] The special rapporteur of the United Nations High Commissioner for Human Rights Report, Fatma Zohra Ksentini, proclaimed that '[i]nternational environmental regulations . . . have finally attained a global dimension, which has made

216 *Johannesburg Declaration on Sustainable Development* annex and *Plan of Implementation of the World Summit on Sustainable Development* annex.
217 *Stockholm* Principle 1.
218 *ICESCR* art 12.
219 The *Brundtland Report* recognises the existence of *environmental rights* as *human rights*. See also, art 24 of *African Charter on Human and Peoples' Rights* and art 11 of *Additional Protocol to the American Convention on Human Rights in the Area of Economic, Social, and Cultural Rights.*

possible the shift from environmental law to the right to a healthy and decent environment'.[220] Unsurprisingly, this right has *not* been enshrined in the national constitutions of only 15 countries in the world:[221]

> The increasing constitutional recognition of environmental rights and responsibilities globally reflects growing awareness of the importance of environmental values and *greater acceptance of a right to a healthy environment.* The practice of States in this area may eventually set the stage for renewed debate on the status of customary law on the right to a healthy environment.[222]

Although a self-standing right to a healthy environment is codified only in a few binding international legal instruments, such as Article 24 of the *African (Banjul) Charter on Human and Peoples' Rights*, there is an undeniable link between the enjoyment of fundamental human rights, including the *right to health* and *right to life*, and a healthy environment. After all, 'the environment is essential to all forms of life, and all human rights are indivisible and interdependent'.[223] This allows for the argument that WTO rules should take into account the *right to a healthy environment.* This is especially true considering that member states are required to trade with a view to protect and preserve the environment.[224] Building on this argument, the following section discusses further obligations of WTO member states stemming from multilateral environmental agreements.

2.6.2 WTO law and international environmental law

To prevent the potential adverse effects posed by the international trade in biotechnology to the environment, many WTO states are bound by international

220 Fatma Zohra Ksentini, *Final Report on Review of Further Developments in Fields with which the Sub-commission Has Been Concerned, Human Rights and the Environment*, UN Doc E/CN.4/Sub.2/1994/9 (6 July 1994).

221 Revel Pointon and Justine Bell-James, 'The Right to a Healthy Environment in Australia' (2019) 7(2) *Griffith Journal of Law & Human Dignity* 76. See also Revel Pointon and Justine Bell-James, 'Legal Analysis: The Right to a Healthy Environment in Australia' *Environmental Defenders Office* (Web Page, 9 January 2020), www.edo.org.au/2020/01/09/right-to-healthy-environment-in-australia/?fbclid=IwAR2SyHBhN9Im1VAltnRiinmFuuve1QixaSfGg67hZgpZ-E0MCncoJuZQFQ0.

222 Human Rights Council, *Analytical Study on the Relationship between Human Rights and the Environment – Report of the United Nations High Commissioner for Human Rights*, UN GAOR, 19th sess, Agenda Items 2 and 3, UN Doc A/HRC/19/34 (16 December 2011) para V [31] (emphasis added).

223 T Simpson and V Jackson, 'Human Rights and the Environment' (1997) *Environmental and Planning Law Journal* 269; Islam (n 139). Similarly, some international courts have established a clear link between the safeguard of the environment and other human rights. In this respect, see the Inter-American Court of Human Rights case law and, in particular, *Kawas Fernandez v Honduras*; *Yakye Axa Indigenous Community v Paraguay*; *Mayagna Community (Sumo) Awas Tingni*, as cited in Ibid 645 nn 89.

224 *WTO Agreement* preamble.

(and domestic) environmental obligations. This section discusses the main international environmental law obligations on most WTO states with a focus on biological diversity (see Section 2.6.2.1) and the use of pesticides (see Section 2.6.2.2), which are both relevant to trading biotechnology.

2.6.2.1 Responsibility and obligations to address loss of biological diversity

Preventing the loss of biological diversity is of paramount importance. This loss can affect the enjoyment of fundamental human rights, such as the rights to life, health, food and water.[225] As mentioned previously, trading biotech products can cause loss of biological diversity because of the introduction of invasive alien species and impacts on native or non-target species in terrestrial and marine ecosystems.[226] It is hardly surprising, then, that there are numerous obligations on several WTO states to protect biodiversity. These obligations include the adoption of a precautionary approach, conservation and sustainable use of biological diversity and adoption of affirmative governmental actions to address risks for the loss of biological diversity.

2.6.2.1.1 OBLIGATION TO PREVENT LOSS OF BIOLOGICAL DIVERSITY AND TO ADOPT A PRECAUTIONARY APPROACH

At the Earth Summit in 1992, all WTO states except the United States signed the *Rio Declaration on Environment and Development* (*Rio Declaration*), which enshrines the precautionary principle:

> In order to protect the environment, the precautionary approach shall be widely applied by States according to their capabilities. Where there are threats of serious or irreversible damage, lack of full scientific certainty shall not be used as a reason for postponing cost-effective measures to prevent environmental degradation.[227]

Also, the *Convention on Biological Diversity* (*CBD*) stresses the 'vital' importance of 'anticipat[ing], prevent[ing] and attack[ing] the causes of significant reduction or loss of biological diversity at source'.[228] It is noteworthy that 158 WTO member states are also parties to the CBD.[229]

225 John H Knox, *Report of the Special Rapporteur on the Issue of Human Rights Obligations Relating to the Enjoyment of a Safe, Clean, Healthy and Sustainable Environment*, UN Doc A/HRC/34/49 (19 January 2017). See also, *Aarhus Convention* preamble. See also *Stockholm Declaration* preamble [1].

226 See Section 1.2.2.

227 *Rio Declaration* Principle 15.

228 *CBD* preamble.

229 Hong Kong-China, Kyrgyz Republic, Macao-China, Chinese Taipei, Tanzania are the WTO states not party to the CBD while the United States is the only signatory state.

Similarly, the *Cartagena Protocol on Biosafety* and the *Nagoya Protocol* require a precautionary approach with respect to managing biodiversity.[230] What is more, states parties to the CBD have agreed to apply a precautionary approach to the management of GM alien species associated with intensive land use for biotech crops:[231]

> Given the unpredictability of the pathways and impacts on biological diversity of invasive alien species, efforts to identify and prevent unintentional introductions as well as decisions concerning intentional introductions should be based on the precautionary approach . . . [that] should also be applied when considering eradication, containment and control measures in relation to alien species that have become established.[232]

In sum, the adoption of a precautionary approach takes a central role in protecting biodiversity, including from alien species. Nevertheless, giving practical effect to these international legal commitments to adopting a precautionary approach to the management of biological diversity is no simple task for WTO states. As mentioned earlier in this chapter, there is a judicial reluctance towards implementing precaution under the WTO, as aptly demonstrated by Wirth's quote:

> [F]rom a trade point of view the precautionary exhortation to anticipate and prevent harm in response to uncertain science appears to be an invitation to overregulation and hence abuse. This concern plays out in parallel fashion in the dispute-settlement process, in which a precautionary justification regulation gives the appearance of an argument of last resort for a respondent state that cannot justify a measure by reference to 'hard' or ostensibly 'sound' science.[233]

There are several legal disputes in which member states' attempts to implement precautionary actions to prevent environmental degradation were rejected by WTO judicial bodies. For example, in 1998 *Australia – Salmon*, the panel rejected the Australian government's request to implement a precautionary ban on fresh chilled or frozen salmon to protect domestic salmon from disease.[234] In

230 The *Cartagena Protocol on Biosafety* preamble, art 1; The *Nagoya Protocol* preamble.

231 *Cartagena Protocol on Biosafety* preamble, art 1; *Nagoya Protocol* preamble.

232 Conference of the Parties, Convention on Biological Diversity, *Decision VI/23 – Alien Species that Threaten Ecosystems, Habitats or Species,* Doc UNEP/CBD/COP/6/20 (April 2002) annex ('*Guiding Principles for the Prevention, Introduction and Mitigation of Impacts of Alien Species that Threaten Ecosystems, Habitats or Species, Guiding Principle 1: Precautionary Approach*'), 257; *CBD* art 8(h).

233 David A Wirth, 'The World Trade Organization Dispute Concerning Genetically Modified Organisms: Precaution Meets International Trade Law' (2013) 37 *Vermont Law Review* 1153, 1162.

234 See, e.g., Panel report, *Australia – Salmon*.

1999 *Japan – Agricultural Products II*, the Japanese government's precautionary request to protect certain agricultural products from the risks posed by the introduction of coddling moths was found to be noncompliant with WTO law.[235] In 2003 *Japan – Apples*, the Japanese government's precautionary request to prohibit the import of certain apples to prevent the spread of fire blight, a plant disease, was rejected.[236]

Also in the context of biotechnology, the analysis of *EC – Biotech* in Part III of this study illustrates the failure of the EU to implement a precautionary ban on certain GM products endangering, inter alia, native fauna.[237] It is interesting that in this case, the panel chose not to explore '[o]ne of the most interesting arguments'[238] of the dispute: whether the adoption of the invoked precautionary measures under the WTO can be triggered by referring to the *Cartagena Protocol on Biosafety*. One might argue that since WTO law is in tension with international environmental law, the panel preferred to avoid addressing the thorny question on the interrelation between these two legal regimes. Whatever the reason behind the panel's choice, it would be appropriate to consider the following:

> While the Appellate Body and the GMO panel speak as if precaution were a separate body of law existing in an alternate universe, the 100 heads of state or government that adopted the Rio Declaration are representatives of the same states that are Members of the WTO. It is no coincidence that it is only in the context of international trade, and in particular the potential for restricting market access, that precaution is routinely assailed as a potentially counterproductive policy.[239]

2.6.2.1.2 OBLIGATIONS TO ENSURE CONSERVATION AND SUSTAINABLE USE OF BIOLOGICAL DIVERSITY

Preventing the loss of biological diversity is intrinsically linked to a need to adopt sustainable practices and use of biological diversity. In this respect, the *CBD*, the *Cartagena Protocol on Biosafety* and the *Treaty on Plant Genetic Resources* are only three of many international treaties requiring states parties, including numerous WTO states, to ensure conservation and sustainable use of biological diversity.[240] These obligations align with the objective of achieving sustainable development,

235 AB report, *Japan – Agricultural Products II.*
236 AB report, *Japan – Apples.*
237 Panel report, *EC – Biotech.*
238 Ilona Cheyne, 'Life After the Biotech Products Dispute' (2008) *Environmental Law Review* 52, 61.
239 Wirth (n 233) 1186.
240 *CBD* preamble, art 5; *Cartagena Protocol on Biosafety* arts 16(2), 10(6), 11(8). See also, *The Treaty on Plant Genetic Resources* art 6(1).

which is acknowledged as a WTO goal[241] and enshrined in a plethora of international instruments that, though not legally binding, have received strong political support.[242]

Nevertheless, WTO states might find it difficult to ensure the sustainable use of biological diversity and, more generally, to attain sustainable development for at least two reasons. First, as long as there is an implicit prima facie pre-eminence of free trade that creates a hierarchy between WTO goals, the achievement of sustainable development is unlikely.[243] Second, the analysis in Chapter 4 highlights that effective adoption of the precautionary principle is a substantial condition to achieve sustainable development.[244] As such, the discussed judicial reluctance to implement precaution under the WTO can hinder the achievement of sustainable development.

2.6.2.1.3 OBLIGATIONS TO TAKE AFFIRMATIVE GOVERNMENTAL ACTIONS TO ADDRESS RISKS FOR THE LOSS OF BIOLOGICAL DIVERSITY

The *Cartagena Protocol on Biosafety* and the *Nagoya Protocol* require states to take affirmative governmental interventions to address biological diversity loss. The former enshrines the obligation to 'regulate, manage, and control risks associated with the use, handling and transboundary movement of living modified organisms by establishing and maintaining 'appropriate mechanisms, measures and strategies'.[245] The latter imposes the duty to '[r]estore biological diversity'.[246] In addition, the CBD supports affirmative governmental interventions to prevent the introduction of alien species, by requiring states to:

> Rehabilitate and restore degraded ecosystems and promote the recovery of threatened species, inter alia, through the development and implementation of plans or other management strategies.[247]

Focusing on the marine environment, which, as Chapter 1 highlights, is potentially threatened by the introduction of GM animals, the *United Nations*

241 *WTO Agreement* preamble.

242 See, e.g., the *Rio Declaration* Principle 12; *Plan of Implementation of the World Summit on Sustainable Development*; *World Summit Outcome*; *New Delhi Declaration* Principle 4; *The Future We Want*; *Implementation of Agenda 21*. *The Future We Want* is the outcome document of the UN Conference on Sustainable Development. *Moreover, some cases of the International Court of Justice (ICJ) suggest the employment of the principle of sustainable development to strike a balance between economic development and the safeguard of the environment. See, e.g., Gabčíkovo–Nagymaros Project (Hungary v Slovakia).*

243 See Section 2.5.

244 See Section 4.3.2.

245 *Cartagena Protocol on Biosafety* art 16(1).

246 *Nagoya Protocol* art 2.

247 *CBD* art 8(f).

Convention on the Law of the Sea (UNCLOS) requires states parties, many of which are WTO member states to:

> [T]ake all measures necessary to prevent, reduce and control pollution of the marine environment resulting from the use of technologies under their jurisdiction or control, or the intentional or accidental introduction of species, alien or new, to a particular part of the marine environment, which may cause significant and harmful changes thereto.[248]

Contracting states are also required to take measures 'necessary to protect and preserve rare or fragile ecosystems as well as the habitat of depleted, threatened or endangered species and other forms of marine life'.[249]

While these international environmental legal obligations call for affirmative governmental interventions, WTO obligations are, by contrast, 'negative' in the sense that they constrain governmental actions.[250] Indeed, 'trade agreements focus on environmental measures as potential impediments to international trade'.[251] This makes it difficult for WTO member states to realise their obligations under multilateral environmental agreements and reflects a normative tension between international environmental law and WTO law.[252]

2.6.2.2 Responsibility and obligations to address the use of pesticides

The analysis of risks in trading biotechnology illustrates that intense cultivation of biotech products for trade purposes may lead farmers to use a significant amount of pesticides.[253] Pesticide usage negatively affects the environment and contributes, to a certain extent, to climate change.[254] The use of pesticides is addressed in a number of treaties, including the *Basel Convention*, the *Rotterdam Convention on the Prior Informed Consent (PIC) Procedure for Certain Hazardous Chemicals and Pesticides in International Trade* (*Rotterdam Convention*), the *Stockholm*

248 *UNCLOS* art 196(1); see also art 192.145 WTO states are party to the UNCLOS while 11 states are not party (i.e., Hong Kong–China, Israel, Kazakhstan, Kyrgyz Republic, Macao–China, Peru, Chinese Taipei, Tajikistan, Turkey, United States, Venezuela (Bolivarian Republic of)) and 8 WTO states are signatory (i.e., Afghanistan, Cambodia, Central African Republic, Colombia, El Salvador, Liechtenstein, Rwanda, United Arab Emirates).
249 Ibid art 194(5).
250 Wirth (n 233) 1161.
251 Ibid 1162.
252 Ibid 1161–1162.
253 See Section 1.2.3.
254 See *Proceedings of the Governing Council at its Nineteenth Session*, GC 19/34, 19th sess, 8th mtg, UN Doc UNEP/GC.19/34 (17 June 1997), annex I ('Decisions adopted by the Governing Council at its nineteenth session – *Decision No 19/13 Chemicals management – C International Action to Protect Human Health and the Environment through Measures which will Reduce and/or Eliminate Emissions and Discharges of Persistent Organic Pollutants, including the Development of an International Legally Binding Instrument*') 74.

Convention on Persistent Organic Pollutants (*Stockholm Convention*), *UNCLOS*, and the *UNFCCC*;[255] The first three are generally described as '*BRS Conventions*'.

2.6.2.2.1 OBLIGATIONS UNDER THE *BRS CONVENTIONS*

The *BRS Conventions* represent the internationally agreed ground rules for developing laws ensuring the sound management of chemicals and waste, including pesticides used for GM crops.[256] The *Stockholm Convention*, '[m]indful of the precautionary approach',[257] was adopted to protect human health and the environment from persistent organic pollutants (POPs).[258] In short, when a chemical is deemed a POP, states party to the *Stockholm Convention* are obliged to ban or restrict the use and production of the chemical involved, which includes those used in pesticides. Even in this case, most (i.e., 160) WTO member states are parties to the *Stockholm Convention*.[259]

States parties to the *Rotterdam Convention* are required to submit chemicals listed in annex III of the Convention to the PIC procedure. The *Rotterdam Convention* aims to promote responsibility and cooperation among parties in the international trade of certain hazardous chemicals. It requires states, 147 of which are also WTO member states, to 'exchange . . . scientific, technical, economic and legal information concerning the chemicals' covered by the Convention.[260] A similar duty is enshrined in the *Basel Convention*, which requires contracting states to cooperate in sharing pertinent and relevant information about the transboundary management of hazardous wastes and other wastes.[261]

Importantly, the WTO is mandated under Article 31(ii) of the *Doha Ministerial Declaration* to negotiate 'procedures for regular information exchange

255 *Stockholm Convention*. The Conference of the Parties subsequently amended the text in 2009, 2011, 2013, 2015 and 2017.

256 Rolph Payet, 'Full-Steam Ahead to UNEA, to Beat Pollution – Greetings from the BRS Secretariat' *Synergies among the Basel, Rotterdam and Stockholm Conventions* (Web Page, 8 November 2017), www.brsmeas.org/Implementation/MediaResources/TheBRSBlog/tabid/4332/language/en-US/Default.aspx.

257 *Stockholm Convention* art 1.

258 Ibid art 1. See Katy Askew, 'Germany Could Introduce National Glyphosate Ban' *FOOD navigator.com* (Web Page, 18 December 2017), www.bundestag.de/blob/533904/d12b1a10a8e5b8b920b7ed7bcca8cba8/pe-6-095-17-pdf-data.pdf. *IPPC* (n 227) art 7(1) (emphasis added).

259 Grenada and Chinese Taipei are the only WTO states not party to the *Stockholm Convention*, while Brunei Darussalam, Haiti, Malaysia and the United States are the WTO signatory states.

260 *Rotterdam Convention* art 14.1(a). See also *Rotterdam Convention* art 1. Bangladesh, Brunei Darussalam, Central African Republic, Egypt, Fiji, Grenada, Haiti, Hong Kong-China, Iceland, Papua New Guinea, Solomon Islands, Chinese Taipei are the WTO states not party to the *Rotterdam Convention* and Angola, Barbados, Saint Lucia, Tajikistan, the United States are the WTO signatory states.

261 While art 10 of the *Basel Convention* outlines the ways through which states are required to cooperate, art 13 highlights which cases require the immediate transmission of specific information to other parties.

between MEA Secretariats and the relevant WTO committees'.[262] Such procedures support WTO states in meeting their duty of cooperation enshrined in the *Rotterdam* and *Basel Conventions*. A similar mechanism could be adopted for exchanging information on the impact of trade on human rights, including the right to health.

Further, it must be considered that the *Basel Convention* aims to reduce harmful effects deriving from transboundary movements of hazardous waste. This is particularly relevant in trading biotechnology for several reasons. First, the IARC and WHO recently classified glyphosate, the most widely used pesticide on GM cultivations, as 'probably carcinogenic to humans'.[263] In light of this classification, the potential transboundary damages to the environment caused by using this pesticide on GM cultivations and products can fall under the scope of annex III of the *Basel Convention*, which defines ***hazardous wastes*** as '[s]ubstances or wastes liable either to cause death or serious injury or to harm human health if swallowed or inhaled or by skin contact' and '[s]ubstances or wastes which, if they are inhaled or ingested or if they penetrate the skin, ***may involve delayed or chronic effects, including carcinogenicity***'.[264]

Accordingly, in trading biotechnology, each state party to the *Basel Convention* is obliged to ***prevent*** 'the import of hazardous wastes and other wastes if it has reason to believe that the wastes in question will not be managed in an environmentally sound manner'.[265] States are also required to ***reduce to the minimum*** the transboundary movement of hazardous wastes and other wastes.[266]

The obligations to prevent and reduce to a minimum the movement of hazardous and other wastes can have significant implications for international trade relations. For example, in 1996, it was estimated that an export ban on recycling materials from rich to poor nations might terminate a US$50 billion trading relationship.[267] If applied to biotech products, a potential European import ban of (only) GM maize would cancel trade of between 2.5 million and 4 million tonnes per year.[268] This can make the implementation of measures around transboundary movement of hazardous and other wastes particularly challenging under the

262 *Doha Ministerial Declaration* art 31(ii). See also, *Report of the Conference of the Parties to the Basel Convention on the Control of Transboundary Movements of Hazardous Wastes and their Disposal*, Distr GEN 6th mtg, UN Doc UNEP/CHW.6/40 (10 February 2003).

263 See IARC and WHO (n 204).

264 *Basel Convention* annex III. See also FAO and WHO, 'International Code of Conduct on Pesticide Management Guidelines on Pesticide Legislation' *FAO* (Web Page, 2014) 52, www.fao.org/fileadmin/templates/agphome/documents/Pests_Pesticides/Code/Annotated_Guidelines2014.pdf.

265 *Basel Convention* art 4[2](g).

266 Ibid art 4[2](d) (emphasis added).

267 James M Sheehan, 'Trashing Free Trade: The Basel Convention's Impact' *Competitive Enterprise Institute* (Web Page, 1 October 1996), https://cei.org/studies-issue-analysis/trashing-free-trade-basel-conventions-impact.

268 European Commission, 'Economic Impact of Unapproved GMOs on EU Feed Imports and Livestock Production' *DG AGRI Report* (Web Page, 2007) 3, https://ec.europa.eu/

WTO. Unsurprisingly, Wirth observes that '[b]eginning with the first tuna Panel report, there has been considerable concern over potential conflicts between . . . the Basel Convention . . . and GATT/WTO rules'.[269]

Additionally, the *Basel Convention* requires contracting states to conduct transboundary movement 'in a manner which will protect human health and the environment against the adverse effects which *may* result from such movement'.[270] This means that in trading biotechnology, states party to the *Basel Convention* are required to take (positive) protective measures whenever there is a mere risk of adverse effects from the transboundary movement. Again, this stands in contrast to WTO rules, which do not include affirmative obligations to safeguard the environment in conducting trade relations.

2.6.2.2.2 OBLIGATIONS UNDER THE *UNCLOS*

Obligations deriving from potential harmful impact of pesticides on the marine environment are established in Article 194 of the *UNCLOS*, which requires contracting states to take *all* measures 'necessary to *prevent*, *reduce* and *control* pollution of the marine environment *from any source*'.[271] These measures seem to refer also to the release of pesticides, since they have to include 'those designed to minimize to the fullest possible extent . . . the release of toxic, harmful or noxious substances, especially those which are persistent, from land-based sources, from or through the atmosphere or by dumping'.[272] Consequently, this obligation is relevant for WTO states that trade biotechnology and are also parties to *UNCLOS*.

2.6.2.2.3 OBLIGATIONS UNDER THE *UNFCCC*

Since the increasing use of pesticides contributes to climate change, the provisions enshrined in the *UNFCCC* find application in biotechnology contexts. In particular, parties to this Convention, almost all of which (i.e., 158) are also WTO member states, are required to '*anticipate, prevent* or *minimize* the causes of climate change and *mitigate* its adverse effects'.[273] To this end, they 'should

agriculture/sites/agriculture/files/publi/reports/gmo/economic_impact_unapproved_gmos_en.pdf.

269 David A Wirth, 'Trade Implications of the Basel Convention Amendment Banning North – South Trade in Hazardous Wastes' (1998) 7(3) *RECIEL* 237, 240–1. See *Tuna–Dolphin* (n 58).

270 *Basel Convention* art 4[2](d) (emphasis added).

271 *UNCLOS* art 194(1) (emphasis added).

272 Ibid art 194[3](a). See Angela Del Vecchio and Roberto Virzo, *Interpretations of the United Nations Convention on the Law of the Sea by International Courts and Tribunals* (Springer, 2019); Alexander Proelß, *The United Nations Convention on the Law of the Sea – A Commentary* (Hart Publishing, 2017).

273 *UNFCCC* art 3(3). See also, *Montreal Protocol* preamble. All WTO states are party to the UNFCCC except Macao–China and Chinese Taipei.

take *precautionary measures*',[274] though as this study demonstrates, WTO states face an uphill battle when attempting to invoke precautionary measures.

To conclude, as Table 2.4 illustrates, the vast majority of WTO states have international responsibilities and obligations aimed to protect terrestrial and marine environments from risks posed by the international trade in biotechnology.[275] These international obligations must be added to the plethora of domestic obligations in this regard, including the approximately 150 states that have enshrined environmental protection in their constitutions.[276] This means that 'more than 70 per cent of the world's national constitutions refer to the safeguard of the environment as a constitutional *right*'.[277]

The analysis of responsibilities and obligations in international environmental law shows that the WTO must still take remarkable steps to ensure that trade and environmental regimes develop coherently. After all, the importance of coordinating policies on trade and the environment is enshrined in the preamble of the *WTO Agreement*.[278] Conversely, taking a measure to protect the environment (or human health) can be required by international environmental law (or international human rights law) and simultaneously prohibited by WTO norms. This underlines the existence of normative antinomies between WTO law and other international law regimes. Such antinomies might stem from the implicit pre-eminence of free trade under the WTO, which hinders a reasoned judicial balance between trade and non-trade interests. Nevertheless, as the following section highlights, judicial and epistemic issues make a reasoned judicial balance between trade and non-trade interests even more difficult.

2.7 WTO judicial and epistemic challenges

The normative issues discussed previously (i.e., the prima facie pre-eminence of free trade under the WTO, and the normative antinomies between WTO law and international human rights law/international environmental law) affect not only the capacity of member states to adopt biosafety measures under and beyond the WTO; they also have implications for the WTO judicial organs. In this respect, it is argued that when trade and non-trade interests stand in opposition with one another in the context of a WTO dispute, as is the case for disputes involving

274 *UNFCCC* art 3(3) (emphasis added); *Montreal Protocol* preamble.

275 The synergy between WTO law and international environmental law is greater than the coordination of the former with international human rights law, as discussed in Section 2.6.1.

276 See Section 2.6.1.2. See also Pointon and Bell-James (n 221) 76. Human Rights Council, *Analytical Study on the Relationship between Human Rights and the Environment – Report of the United Nations High Commissioner for Human Rights* [30].

277 Human Rights Council, *Analytical Study on the Relationship between Human Rights and the Environment – Report of the United Nations High Commissioner for Human Rights* para V [30].

278 *WTO Agreement* preamble.

Table 2.4 Summary of possible normative antinomies between international environmental law and WTO law

International Law		*WTO Law*
WTO States' obligation(s) to . . .		*Possible Normative Antinomies*
. . . regulate, manage, and control	• 'risks associated with the use and release of living modified organisms resulting from biotechnology which are likely to have adverse environmental impacts that could affect the conservation and sustainable use of biological diversity, taking also into account the risks to human health'[i] • 'risks associated with the use, handling and transboundary movement of living modified organisms [by establishing] appropriate mechanisms, measures and strategies'[ii]	International law provides *affirmative* governmental actions to ensure the environment, while WTO obligations are, by contrast, only *negative*, in the sense that they place constraints on governmental actions.
. . . rehabilitate and restore	• degraded ecosystems[iii]	
. . . promote the recovery	• of threatened species[iv]	
. . . prevent, reduce, and control	• 'pollution of the marine environment resulting from the use of technologies under their jurisdiction or control the intentional or accidental introduction of species, alien or new, to a particular part of the marine environment, which may cause significant and harmful changes thereto'[v] • 'pollution of the marine environment from any source'[vi]	
. . . take necessary measures	• 'to protect and preserve rare or fragile ecosystems as well as the habitat of depleted, threatened or endangered species and other forms of marine life'[vii]	
. . . protect	• human health and the environment against the adverse effects that may result from the transboundary movement of hazardous wastes and other wastes[viii]	

(*Continued*)

Table 2.4 (Continued)

International Law		*WTO Law*
WTO States' obligation(s) to . . .		*Possible Normative Antinomies*
. . . preserve	• 'rare or fragile [marine] ecosystems'[ix] • 'the habitat of depleted, threatened or endangered species and other forms of marine life'[x]	
. . . mitigate	• adverse effects caused by climate change[xi]	
. . . promote	• 'the recovery of threatened species'[xii]	
. . . rehabilitate and restore	• 'degraded ecosystems'[xiii]	
. . . cooperate with other states	• for the conservation of biological diversity[xiv] • for sustainable use of biological diversity[xv] • for sharing relevant information regarding environmental matters[xvi]	
. . . guarantee	• the enjoyment of the right to a healthy environment[xvii]	
. . . prevent	• 'adverse effects of the living modified organism on the conservation and sustainable use of biological diversity . . . within the territory of the [importer state]' [xviii] • 'unintentional transboundary movements of living modified organisms' [xix] • '[to] [p]revent the introduction of, control or eradicate those alien species which threaten ecosystems, habitats or species' [xx] • 'the import of hazardous wastes and other wastes if it has reason to believe that the wastes in question will not be managed in an environmentally sound manner' [xxi]	As the obligations to prevent, avoid and/or reduce to minimum adverse effects to the environment and the movement of hazardous wastes and other wastes can have significant economic implications for international trade relations, implementing protective measures in this regard might be particularly challenging under the WTO.
. . . avoid or reduce to the minimum	• potential adverse effects 'on the conservation and sustainable use of biological diversity in the Party of import' [xxii]	

International Law		*WTO Law*
WTO States' obligation(s) to . . .		*Possible Normative Antinomies*
	• the transboundary movement of hazardous wastes and other wastes [xxiii] • 'the causes of significant reduction or loss of biological diversity at source' [xxiv]	
. . . anticipate, prevent, minimize, contain, or otherwise avoid	• 'risks to biological diversity' [xxv] by means of the precautionary approach [xxvi] • 'the causes of climate change and mitigate its adverse effects' [xxvii] by means of precautionary measures	The adoption of precautionary actions preventing or reducing environmental risks is neither explicitly provided under the WTO nor facilitated by the WTO judicial bodies
. . . ensure conservation and sustainable use	• of biological diversity [xxviii]	Ensuring the sustainable use of biological diversity and attaining sustainable development under the WTO is hindered by the prima facie pre-eminence of free trade – which creates a hierarchy between the three pillars of sustainable development – and by the WTO judicial bodies' reluctance to implement the precautionary principle – which is a substantial condition for achieving sustainable development.

i *CBD* art 8(g); *Aarhus Convention* Preamble; art 1.
ii *Cartagena Protocol on Biosafety* art 16(1).
iii *CBD* art 8(f).
iv Ibid art 8(f).
v *UNCLOS* art 196(1); art 192.
vi Ibid art 194(1).
vii Ibid art 194(5).
viii *Basel Convention* art 4 para 2(d).
ix *UNCLOS* art 194 para 5.
x Ibid art 194 para 5.

(*Continued*)

Table 2.4 (Continued)

[xi] *UNFCCC* art 3(3).
[xii] *CBD* art 8(f).
[xiii] Ibid art 8(f).
[xiv] *Cartagena Protocol on Biosafety* art 16(5).
[xv] *CBD* Preamble, art 5; *Cartagena Protocol on Biosafety* art 16(5).
[xvi] *Cartagena Protocol on Biosafety* art 23; *CBD* art 17; *IPPC* art 8; *UNCLOS* art 244; *Rotterdam Convention* art 14(1); *Vienna Convention for the Protection of the Ozone Layer* Annex II.1; *Treaty on Plant Genetic Resources* art 13.2(a); *Basel Convention* arts 10 and 13.
[xvii] See the sources supporting the analysis in Section 2.6.1.2.
[xviii] *Cartagena Protocol on Biosafety* art 16(2).
[xix] Ibid art 16(3).
[xx] *CBD* art 8(h).
[xxi] *Basel Convention* art 4 para 2(g).
[xxii] *Cartagena Protocol on Biosafety* arts 10(6), 11(8).
[xxiii] *Basel Convention* art 4 para 2(d).
[xxiv] *CBD* Preamble.
[xxv] *Cartagena Protocol on Biosafety* art 2.2.
[xxvi] Ibid Preamble, art 1.
[xxvii] *UNFCCC* art 3(3).
[xxviii] *CBD* Preamble, art 5; *Cartagena Protocol on Biosafety* arts 16(2), 10(6), 11(8); *Treaty on Plant Genetic Resources* Preamble, art 6(1); *CITES* Preamble.

biotechnology, the WTO's tendency to favour free trade might not be the result of a reasoned judicial balance.

> [T]he WTO does not provide for a true balancing of trade and non-trade interests, as the latter only become relevant when States choose to invoke them as justifications to restrict trade (and thus risk non-compliance with the WTO), rather than when States might threaten non-trade interests by removing barriers to trade in, for example, a harmful product.[279]

Performing a reasoned balance between the competing interests in the context of biotechnology is even more difficult considering that 'the WTO is institutionally not ready for such a fundamental balancing of values and interests (mainly economic versus non-economic)'.[280] This deficit is demonstrated by the WTO's lack of an analytical structure that guides WTO judicial bodies in balancing trade and non-trade interests. A contributing factor is the absence of committees informing decision-makers on the impact of trade rules on human rights, as discussed in Section 2.4.3.

The challenges for the WTO dispute settlement bodies in performing an analytical balance are further complicated by the epistemic uncertainties in the contexts of biotechnology.[281] No WTO provision specifically regulates cases in

279 Joseph (n 23) 59. See also Anne Orford, 'Beyond Harmonization: Trade, Human Rights and the Economy of Sacrifice' (2005) 18(2) *Leiden Journal of International Law* 179.

280 Mads Andenas and Stefan Zleptnig, 'Proportionality: WTO Law: In Comparative Perspective' (2007) 42 *Texas International Law Journal* 371, 373; Jan Neumann and Elisabeth Turk, 'Necessity Revisited: Proportionality in World Trade Organization Law after *Korea – Beef, EC – Asbestos* and *EC – Sardines*' (2003) 37(1) *World Trade Journal* 199.

281 See Section 1.2.

which scientific uncertainty occurs. The *SPS Agreement* addresses circumstances of ***insufficient scientific evidence***[282] that, however, do not cover situations of scientific uncertainty, as WTO dispute settlement bodies have made clear in the past.[283] Chapters 4 and 8 provide more insights on the implications stemming from the judicial distinction between ***scientific uncertainty*** and ***insufficient scientific evidence***.[284] For the purposes of this chapter, it is sufficient to stress that WTO law overlooks the regulation of situations characterised by scientific uncertainty. Scientific uncertainty is not considered when the WTO seeks to establish whether the contested biosafety measures justify trade limitations under WTO law.[285] This calls for two observations.

First, most WTO states have international responsibilities and obligations to safeguard human health and/or the environment, even when scientific uncertainties remain. Indeed, numerous international treaties require most WTO states to adopt a precautionary approach to prevent and address even potential damages to human health and/or the environment.[286] Unsurprisingly, the request to employ the precautionary principle in order to adopt human health and environmental measures in the face of uncertainties was advanced in all three WTO biotechnology cases but was consistently rejected by the WTO judicial bodies. The lack of consideration of scientific uncertainty under the WTO hinders effective implementation of precautionary measures in trade contexts.

Second, while WTO law disregards scientific uncertainty, WTO judicial bodies facing biotechnology cases cannot avoid addressing the epistemic issues surrounding this technology. Put differently, in evaluating requests to trade biotechnology and ensure biosafety, WTO judicial bodies inevitably face reams of scientifically uncertain and antithetical evidence, the evaluation of which is conducted without any guideline provided by WTO law. This, in turn, has implications for the objectivity of the judicial balance, which is confined to the discretion of the appointed panel. Moreover, such judicial epistemic discretion is almost total in cases, generally termed ***stalemates***, in which in the view of WTO decision-makers, no interest prevails over (an)other(s).

To conclude, the discussed normative issues and gaps under the WTO exacerbate the judicial difficulties in balancing the competing interests in trading biotechnology and managing the epistemic problems stemming from the uncertainties surrounding this technology. Thus, investigating how WTO normative, judicial and epistemic issues can be overcome to perform a structured judicial balance in the context of biotechnology becomes paramount. This study seeks to do just that.

282 *SPS Agreement*, art 5.7.

283 AB report, *Japan–Apples* [184].

284 See Sections 4.4.1.1 and 8.3.

285 As the analyses in Chapters 7 and 8 illustrate, judicial analysis revolves around the evaluation of whether there is 'sufficient' or 'insufficient' scientific evidence supporting the request(s) for trade limitations.

286 See Sections 2.6.1 and 2.6.2.

2.8 Conclusion

This chapter highlights that the WTO was established with several overriding and paramount goals. If the objective of expanding the production of, and trade in, goods and services is as important as 'green goals' (e.g., objectives of sustainable development and safeguarding of the environment), then free trade in biotechnology should have the same relevance as the interest in ensuring human health and the environment in trade contexts. As the analysis in this chapter reveals, member states can indeed limit free trade to implement protective measures, although a range of strict criteria must be fulfilled. Nevertheless, the capacity of member states to implement protective measures under, and beyond, the WTO framework is undermined by an implicit prima facie pre-eminence of free trade under the WTO, and normative antinomies between WTO law and other international law regimes.

Regarding the implicit prima facie pre-eminence of free trade, this chapter identifies five factors that indicate a bias towards trade liberalisation under the WTO:

1. a 'democratic deficit' regarding non-trade interests,
2. a range of criteria undermining flexibility of member states to adopt health and environmental policy flexibility of member states,
3. a normative and judicial consideration of protective measures as exceptions to substantive obligations concerning trade liberalisation,
4. the lack of provisions designed with the primary purpose of ensuring human health and the environment, and
5. the lack of a process for challenging trade measures that negatively affect human health.

In ascribing greater importance to trade liberalisation than other WTO goals, sustainable development becomes unattainable, if only because it requires a lack of hierarchy between economic growth, environmental protection and social development.

Moreover, the implicit WTO pre-eminence of free trade affects the capacity of member states to fulfil international obligations to protect human health and the environment from the risks of biotechnology. This underpins the existence of normative antinomies between WTO law and international human rights law on the one hand, and international environmental law on the other hand. Taking a measure to protect health or the environment can simultaneously be required by human rights law or international environmental law and prohibited (or at least not supported) by WTO norms.

Neither WTO law nor WTO judicial bodies provide criteria to solve the implicit prima facie pre-eminence of free trade or the normative antinomies. Additionally, it is not clear under which jurisdiction the antinomies ought to be resolved. Wherever the answer lies, WTO judicial bodies cannot escape all international commitments that seek the harmonisation of international law regimes.[287] Nevertheless, balancing competing interests and harmonising norms stemming from different international law regimes might be arduous for WTO judicial bodies. Indeed, this chapter highlights that because of the dominant commercial ethos characterising the WTO normative framework, when trade and non-trade interests stand in opposition with one another in the context of a WTO dispute, as is the case for disputes involving biotechnology, the WTO's tendency to favour free trade might not be the result of a reasoned judicial balance. This is because, first, non-trade interests 'only become relevant when States choose to invoke them as justifications to restrict trade (and thus risk non-compliance with the WTO), rather than when States might threaten non-trade interests by removing barriers to trade in, for example, a harmful product'.[288] Second, WTO judicial bodies are considered institutionally unprepared to balance economic and non-economic values.[289] Third, the WTO lacks an analytical structure guiding WTO judicial bodies in balancing trade and non-trade interests. Fourth, a reasoned judicial balance between the competing interests in trading biotechnology is even more difficult considering the epistemic uncertainties on the effects posed by trading biotechnology to biosafety, and the unknowns carried by stalemate cases. Fifth, WTO law does not regulate circumstances in which scientific uncertainty occurs. This hinders effective operationalisation of precautionary measures and makes a reasoned judicial balance between trade and non-trade interests particularly difficult.

Against the background of these findings, Chapters 3 and 4 discuss how the WTO can become a forum in which normative, judicial and epistemic issues can be overcome to enable WTO decision-makers to perform a reasoned judicial balance between trade and non-trade interests.

287 Julia Ya Qin, 'Managing Conflicts Between Rulings of the World Trade Organization and Regional Trade Tribunals: Reflections on the Brazil–Tyres Case' (2010) *Making Transnational Law Work in the Global Economy* 601, 624–627.

288 Joseph (n 23) 59. See also Orford (n 282).

289 Andenas and Zleptnig (n 283) 373; Neumann and Turk (n 283). See also Center for International Environmental Law, 'Second Guessing National Level Policy Choices: Necessity, Proportionality and Balance in the WTO Services Negotiations' *CIEL* (Web Page, 2003) 4, www.ciel.org/wp-content/uploads/2015/03/Necessity_3Sep03.pdf.

3 Proportionality analysis to address WTO normative and judicial challenges in the context of biotechnology

3.1 Introduction

This chapter discusses whether, and if so how, proportionality analysis can aid in overcoming the normative antinomies under and beyond the WTO and the judicial challenges discussed in Chapter 2. As mentioned previously, WTO law is characterised by an implicit prima facie pre-eminence of free trade and normative antinomies with human rights law and international environmental law. These normative issues undermine the capacity of member states to implement biosafety measures (under the WTO) and fulfil international obligations to ensure biosafety from risks in trading biotechnology (beyond the WTO).

The WTO normative framework neither provides criteria to address the implicit pre-eminence of free trade nor suggests solutions to address the normative antinomies. However, it might be possible to overcome these problems via interpretation. In interpreting WTO provisions enabling member states to ensure biosafety, WTO judicial bodies could give greater weight to biosafety. Nevertheless, as Chapter 2 highlights, WTO judicial bodies are institutionally not ready to perform a reasoned balance between the competing interests in the context of biotechnology:[1]

> Challenges occur when trade and non-trade values collide, when certain types of products are unwanted on a market because of their incompatibilities with non-trade values.[2]

Against this background, this chapter shows how WTO decision-makers could use proportionality analysis to achieve a reasoned (or structured) balance

1 Mads Andenas and Stefan Zleptnig, 'Proportionality: WTO Law: In Comparative Perspective' (2007) 42 *Texas International Law Journal* 371, 373; Jan Neumann and Elisabeth Turk, 'Necessity Revisited: Proportionality in World Trade Organization Law after Korea – Beef EC – Asbestos and EC – Sardines' (2003) 37(1) *World Trade Journal* 199.

2 Henrik Andersen, 'Protection of Non-Trade Values in WTO Appellate Body Jurisprudence: Exceptions, Economic Arguments, and Eluding Questions' (2015) 18(2) *Journal of International Economic Law* 383–384.

DOI: 10.4324/9781003325741-5

between the protection of trade, health and environment when conflict arises. 'The appeal of P[roportionality] . . . lies in its accommodating character in the face of conflicting interests'.[3] At the core of proportionality analysis is a 'structure' under which Judges adjudicate which competing interest weighs more in light of the applicable law and the facts.[4] As Kuo stressed, 'the key component of this reasoning structure is balancing'.[5] 'Whenever there is a conflict of rights, values and interests', Andenas and Zleptnig add, 'this conflict will often need to be resolved through a judicial balancing act'.[6] This chapter argues that WTO judicial decision-makers should adopt proportionality analysis to mitigate the normative antinomies between WTO law and international human rights and international environmental law. Besides being a tool for addressing the judicial deficit to strike a structured balance between competing interests under the WTO, proportionality is also a tool to harmonise norms from different international law regimes.[7]

This chapter develops as follows. Section 3.2 begins with a general overview of the meaning, structure and migration of proportionality across jurisdictions. Section 3.3 provides justification for the use of proportionality under WTO law. This sheds light on the interpretation of proportionality under the WTO (see Section 3.3.1). It also explains why proportionality, in particular its third limb – balancing – is rational (see Section 3.3.2) and why WTO decision-makers should use it to balance economic and non-economic interests in the context of biotechnology (see Section 3.3.3). Section 3.4 discusses the structure of reasoning WTO judicial balance should have in the context of biotechnology. Approaching this investigation illustrates Robert Alexy's theory of balancing, which is a valuable model to support a rational structure of judicial reasoning under the WTO. Section 3.5 builds on this line of reasoning and provides a step-by-step explanation of how WTO decision-makers can perform a well-structured proportionality analysis to address biotechnology cases. Section 3.6 sheds lights on the limits of transplanting proportionality analysis to this field and offers suggestions to refine Alexy's theory to adjust it to the context of biotechnology. Finally, Section 3.7 outlines the conclusions.

3 Ming Sung Kuo, 'Resolving the Question of Inter-Scalar Legitimacy into Law? A Hard Look at Proportionality Balancing in Global Governance' (2018) 31(4) *Leiden Journal of International Law* 793, 799.

4 Kai Möller, *The Global Model of Constitutional Rights* (Oxford Constitutional Theory, 2012); Kuo (n 3).

5 Kuo (n 3).

6 Andenas and Zleptnig (n 1) 385.

7 The analysis in this chapter is based on the article of Alessandra Guida, 'The Reasoning Structure in Legal Disputes on International Trade of Biotechnology: From a Judicial Balance by Chance to a Judicial Balance by Design' (2021) 12(3) *European Journal of Risk Regulation* 602.

3.2 Proportionality: meaning, structure and use of a migrant legal criterion

3.2.1 The concept of proportionality

As Cannizzaro states and Cottier emphasises, 'the requirement of proportionality is almost universally affirmed'.[8] Nevertheless, defining proportionality is not a straightforward task. This is because there are several conceptions of proportionality,[9] the meaning of which depends on the context to which it applies.[10] When conceived as a legal concept,[11] proportionality – which the literature considers a 'principle', 'test' or 'analysis' – is a criterion that decision-makers use to justify decisions involving conflicting values, principles, rights or interests.[12]

Proportionality is viewed as a doctrinal tool that can solve conflicts with 'mathematica[l]' precision[13] by offering an 'arithmetic' balance,[14] and an analytical framework guiding decision-makers to assess competing rights, interests and values[15] or 'to establish whether a limitation of rights is justifiable'.[16] It is also defined as 'a goal of government'[17] and a 'model of optimization of values in conflicts'.[18] Even more noteworthy, proportionality 'lies at the core of justice'.[19] This

8 Enzo Cannizzaro, 'The Role of Proportionality in the Law of International Countermeasures' (2001) 12 *EJIL* 889; Thomas Cottier et al., 'The Principle of Proportionality in International Law: Foundations and Variations' (2017) 18(4) *The Journal of World Investment & Trade* 628.

9 See Bernhard Schlink, 'Proportionality (1)' (2012) (February) *The Oxford Handbook of Comparative Constitutional Law* 719.

10 See especially Valentina Vadi, *Proportionality, Reasonableness and Standards of Review in International Investment Law and Arbitration* (Edward Elgar, 2018) 57–62.

11 For the purposes of this investigation, this study discusses proportionality only as a legal concept.

12 Andenas and Zleptnig (n 1); Valentina Vadi, 'The Migration of Constitutional Ideas to Regional and International Economic Law: The Case of Proportionality' (2015) 35(3) *Northwestern Journal of International Law & Business* 557; Jacco Bomhoff, 'Balancing, the Global and the Local: Judicial Balancing as a Problematic Topic in Comparative (Constitutional) Law' (2008) 31 *Hastings International & Comparative Law Review* 555.

13 Kai Möller, 'Proportionality: Challenging the Critics' (2012) 10(3) *International Journal of Constitutional Law* 709, 724.

14 N Jansen Calamita, 'The Principle of Proportionality and the Problem of Indeterminacy in International Investment Treaties' (2014) *Yearbook of International Investment Law and Policy* 157, 174.

15 Möller (n 13) 726.

16 Julian Rivers, 'Proportionality and Variable Intensity of Review' (2006) 65(1) *Cambridge Law Journal* 174.

17 Vicki C Jackson, 'Constitutional Law in an Age of Proportionality' (2015) 124(8) *Yale Law Journal* 3094, 3098.

18 Luc B Tremblay, 'An Egalitarian Defence of Proportionality-Based Balancing' (2014) 12(4) *International Journal of Constitutional Law* 864.

19 Vadi (n 10) 57; Aurelien Portuese, 'Principle of Proportionality as Principle of Economic Efficiency' (2013) 19(5) *European Law Journal* 612. As Crawford added, it originates from the ideas of 'equity' and 'distributive justice', which emerged in ancient legal Greek and Roman texts. See Emily Crawford, 'Proportionality' in Rüdiger Wolfrum (ed), *Max Planck*

was already noted by Aristotle, according to whom 'the just is the proportional, the unjust is what violates the proportion'.[20]

Despite the different conceptions of proportionality, the discussion of which is not particularly relevant for the purposes of the present investigation, the common denominator is the capacity of this criterion to solve cases concerning conflicting legal interests or principles. Additionally, it is agreed that balancing is at the core of proportionality[21] and, as Barak underlines, it represents 'the best way' to resolve the tension between competing values.[22] Unsurprisingly, proportionality analysis is also termed 'proportionality balancing'.[23] Balancing is, however, only the last step of the analytical structure supporting proportionality, as illustrated in Section 3.2.2.

3.2.2 The structure of proportionality

The key feature of proportionality lies in its analytical structure. In the view of most courts and scholars, proportionality has a triadic structure that is supported by three tests,[24] otherwise termed subprinciples:[25] suitability, necessity and balancing (or proportionality *stricto sensu*).

The *suitability test* requires that a state measure must be appropriate to achieve the desired and legitimate end.[26] This, accordingly, presupposes the existence of a causal linkage between the objective and the measure. The *necessity test* requires

---

Encyclopedia of Public International Law (Oxford University Press, 2011). Similarly, Schlink observes that proportionality 'played and plays a crucial role in the philosophical quest for justice': Schlink (n 9) 728. See also Cottier et al. (n 8).

20 Aristotle, 'Nicomachean Ethics Bk 5, 1131b (15)' in Jonathan Barnes (ed), *The Complete Works of Aristotle- The Revised Oxford Translation* (Princeton University Press, 1995) 1786; Schlink (n 9) 719.

21 Aharon Barak, 'Proportionality (2)' (2012) (February) *The Oxford Handbook of Comparative Constitutional Law* 1.

22 Aharon Barak, *Proportionality: Constitutional Rights and Their Limitations* (Cambridge University Press, 2012) 221.

23 See, e.g., Alec Stone Sweet and Jud Mathews, *Proportionality Balancing and Constitutional Governance: A Comparative and Global Approach* (Oxford University Press, 2019) 162 (*Proportionality Balanc. Const Gov A Comp Glob Approach*); Kuo (n 3); Federico Ortino, 'Investment Treaties, Sustainable Development and Reasonableness Review: A Case Against Strict Proportionality Balancing' (2017) 30(1) *Leiden Journal of International Law* 71; Alec Stone Sweet and Jud Mathews, 'Proportionality Balancing and Global Constitutionalism' (2008) 1 *Faculty Scholarship Series* 1.

24 Schlink (n 9) 723–725; Thomas Kleinlein, 'Judicial Lawmaking by Judicial Restraint? The Potential of Balancing in International Economic Law' (2011) 12(5) *German Law Journal* 1141, 1149.

25 Robert Alexy, 'Proportionality, Constitutional Law, and Sub-Constitutional Law: A Reply to Aharon Barak' (2018) 16(3) *International Journal of Constitutional Law* 871, 872; Carlos Bernal Pulido, 'The Migration of Proportionality across Europe' (2013) 11 *NZJPIL* 483. See also Alec Stone Sweet, 'Investor – State Arbitration: Proportionality's New Frontier' (2010) 4 *Law and Ethics of Human Rights* 47.

26 Some authors have addressed the two elements of the suitability test (i.e., the factual appropriateness and legitimate end) separately to state that proportionality has four tests (or

the adoption of necessary measures, meaning the least restrictive and least onerous among equally effective alternatives.

Finally, the *balancing test* (or proportionality *stricto sensu*) requires the adoption of a measure that is not excessive or disproportionate in relation to the pursued objective. This means that 'the limitation[s] achieve the pursued end to a degree that justifies the extent of the constraint on the constitutional right'.[27]

While scholars and judges agree on approaching proportionality through these steps (or subprinciples), its use has raised conflicting views. Leading scholars embrace proportionality because of its merits. Sweet, for instance, claims that 'proportionality provides judges with the most appropriate analytical procedure currently available for adjudicating disputes involving conflicts between two principles (or interests, or values)'.[28] Bernal Pulido, in line with Kumm, adds that '[i]t also prevents arbitrariness as it requires that judges and political authorities justify rights limitations after having taken into account all these reasons and interests'.[29] Alexy maintains that proportionality is unavoidable and the only rational criterion allowing decision-makers to consider the reasons to limit the enjoyment of some right(s) and the right(s) itself.[30] In line with Alexy, Barak states that 'proportionality is a key criterion in solving the constant conflicts between legal principles'.[31] In Beatty's view, 'the law's golden rule'[32] of proportionality possesses 'neutrality' and 'a capacity of rationality'.[33] Put differently, proportionality seeks to achieve a 'calibration through a structured approach to limitations on rights'.[34] These are just a few examples of the widespread support that proportionality has received in the literature.[35]

subprinciples). See Stone Sweet and Mathews, *Proportionality Balancing and Constitutional Governance* (n 23) 75; Barak (n 21) 743–744; Vadi (n 10) 60.

27 Pulido (n 25) 484.

28 Stone Sweet (n 25) 48.

29 Pulido (n 25) 514; Mattias Kumm, 'The Idea of Socratic Contestation and the Right to Justification: The Point of Rights-Based Proportionality Review' (2010) 4 *LEHR* 142. See also Mattias Kumm, 'Constitutional Rights as Principles: On the Structure and Domain of Constitutional Justice. A Review Essay on *A Theory of Constitutional Rights*' (2004) 2(3) *International Journal of Constitutional Law* 574.

30 Robert Alexy, *A Theory of Constitutional Rights* (Oxford University Press, 2002) 74.

31 Barak (n 22) 237; Alexy (n 30).

32 David Beatty, 'Law's Golden Rule' in Gianluigi Palombella and Neil Walker (eds), *Relocating the Rule of Law* (Hart Publishing, 2009) 99, 103.

33 David Beatty, *The Ultimate Rule of Law* (Oxford University Press, 2004) 171, quoted in Pulido (n 25) 484.

34 Jamal Greene, 'Foreword: Rights as Trumps ?' (2018) 132(1) *Harvard Law Review* 28, 58; Jackson (n 17) 3098–3099; Joseph Blocher, 'Response Rights as Trumps of What?' (2019) 132(6) *Harvard Law Review Forum* 120.

35 See, e.g., Stephen Gardbaum, 'A Democratic Defense of Constitutional Balancing' (2010) 4 *LEHR* 78; Schlink (n 9); Caroline Henckels, *Proportionality and Deference in Investor–State Arbitration – Balancing Investment Protection and Regulatory Autonomy* (Cambridge University Press, 2015); M Cohen-Eliya and I Porat, 'Proportionality and the Culture of

Nevertheless, proportionality is the target of numerous criticisms. Jackson, for example, argues that the broad support that proportionality received does not make it a 'superior mode of analysis',[36] while Lacey and Pickard contended that proportionality is a mere 'chimera'.[37] Tsakyrakis considered proportionality 'a genuine assault on the very concept of human rights'[38] and a 'misguided quest for precision and objectivity'.[39] Habermas held that proportionality undermines the 'firmness' of constitutional rights,[40] while Webber affirmed that proportionality 'would appear to make no claim to correctness in any morally significant way'.[41]

This profound disagreement on the use of proportionality raises a range of challenges regarding the justifiability of its migration across international legal spheres.[42] Section 3.2.3 casts light on the origin and migration of proportionality across jurisdictions and areas of law, while Section 3.3 narrows the investigative lens to the justification to use proportionality analysis to biotechnology cases in the context of the WTO.

3.2.3 Migration of proportionality across jurisdictions

The concept of proportion is 'present in virtually all legal systems of the world'.[43] While historical references to proportionality as a legal concept can be found in the Babylonian code of Hammurabi, enacted in 1772 BC,[44] its origins as a legal principle are commonly traced back to the late eighteenth century, when it was introduced into German administrative law (*Verhältnismäßigkeitsgrundsatz*) and adopted by police to ensure public safety.[45]

Justification' (2011) 59 *AJCL* 463; Mads Andenas and Stefan Zleptnig, 'Proportionality and Balancing in WTO Law: A Comparative Perspective' (2007) 20(1) *Cambridge Review of International Affairs* 71; Manuel Atienza, *Las Razones Del Derecho – Teorías de La Argumentación Jurídica* (Universidad Nacional Autónoma de México, 2005).

36 Vicki C Jackson, 'Being Proportional about Proportionality' (2004) 40(1996) *Constitutional Commentary* 803, 818.

37 Nicola Lacey and Hanna Pickard, 'The Chimera of Proportionality' (2015) 78 *Modern Law Review* 216.

38 Stavros Tsakyrakis, 'Proportionality: An Assault on Human Rights?' (2009) 7(3) *International Journal of Constitutional Law* 468, 491.

39 Ibid.

40 Jirgen Habermas, *Between Facts and Norms* (MIT Press, 1996) 254, cited in Pulido (n 25).

41 Grégoire CN Webber, 'Proportionality, Balancing, and the Cult of Constitutional Rights Scholarship' (2010) XXIII(1) *The Canadian Journal of Law and Jurisprudence* 179, 181.

42 Vadi (n 10); Pulido (n 25).

43 Portuese (n 19) 612; Vadi (n 10) 57.

44 Vadi (n 10) 58.

45 Schlink (n 9) 728. See also Diana-Urania Galetta, 'General Principles of EU Law as Evidence of the Development of a Common European Legal Thinking: The Example of the Proportionality Principle (from the Italian Perspective)' in Hermann-Josef Blanke et al. (eds), *Common European Legal Thinking: Essays in Honour of Albrecht Weber* (Springer, 2015) 221, 288. See also Stone Sweet and Mathews, *Proportionality Balancing and Constitutional*

'Since its genesis in the Prussian law governing police power, proportionality has grown and has been expanded within European public law'.[46] Indeed, the migration of proportionality analysis to European law is 'a paradigm of successful legal transplant'.[47] Unsurprisingly, the European Court of Justice (ECJ)[48] and the European Court of Human Rights (ECtHR)[49] have frequently adopted the principle of proportionality to, respectively, provide solutions relating to issues associated with the 'four fundamental freedoms' of the European Union[50] and establish whether states' limitations on individual rights under the *European Convention of Human Rights* are in breach with this Convention.[51]

Over the years, other international courts have increasingly adopted proportionality analysis.[52] For example, the Inter-American Court of Human Rights (IACtHR) and the United Nations Human Rights Committee (UNHRC) have consistently adopted proportionality to, inter alia, determine the permissibility of interference with rights.[53]

Governance (n 23) 97; Moshem Cohen-Eliya and Iddo Porat, 'American Balancing and German Proportionality: The Historical Origins' (2010) 8(2) *International Journal of Constitutional Law* 263, 271.

46 Pulido (n 25) 492.

47 Vadi (n 10) 75.

48 Among other cases, see *Cassis de Dijon* [13]–[14]; *Commission v Denmark (Danish Bottles)*; *Commission v Germany (Beer Purity)*.

49 The ECtHR applied proportionality in, for instance, *Fayed v United Kingdom*; *Lithgow and Others v United Kingdom*; *Open Door and Dublin Well Woman v Ireland*.

50 The 'four fundamental freedoms' of the European Union are freedom of movement of goods, persons, services and capital. See Jukka Snell, *Goods and Services in EC Law: A Study of the Relationship Between the Freedoms* (Oxford University Press, 2002) 194; Jan H Jans, 'Proportionality Revisited' (2000) 27 *LIEI* 239; Stefan Enchelmaier, 'Four Freedoms, How Many Principles?' (2004) 24 *OJLS* 169.

51 Pulido (n 25) 497. On the application of proportionality by European courts, see also Vadi (n 10) 75–82; Gráinne de Búrca, 'The Principle of Proportionality and Its Application in EC Law' (1993) 13(1) *Yearbook of European Law* 105; Takis Tridimas, *The General Principles of EU Law* (Oxford University Press, 2006); Tor Inge Harbo, 'The Function of the Proportionality Principle in EU Law' (2010) 16(2) *European Law Journal* 158; Tor-Inge Harbo, *The Function of Proportionality Analysis in European Law* (Brill, 2015).

52 See Alec Stone Sweet and Jud Mathews, 'Proportionality and Rights Protection in Asia: Hong Kong, Malaysia, South Korea, Taiwan – Whither Singapore?' (2017) 29 *Singapore Academy of Law Journal* 774; Stone Sweet and Mathews, 'Proportionality Balancing and Global Constitutionalism' (n 23); Kuo (n 3).

53 Henckels (n 35) 18; Andreas Follesdal, 'Exporting the Margin of Appreciation: Lessons for the Inter-American Court of Human Rights' (2017) 15(2) *International Journal of Constitutional Law* 359. See, e.g., *Handyside v United Kingdom*, 24 Eur Ct HR 523 EHRR (1976); *James and Others v United Kingdom*, 8 EHRR 123 (1986); *Hirst v United Kingdom* (No 2), 42 EHRR 849 (2005).

Further, in cases concerning the use of force and self-defence,[54] maritime delimitations[55] and countermeasures,[56] the International Court of Justice (ICJ) has repeatedly emphasised the importance of imposing proportional measures.[57]

Over the past half-century, international courts along with domestic tribunals[58] have become major sites for the development and use of general principles.[59] Thus, it is unsurprising that 'the world's most important international courts have embraced proportionality as a general principle of law'.[60] Nevertheless, the question of whether proportionality has migrated to international trade law remains debated.[61] Section 3.3 clarifies whether proportionality can be interpreted under the WTO and, if so, whether there is any justification for its migration to such an economic context.

3.3 Justification to use proportionality analysis in WTO biotechnology cases

Even though proportionality is not specified in any *WTO Agreement*, several courts in other regimes apply it without explicit entrenchment in their constitution. Hence, the question arises as to whether the WTO should do the same. This section argues for the affirmative in relation to WTO biotechnology cases. In so doing, three main arguments are discussed: The interpretation of proportionality

54 See *Military and Paramilitary Activities in and against Nicaragua (Nicaragua v United States of America) (Merits)* [210].

55 *North Sea Continental Shelf Cases (Federal Republic of Germany/Denmark; Federal Republic of Germany/Netherlands)* [54].

56 See, e.g., *Gabčíkovo-Nagymaros Project (Hungary v Slovakia)* [56].

57 Crawford (n 19) 3. See also Rosalyn Higgins, *Problems and Process: International Law and How We Use It* (Clarendon Oxford, 1994) 231. The ICJ has also provided insights on reasonableness, which is a context-specific concept: Olivier Corten, 'Reasonableness in International Law' in Rüdiger Wolfrum (ed), *Max Planck Encyclopedia of Public International Law* (Oxford University Press, 2013) 16. For a detailed discussion of the adoption of reasonableness by international courts, see Vadi (n 10) 131–143. For further insights on proportionality in relation to reasonableness, see especially Andrea Morrone, 'Constitutional Adjudication and the Principle of Reasonableness' in Giorgio Bongiovanni, Giovanni Sartor and Chiara Valentini (eds), *Reasonableness and Law* (Springer, 2009) 215; Giuseppe Scaccia, *Gli 'Strumenti' Della Ragionevolezza Nel Giudizio Costituzionale* (Giuffrk, 2000); Pulido (n 25).

58 For instance, Bangladesh's International Crimes Tribunal (ICT) has acknowledged the importance of adopting proportionality. See *Sakhawat and others judgment* [1091]; *Liakat and Aminul judgment* [792]–[793]. For further insights on the application of proportionality by the International Crimes Tribunal, see M Rafiqul Islam, *National Trials of International Crimes in Bangladesh – Transitional Justice as Reflected in Judgments* (Brill Nijhoff, 2019).

59 Stone Sweet and Mathews, 'Proportionality Balancing and Global Constitutionalism' (n 23) 162.

60 Ibid. Unlike most international courts, the adoption of proportionality in international investment law and arbitration is still highly debated. In this respect, see especially Henckels (n 35); Vadi (n 10) 88–106.

61 Vadi (n 10) 82.

under the WTO (see Section 3.3.1), the application of proportionality *stricto sensu* (or balancing test) – which is the last and most contested step of the proportionality structure – under the WTO (see Section 3.3.2) and the main reasons to adopt proportionality analysis in the context of biotechnology (see Section 3.3.3).

3.3.1 Proportionality under the WTO

No *WTO Agreement* refers to proportionality *expressis verbis*. However, several WTO provisions and judicial reasoning are sources that interpreters can use to justify the use of proportionality under WTO law.[62] More specifically, in the context of the *GATT*, *SPS*, *TBT* and *TRIPs Agreements*, there are terms, such as 'proportionate', 'necessary', 'commensurate', 'less trade restrictive' and 'weighing and balancing exercise', that, along with the interpretation ascribed to them by panels and the AB, reflect elements of the proportionality analysis.[63]

For example, in interpreting the necessity requirement under Article XX(b) of the *GATT Agreement*, the AB developed the 'necessity test' in 2000 *Korea – Various Measures on Beef*, which recalls the second step of the proportionality analysis.[64] The WTO secretariat went further, stressing that the necessity test in the context of this provision 'explicitly recognizes the WTO's prerogative to *balance conflicting policy objectives*'.[65] In doing so, the secretariat refers to proportionality by mentioning its second test (i.e., the necessity test) and, simultaneously, relates such a test to the judicial balance between competing objectives. This, in turn, underlines the close relationship between proportionality analysis and balancing.

Some might argue that if WTO decision-makers developed the necessity test, rather than a proportionality test, decision-makers should adopt the former to weigh and balance competing values under the WTO. However, the necessity test adopted by the AB is 'overbroad and underinclusive'[66] and, conversely, 'it seems to elevate trade values to a pre-eminent status'.[67] Moreover, it does not consider the chosen national level of protection.[68] Therefore, the necessity test cannot (and should not) replace a well-structured proportionality analysis.

62 Cottier et al. (n 8).

63 Vadi (n 10) 83; Cottier et al. (n 8); Andrew D Mitchell, 'Proportionality and Remedies in WTO Disputes' (2007) 17(5) *European Journal of International Law* 985, 987.

64 Section 2.4.1.2 discusses the judicial interpretation of the necessary parameter in great detail.

65 Center for International Environmental Law, 'Second Guessing National Level Policy Choices: Necessity, Proportionality and Balance in the WTO Services Negotiations' *CIEL* (Web Page, 2003) 2, www.ciel.org/wp-content/uploads/2015/03/Necessity_3Sep03.pdf (emphasis added) citing WTO, unpublished note by the Secretariat, Working Party on Domestic Regulation, 'Application of the Necessity Test: Issues for Consideration' Job No 5929 (19 March 2000).

66 Joel P Trachtman, 'Trade and . . . Problems, Cost-Benefit Analysis and Subsidiarity' (1998) 9 *EJIL* 32, 72; Vadi (n 10) 85.

67 Vadi (n 10) 85; Trachtman (n 66).

68 Vadi (n 10) 85.

Further, there is judicial reasoning suggesting that the necessity test is not the only element of proportionality analysis that has been adopted under the WTO. For example, in *Korea – Various Measures on Beef*, the AB emphasises the importance of establishing whether the contested necessary measures ***contribute to attain the declared objective***. This suggests the judicial adoption of a 'suitability test',[69] which is another component of the proportionality analysis.[70]

Further elements of proportionality analysis can be found in the chapeau of Article XX of the *GATT Agreement*. As the analysis in Chapter 2 indicates, according to the chapeau, protective measures can be adopted in the context of the *GATT*, *SPS* and *TBT Agreements* if they are assessed as, inter alia, (1) not more trade restrictive than necessary, (2) not applied in a manner that would constitute a means of arbitrary or (3) unjustifiable discrimination between countries, or (4) a disguised restriction on international trade.[71] In other words, the contested biosafety measures must be assessed as ***proportionate*** to free trade. This entails, as Cottier and others noted, a 'weighing and balancing exercise along the lines of the proportionality principle'.[72] The AB in *US – Shrimp* points out that the chapeau 'embodies the recognition on the part of the WTO members of the need to maintain a balance of [inter alia] rights and obligations [of member states]'.[73] To remind us, balancing is the central element of proportionality.[74]

There are implicit references to proportionality analysis also in the context of the *SPS* and *TBT Agreements*. For example, Article 5.6 of the *SPS Agreement* clarifies that 'Members shall ensure that [SPS] measures are ***not more trade-restrictive than required*** to achieve their appropriate level of sanitary or phytosanitary protection'.[75] This is reminiscent of the necessity test.

Moreover, in *Japan – Apples*, the AB held that the requirement under Article 2.2 of the *SPS Agreement*, to support sanitary and phytosanitary measures through 'sufficient scientific evidence', is satisfied when these measures demonstrate a '***rational relationship***' with the objective pursued.[76] The assessment of this requirement entails a judicial proportionality analysis. Similarly, in the context of the *TBT Agreement*, WTO judicial bodies should establish whether states' technical regulations are 'prepared, adopted or applied with a view to or with the effect of creating ***unnecessary obstacles*** to international trade'.[77] This evaluation can be duly conducted through the proportionality analysis.

69 AB report, *Korea–Various Measures on Beef* [161].
70 Ibid; AB report, *Brazil–Retreaded Tyres.*
71 *GATT Agreement* art XX, chapeau; see Section 2.4.1.1.
72 Cottier et al. (n 8).
73 AB report, *US – Shrimp* [156]. The AB adds that the chapeau of *GATT Agreement* art XX can be viewed as a 'line of equilibrium', which evokes a sense of proportion.
74 Barak (n 21) 746.
75 *SPS Agreement* art 5.6 (emphasis added).
76 AB report, *Japan–Apples.*
77 *TBT Agreement* art 2.2 (emphasis added).

Elements of proportionality analysis can also be found in the *TRIPs Agreement*. For instance, in Article 46 it stresses 'the *need for proportionality* between the seriousness of the infringement and the remedies ordered as well as the interests of third parties'.[78]

Panels and the AB are not the only WTO authorities that have underlined (more or less explicitly) the importance of proportionality under the WTO. Indeed, WTO arbitrators recognise the 'general international principle of proportionality'.[79]

Further, the interpretation of proportionality under WTO law is supported by several commentators who refer to this concept to emphasise the importance of balancing competing interests.[80] Some note that because the need for balancing member states' trade interests and other legitimate policy goals is 'implicit to the WTO framework',[81] proportionality '*therefore* is of inherent importance to international trade regulation in balancing divergent interests at stake'.[82] Hilf adds:

> [T]he principle of proportionality is one of the more basic principles underlying the multilateral trading system, although there is no explicit reference to it in WTO law. However, the basic idea of proportionality, ie, the due balancing of competing rights, is reflected several times in WTO agreements.[83]

Mitchell notes that proportionality is manifested under the WTO in 'retaliatory actions' that are suspensions of concessions required by complainant states in circumstances in which respondent states fail to bring inconsistent measures into conformity within a reasonable period.[84] In these circumstances, WTO judicial bodies have to assess which retaliatory measure can be considered 'equivalent' to the level of nullification or impairment; thus, a proportionality analysis is implicitly conducted.[85]

78 *TRIPs Agreement* art 4.6 (emphasis added). Further elements of proportionality can be found in the *SCM Agreement* clarifying under art 4.10 nn 9 that countermeasures must not be 'disproportionate'. See Vadi (n 10) 87.

79 Decision by the Arbitrators, *European Communities – Regime for the Importation, Sale and Distribution of Bananas – Recourse to Arbitration by the European Communities under Article 22.6 of the DSU* [6.16].

80 Stone Sweet and Mathews, 'Proportionality Balancing and Global Constitutionalism' (n 23) 166. See also Mitchell (n 63); Neumann and Turk (n 1); Alan Sykest, 'The Least Restrictive Means' (2003) 70(1) *The University of Chicago Law Review* 403; Vadi (n 12); Tamar Megiddo, 'Beyond Fragmentation: On International Law's Integrationist Forces' (2019) 44(1) *Yale Journal of International Law* 4.

81 Cottier et al. (n 8) 644.

82 Peter Van den Bossche, 'Looking for Proportionality in WTO Law' (2008) 35(3) *LIEI* 284 (emphasis added) cited in Cottier et al. (n 8) 644.

83 Meinhard Hilf, 'Power, Rules and Principles – Which Orientation for WTO/GATT Law?' (2001) 4(1) *Journal of International Economic Law* 111, 120–121, quoted in.Mitchell (n 63).

84 Mitchell (n 63) 986–987.

85 Ibid. In this respect, see Decision by the Arbitrators, *Brazil – Export Financing Programme for Aircraft – Recourse to Arbitration by Brazil* [3.55]; *EC – Hormones* [5.5]–[5.8]; Decision

To conclude, several provisions and decisions demonstrate that proportionality can be justified under WTO law and, indeed, should be applied. In the view of the AB, proportionality is a recognised principle of customary international law,[86] though its status is still debated in the literature.[87] Nonetheless, no WTO source explicitly requires consideration of proportionality in WTO disputes.[88] Nonetheless, even if deciding *proportionally* is not a requirement, the use of this legal criterion can bring clarity, transparency and equilibrium in balancing conflicting interests under the WTO framework. This is particularly important considering there is 'a sort of balancing obligation' under the WTO.[89] This, accordingly, enhances the key role that proportionality analysis might have in guiding WTO decision-makers in performing a reasoned judicial balance between competing interests in trading biotechnology.

While there seem to be no objections to applying the first two tests of proportionality analysis (i.e., suitability test and necessity test) under the WTO, several commentators[90] claim that WTO judicial bodies should not perform the balancing test (i.e., the last test of proportionality analysis) for the reasons discussed in the following section.

3.3.2 Balancing test (or proportionality stricto sensu*) under the WTO*

As explained previously, the balancing test is the last step of the triadic structure of proportionality. Decision-makers are called in this final stage to effectively balance and weigh the competing rights, principles or interests to achieve a concrete outcome. The balancing test 'requires a proper relationship between the social

---

by the Arbitrators, *European Communities – Regime for the Importation, Sale and Distribution of Bananas* [76]; AB report, *US – Cotton from Pakistan* [120]; AB report, *US – Line Pipe* [252]. See also Joost Pauwelyn, 'Enforcement and Countermeasures in the WTO: Rules Are Rules – Toward a More Collective Approach' (2000) 94 *AJIL* 335, 343.

86 *US – Line Pipe* [259].

87 In this respect see, Eric Engle, 'The History of the General Principle of Proportionality: An Overview' (2012) 10(1) *Dartmouth Law Journal* 1, 3. In the same view, Margherita Poto, 'The Principle of Proportionality in Comparative Perspective' (2007) 8 *German Law Journal* 835; Andenas and Zleptnig (n 1). For a different view on proportionality, see Cottier et al. (n 8).

88 Claiming that proportionality is an obligation would imply that if a panel fails to use proportionality, it has violated WTO law. This would be a reason for annulment of the decision, which is highly unlikely under the WTO, in which panels have substantial discretion in taking decisions.

89 Federico Ortino, *Basic Legal Instruments for the Liberalisation of Trade – A Comparative Analysis of EC and WTO Law* (Hart Publishing, 2004) 467.

90 See, e.g., Axel Desmedt, 'Proportionality in WTO Law' (2001) *Journal of International Economic Law* 441; Neumann and Turk (n 1) 232–233; Ortino (n 89) 472; Gregory Charles Shaffer, 'A Structural Approach to WTO Jurisprudence: Why Institutional Choice Lies at the Center of the GMO Case' (2008) 4(1) *New York University Journal of International Law and Politics* 1, 60; Bossche (n 82) 284.

benefit of realizing the proper purpose and the social benefit of avoiding the limitation of the constitutional right'.[91] Put differently, at this stage, a true 'weighing and balancing' of competing values takes place.[92]

The operationalisation of the balancing test under the WTO is highly criticised for three reasons. First, some claim that implementing the balancing test becomes a political tool (mis)used by decision-makers for judicial activism in legal decision-making.[93] The fear usually relates to the balancing test affording judges subjective and excessive discretion.[94]

This concern is only partially substantiated. As Barak observes:

> Certainly, the balancing component affords the judge discretion. But by what standard can that discretion be said to be too broad? . . . Proportionality is a framework that needs to be filled with content, and it allows for varied degrees of protection.[95]

Moreover, no proof has been offered that applying the balancing test has shaped decisions infused with broad judicial epistemic discretion. This criticism is 'not based on a systematic analysis of judicial practice. At best, it refers to individual cases as anecdotal evidence'.[96]

Further, although the balancing test cannot exclude the subjective appraisals of judges, 'this does mean that balancing is irrational and based only on these subjective appraisals'.[97] Rather, as Bernal Pulido adds, criticisms about the excessive discretion that the balancing test grants, and more generally the criticisms on the limitations of the rationality of balancing, should be rejected because they often reflect *hyper-rationality*:

> [B]alancing is no guarantee of objectivity. This is due, above all, to the fact that objectivity is an ideal that is unlikely to be achieved in any normative field.[98]

91 Barak (n 21) 744; See also Dieter Grimm, 'Proportionality in Canadian and German Constitutional Jurisprudence' (2007) 57 *University of Toronto Law Journal* 383, 388; Barak (n 22) 236; Alexy (n 30) 67.

92 Pulido (n 25).

93 See, e.g., Grant Huscroft, 'Proportionality and Pretense' (2014) 29 *Constitutional Commentary* 229, 255; Jochen von Bernstorff, 'Proportionality without Balancing – Why Judicial Ad Hoc-Balancing Is Unnecessary and Potentially Detrimental to the Realization of Individual and Collective Self-Determination' in Liora Lazarus, Christopher McCrudden and Nigel Bowles (eds), *Reasoning Rights: Comparative Judicial Engagement* (Hart Publishing, 2014) 63, 66; Duncan Kennedy, 'A Transnational Genealogy of Proportionality in Private Law' in Brownsword et al. (eds), *The Foundations of European Private Law* (Hart Publishing, 2011) 185, 187.

94 Huscroft (n 93) 255; Bernstorff (n 93) 66; Kennedy (n 93) 187.

95 Barak (n 21) 750.

96 Niels Petersen, *Proportionality and Judicial Activism – Fundamental Rights Adjudication in Canada, Germany and South Africa* (Cambridge University Press, 2017) 61.

97 Carlos Bernal Pulido, 'The Rationality of Balancing' (2006) 92(2) *Archiv fuer Rechts- und Sozial Philosophie* 195.

98 Ibid 197. For further insights on objectivity in normative fiels, see Martin Borowski, 'La Restricción de Los Derechos Fundamentales' (2000) *Revista Española de Derecho Constitucional* 59, 46.

This means that not recognising the limitations of rationality would be irrational.[99]

A second criticism highlights that in performing the balancing test, WTO judicial bodies should weigh and balance incommensurable values,[100] meaning values that do not have a common metric allowing WTO decision-makers to evaluate and compare their importance.[101] According to Da Silva, the objections based on alleged incommensurability can be addressed by stressing the following:

> [T]his type of objection is often based solely on intuition, as if it were enough to point out the incomparability of apples and oranges. Just as it is possible to compare apples and oranges relative to a given covering value (vitamin content, for instance), it is also possible to compare and balance constitutional rights relative to a given covering value: their degrees of satisfaction and non-satisfaction. The fact that these rights may be incommensurable in the abstract does not alter their comparability in concrete situations.[102]

In addition, Alexy's theory of balancing adopts triadic scales for the elements that decision-makers must consider in balancing competing rights or interests.[103] Such scales (as outlined in Section 3.4) represent a common metric to compare, balance and weight the values at stake. Thus, performing a balancing test in light of Alexy's theory of balancing should circumvent the criticism on the incommensurability of values. Alexy's balancing model offers a structure for 'a common measure for comparing principles', thereby 'providing a predictable result that can be correctly justified in the law'.[104]

Third, it has been argued that 'WTO law *does* not, and . . . *should* not include . . . the principle of "proportionality *stricto sensu*"'[105] because it 'constitutes an extraordinary intrusion into national regulatory sovereignty'.[106] Its application would lead to unreasonable judgments in which WTO decision-makers tend 'to

99 Pulido (n 97) 197. For an in-depth analysis of the concept of rationality, see Pulido (n 97) 199–200.

100 On the concept of incommensurability, see Joseph Raz, 'Incommensurability and Agency' in Joseph Raz (ed), *Engaging Reason* (Oxford University Press, 2001) 46; Robert Alexy, *A Theory of Legal Argumentation: The Theory of Rational Discourse as Theory of Legal Justification* (Oxford University Press, 2009); Stone Sweet and Mathews, 'Proportionality Balancing and Global Constitutionalism' (n 23) 38–40.

101 For criticisms on the balancing test in relation to incommensurability, see, e.g., Thomas Alexander Aleinikoff, 'Constitutional Law in the Age of Balancing' (1987) *Yale Law Journal* 96, 973; Lawrence Tribe, 'Constitutional Calculus: Equal Justice or Economic Efficiency' (1985) *Harvard Law Review* 98, 595; Cass Sunstein, 'Incommensurability and Valuation in Law' (1994) 92 *Michigan Law Review* 779.

102 Virgílio Afonso Da Silva, 'Comparing the Incommensurable: Constitutional Principles, Balancing and Rational Decision' (2011) 31(2) *Oxford Journal of Legal Studies* 273, 301.

103 Robert Alexy, 'Discourse Theory and Fundamental Rights' in Agustín José Menéndez and Erik Oddvar Eriksen (eds), *Arguing Fundamental Rights* (Springer, 2006) 15, 24–26.

104 Pulido (n 97) 200. see also Alexy (n 30); Barak (n 22).

105 Ortino (n 89) 472 (emphasis in original).

106 Ibid. See also Desmedt (n 90); Neumann and Turk (n 1); Shaffer (n 90); Bossche (n 82).

prefer "trade" (and thus "deregulation") to "health [and/or environmental] protection" (and thus Member States' regulation)'.[107]

Such criticism disregards the fact that when WTO judicial bodies are called to examine competing requests, the resulting judicial decisions will inevitably interfere with sovereign policy choices of at least one party involved. In fact, asking WTO judicial bodies to justify their decisions in light of a structured balancing test would only enhance transparency and objectivity of final decisions, which should be in the interests of states. Put differently, '[t]he more structured and rational a test, the more the courts will have to engage in a transparent judicial discourse with regard to trade-offs they are constantly required to make. . .. [I]t may contribute to reducing the vagueness and unpredictability of judicial reasoning in the WTO'.[108]

Moreover, although the balancing test might expose courts to allegations that they arrogate themselves to a legislative function, Stone Sweet and Mathews highlight:

> there is less to the charge than might appear at first blush. After all, the constitutional legislator, acting on behalf of the People, has entrusted the function of rights protection to the constitutional court, and relegated legislative authority to a lower echelon on the hierarchy of norms that constitutes the polity.[109]

In light of all these considerations, the balancing test becomes necessary to obtain a transparent and concrete balancing outcome in biotechnology legal disputes and, simultaneously, it can also limit the substantial discretion of panels:[110] '[b]y limiting discretion, one central purpose of the rule of law is served'.[111]

Although 'proportionality – like any conceptual framework – is not a neutral process',[112] the analysis in this section shows that the three main counterarguments against the balancing test under the WTO should not discourage its application. On the contrary, performing a full proportionality analysis, which means taking the three steps of suitability, necessity and balancing test (or proportionality *stricto sensu*), is highly desirable in the context of biotechnology for the reasons discussed in Section 3.3.3.

107 Ortino (n 89) 420.

108 Andenas and Zleptnig (n 35) 90.

109 Stone Sweet and Mathews, *Proportionality Balancing and Constitutional Governance* (n 23) 38.

110 This criticism to the application of the balancing test under the WTO is rebutted in Dominic McGoldrick, 'A Defence of the Margin of Appreciation and an Argument for Its Application by the Human Rights Committee' (2015) 65(1) *International and Comparative Law Quarterly* 21; Enzo Cannizzaro, 'Proportionality and Margin of Appreciation in the Whaling Case: Reconciling Antithetical Doctrines?' (2016) 27(4) *European Journal of International Law* 1061.

111 Andenas and Zleptnig (n 35) 90.

112 Vadi (n 12).

3.3.3 Reasons to apply proportionality analysis to biotechnology cases

There are four key reasons to manage WTO biotechnology cases by performing proportionality analysis:

1. Proportionality analysis guides the balancing process whenever a conflict of rights, principles, interests or values occurs.[113] International trade in biotechnology favours the economic development of states importing and exporting these products and enhances the world food production. Conversely, it creates risks to human health and the environment. Accordingly, proportionality analysis would be a valuable judicial tool to address the competing interests in the context of biotechnology.
2. As outlined in Chapter 2, 'a close examination [of the WTO jurisprudence] reveals that [panels and] the Appellate Body did not really balance free trade with non-trade values'.[114] The implicit prima facie pre-eminence of free trade along with the lack of a structure supporting a reasoned judicial balance are the two main factors behind this judicial deficit. Conducting proportionality analysis can aid decision-makers to address both these factors for the following reasons. Proportionality analysis can be a tool to disclose the implicit prima facie pre-eminence of free trade under the WTO. The appeal of proportionality lies in the transparency it brings to balancing.[115] Given that, performing proportionality analysis would entail important advantages. If there is pre-eminence of free trade, proportionality renders it transparent; if there is no justification for the pre-eminence, it would be apparent if WTO judicial bodies grant it to trade or not. As '[p]roportionality balancing is an "analytical structure" ',[116] its performance can also be a means to fill the WTO's lack of a structure supporting a reasoned judicial balance.[117]
3. Further, proportionality provides WTO judicial bodies with a chance to foster a solution to the fragmentation of international law. This is because proportionality is viewed as a valid approach to 'defragmentation' of international law.[118] Additionally, WTO judicial bodies in general, and the AB in

113 Andenas and Zleptnig (n 1) 385.

114 Desmedt (n 90) 476; See also Neumann and Turk (n 1) 227; Anne Orford, 'Beyond Harmonization: Trade, Human Rights and the Economy of Sacrifice' (2005) 18(2) *Leiden Journal of International Law* 179; Sarah Joseph, *Blame It on the WTO? A Human Rights Critique* (Oxford University Press, 2011) 59; Kleinlein (n 24).

115 Stephen Breyer, *The Court and the World: American Law and the New Global Realities Paperback* (Vintage, 2016); Greene (n 34) 55.

116 Kumm, 'The Idea of Socratic Contestation and the Right to Justification' (n 29) 579, quoted by Kleinlein (n 24) 1148.

117 This is because the WTO is considered 'institutionally not ready' for balancing economic and non-economic values. Andenas and Zleptnig (n 1) 373.

118 See, e.g., Adamantia Rachovitsa, 'Fragmentation of International Law Revisited: Insights, Good Practices, and Lessons to Be Learned from the Case Law of the European Court of

particular, might have a key role in employing proportionality to address the fragmentation of international law. As Megiddo observes, the AB represents an 'important, exceptionally powerful judicial body that can hardly be called a beacon of international legal harmonization'.[119] By adopting proportionality analysis in biotechnology cases that, importantly, show normative tensions between WTO norms and norms in international human rights law and international environmental law, the AB could contribute to overcoming the fragmentation of international law. This would require a structured judicial balance between human rights and other international principles as well as trade rules. Proportionality analysis can be the means to guide WTO decision-makers to perform such a balance.

4. The judicial performance of proportionality analysis would also limit the 'substantial margin of discretion'[120] given to panels to:

   a. decide '*which evidence [they] choos[e]* to utilize in making findings',[121]
   b. determine 'the *credibility and weight* properly to be ascribed to (that is, the appreciation of) a given piece of evidence',[122] and
   c. decide whether the information disclosed by the appointed experts 'is likely to affect or give rise to justifiable doubts as to the person's independence or impartiality'.[123]

This is because proportionality brings transparency to balancing. Moreover, the performance of proportionality analysis can reduce the discretion of panels facing cases in which the weight of the competing interests is identical and, as a consequence, the scales of justice are in equipoise. Sections 3.4 and 3.5 discuss in greater detail how proportionality analysis can limit the discretion of panels in these stalemate cases.

There is, therefore, merit in performing proportionality analysis in the context of biotechnology under the WTO. The question is: What structure of reasoning should be used to achieve a reasoned and rational outcome? Section 3.4 illustrates Alexy's theory of balancing, which is a valuable model to support a rational structure of judicial reasoning under the WTO.

Human Rights' (2015) 28(4) *Leiden Journal of International Law* 863; Martti Koskenniemi and Päivi Leino, 'Fragmentation of International Law? Postmodern Anxieties' (2002) 15(3) *Leiden Journal of International Law* 553; Stone Sweet and Mathews, *Proportionality Balancing and Constitutional Governance* (n 23); Stephan W Schill, 'Cross-Regime Harmonization through Proportionality Analysis: The Case of International Investment Law, the Law of State Immunity Proposal' (2009) 16 *Indiana Journal of Global Studies* 483; Anne van Aaken, 'Defragmentation of Public International Law Through Interpretation: A Methodological Proposal' (2009) 16(2) *Indiana Journal of Global Studies* 483; Kleinlein (n 24).

119 Megiddo (n 80) 131.

120 AB report, *EC – Hormones* [135].

121 Ibid.

122 Ibid [132]. See also AB report, *US/Canada – Hormones Continued Suspension* [439].

123 AB report, *US/Canada – Hormones Continued Suspension* [446].

3.4 The structure of balancing according to Robert Alexy

Balancing has become 'an essential methodological criterion for adjudication'.[124] Indeed, every modern legal system is composed of two kinds of norms: *rules*, which are applied by means of subsumption, and *principles*, which are applied by means of balancing.[125] As Alexy explains, any judicial balance 'consists in nothing else than optimization relative to competing principles'.[126] This is because principles can be satisfied to varying degrees, while 'rules are norms that are always either fulfilled or not'.[127] This means that WTO decision-makers facing biotechnology legal disputes have to balance – or, in other words, *optimise* – the *principle of trade liberalisation*[128] ('interest in trading biotechnology')[129] and the *principle of ensuring biosafety from risks posed by trading biotechnology* ('interest in ensuring biosafety').[130]

Balancing is, however, not a straightforward procedure, especially under the WTO, which is considered institutionally unprepared for balancing economic and non-economic values. Additionally, there are ongoing theoretical and practical discussions on whether balancing is a rational procedure or a purely rhetorical device.[131] This invites the question of what structure of reasoning balancing should have to be reasoned and rational under the WTO. More specifically, how should WTO decision-makers balance the interest in trading biotechnology and the interest in ensuring biosafety given the normative issues (stemming from an implicit prima facie pre-eminence of free trade, the normative antinomies between WTO law and international human rights law and international environmental law), the judicial issues in balancing economic and non-economic values and the epistemic uncertainties surrounding the international trade of such products? Jurist and legal philosopher Alexy, in *A Theory of Constitutional Rights*,[132]

124 Pulido (n 97) 195.

125 Ibid.

126 Robert Alexy, *A Theory of Constitutional Rights* (J Rivers trans, Oxford University Press, 2002) 47–48 [trans of *Theorie Der Grundrechte* (first published 1985)]; Robert Alexy, 'Balancing, Constitutional Review, and Representation' (2005) 3(4) *International Journal of Constitutional Law* 572, 573.

127 Matthias Klatt and Moritz Meister, *The Constitutional Structure of Proportionality* (Oxford University Press, 2012) 10; Alexy, *A Theory of Constitutional Rights* (n 126) 47–48.

128 In discussing proportionality under the WTO, Ortino referred to free trade as *principle of trade liberalisation*. See Ortino (n 89) 465.

129 Although a narrow interpretation of the concept of 'interests' would encompass it under the anthropological realm, here its interpretation is broader.

130 In this respect, Alexy's elucidation of the so-called 'optimisation requirement' aids understanding that while free trade and biosafety in trading biotechnology are WTO goals, the enhancement of free trade and the protection of biosafety in conducting trade relations are legal principles. See Alexy, *A Theory of Constitutional Rights* (n 126) 47–48. See also Klatt and Meister (n 127) 328.

131 See Pulido (n 97) 195.

132 Stone Sweet and Mathews, *Proportionality Balancing and Constitutional Governance* (n 23).

developed a conception of the structure of balancing that helps answer these questions.[133]

In Alexy's view, three elements form a rational structure of balancing: the law of balancing, the weight formula and the burden of argumentation.[134] By considering these three elements – which are explained in this section – the judicial balance of competing rights or principles can become a rational procedure[135] based on a well-structured proportionality analysis.

1. The *law of balancing* comprises and relates the three factors to be considered in any balancing process: the abstract weight, the intensity of interference and the reliability of empirical premises of the principles or rights at stake.

    a. According to Dworkin and Alexy, unlike rules, principles 'operate as reasons that can be accorded different degrees of "weight" according to both the case at hand and interplay with other principles'.[136] The 'weight' of a principle can be assessed in abstract (without any link to a concrete case) or in concrete (under the circumstances of a case).[137]

Thus, the *abstract weight* (i.e., the first factor of the law of balancing) considers the possible different legal hierarchies between the competing principles or rights under examination. It might be argued, for instance, that the right to life has a greater abstract weight than the right to development, if only because, unlike the right to development, the right to life is non-derogable.[138] It can also be argued that the right to health, which is potentially jeopardised by the international trade in biotechnology, has a greater abstract weight than the right to trade, which is enhanced by importing and exporting those products. This is because 'no right to trade as such is recognized in human rights law'.[139]

b. The *intensity of interference* (i.e., the second factor of the law of balancing) stands for the intensity of interference by non-satisfaction of, or detriment to, the principles or rights at stake. For instance, spraying GM crops with much more herbicides than the maximum amount allowed by the competent authorities would inevitably interfere with the enjoyment of the right to

133 Alexy, *A Theory of Constitutional Rights* (n 126) 47–48.
134 Robert Alexy, 'On Balancing and Subsumption. A Structural Comparison' (2003) 16(4) *Ratio Juris* 433.
135 Ibid.
136 Richard Bellamy, 'Ronald Dworkin, Taking Rights Seriously' (2017) *The Oxford Handbook of Classics in Contemporary Political Theory* 1, 4; Ronald Dworkin, *Taking Rights Seriously* (Harvard University Press, 1978) 14; Alexy (n 30) 44.
137 Dworkin (n 136); Alexy (n 30).
138 United Nations Human Rights, 'Core Human Rights in the Two Covenants' *UNHR* (Web Page, September 2013), https://nhri.ohchr.org/EN/IHRS/TreatyBodies/Page%20Documents/Core%20Human%20Rights.pdf.
139 Joseph (n 114) 36.

health of people living in areas surrounding fields of GM crops. Numerous scientific studies show the adverse effects on the health of people exposed to massive doses of herbicides.[140]

Importantly, Alexy identified a close link between the degree of non-satisfaction of one interest and the abstract weight of the other(s) at stake, a link that is expressed through the so-called *first law of balancing*, according to which, '[t]he greater the degree of non-satisfaction of, or detriment to, one principle [right], the greater must be the importance of satisfying the other'.[141]

At this point, the question is how the degree of non-satisfaction of an interest or the abstract weight of the interests at stake can be expressed and compared. In this respect, Alexy adopted the triadic scale of *light*, *moderate* and *serious*, which was developed by the German Federal Constitutional Court in *Tobacco*.[142]

c. The third factor of Alexy's law of balancing is the *reliability of empirical premises*, in the sense of certainty of the underlying empirical assumptions. Reliability of empirical premises refers to the degree of knowledge of factual data of a concrete case. The intensity of interference and reliability of empirical premises are interrelated according to Alexy's *second law of balancing*, which reads as follows:

> [t]he more heavily an interference in a constitutional right [or legal principle] weighs, the greater must be the certainty of its underlying premises.[143]

After all, even by logic, it is possible to state that reliability of assumptions decreases when uncertainties regarding such assumptions increase, as illustrated in Figure 3.1.

140 See, e.g., Ki-Hyun Kima, Ehsanul Kabirb and Shamin Ara Jahanc, 'Exposure to Pesticides and the Associated Human Health Effects' (2017) 575 *Science of the Total Environment* 525; Antonio F Hernándeza et al., 'Toxic Effects of Pesticide Mixtures at a Molecular Level: Their Relevance to Human Health' (2013) 307 *Toxicology* 136; Virginie Rizzatia et al., 'Effects of Pesticide Mixtures in Human and Animal Models: An Update of the Recent Literature' (2016) 254 *Chemico-Biological Interactions* 231; David C Bellinger, 'A Strategy for Comparing the Contributions of Environmental Chemicals and Other Risk Factors to Neurodevelopment of Children' (2012) 120(4) *Environmental Health Perspectives* 501.

141 Robert Alexy, 'Formal Principles: Some Replies to Critics' (2014) 12(3) *International Journal of Constitutional Law* 511, 513.

142 *Decisions of the German Federal Constitutional Court*, (BVerfGE) 95, 173. This triadic scale can be 'facilitated' by using numbers, following the geometrical sequence of 2^0, 2^1, 2^2, namely respectively 1, 2, and 4, for respectively 'light' (l) 'moderate' (m) and 'serious' (s) intensity of interference. Alexy explains that '[t]he Court qualifies the duty of tobacco producers to place health warnings respecting the dangers of smoking on their products as a relatively minor or light interference with freedom to pursue one's profession. By contrast, a total ban on all tobacco products would count as a serious interference. Between such minor and serious cases, others of moderate intensity of interference can be found': Alexy (n 103) 25.

143 Alexy (n 141) 514.

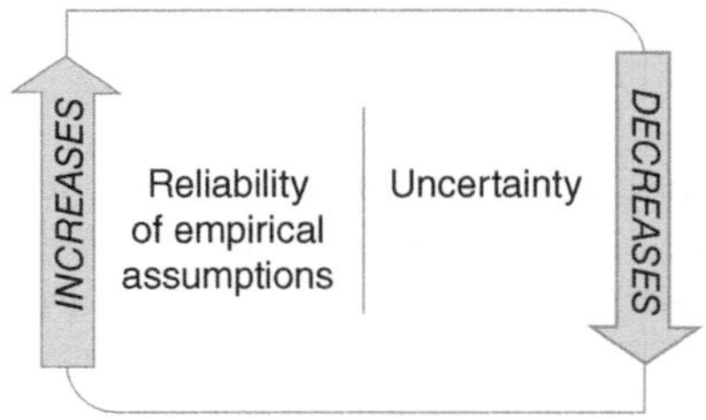

Figure 3.1 Reliability and uncertainty in relation

Similarly to the first two factors, even for the reliability of empirical assumption, Alexy adopted a triadic scale developed by the German Federal Constitutional Court that in the cannabis judgment refers to ***reliable/certain***, ***average or plausible*** and ***uncertain*** empirical premises.[144] As anticipated, the triadic scales adopted by Alexy in relation to the three elements of the law of balancing offer a common metric to evaluate the relative importance of the values at stake. This, in turn, offers a solution to the criticism that any judicial balance compares incommensurable values.[145]

2. Alexy's ***weight formula*** (i.e., the second factor of the structure of balancing) answers the question of how the theoretical law of balancing can aid decision-makers to manage real cases and obtain a concrete balancing outcome.[146] The weight formula is certainly the most innovative and, simultaneously, the most criticised element of Alexy's balancing theory. As Bernal Pulido observes, 'there are diverse rationality limits that leave a margin of discretion to judges' without, nonetheless, impairing 'the analytical value of the weight formula'.[147] This formula encompasses the three factors of the law of balancing (i.e., abstract weight, intensity of interference and reliability of

144 *Decisions of the German Federal Constitutional Court* (BVerfGE) 90, 145. Alexy (n 30). As for the abstract weight and intensity of interference, the triadic scale in relation to the reliability of empirical premises can be exemplified by assigning numerical values: certain = $2^0 = 1$; average = $2^{-1} = \frac{1}{2}$; uncertain = $2^{-2} = \frac{1}{4}$. Klatt and Meister observe that the reliability scale proposed by Alexy refers only to empirical premises. However, in 'Formal Principles: Some Replies to Critics', Alexy clarifies that his second law of balancing refers to both empirical and normative premises. See Alexy (n 141) 514.

145 See Section 3.3.2.

146 In rationalising the judicial balance, Alexy distinguished the ***internal*** justification of balancing, expressed through the so-called 'weight formula', from the ***external*** justification of balancing referring to the values attributed to factors inserted in such a formula. See Alexy (n 134) 435.

147 Carlos Bernal Pulido, 'On Alexy's Weight Formula' in Menéndez Agustín José and Erik Oddvar Eriksen (eds), *Arguing Fundamental Rights* (Springer, 2006) 101, 109.

empirical premises) to obtain the concrete weight (CW) of the competing interests to reveal which one weighs more.[148]

When translated to our context of investigation, the judicial application of the weight formula should consider abstract weight (AW), intensity of interference (IoI), reliability of empirical premises (R^e) pertaining to the interest in trading biotechnology, which is indicated with (t), and the interest in ensuring biosafety from risks posed by trading biotechnology, which is exemplified with (b):

$$\text{CW}(\text{t})(\text{b}) = \frac{AW(t) * IoI(t) * R^e(t)}{AW(b) * IoI(b) * R^e(b)}$$

'The weight formula is thus proposed as a developed complement to the rule of balancing, which Alexy states on the basis of a classical formulation of the third limb of the proportionality principle',[149] which is the balancing test (or proportionality *stricto sensu*).

3. The third element of Alexy's structure of balancing is ***the burden of argumentation*** that operates when the application of the 'weight formula' results in a stalemate (i.e., when the weights of the principles are identical).[150] However, Alexy did not provide a straightforward explanation of how to break a stalemate by means of this third element.[151] In this respect, Section 3.6 suggests addressing stalemates in biotechnology legal disputes by reversing the burden of proof through the precautionary principle.

In sum, according to Alexy, balancing is a rational process with three main elements. The law of balancing (i.e., the first element) comprises and relates the relevant factors to balance two competing rights, principles or legal interests: abstract weight, intensity of interference and reliability of empirical premises. The weight formula (i.e., the second element) is the means to reach a concrete balancing outcome. Finally, the burden of argumentation (i.e., the third element) aids decision-makers to address stalemate cases, though how to do so is not well defined. Adopting this rational balancing process under the WTO would allow

148 Alexy demonstrates that the determination of the concrete weight of the values is facilitated by applying numerical values to the weight formula. The numerical values are ascribed to the three factors inserted in the weight formula by referring to the triadic scales adopted for the abstract weight (AW), intensity of interference (IoI) and reliability of empirical premises (R^e). See Klatt and Meister (n 127) 12; Alexy, 'On Balancing and Subsumption. A Structural Comparison' (n 134).

149 Pulido (n 97) 204. See, e.g., *Decision of the German Constitutional Court in BVerfGE* 30, 296 (316).

150 Robert Alexy, 'The Absolute and the Relative Dimensions of Constitutional Rights' (2017) 37(1) *Oxford Journal of Legal Studies* 31; Pulido (n 147).

151 Pulido (n 147) 104.

panels to perform a reasoned and rational proportionality analysis of legal disputes concerning biotechnology. Bearing this in mind, Section 3.5 provides a step-by-step explanation of how WTO judicial bodies can apply this theory to address biotechnology legal disputes.

3.5 Proportionality analysis applied to biotechnology scenarios

This section illustrates how a well-structured proportionality analysis, the core of which lies in balancing the competing rights or principles at stake by means of Alexy's theory of balancing, can lead WTO judicial bodies to obtain a concrete outcome in biotechnology cases.

First – Identification of the competing interests at stake: As the first step, it is necessary to identify the competing rights, principles or interests to balance that, in this case, are the interests in trading biotechnology and ensuring biosafety.[152]

Second – Ascribing values to the abstract weight of the interests in trading biotechnology and ensuring biosafety: In establishing the abstract weight of the interests at stake, WTO decision-makers might decide that the interest in trading biotechnology has the same, minor or greater, abstract weight than the interest in ensuring biosafety.

Considering the discussed implicit prima facie pre-eminence of free trade under the WTO,[153] it is plausible that requests to enhance free trade in biotechnology would receive *greater abstract weight* than requests for ensuring biosafety. This, however, would contradict the panels' and AB's acknowledgement that 'few interests are more "vital" and "important" than protecting human beings from health risks'.[154] This assertion suggests the judicial attachment of a high abstract weight to the interest in ensuring biosafety, arguably higher than the one assigned to the interest in trading products potentially harmful to human health and the environment. Yet, the analysis in Chapter 2 of some provisions permitting member states to ensure the protection of human health and the environment under the WTO shows that commercial values, like free trade in biotechnology, seem to be implicitly more important than non-commercial values, such as biosafety.[155] This confirms that requests to trade biotechnology might, at present, receive a greater abstract weight than requests for ensuring biosafety.

152 In applying the weight formula to biotechnology cases, we must remember that the interest in trading biotechnology mirrors the right to development of states that export, import and cultivate such products. Simultaneously, the interests in ensuring biosafety from adverse effects posed by trading biotechnology reflects the right to health and the right to a healthy environment.

153 See Section 2.5.

154 Panel report, *Brazil – Retreaded Tyres* [7.108]; AB report, *Brazil – Retreaded Tyres* [144], [179]; AB report, *EC – Asbestos* [172]; Panel report, *Brazil – Taxation* [7.873].

155 See Section 2.4.

At this point, we have to recall that WTO law does not establish a paramount goal to be pursued or facilitated.[156] This might lead to assumptions that the scales of justice should be in equipoise at the beginning of WTO legal disputes.[157] In other words, if the scales of justice should not tip towards one side, interests in trading biotechnology and ensuring biosafety should receive the ***same abstract weight***. After all, they reflect ***equal*** WTO goals: facilitation of trade relations and free trade, and the protection of human health and the environment in trade relations.[158] Although establishing that the two interests have the same abstract weight would properly echo the lack of an overriding WTO goal, it would overlook human rights implications in trade contexts.[159]

Thus, establishing the values of the abstract weight of the competing interests in the context of biotechnology might be particularly difficult for WTO decision-makers. As neither WTO law nor Alexy's theory of balancing suggests how to address this challenge, Section 3.6 refines Alexy's theory to adjust it to the context of biotechnology.

Third – Ascribing the values of the intensity of interference of the interests in trading biotechnology and ensuring biosafety: Because the degree of interference is not a variable that WTO decision-makers should assess in abstract, the values of the intensity of interference of the interests depend on the concrete case. For instance, a total ban on the import/export of a contested GMO represents a *serious* interference with trade.[160] A high tax on the import/export of such product is, arguably, a *moderate* interference,[161] while a low tax on the contested product reflects a *light* interference with trade.[162]

Although establishing the intensity of interference requires a case-by-case analysis, it is important to bear in mind that the chapeau of Article XX of the *GATT Agreement* clarifies that protective measures triggered in the context of the *GATT*, *SPS* and *TBT Agreements* do not apply in a manner that would constitute 'a means of arbitrary or unjustifiable discrimination between countries where the same conditions prevail, or a disguised restriction on international trade [occurs]'.[163] Accordingly, performing the necessity test (i.e., the second step of proportionality analysis) can guide WTO judicial bodies in determining

156 See Section 2.3.

157 Peter-Tobias Stoll and Frank Schorkopf, *WTO – World Economic Order, World Trade Law* (Martinus Nijhoff, 2006) 33; Franz Xaver Perrez, 'The Mutual Supportiveness of Trade and Environment International Law Stable' (2006) 100 *Cambridge University Press on Behalf of the American Society of International Law* 65.

158 See Section 2.3. By assuming that the abstract weights of the interests in trading biotechnology and ensuring biosafety are identical, their values can be ignored because they cancel each other out and, consequently, should not be inserted in the weight formula.

159 See Section 2.6.1.

160 $IoI(t) = s = 2^2 = 4$. See the triadic scale of reference in n 142.

161 $IoI(t) = m = 2^1 = 2$. See the triadic scale of reference in n 142.

162 $IoI(t) = l = 2^0 = 1$. See the triadic scale of reference in n 142.

163 *GATT Agreement* chapeau; *SPS Agreement* art 2[3].

whether the contested biosafety measure represents the least restrictive and least onerous among equally effective alternatives.

It is also important to remember that the AB in *Korea – Various Measures on Beef* underlines the importance of implementing protective measures that *contribute to attain the declared objective.*[164] As such, in establishing the intensity of interference of the interest in trading biotechnology with the interest in ensuring biosafety, WTO judicial bodies can (and should) perform the suitability test (i.e., the first step of proportionality analysis). This would aid the appointed panel to determine whether there is a causal linkage between the objective and the contested measure and, as such, whether the contested measure is appropriate to achieve the desired and legitimate end.

Therefore, performing the first two tests of proportionality analysis can support the judicial determination of the intensity of interference of the interests in the context of biotechnology. Nevertheless, the still-high level of scientific uncertainty can make such a determination quite challenging, as explained in relation to the reliability of empirical premises outlined in the fourth step.

Fourth – Ascribing the values of the reliability of empirical premises of the interests in trading biotechnology and ensuring biosafety: As for the intensity of interference, the reliability of empirical premises is a variable to assess under concrete circumstances. This means that under the circumstances of concrete trade-restrictive measures adopted by member states, WTO judicial bodies should assess whether the justification based on risks to health and environment is grounded on reliable or unreliable knowledge about the biotechnology in question.

The still-high level of scientific uncertainty on the effects of trading biotechnology on biosafety makes such judicial evaluation particularly difficult. Facing contrasting scientific evidence claiming, on one hand, the safety of biotechnology, and on the other, their harmfulness to biosafety, the question is: How should a panel determine the reliability of related empirical assumptions?

Before answering this question, it must be preliminarily clarified that real cases can present two different situations of unreliability concerning empirical premises. 'In the first situation, there is fully reliable knowledge of the intensity of interference, but the underlying empirical premises are unreliable'.[165] Facing these cases, WTO decision-makers can refer to Alexy's second law of balancing that, as explained earlier, establishes the following:

> The more heavily an interference in a constitutional right [or legal principle] weighs, the greater must be the certainty of its underlying premises.[166]

Since in biotechnology cases there is no fully reliable knowledge of the intensity of interference of the interest in trading biotechnology with the interest in ensuring biosafety, WTO biotechnology legal disputes do not reflect this first scenario.

164 AB report, *Korea – Various Measures on Beef* [161].
165 Klatt and Meister (n 127) 128.
166 Alexy (n 141) 514.

'In the second situation, the classification of the intensity of interference itself is unreliable due to empirical unreliability'.[167] Put differently, the unreliability of empirical premises makes also unreliable the intensity of interference of the interests at stake. This second situation of unreliability concerning empirical premises seems to fit the biotechnology scenarios, in which, although it is not completely uncertain, it is difficult to establish the intensity of interference of the interest in trading biotechnology with the interest in ensuring biosafety. This is because the knowledge, and consequently the empirical premises, on the impact of biotechnology on human health and/or the environment remain unreliable, as currently supported by scientifically uncertain and conflicting evidence.

As a result of the broad judicial epistemic discretion given to WTO panels, WTO law does not provide guidelines on how decision-makers should examine the reliability of empirical premises and, consequently, the reliability of evidence supporting such premises. The question becomes even more intricate considering that Alexy's second law of balancing cannot guide decision-makers in managing this second situation of unreliability of empirical premises. Therefore, Section 3.6 offers a potential solution to fill this lacuna in Alexy's theory of balancing.

Fifth – Operationalisation of Alexy's weight formula: Once the values of the abstract weight, the intensity of interference and the reliability of empirical premises have been established, WTO judicial bodies can insert them in Alexy's weight formula. Indeed, the operationalisation of such formula allows decision-makers to obtain the concrete weight of the interest in trading biotechnology in a given case relating to the interest in ensuring biosafety from risks posed by trading biotechnology.[168]

The scenarios that might be brought to the attention of WTO judicial bodies are manifold because they depend on the concrete circumstances of each case. Nonetheless, the application of the weight formula can result in three possible outcomes.

In the first scenario, the operationalisation of the formula shows that the interest in ensuring biosafety weighs more than the interest in trading biotechnology. In this case, WTO judicial bodies should not have discretion but should support national requests to protect biosafety from adverse risks posed by the international trade of these products.

In the second scenario, the application of the formula highlights that the interest in trading biotechnology weighs more than the interest in ensuring biosafety. As such, national requests to enhance international trade in biotechnology should be supported in WTO courtrooms.

In the third possible scenario, the judicial balance results in a stalemate, meaning that the two interests have the same concrete weight. Accordingly, 'the choice between the two does not make any difference in the balancing [process]'.[169]

167 Klatt and Meister (n 127) 128.
168 See Alexy's weight formula in its basic form illustrated in Section 3.4.
169 Klatt and Meister (n 127) 134.

Therefore, the judicial balance through Alexy's weight formula is meaningless.[170] This means that WTO judicial bodies have (only in this case) 'genuine empirical epistemic discretion', that is, the situation in which decision-makers have complete discretion because uncertainty concerning empirical premises is given.[171]

To summarise, performing a well-structured proportionality analysis involves five steps and would require WTO judicial bodies to identify the interests to be balanced, ascribe the values of their abstract weight, intensity of interference and reliability of empirical premises, and operationalise Alexy's weight formula by adopting the established values of these three factors.

This step-by-step discussion of how to perform proportionality analysis in the context of biotechnology under the WTO identifies three key unsolved questions, however. First, how should the abstract weight of the interests in trading biotechnology and ensuring biosafety be determined? Second, how can the reliability of empirical premises be determined when scientifically uncertain and conflicting evidence supports such premises? Third, how should the burden of argumentation operate to break stalemates and, simultaneously, reduce the epistemic discretion of panels in stalemate cases? Section 3.6 addresses these three questions.

3.6 Refining proportionality analysis: new factors for the balancing process in the context of biotechnology

Having illustrated how a well-structured proportionality analysis can guide WTO decision-makers in balancing the competing interests involved in trading biotechnology, this section refines Alexy's theory of balancing to address the discussed remaining issues in applying this theory to biotechnology cases. In approaching this task, this section suggests the judicial consideration of three new factors in balancing the interests in trading biotechnology and ensuring biosafety: The *pro homine* (or *pro personae*) *principle* to overcome the issues concerning the determination of the abstract weight of these interests (see Section 3.6.1); the *reliability of evidence* to guide WTO decision-makers in determining the reliability of empirical premises (see Section 3.6.2) and the *precautionary principle* to break stalemate cases and, accordingly, reduce the epistemic discretion of panels in these cases (see Section 3.6.3). The reasons underneath these suggestions are respectively discussed in Sections 3.6.1–3.6.3.[172]

170 Klatt and Meister highlight that if the value of $C(b)_{1,2}$ is greater than 1 or below 1 is greater than 1 or below 1, the values interference and reliability are to be inserted in the weight formula. See Matthias Klatt and Johannes Schmidt, 'Epistemic Discretion in Constitutional Law' (2012) 10(1) *International Journal of Constitutional Law* 69, 15. See also Klatt and Meister (n 127) 119; Alexy (n 103).

171 Klatt and Meister (n 127) 120–121.

172 These new three factors would enrich the 'external' justification of balancing, which means they should be added to the 'abstract weight', 'intensity of interference' and 'reliability (both

3.6.1 **Pro Homine** *(or* **pro personae***)* **principle** ***as a new factor to establish the abstract weight of the competing interests in the balancing process***

The difficulty in determining the abstract weight of the interests in trading biotechnology and ensuring biosafety mainly stems from the fact that an implicit prima facie pre-eminence of free trade characterises the WTO. Consequently, the dominant commercial ethos under the WTO might arguably lead WTO decision-makers to consider the abstract weight of the interest in trading biotechnology as greater than the abstract weight of the interest in ensuring biosafety. This is despite the fact that both interests reflect equal WTO goals.[173] Thus, the present study suggests the judicial consideration of the *pro homine* (or *pro personae*) principle to establish the abstract weight of the interests in trading biotechnology and ensuring biosafety.

The *pro homine* principle embodies the broad acknowledgement that:

> individuals [rather than states] are subjects of international human rights law and, consequently, have interests that need to be taken into consideration in developing and applying international law. This is the core aspect of the *pro homine* principle.[174]

Importantly, human rights courts, such as the ECtHR and the IACtHR, are not the only judicial bodies that consider the *pro homine* principle.[175] The ICJ, for example, adopted this principle on several occasions.[176] Indeed, '[t]his principle sets an imperative rule to all international law actors',[177] which should consider the *pro homine* principle if only because it pursues the joint goal of protecting humans.[178]

As De Oliveira Mazzuoli and Ribeiro point out, the *pro homine* principle 'is not an abstract and philosophical term'.[179] Rather, as Berbera clarifies, it is an interpretative principle and a normative conflict-resolution technique.[180]

---

empirical and normative) of premises' of the interests at stake. The distinction between 'internal' and 'external' justification of balancing is outlined in note 146.

173 This might suggest ascribing the same abstract weight to the interests at stake to properly echo the lack of an overriding WTO goal. Nevertheless, as previously mentioned, this decision would not consider human rights implications in trade contexts.

174 Valerio De Oliveira Mazzuoli and Dilton Ribeiro, 'The Pro Homine Principle as a Fundamental Aspect of International Human Rights Law' (2016) 17(e17003) *Meridiano 47 Journal of Global Studies* 1, 3.

175 Generally, these courts invoke art 29 of the *American Convention on Human Rights* ('*ACHR*') or art 31(1) of the *VCLT* to adopt the *pro homine* principle. Hayde Rodarte Berbera, 'The Pro Personae Principle and Its Application by Mexican Courts' (2017) 4(1) *QMHRR* 1, 10.

176 See, e.g., *LaGrand Case (Germany v United States of America)* [2001] ICJ Rep 466; Case Concerning Ahmadou Sadio Diallo [2010] ICJ Rep 639. See also De Oliveira Mazzuoli and Ribeiro (n 174) 5–7.

177 De Oliveira Mazzuoli and Ribeiro (n 174) 1.

178 Ibid 5.

179 Ibid 1.

180 Berbera (n 175) 10.

Approaching the *pro homine principle as an interpretative principle* implies:

> [T]he need to choose, among the different possible ways of interpretation, the one that better protects the human rights of the person concerned, either by extending . . . or by limiting . . . the meaning, content and scope of the norm.[181]

In other words, by adopting the *pro homine* principle, the WTO decision-maker should ascribe a prima facie higher weight to the protection of human health and, arguably, the environment, the safeguard of which is directly related to the well-being of humans. After all, 'the constitutional scope of the WTO leaves a wide space for the Appellate Body to protect non-trade values'.[182] Moreover, as Pauwelyn and Elsig outline, 'if investment tribunals interpret pro investors; human rights tribunals interpret *pro homine* and WTO tribunals construe pro traders, the risk of inconsistent outcomes is higher'.[183] Adopting the *pro homine* principle would be a valuable solution in this regard and, even more noteworthy, it would be a valuable tool to tackle the implicit prima facie pre-eminence of free trade under the WTO that, as Chapter 2 extensively discusses, is legally groundless.[184]

Further, the fact that the *pro homine* principle is also a *normative conflict-resolution technique* means that when facing conflicting norms, the norm that better protects the rights of individuals should prevail. This would require WTO decision-makers to prioritise the norms that most benefit the person(s) concerned,[185] which, in biotechnology legal disputes, would be the people potentially affected by the adverse risks to biosafety posed by the international trade in biotechnology.

By adopting the *pro homine* principle, WTO judicial bodies might, accordingly, foster (at least to some extent) a solution to the fragmentation of international law. Indeed, its use promotes, according to Freitas Mohallem, the unity of international law via dialogue[186] and simultaneously mitigates, in Lixinski's view, its fragmentation.[187] Accordingly, the employment of the *pro homine* principle would be viewed as a valuable effort to harmonise WTO law and human rights

181 Ibid; see also Carpio Marcos Edgar, *La Interpretación de Los Derechos Fundamentales* (Palestra Editores, 2004) 470–473.

182 Andersen (n 2) 383.

183 Joost Pauwelyn and Manfred Elsig, 'The Politics of Treaty Interpretation: Variations and Explanations across International Tribunals' (2011) (Weiler 2010) *SSRN Electronic Journal* 445, 7.

184 See Section 2.3.

185 Karlos Castilla, 'El Principio Pro Persona En La Administración de Justicia' (2009) 20 *Revista Mexicana de Derecho Constitucional* 68, 71–78; Berbera (n 175) 10.

186 Michael Freitas Mohallem, 'Horizontal Judicial Dialogue on Human Rights: The Practice of Constitutional Courts in South America' in Amrei Müller (ed), *Judicial Dialogue and Human Rights* (Cambridge University Press, 2017) 67; Berbera (n 175) 13.

187 Lucas Lixinski, 'Treaty Interpretation by the Inter-American Court of Human Rights: Expansionism at the Service of the Unity of International Law' (2010) 21(3) *The European Journal of International Law* 585, 586; Berbera (n 175) 13.

law. This is particularly important considering the discussed normative antinomies between WTO rules and human rights law[188] and the lack of sufficient efforts under the WTO to harmonise the trade law system with human rights.[189]

3.6.2 Reliability of evidence *as a new factor to determine the reliability of empirical premises in the balancing process*

Alexy's theory of balancing does not provide indications to address the circumstances raised by the international trade in biotechnology in relation to the unreliability of empirical premises. Indeed, his second law of balancing (i.e., *the more heavily an interference in a constitutional right [or legal principle] weighs, the greater must be the certainty of its underlying premises*)[190] applies only to circumstances in which there is fully reliable knowledge of the intensity of interference, though the underlying empirical premises are unreliable.[191] In trading biotech products, there is, however, no fully reliable knowledge of the intensity of interference of the interest in trading biotechnology with that of ensuring biosafety. The intensity of interference itself is unreliable because of the unreliability of the knowledge (i.e., empirical premises) on the effects posed by trading biotechnology to biosafety, which is caused by the high level of scientific uncertainty surrounding the effects of biotechnology.

Considering that Alexy's theory does not provide suggestions in this regard, the question, therefore, is how WTO decision-makers should determine the reliability of empirical premises in balancing the competing interests in the context of biotechnology. This section suggests performing a thorough evaluation of the *reliability of evidence* to fill the lacuna in Alexy's theory.[192]

The reliability of evidence is a factor highly relevant in the context of biotechnology, which is characterised by ample scientific literature supporting either the safety or the harmfulness of biotechnology. Nevertheless, WTO panels seem to overlook this key factor in assessing the quality of evidence.[193] Indeed, the AB stresses that panels determine the *appreciation* (or quality) *of evidence* by assessing '*credibility* and *weight* . . . ascribed to . . . a given *piece* of evidence'.[194] This description of the process of appreciation of evidence under the WTO does not align with the general understanding of this judicial task. Indeed, the judicial

188 See Section 2.6.
189 See Sections 2.4 and 2.5.
190 Alexy (n 141) 514.
191 See Section 3.5.
192 Some suggestions in the literature attempt to fill the gap in the doctrine of balancing proposed by Alexy. See, e.g., Klatt and Meister (n 127) 10.
193 Arguably, the reason lies in the fact that '[b]ecause weighing evidence is so common, the importance of the process is often overlooked and as a result, it is generally performed informally and presented as a narrative'. US EPA Office of Research and Development, EPA/100/R-16/001 (Web Record, 2016) 1, https://cfpub.epa.gov/si/si_public_record_report.cfm?Lab=OSA&dirEntryId=335523.
194 *EC – Hormones* (n 120) [132] (emphasis added).

appreciation of evidence is generally described as a process, also termed weight of evidence (WoE), weighing, among other elements, the *credibility* and *reliability* of evidence to determine the quality of the body of evidence submitted by parties.[195]

Thus, the judicial appreciation of evidence should be the result of a transparent evaluation process that also encompasses the reliability of evidence. A pertinent question at this point might be: What makes a piece of evidence *reliable*? Arguably, there is no single answer. Nonetheless, three suggestions might certainly enhance the reliability of evidence.

As the first step to enhance the reliability of evidence, panels might invite all experts involved (i.e., parties' experts and those appointed by panellists) to submit evidence arising from the same scientific process. For the sake of consistency, panels might, for instance, require risk assessors to perform their analyses by referring to *the same WoE process*. The WoE process developed in the 2016 Report of the US Environmental Protection Agency (EPA Report) might be a good example in this regard. With the main purpose of judging the relevance, strength and reliability of evidence in ecological assessment, the 2016 EPA Report shaped a detailed WoE process, which involves the following steps:

> (1) assembling evidence, (2) weighting evidence with respect to properties, and (3) weighing the integrated body of evidence. This WoE process is embedded in larger assessment processes, which include planning, problem formulation, analysis, synthesis, and communicating results.[196]

A consistent risk assessors' adoption of a WoE process would enhance transparency and consistency in performing risk assessments. This would aid WTO decision-makers to assess the reliability of evidence and, accordingly, the reliability of related empirical premises.

As a second step, a comprehensive judicial assessment of the reliability of evidence should entail a thorough *evaluation of the appropriateness of risk assessments* supporting the evidence brought to the attention of the appointed panel. Risk assessment is the process that generates the body of evidence supporting requests in biotechnology legal disputes. Nevertheless, the WTO normative framework

195 See, e.g., Florentin Smarandache and Jean Dezert, *Advances and Applications of DSmT for Information Fusion* (Infinite Study, vol IV, 2015) 413; Glenn Suter, Susan Cormier and Mace Barron, 'A Weight of Evidence Framework for Environmental Assessments: Inferring Qualities' (2017) 13(6) *Integrated Environmental Assessment and Management* 1038; A Tilghman Hall et al., 'New Approach to Weight-of-Evidence Assessment of Ecotoxicological Effects in Regulatory Decision-Making' (2017) 13(4) *Integrated Environmental Assessment and Management* 573; Michael Balls et al., 'The Principles of Weight of Evidence Validation of Test Methods and Testing Strategies: The Report and Recommendations of ECVAM Workshop 58a' (2006) 34(6) *ATLA Alternatives to Laboratory Animals* 603.

196 US EPA Office of Research and Development (n 193).

and the WTO jurisprudence neglect to define what can be considered 'appropriate' in circumstances involving scientific uncertainties. For example, in the context of the *SPS Agreement*, any risk assessment complying with Article 5.1 and annex A.4 of this Agreement is considered 'appropriate'. Nevertheless, both the Article and annex are science-centric and, thus, do not suit the scientifically uncertain circumstances surrounding the international trade in biotechnology.[197] In light of this, and considering that risk assessment of biotechnology cannot be reduced to a scientific matter, Chapter 7 highlights what makes a risk assessment 'appropriate' in the view of WTO law and judicial bodies.

As a third and final point, a comprehensive process of evaluation of the reliability of evidence would also consider the ***reliability of experts advising parties and panels***. This is particularly important considering that a vast part of research on biotechnology is financed by the largest biotech companies (Monsanto, Bayer CropScience, Dupont, Syngenta and Groupe Limagrain) and, accordingly, the reliability of financially supported studies should be investigated:[198]

> One problem, identified by independent scientists, is that much of the relevant information and technical expertise resides with the industrial interests that have a stake in marketing [biotechnology], or with scientists and researchers with strong industry affiliations.[199]

Consequently, WTO judicial bodies face information asymmetries that, as Eliason observes, cast doubt on the impartiality of scientific evidence adopted to perform risk assessments.[200] Further, as Howse and Horn point out, biotech cases raise an important challenge: Public trust in multinational corporations that are 'very much behind the use of trade-law litigation to expand market access for GMOs'.[201]

Appointing and consulting reliable experts is, as such, paramount, and importantly, it is a task confined to panels' discretion.[202] Nevertheless, because of the obligation to afford due process,[203] experts consulted by a panel must be independent and impartial.[204] Yet, *US/Canada – Hormones Continued Suspension*

197 Chapter 7 provides an in-depth analysis of art 5.1 and annex A.4 of the *SPS Agreement.*

198 See Ruchir Raman, 'The Impact of Genetically Modified (GM) Crops in Modern Agriculture: A Review' (2017) 8(4) *GM Crops and Food* 195, 203.

199 Robert Howse and Petros C Mavroidis, 'Europe's Evolving Regulatory Strategy for GMOs and the Issue of Consistency with WTO Law: Of Kine and Brine' (2000) 24(1) *Fordham International Law Journal* 317, 351.

200 Antonia Eliason, 'Science versus Law in WTO Jurisprudence: The (Mis)Interpretation of the Scientific Process and the (In)Sufficiency of Scientific Evidence in EC-Biotech' (2009) 41 *New York University Journal of International Law & Policy* 341, 402.

201 Robert Howse and Henrik Horn, 'European Communities – Measures Affecting the Approval and Marketing of Biotech Products' (2009) 8(1) *World Trade Review* 49, 52.

202 *US/Canada–Hormones Continued Suspension* (n 122) [436], [444].

203 Ibid [436].

204 Ibid [436], [444].

shows that panels' discretion can result in the appointment of experts whose affiliations 'compromised', according to the AB, 'the adjudicative independence and impartiality of the Panel'.[205] This is because the panel's appointment of Boisseau and Boobis infringed the obligation to afford due process for the following reason:

> [T]he Panel disregarded its "most important objection" that an expert who has participated in the drafting of JECFA [i.e., Joint FAO/WHO Expert Committee on Food Additives] reports cannot be independent and impartial because, in this case, the experts were being asked to evaluate new scientific evidence underlying reports that were directly critical of, or in conflict with, their prior contribution to the JECFA reports.[206]

In light of this, this section suggests normative amendments that might enhance the likelihood to appoint reliable experts advising panels.

1. *Amendment to the Rules of Conduct*: Experts requested to advise panels are currently subject to 'disclose any information that . . . is likely to affect or give rise to justifiable doubts as to their independence or impartiality'.[207] This obligation is set out in Section VI.2 of the *Rules of Conduct*.[208] Disclosing a conflict of interests does not generally imply an automatic exclusion of the declarant. Indeed, the panel in *US/Canada – Hormones Continued Suspension* considered the conflict of interests declared by Boisseau and Boobis an added value rather than a source of concern.[209]

An amendment to the WTO *Rules of Conduct* might reduce the chances for future panels to appoint experts whose impartiality is compromised because of their conflicts of interest. More specifically, annex 2 of the *Rules of Conduct* provides an open list of information that a person called upon to serve in a dispute should disclose. For example, appointed experts must disclose (1) financial interests (e.g., investments and loans), business interests (e.g., directorship or other contractual interests) and property interests relevant to the dispute in question; (2) professional interests (e.g., a past or present relationship with private clients); (3) other active interests that may be relevant to the dispute in question; (4) publications or public statements on issues relevant to the dispute in question; and (5) employment or family interests in providing their consultation.[210]

205 Ibid [481].
206 Ibid [456].
207 Ibid [64].
208 *Rules of Conduct for the Understanding on Rules and Procedures Governing the Settlement of Disputes*, WTO Doc WT/DSB/RC/1 (96–5267) (11 December 1996) s VI.2 ('*Rules of Conduct*').
209 AB report, *US/Canada – Hormones Continued Suspension* [461]; Panel report, *US/Canada – Hormones Continued Suspension* [7.83] (emphasis in original).
210 *Rules of Conduct* annex 2.

Simply put, WTO experts '*shall* disclose any information' that might show a conflict of interest,[211] while panels, in line with almost all other courts, are not required to automatically exclude experts disclosing such information. This might be viewed as problematic because it allows experts who are not independent to give evidence before WTO panels. How can, for instance, an expert who received funds from multinationals supporting biotechnology be 'independent'? How can the opinion of an expert who openly made public statements on the harmfulness of biotechnology be considered 'impartial'? Nevertheless, an automatic exclusion of experts previously involved in one of the circumstances listed under annex 2 would lead to the problem of excluding any relevant person with knowledge about the matter.

Therefore, this study suggests the following. The disclosure rule section under Section VI.2 of the *Rules of Conduct* should be maintained. However, a recusation procedure should be added. The *Rules of Conduct* should, first, set out specific conditions for recusation, such as, for example, having received funding from parties or having expressed views about the matter in question; and second, it should impose a restrictive interpretation of such conditions. This amendment would considerably reduce the possibility of appointing experts whose impartiality and, accordingly, reliability, might jeopardise the fairness of proceedings and the impartiality of decision-making.

2. *Amendment to Article 13 of the DSU*: A further improvement that might enhance the impartiality of decision-making and, simultaneously, the chances of obtaining a clearer picture of the effects of biotechnology would require an amendment to Article 13, which currently allows panels to consult either individual experts or to constitute an 'expert review group' to prepare an advisory report.[212]

In *US/Canada – Hormones Continued Suspension*, the EC stressed that the panel 'for no good reason declined to follow [its] suggestion to constitute an expert review group'.[213] Panels are indeed not required to support parties' requests to either consult individual experts or constitute an expert review group. It is, however, interesting to note that 'in no case to date has a panel chosen the [option of appointing a group of experts]'.[214]

However, as Eliason observes, the 'panels' decisions to address experts individually rather than as a group have affected the reliability of the responses'.[215] The establishment of an *expert review group* carries the significant advantage of preventing panels from arbitrarily picking and choosing scientific opinions or

211 Ibid s VI.2 (emphasis added).

212 *Dispute Settlement Understanding* art 13.

213 AB report, *US/Canada–Hormones Continued Suspension* [440]; Panel report, *US/Canada–Hormones Continued Suspension* [7.71].

214 Eliason (n 200) 383.

215 Ibid 381.

'rel[ying] extensively' on only some of the scientific opinions provided, as happened in *US/Canada – Hormones Continued Suspension*.[216]

In light of these advantages, and considering that the recurring preference of panels to address individual experts rather than groups of experts mitigates the value of expert scientific testimony,[217] an amendment to Article 13 of the *DSU* might be considered. When facing biotechnology matters 'involving highly complex scientific issues',[218] panels seeking advice should step away from their preference of appointing individual scientists and be required to appoint an expert review group. As Crawford-Brown, Pauwelyn and Smith emphasise, '[t]his group, with its own mandate set by the panel, can then discuss and evaluate matters internally before submitting its balanced conclusions to the judicial decision maker'.[219] What is more, the appointment of an expert review group would both echo panels' wish to hear majority and minority views and, at the same time, prevent judges from deciding which view is a majority/minority view in the scientific community. Indeed, judges may not be best placed to determine that.

At this point, a pertinent question is who can participate in expert review groups. Appendix 4, paragraph 2 of the *DSU* establishes that '[p]articipation in expert review groups shall be restricted to persons of professional standing and experience in the field in question'.[220] This is assessed based on the number of peer-reviewed publications of an expert.[221] The EU criticises this point in *US/Canada – Hormones Continued Suspension*,[222] when it asks 'whether an expert that has been the author of a given report is impartial and independent to act as a "peer" in "reviewing" reports that explicitly criticise the report where the "peer" is a co-author'.[223] This pertinent point clearly demonstrates the value of impartiality over the number of peer-reviewed papers a scientist has published.

However, peer review is widely recognised in the scientific community (and beyond) as the process through which scientific analyses should be validated. This process is deemed the means to 'separate valid science from nonsense'.[224] Thus, it is understandable that the selection of experts will take into account the number of peer-reviewed publications an individual has achieved. However, the quantitative output of a scientist should not be the only factor that determines

216 AB report, *US/Canada–Hormones Continued Suspension* [484].
217 Eliason (n 200) 383.
218 AB report, *US/Canada–Hormones Continued Suspension* [436].
219 Douglas Crawford-Brown, Joost Pauwelyn and Kelly Smith, 'Environmental Risk, Precaution, and Scientific Rationality in the Context of WTO/NAFTA Trade Rules' (2004) 24 *Risk Analysis* 461, 468.
220 *Dispute Settlement Understanding* Appendix 4[2].
221 Panel report, *US/Canada–Hormones Continued Suspension* [6.22].
222 AB report, *US/Canada–Hormones Continued Suspension* [476].
223 Ibid [476].
224 David Goodstein, 'How Science Works' in Committee on the Development of the Third Edition of the Reference Manual on Scientific Evidence & Committee on Science, Technology, and Law Policy and Global Affairs (ed), *Reference Manual on Scientific Evidence* (The National Academies Press, 3rd ed, 2011) 37, 44–45.

expertise. Indeed, Appendix 4, paragraph 2 of the *DSU* restricts participation in review groups to those showing 'professional standing and experience in the field in question', which can be broader than the number of publications achieved.

Regardless of the peer review debate,[225] it is argued that the restrictions on participating in expert review groups, set out in Appendix 4, paragraph 2, do not fit the complex and still-unexplored field of biotechnology. As discussed in Section 7.4.2, a rethink of what constitutes an 'expert' is required to include non-scientific members. An amendment to that affect would align with Article 13.1 of the *DSU*, permitting panels 'to seek information and technical advice *from any individual or body which it deems appropriate*'.[226]

To conclude, this section highlights that facing the unreliability of the intensity of interference caused by the unreliability of empirical assumptions on the adverse effects posed by trading biotechnology to biosafety, WTO decision-makers should evaluate the reliability of evidence in their balancing process or, more specifically, in their assessment of the reliability of empirical premises of the interests. Considering the numerous opposing scientific studies about biotechnology and remembering that a large portion of research in biotechnology is financed by the five main biotech companies, judicial evaluation of the reliability of evidence might be difficult. This section points out three means to improve the reliability of evidence: (1) asking the appointed experts to adopt the same WoE, (2) conducting a thorough evaluation of the appropriateness of risk assessments, and (3) enhancing the likelihood of appointing reliable experts to advise panels. Further, they would support transparency and consistency in performing risk assessment, aid panels in determining the *quality* of evidence, and align the WTO process of appreciation of evidence with the general understanding of this process, which involves the reliability of evidence.

3.6.3 The **precautionary principle** *as a new criterion to break stalemates and reduce judicial epistemic discretion*

A further refinement of Alexy's theory of balancing concerns the way the burden of argumentation should operate to break stalemate cases. Although it is indicated that the burden of argumentation operates when the application of the weight formula results in a stalemate, there are scant contributions illustrating how this third element of Alexy's structure of balancing can break a stalemate.[227] Arguably, the reason lies in the fact that scholars agree on the following: stalemates entail circumstances of a pure judicial empirical epistemic discretion ('judicial epistemic discretion').[228]

225 Ibid.

226 *Dispute Settlement Understanding* Appendix 4 [4] (emphasis added).

227 Alexy offered several solutions to break stalemate cases by means of the burden of argumentation. However, Alexy's solutions have been identified as problematic because they could lead to different results. See Pulido (n 147) 104.

228 Klatt and Schmidt (n 170) 19.

Nevertheless, the uncertainties surrounding stalemate cases leave numerous unknowns. For instance, it is doubtful which values decision-makers must use to assess the abstract weight and the intensity of interference in balancing the competing rights, principles and interests considered. This uncertainty makes the normative premises unreliable. The reliability of normative premises refers to the legal position of principles or rights at stake. Specifically, any legal principle has a semantic domain in which there are different legal positions. The protection of fauna and the safeguard of forestry are, for instance, different legal positions within the same domain of environmental protection. In real cases, the reliability of normative premises determines both the abstract weight and the intensity of interference of the competing rights, principles or interests at stake. For example, although the right to health is a fundamental right with a high abstract weight, in the context of biotechnology, the legal position of (the legal interest of ensuring) human health from risks posed by trading biotechnology changes according to the circumstances. It can be higher or lower depending on whether such products cause irreversible (e.g., terminal diseases) or reversible damages to humans (e.g., allergies).[229]

Also, the uncertainty surrounding stalemate cases extends further the already broad discretion given to panels to select evidence,[230] determine the credibility and WoE[231] and appoint experts.[232] This might, accordingly, undermine the transparency and objectivity of final judgments.

Therefore, the present analysis suggests breaking stalemates, and thereby reducing judicial epistemic discretion, by considering the *precautionary principle.* The precautionary principle, which is thoroughly discussed in Chapter 4, is an international environmental law principle that 'calls for actions at an earlier stage, even in a time of doubt when there is not yet conclusive scientific evidence as to the harmfulness'.[233] Thus, it plays a key role in the field of biotechnology, which is perforated by uncertainties. Unsurprisingly, the jurisprudence of international courts contains plenty of cases in which precaution was invoked to support biosafety requests to address risks to human health and/or the environment caused by biotechnology.[234] Moreover, the precautionary principle can be implemented in judicial contexts through procedural means including reversing the burden of proof:

229 Unreliability of normative premises also raises problems of 'normative epistemic discretion'. See especially Klatt and Meister (n 127) 133; Alexy (n 141) 514.

230 AB report, *EC – Hormones* [135].

231 Ibid [132].

232 AB report, *US/Canada – Hormones Continued Suspension* [446].

233 Aline L Jaeckel, *The International Seabed Authority and the Precautionary Principle – Balancing Deep Seabed Mineral Mining and Marine Environmental Protection* (Brill Nijhoff, 2017) 29.

234 See, e.g., AB report, *EC – Hormones*; AB report, *US/Canada – Hormones Continued Suspension*; Panel report, *EC – Biotech*; *Giorgio Fidenato and Others*; *France Monsanto*; *Austrian case*; *Monsanto Italy*; *Cassis de Dijon*.

> [N]ormative rules such as the P[recautionary] P[rinciple] can be regarded as fair when they ensure 'distributive justice' – that is, when 'an appropriate or proper allocation of burdens and benefits' [is] secured by the rules themselves.[235]

In other words, the precautionary principle can reverse the burden of proof and place it on the proponent of biotechnology. Further, the precautionary approach affects the standard of proof by lowering the evidentiary threshold.[236] By reversing the burden of proof, or simply by affecting the standard of proof, precaution represents a valid means to break a stalemate.[237]

Simultaneously, the consideration of precaution as an additional factor in the balancing process might alleviate the concern of some commentators discouraging the application of the proportionality *stricto sensu* (or balancing test) because it would lead WTO decision-makers 'to prefer "trade" (and thus "deregulation") to "health [and/or environmental] protection" (and thus Member States' regulation)'.[238] Indeed, although precaution does not dictate an outcome, it requires decision-makers to consider biosafety measures despite remaining uncertainties. This means that precaution can mitigate the implicit prima facie pre-eminence of free trade and the science-centric requirements of the *SPS Agreement* to trigger biosafety measures.[239] It can also be a valid means to address, to some extent, the lack of reliability of empirical assumptions concerning the impact of trading biotechnology on biosafety, as discussed in Chapter 4: *in dubio pro biosafety*. Moreover, the judicial operationalisation of the precautionary principle would also be a coherent consequence of the judicial adoption of the *pro homine* principle, which ascribes a prima facie priority to rights protecting individuals from, in this case, risks posed by trading biotechnology.

To conclude, the precautionary principle can break stalemates and, accordingly, reduce the discretion of panels by reversing or affecting the standard of

235 Iain Scobbie, 'Tom Franck's Fairness' (2002) 13(4) *European Journal of International Law* 909, 910, quoted in Monika Ambrus, 'The Precautionary Principle and a Fair Allocation of the Burden of Proof in International Environmental Law' (2012) 21(3) *Review of European Community and International Environmental Law* 259, 260.

236 Jaeckel (n 233) 55; Arie Trouwborst, 'The Precautionary Principle in General International Law: Combating the Babylonian Confusion' (2007) 16 *Review of European Community & International Environmental Law* 185, 192; David Freestone and Ellen Hey, 'Implementing the Precautionary Principle: Challenges and Opportunities' in David Freestone and Ellen Hey (eds), *The Precautionary Principle and International Law: The Challenge of Implementation* (Kluwer Law International, 1996) 249; Jacqueline Peel, *The Precautionary Principle in Practice: Environmental Decision-Making and Scientific Uncertainty* (Federation Press, 2005) 6.

237 For an in-depth discussion of the precautionary principle and the burden of proof, see Section 4.4.2.

238 Ortino (n 89) 420.

239 Regarding the requirements under the *SPS Agreement* to trigger safeguarding measures, see Section 2.4.2.

proof. Nevertheless, the interpretation of the precautionary principle as a procedural tool is debated as much as its application under the WTO. Chapter 4 offers an in-depth discussion of the implementation of the precautionary principle, particularly relating to the burden of proof under the WTO.

3.7 Conclusion

The analysis in this chapter demonstrates that performing proportionality analysis in the context of biotechnology under the WTO has compelling justifications despite the lack of explicit reference to proportionality in the WTO agreements and the scepticism of the balancing test (i.e., the third test of proportionality analysis). In light of the foundations provided by Alexy's theory of balancing, the WTO judicial balance between trade and non-trade interests can be the result of a well-structured proportionality analysis, rather than a decision confined to the epistemic discretion of the appointed panel.

Transplanting proportionality analysis to the field of biotechnology carries some limits. This chapter overcomes those limits by suggesting the judicial consideration of three new factors in the balancing process: the *pro homine* principle, the reliability of evidence and the precautionary principle.

By adopting the *pro homine* principle, WTO decision-makers could ascribe a prima facie higher weight to human rights and, accordingly, biosafety protection (the *pro homine* principle as an interpretative principle). Moreover, facing conflicting norms, the *pro homine* principle would require WTO decision-makers to prioritise the norms that most benefit the person(s) concerned, which, in biotechnology legal disputes, would be the people potentially affected by the adverse risks posed by the international trade in biotechnology to biosafety (the *pro homine* principle as a normative conflict-resolution technique). In this view, the judicial consideration of the *pro homine* principle in the balancing process would (1) aid decision-makers to ascribe the abstract weight of the interests in trading biotechnology and ensuring biosafety, (2) tackle the implicit prima facie pre-eminence of free trade under the WTO and (3) address (at least to some extent) the fragmentation of international law.

Considering the *reliability of evidence* as a further factor to take account of in balancing the competing interests in trading biotechnology would help WTO decision-makers establish the reliability of empirical premises, the determination of which might be difficult in the chasm of antithetical scientific studies on biotechnology. The analysis in this chapter underlines that (1) the consistent risk assessors' adoption of a WoE process, along with (2) a comprehensive judicial evaluation of 'appropriateness' of risk assessment and (3) normative suggestions for improving the likelihood of appointing reliable experts, might enhance the reliability of evidence-supporting requests in biotechnology cases.

Finally, the *precautionary principle* should be considered by decision-makers managing biotechnology cases for two reasons. First, by reversing the burden of proof and affecting the standard of proof, the precautionary principle can break stalemates. This would reduce the judicial epistemic discretion of panels in these cases. Second, Chapter 4 shows that the judicial adoption of this principle can aid WTO decision-makers to address the scientific uncertainties surrounding the international trade in biotechnology. This means that effective implementation of the precautionary principle might guide WTO decision-makers to address the epistemic challenges surrounding the international trade in biotechnology. Simply put, trading biotechnology raises not only ***normative*** and ***judicial*** issues, which can be addressed by performing a proportionality analysis in light of Alexy's theory of balancing and the suggested refinements to this theory, but also *epistemic* problems, which are twofold. As Chapter 1 highlights, the first epistemic problem is raised by the fact that risks posed by the international trade in biotechnology are uncertain. This uncertainty of the effects of trading biotechnology on biosafety also makes uncertain the reliability of empirical assumptions concerning the effects posed by trading biotechnology to biosafety. This raises epistemic challenges for WTO decision-makers required to make decisions on biotechnology legal disputes. Second, stalemate cases entail numerous unknowns, which are confined to the almost total epistemic discretion of decision-makers. This, in turn, entails uncertainties on the objectivity of final judicial decisions in stalemate cases.

Building on the discussion in this chapter, Chapter 4 focuses on how effective operationalisation of the precautionary principle can guide WTO decision-makers in addressing the epistemic issues surrounding the international trade in biotechnology.

4 The precautionary principle to address WTO epistemic challenges in the context of biotechnology

4.1 Introduction

In discussing proportionality analysis in the previous chapter, the precautionary principle appears as an element that WTO judicial bodies should take account of in balancing the competing interests in the context of biotechnology. This is because while performing a well-structured proportionality analysis can aid WTO decision-makers to address normative and judicial issues surrounding the international trade in biotechnology, effective operationalisation of the precautionary principle can guide panels and the AB to handle the epistemic issues in the context of biotechnology.

To return to a point made earlier, the epistemic issues raised by the international trade in biotechnology stem from the still-high level of scientific uncertainty about the effects of these products to human health and the environment.[1] The unknowns carried by stalemate cases raise further epistemic challenges for WTO decision-makers who, facing complex and antithetical scientific studies on biotechnology, have almost total discretion.[2]

The judicial consideration of the precautionary principle in balancing the competing interests in trading biotechnology can be a valid means to overcome these epistemic issues. As the principle requires taking actions even where uncertainty remains,[3] its implementation can be key to addressing scientific uncertainties surrounding the international trade in biotechnology: 'Under the precautionary principle, the benefit of any such doubt is to go to the environment. *In dubio pro nature*'[4] or, if applied to the context of biotechnology, *in*

1 The analysis of benefits and risks in trading biotechnology highlights that the scientific community is deeply divided on both the positive and negative impacts on biosafety. See Section 1.2.

2 As discussed in Section 3.5, facing stalemate cases, the operationalisation of Alexy's 'weight formula' would be meaningless. See Matthias Klatt and Moritz Meister, *The Constitutional Structure of Proportionality* (Oxford University Press, 2012) 120–121.

3 Arie Trouwborst, *Evolution and Status of the Precautionary Principle in International Law* (Kluwer Law International, 2002) 10.

4 Arie Trouwborst, 'The Precautionary Principle in General International Law: Combating the Babylonian Confusion' (2007) 16 *Review of European Community & International Environmental Law* 185, 187.

DOI: 10.4324/9781003325741-6

dubio pro biosafety.[5] This means that the adoption of the precautionary principle under the WTO might mitigate the *pro trade* ethos within the WTO, which is discussed in Chapter 2. In fostering a solution to handle scientific uncertainties, the precautionary principle can, in turn, be a valid means to address, to some extent, the lack of reliability of empirical assumptions concerning the impact of trading biotechnology to biosafety.

What is more, precaution can also be a valid means to break stalemate cases and, accordingly, reduce the judicial discretion in these cases by lowering the standard of proof or reversing the burden of proof and placing it on the proponent of biotechnology. In doing so, the judicial adoption of precaution would reduce the numerous unknowns carried by stalemate scenarios, which undermine transparency and objectivity of final decisions.

Nevertheless, the interpretation and application of precaution under the WTO, especially its operationalisation through procedural means such as reversing the burden of proof, is still debated. Additionally, WTO judicial bodies are reticent in allowing its operationalisation. Unsurprisingly, the 2005 Report of the former secretary to the Committee on Trade and Environment (CTE) emphasises that member states 'face *real challenges* when defending a precautionary action before the WTO Dispute Settlement Body'.[6]

In light of this, the present chapter discusses the precautionary principle with a focus on its judicial operationalisation. Although offering a general overview of the most relevant aspects of precaution, the focus lies on those issues that are relevant for enhancing a reasoned judicial balance between the interests in trading biotechnology and ensuring biosafety. In so doing, this analysis aims to show that the WTO judicial bodies' reticence in adopting the precautionary principle is unjustified.

In approaching this investigation, this chapter develops as follows. Section 4.2 introduces the concept of precaution by highlighting its rationale, status and adoption in international law. This includes discussing the migration of this principle across jurisdictions and providing examples of its adoption in contexts other than trade to map out the features of precaution. This is because WTO law does not yet offer many examples of the precautionary principle. Section 4.3 turns to the applicability of precaution under the WTO framework and, in doing so, identifies three grounds allowing precaution to be encompassed under WTO law. Section 4.4 discusses the implementation of the precautionary principle in the context of biotechnology under the WTO with the main purpose of showing how effective adoption of this legal tool can aid WTO decision-makers to

5 The *Cartagena Protocol on Biosafety* defines *biosafety* as the protection of 'human health and the environment from the possible adverse effects of the products of modern biotechnology': *Cartagena Protocol on Biosafety* 1.

6 Sabrina Shaw and Risa Schwartz, 'UNU-IAS Report Trading Precaution: The Precautionary Principle and the WTO United' (Web Page, November 2005) 11, http://collections.unu.edu/eserv/UNU:3103/Precautionary_Principle_and_WTO.pdf (emphasis added).

overcome the epistemic issues raised by the international trade in biotechnology. Final remarks are set out in Section 4.5.

4.2 Precaution: main features, migration across jurisdictions and implementing dimensions

4.2.1 Concept, formulation(s) and elements of precaution

The concept of precaution responds to a growing awareness about the fact that the remedial approach traditionally adopted by international environmental law to environmental damages was insufficient to prevent environmental degradation. The concept of being *pre*-cautionary originates from the idea of *Vorsorge* (Precaution) or foresight beyond immediate cause and effects.[7] Indeed, precaution overcomes the need for proving 'clear and convincing evidence' of environmental harm[8] as it operates with a more proactive (rather than reactive) rationale.

Since its inclusion in German law in the 1970s, numerous international conventions,[9] agreements,[10] protocols[11] and declarations[12] adopted the pre-

7 Aline L Jaeckel, *The International Seabed Authority and the Precautionary Principle – Balancing Deep Seabed Mineral Mining and Marine Environmental Protection* (Brill Nijhoff, 2017) 29.

8 See, e.g., *Trail Smelter Case (US v Canada) (Arbitration Award,* 16 April 1938 and 11 March 1941) 3 RIAA 1905, 1965.

9 See *Vienna Convention* preamble; *UNFCCC* art 3; *International Convention on Oil Pollution Preparedness, Response, and Co-operation* preamble; *Convention on the Protection of the Marine Environment of the Baltic Sea Area* art 3(2); *Convention for the Protection of the Marine Environment of the North East Atlantic* art 2; *United Nations Convention on the Protection and Use of Transboundary Watercourses and International Lakes*; *Convention on the Protection of the Rhine* art 4; *Convention on Cooperation for the Protection and Sustainable Use of the River Danube* arts 2(4) and 2(5); *Stockholm Convention* arts 1 and 8(9); *Convention on the Ban of the Import of Hazardous Wastes into Africa and on the Control of Their Transboundary Movements within Africa* art 3(f); *Convention to Ban the Importation into Forum Island Countries of Hazardous and Radioactive Wastes and to Control the Transboundary Movement and Management of Hazardous Wastes within the South Pacific Region* arts 1 and 13(3); *CCAMLR* art 2(3).

10 See *Agreement on the Conservation of Cetaceans of the Black Sea, Mediterranean Sea and Contiguous Atlantic Area* art II(4); *Agreement for the Implementation of the Provisions of the United Nations Convention on the Law of the Sea of 10 December 1982 Relating to the Conservation and Management of Straddling Fish Stocks and Highly Migratory Fish Stocks* art 5(c); *Agreement on the Protection of the River Scheldt* art 3(2). Moreover, the discussion in Section 4.3.1 highlights that the precautionary principle is indirectly enshrined in, inter alia, the *SPS* and *GATT Agreements.*

11 See, e.g., *Montreal Protocol* preamble; *Protocol to the 1979 Convention on Long-Range Transboundary Air Pollution on Further Reduction of Sulphur Emissions*, preamble.

12 See, e.g., *Rio Declaration* Principle 15; *Bergen Ministerial Declaration on Sustainable Development in the ECE Region*; *Malmo Ministerial Declaration, First Global Ministerial Environment Forum* arts 3 and 11; *Ministerial Declaration of the First International Conference on the Protection of the North Sea* arts A(7), D(3), H(7); *Ministerial Declaration of the Second International Conference on the Protection of the North Sea* annex F; *Ministerial Declaration*

cautionary principle. Most WTO states are also parties to several of these international treaties enshrining the precautionary principle.[13] These member states are required to adopt the precautionary principle to prevent environmental harm from human activities in relation to the issues that the various legal instruments deal with.

Its incorporation into Principle 15 of the 1992 Rio Declaration sealed its almost universal acceptance. It states:

> In order to protect the environment, the precautionary approach shall be widely applied by States according to their capabilities. Where there are threats of serious or irreversible damage, lack of full scientific certainty shall not be used as a reason for postponing cost-effective measures to prevent environmental degradation.[14]

Precaution lacks a single formulation, however. Some international instruments refer to the precautionary *principle*, while others address it as precautionary *approach*.[15] It has been argued that the term *approach* entails greater flexibility.[16] This might explain the trend in recent practice to adopt approach rather than principle.[17] The greater flexibility of the term *approach* might also be implied from the fact that in *EC – Biotech*, the United States, which opposed the implementation of European precautionary measures, argues for the use of approach instead of principle, arguably because the term *principle* entails a legally binding nature.[18]

However, a comprehensive study of legal instruments that refer to the precautionary principle or approach demonstrates that the substantive obligations behind both terms are similar.[19] Therefore, in line with other scholars who con-

of the Fourth International Conference on Protection of the North Sea arts 17, 43(2), 54, 58, Recommendations 1 and 2; *Ministerial Declaration of the Third International Conference on Protection of the North Sea* art 25; *Ministerial Declaration of the Fifth International Conference on the Protection of the North Sea* arts 10, 11, 15, 16, 19, 29; *Ministerial Declaration on the Protection of the Black Sea* preamble; *Baltic Sea Declaration*; *Declaration on the Protection of the Marine Environment of the Baltic Sea by the Ministers Responsible for the Environmental Protection of the Baltic Sea States* preamble; *Ministerial Declaration of the Seventh Trilateral Government Conference on the Protection of the Wadden Sea.*

13 See the analysis and graphs in Sections 2.6.1 and 2.6.2.

14 *Rio Declaration* Principle 15.

15 Further insights on the differences between precautionary approach and precautionary principle are in Arie Trouwborst, *Precautionary Rights and Duties of States* (Martinus Nijhoff, 2006) 10–12; 21–26; Joakim Zander, *The Application of the Precautionary Principle in Practice – Comparative Dimensions* (Cambridge University Press, 2010) 3–7.

16 *Southern Bluefin Tuna Cases (New Zealand v Japan; Australia v Japan)* (Provisional Measures) [19]; see also the separate opinion of Judge Ad Hoc Shearer.

17 Alex G Oude Elferink, 'Governance Principles for Areas beyond National Jurisdiction' (2012) 27 *The International Journal of Marine and Coastal Law* 205; Jaeckel (n 7).

18 Panel report, *EC – Biotech* [4.541].

19 Trouwborst (n 3) 10. See also Trouwborst (n 15) 10–12; 21–26; Zander (n 15) 3–7.

sider the debate over terminology to be mainly a 'semantic squabble',[20] this study refers to precautionary principle, approach and plain precaution interchangeably. It also uses the term *precautionary measures*, which refer to measures adopted in light of the precautionary principle.[21]

Despite the lack of a single formulation of precaution, scholars and decision-makers widely agree on the three components defining the precautionary principle:[22] (1) *risk* of environmental or human health harm, (2) *uncertainty* about harm to human health and/or the environment, and (3) *action* at an early stage.[23] Each element is briefly discussed as follows:

1. *Risk of environmental harm or harm to human health*: The occurrence of risks, mostly caused by human activities, to the environment or to human health is the first element of precaution.[24] Clearly, it would be unreasonable to invoke precaution for inescapable or daily risks to humans' lives. Therefore, the concept of precaution must necessarily imply a minimum threshold of risk. Yet, 'a substantial number of international instruments omit any specific threshold'.[25] Most of these instruments do not define 'risk', kinds of risks or what effects on human health and/or the environment must be considered. This vagueness is exacerbated by the fact that some common formulations of precaution refer to different thresholds of risks. For example, the *Rio Declaration* requires *serious or irreversible damage*, while for the European *Communication on the Precautionary Principle* (*COMM(2000)*), the precautionary principle applies 'when there are *reasonable grounds* for concern that potential hazards may affect the environment or human, animal

20 Nicolas De Sadeleer, *Environmental Principles: From Political Slogans to Legal Rules* (Oxford University Press, 2002) 92; see also Elferink (n 17); Rosie Cooney, 'A Long and Winding Road? Precaution from Principle to Practice in Biodiversity Conservation' in Elizabeth Fisher, Judith Jones and René von Schomberg (eds), *Implementing the Precautionary Principle: Perspectives and Prospects* (Edward Elgar Publishing, 2006) 223, 224; Malgosia Fitzmaurice, *Contemporary Issues in International Environmental Law* (Edward Elgar Publishing, 2009) 8; Patricia Birnie, Alan Boyle and Catherine Redgwell, *International Law and the Environment* (Oxford University Press, 3rd ed, 2009) 154–157; Jaeckel (n 7) 22.

21 As Chapter 1 clarifies, any protective measure, including biosafety measures, can be adopted in light of the precautionary principle to be here considered precautionary measures. See *Glossary of Terms*.

22 See especially, Trouwborst (n 15) 21–35. See also Mariëlle Matthee and Dominique Vermersch, 'Are the Precautionary Principle and the International Trade of Genetically Modified Organisms Reconcilable?' (2000) 12(1) *Journal of Agricultural and Environmental Ethics* 59, 61; James Cameron and Juli Abouchar, 'The Status of the Precautionary Principle in International Law' in David Freestone and Ellen Hey (eds), *The Precautionary Principle in International Law: The Challenge of Implementation* (Kluwer Law International B.V., 1996) 29, 45.

23 See Trouwborst (n 15) 121–158.

24 Jaeckel (n 7) 42.

25 Trouwborst (n 15) 45–47; Jaeckel (n 7) 38.

or plant health'.[26] Accordingly, the former sets a higher bar for triggering precaution than the latter.

Arguably, there is no general threshold, as the evaluation of risk depends on the concrete case. For example, it might be assumed that the more serious the eventual risk to the health or the environment, the lower the threshold should be for applying the precautionary principle.

As already anticipated in Chapter 2, under the WTO, member states have the right to establish their own appropriate level of protection (ALOP) that, as such, can also be *precautionary*. Thus, the bar for triggering precaution can be higher or lower according to the formulation of precaution adopted and the circumstances in the case at hand. Interestingly, the AB in *EC – Hormones* explains that responsible governments act from a 'precautionary' perspective where irreversible risks, such as life-threatening damage to human health, are concerned.[27] By relating *precautionary* actions to *irreversible risks*, the AB seems to refer to the formulation of precaution under Principle 15 of the *Rio Declaration* and, in turn, to set a high bar for triggering precaution.

2. *Uncertainty on environmental harm or harm to human health*: In regard to the element of uncertainty, it is important to stress that precaution applies *not because of* uncertainty but *despite* it.[28] Concerns over environmental or human health harm are the trigger for precaution, not uncertainty.[29] Put differently, what triggers the application of the precautionary principle is the obligation or responsibility to protect human health and the environment even under conditions of uncertainty. This aspect is particularly relevant considering that in the WTO biotechnology cases analysed in Part III of this book, national adoptions of the precautionary principle were rejected by three panels in part because of the lack of *insufficient* scientific evidence.[30] This, accordingly, underlines a misperception of the relationship between precaution on the one hand and scientific knowledge about the effects posed by biotechnology to biosafety on the other hand, as discussed in Chapter 8.

Further, the precautionary principle covers all types of uncertainty (i.e., epistemic and ontological) but not all levels of uncertainty.[31] Otherwise, precaution would

26 *Rio Declaration*, Principle 15; *COMM(2000)* final, 8. For an in-depth analysis of the precautionary principle under European law, see especially Alessandra Guida, 'The Precautionary Principle and Genetically Modified Organisms: A Bone of Contention Between European Institutions and Member States' (2021) 8(1) *Journal of Law and the Biosciences* 1.

27 AB report, *EC – Hormones* [124].

28 Jaeckel (n 7) 36; Trouwborst (n 15).

29 Jaeckel (n 7) 36; Trouwborst (n 15) 91–96.

30 See the WTO case analysis in Chapters 7 and 8.

31 Jaeckel (n 7) 38–39.

apply for every imaginary risk. As for the risk of environmental or human health harm, the threshold of probability of harm varies across international instruments according to which harm *might*, *may* or *could* occur.[32]

The lack of a well-identified level or threshold of (un)certainty allowing precaution to apply is considered '[t]he most immediate issue, and the one with the most important practical implications'[33] concerning the operationalisation of the precautionary principle. Importantly, the application of precaution is context-dependent and, thus, will vary in different regimes.[34] In discussing how precaution applies in the three WTO biotechnology cases, the present study develops a scale of uncertainties that might guide WTO decision-makers in adopting the precautionary principle under the WTO.[35]

3. *Timely precautionary action*: The third element of precaution is the timely action aiming at avoiding damages to human health and/or the environment.[36] For instance, according to Principle 15 of the *Rio Declaration*, the precautionary approach requires 'measures to prevent environmental degradation'.[37]

Without precautionary action at an early stage, 'precaution would be meaningless. Yet, this is precisely where the challenge lies'.[38] This is because there is no straightforward answer to the central question of how the rhetoric of precaution can be translated into protective measures. In the view of international courts, precaution can entail, inter alia, (1) 'a very cautious'[39] or (2) 'a prudent' approach;[40] (3) appropriate measures 'for the preservation of the environment'[41] or (4) 'to prevent specific potential risks to public health, safety and the environment';[42] (5) 'restrictive measures';[43] (6) 'any measure for the protection

32 Trouwborst (n 15) 99–100.
33 Charles Weiss, 'Can There Be Science-Based Precaution?' (2006) 1 *Environmental Research Letters* 1, 6; Kjell Hausken, 'The Precautionary Principle as Multi-Period Games Where Players Have Different Thresholds for Acceptable Uncertainty' (2021) 206 *Reliability Engineering & System Safety* 1.
34 Jacqueline Peel, *The Precautionary Principle in Practice: Environmental Decision-Making and Scientific Uncertainty* (Federation Press, 2005) 6.
35 See Section 8.4.3.
36 Trouwborst (n 15) 121–158.
37 *Rio Declaration* Principle 15.
38 Jaeckel (n 7) 39.
39 *Vilnes and Others v Norway* [2013] Eur Court HR 1 [244].
40 *Commission v Denmark* (C-192/01) [2003] ECR I-9724, [35].
41 *Gabčíkovo-Nagymaros Project (Hungary–Slovakia)* [117].
42 *Dow AgroSciences v European Commission* (T-475/07) [2008] ECR 214, [144]; *Artegodan and Others v Commission* (T-74/00, T-76/00, T-83/00 to T-85/00, T-132/00, T-137/00 and T-141/00) [2002] ECR II-4948, [121], [184].
43 *Commission v Denmark* (C-192/01) [2003] ECR I-9724, [52]; Opinion of Advocate General Bot, *Giovanni Pesce and Others* (Joined Cases C-78/16 and C-79/16) [2016] ECR 340, [110].

of human health';[44] (7) protective measures;[45] or (8) 'provisional risk management measures'.[46]

We can thus assume that there is no exhaustive list of precautionary measures. Even in trade contexts, as Cordonier Segger and Gehring point out, '[the precautionary principle] leads to various policy options, not just total bans'.[47] In determining precautionary measures, three factors are relevant. Any precautionary measure must be (1) effective in reaching the pursued goal of protecting human health and/or the environment, (2) proportionate to it, meaning no more restrictive than necessary, and (3) precautionary action must be taken early, even if uncertainties remain.

Under the WTO, the ALOPs set by member states should presumably reach that goal. However, in legal disputes where the established ALOP from risks posed by biotechnology is generally contested by the other party at stake, the adopted precautionary measure must be balanced with the competing interest of free trade. In other words, the precautionary principle and related measures are subject to balancing.[48]

As this section demonstrates, the precautionary principle (or approach) lacks a single formulation, but it does have a conceptual core and an undisputed proactive rationale. Since its first appearance as a principle in German law, the precautionary principle has not only been enshrined in numerous international treaties but also migrated across jurisdictions, as Section 4.2.2 outlines.

4.2.2 *Migration of precaution across jurisdictions and its current status*

Precaution finds increasing acceptance also at the judicial level. Already in 1997, the ICJ emphasised in *Gabčíkovo-Nagymaros Project* that both states involved (i.e., Hungary *versus* Slovakia) 'agree[d] on the need to take environmental concerns seriously and to take the required precautionary measures'.[49] Examples of the application of the precautionary principle can also be found in the jurisprudence of the ECJ, which has remarked several times that the principle 'is intended to be applied in order to ensure a high level of protection of health, consumer safety and the environment'.[50] Recently, the Seabed Disputes Chamber

44 *Gowan Comércio v Ministero della Salute* (C-77/09) [2010] ECR I–13555, [74].

45 Ibid; *Commission v Denmark* (C-192/01) [2003] ECR I-9724, [49].

46 *Giorgio Fidenato and Others* (Case C-111/16) [2017] ECR I-00000, [44].

47 Marie-Claire Cordonier Segger and Markus W Gehring, 'The WTO and Precaution: Sustainable Development Implications of the WTO Asbestos Dispute' (2003) 15(3) *Journal of Environmental Law* 289, 297.

48 As further discussed in this chapter and anticipated in Section 3.6.3, the precautionary principle must be interpreted in the Alexian sense of the word, meaning that precaution itself is subject to judicial optimisation and balancing with the other principles/interests at stake.

49 *Gabčíkovo-Nagymaros Project (Hungary v Slovakia)* 113. See also *Pulp Mills* and *Nuclear Tests (New Zealand v France)*.

50 *Artegodan and Others v Commission* [183]. See also *Giorgio Fidenato and Others* [44].

of ITLOS issued its 2011 *Advisory Opinion on Responsibilities and Obligations of States Sponsoring Persons or Entities with Respect to Activities in the Area*,[51] in which the Chamber notes that the precautionary approach is an integral part of the due diligence obligation of states sponsoring specific seabed mining activities.[52] Precaution finds room also in the context of human rights. In this respect, the ECtHR in *Tătar v Romania* underlines the key role of precaution in the context of the *Convention for the Protection of Human Rights and Fundamental Freedoms* (*European Convention on Human Rights*).[53] This judicial decision is particularly relevant for two reasons. First, it points out that when states fail to safeguard health and the environment by omitting to operationalise necessary precautionary measures, an infringement of the human right to respect for private and family life occurs (i.e., infringement of Article 8 of the *European Convention on Human Rights*).[54] Second, it highlights that precaution applies not only to environmental matters but also to ensure human health protection, which is particularly relevant in relation to biosafety which has two dimensions, one relating to human health and another to the environment.[55]

In light of this, it is argued that the migration of the precautionary principle across jurisdictions as well as the judicial transplantation and borrowing of the concept of precaution from one international court to another have shaped this principle.[56]

Given its widespread application, debate about whether the precautionary principle has achieved the status of a customary norm of international law was to be expected. As is well known, 'customary rules are binding on all states, in contrast to treaties, which are specific obligations between contracting states'.[57] In the view of the *Seabed Disputes Chamber*, there is a *trend* towards the precautionary

51 *Responsibilities and Obligations of States Sponsoring Persons and Entities with Respect to Activities in the Area* (Advisory Opinion) para 131. In the previous *Southern Bluefin Tuna*, the *MOX Plant*, the *Straits of Johor* cases the ITLOS gave to precaution an implicit mention. See *Southern Bluefin Tuna Cases (New Zealand v Japan; Australia v Japan)* (Provisional Measures); *The MOX Plant Case (Ireland v UK)* (Provisional Measures; *Case Concerning Land Reclamation by Singapore in and around the Straits of Johor (Malaysia v Singapore)* (Provisional Measures).

52 David VanderZwaag, 'The ICJ, ITLOS and the Precautionary Approach: Paltry Progressions, Jurisprudential Jousting' (2013) 35 *University of Hawai'i Law Review* 617, 625.

53 See *European Convention on Human Rights.*

54 *European Convention on Human Rights* art 8. See *Vilnes and Others v Norway* [244].

55 See *Cartagena Protocol on Biosafety* 1.

56 For more insights on migration, transplants and borrowing of concepts, see especially Vlad Perju, 'Constitutional Transplants, Borrowing, and Migrations' in Michel Rosenfeld and András Sajó (eds), *The Oxford Handbook of Comparative Constitutional Law* (Oxford University Press, 2012) 1304; Valentina Vadi, *Proportionality, Reasonableness and Standards of Review in International Investment Law and Arbitration* (Edward Elgar, 2018) 35–53; Alan Watson, *Legal Transplants: An Approach to Comparative Law* (University of Georgia Press, 1994) 19–20.

57 Daniel M Bodansky, 'The Concept of Customary International Law' (1995) 16(3) *Michigan Journal of International Law* 667, 671.

approach becoming customary law.[58] Leading scholars concur with the finding of precaution having reached customary status.[59] For example, Gehring and Segger observe that '[s]ince the precautionary principle is emerging as customary international law, international trade law should take this into account to help guide judicial decision-making'.[60] A detailed discussion about the status of precaution is beyond the scope of this study. Yet, it is important to acknowledge that controversies on its customary status remain.[61] For present purposes, it suffices to note that precaution is currently 'incorporated into virtually every international environmental regime'[62] and applied to address environmental and human health harm from potentially dangerous human activities, including the adoption and trade in biotechnology that can have adverse impacts on biosafety.[63]

Despite its widespread endorsement, the precautionary principle has not escaped criticism.[64] A key criticism is that precaution, when applied to new tech-

58 *Responsibilities and Obligations of States Sponsoring Persons and Entities with Respect to Activities in the Area* (Advisory Opinion) [135].

59 See, e.g., Trouwborst (n 3); J Cameron, 'The Status of the Precautionary Principle in International Law' in T O'Riordan and J Cameron (eds), *Interpreting the Precautionary Principle* (Earthscan, 1994); De Sadeleer (n 20); Owen McIntyre and Thomas Mosedale, 'The Precautionary Principle as a Norm of Customary International Law' (1997) 9(2) *Journal of Environmental Law* 221; Elferink (n 17); David Freestone, 'International Fisheries Law Since Rio: The Continued Rise of the Precautionary Principle' in Alan Boyle and David Freestone (eds), *International Law and Sustainable Development: Past Achievements and Future Challenges* (Oxford University Press, 2001) 135; Philippe Sands and Jacqueline Peel, *Principles of International Environmental Law* (Cambridge University Press, 2012); Jaeckel (n 7).

60 Markus W Gehring and Marie-Claire Cordonier Segger, *Precaution in World Trade Law: The Precautionary Principle and Its Implications for the World Trade Organisation* (CISDL, 2002) 27. See also Abdul Haseeb Ansari and Sri Wartini, 'Application of Precautionary Principle in International Trade Law and International Environmental Law: A Comparative Assessment' (2014) 13(1) *Journal of International Trade Law and Policy* 19, 22–23.

61 Ole W Pedersen, 'From Abundance to Indeterminacy: The Precautionary Principle and Its Two Camps of Custom' (2014) 3 *Transnational Environmental Law* 323. See also AB report, *EC – Hormones* [123]. For further insights on the status of the precautionary principle, see also Malcolm D Evans, *International Law* (Oxford University Press, 3rd ed, 2010) 695; Birnie, Boyle and Redgwell (n 20) 125–127.

62 Jaeckel (n 7) 31. See also Freestone (n 59) 135; Trouwborst (n 4) 187.

63 See *CBD* preamble; *CPB* preamble, art 1, arts 10(6), 11(8).

64 See, e.g., Giandomenico Majone, 'What Price Safety? The Precautionary Principle and Its Policy Implications' (2002) 40(1) *Journal of Common Market Studies* 89, 93; Daniel Bodansky, 'Scientific Uncertainty and the Precautionary Principle' (1991) 33 *Environment* 4, 34–44; Gary E Marchant and Kenneth Mossman L, *Arbitrary and Capricious: The Precautionary Principle in the European Union Courts* (American Enterprise Institute, 2005) 16; Cass R Sunstein, *Laws of Fear: Beyond the Precautionary Principle* (Cambridge University Press, 2005) 13–34; William J McKinney and H Hammer Hill, 'Of Sustainability and Precaution: The Logical, Epistemological, and Moral Problems of the Precautionary Principle and Their Implications for Sustainable Development' (2000) 5(1) *Ethics and the Environment* 77, 79; Ragnar E Löfstedt, 'Risk Communication and Management in the Twenty-First Century' (2004) 7(3) *International Public Management Journal* 335; Bénédicte Sage-Fuller, *The Precautionary Principle in Marine Environmental Law: With Special*

nologies, hampers socio-economic developments.[65] Yet, Swedish research on precautionary management of chemicals has established that precautionary measures 'seem to have promoted sustainable development from both an environmental and a socio-economic point of view'.[66] Additional comparative analyses of the precautionary principle highlight that its application 'impl[ies] innovation in technology, products, and processes'.[67] In any event, this criticism, or indeed other points of criticism that have been debunked in the literature,[68] did not prevent the integration of the precautionary principle into international law.[69] To conclude with the ECJ's claim in *Gowan Comércio Internacional e Serviços L[da] v Ministero della Salute*, 'it must be accepted that . . . the precautionary principle is an integral part of the decision-making process'.[70] The present study accepts this statement as true and, accordingly, continues with discussing the implementation of the precautionary principle.

4.2.3 Implementation of precaution through three dimensions

Having established the importance of the precautionary principle, this section briefly discusses the three dimensions of its implementation – institutional, procedural, and judicial.

1. *Institutional dimension*: Institutional context – that is, chiefly public administration – has an 'overwhelming influence' on the implementation of precaution.[71] Effective implementation of precaution requires an institutional

---

Reference to High Risk Vessels (Routledge, 2013); Martin Peterson, 'Yes, The Precautionary Principle Is Incoherent' (2017) 37(11) *Risk Analysis* 2035.

65 John Graham, *The Perils of the Precautionary Principle: Lessons from the American and European Experience* (Heritage Foundation, 2004); Majone (n 64).

66 Mikael Karlsson, 'The Precautionary Principle, Swedish Chemicals Policy and Sustainable Development' (2006) 9(4) *Journal of Risk Research* 337.

67 Oliver Todt and José Luis Luján, 'Analyzing Precautionary Regulation: Do Precaution, Science, and Innovation Go Together?' (2014) 34(12) *Risk Analysis* 2163.

68 See. e.g., Alessandra Arcuri, 'Reconstructing Precaution, Deconstructing Misconceptions' (2007) 21 *Ethics and International Affairs* 359; Anne Ingeborg Myhr, 'A Precautionary Approach to Genetically Modified Organisms: Challenges and Implications for Policy and Science' (2010) 23(6) *Journal of Agricultural and Environmental Ethics* 501; Elizabeth Fisher, 'Precaution, Precaution Everywhere: Developing a "Common Understanding" of the Precautionary Principle in the European Community' (2002) 9 *Maastricht Journal of European and Comparative Law* 7–28.

69 Warwick Gullett, 'Environmental Protection and the Precautionary Principle: A Response to Scientific Uncertainty in Environmental Management' (1997) 14 *Environmental and Planning Law Journal* 52.

70 *Gowan Comércio Internacional e Serviços Lda v Ministero della Salute* (C-77/09) [2010] ECR I-13555, [74].

71 Elizabeth Fisher and Ronnie Harding, 'The Precautionary Principle and Administrative Constitutionalism: The Development of Frameworks for Applying the Precautionary Principle' in Elizabeth Fisher, Judith S Jones and René von Schomberg (eds), *Implementing the Precautionary: Perspectives and Prospects* (Edward Elgar Publishing, 2006) 113, 116.

dimension, as precautionary decisions are taken by existing bodies that, in turn, must have the capacity to perform risk assessments and give effects to the chosen measures of risk management.[72] Institutional measures can include, for instance, the establishment of scientific advisory committees.[73] It is noteworthy that the analysis of WTO institutional response to ensure biosafety in Chapter 2 highlights that the WTO does not provide for risk assessments to be performed at the WTO level because of the lack of WTO committees evaluating, for instance, the impact of trade on human rights.[74] Consequently, this WTO institutional deficit might hinder effective operationalisation of precautionary measures on biosafety.

2. *Procedural dimension*: Precaution can be also implemented through procedural measures, both in a judicial and an administrative context.[75] Procedural measures include reversing the burden of proof[76] or applying risk assessments procedures.[77] Nevertheless, in the scholarly literature there are divergent ideas on implementing precaution through procedural measures.[78]

Whether implementing procedural measures implies a successful or unsuccessful adoption of the precautionary principle depends on the context of reference. Therefore, rather than discussing the operationalisation of the precautionary principle by means of procedural measures in general terms, the analysis of precaution under the WTO in Section 4.4.2 adds context to this aspect by conducting an in-depth discussion of why and when effective implementation of precaution in trade contexts might require reversing the burden of proof.

3. *Judicial dimension*: As the final decision of whether precautionary measures can be adopted is often established in courtrooms, effective implementation of precaution entails a judicial dimension. This dimension refers to the judicial capacity and competencies to examine risk assessments associated with biosafety measures and ensure member states' enjoyment of their right to establish a *precautionary* ALOP, even in cases in which the other party adopts a less cautionary approach to the management of risks posed by trading biotechnology.

72 Jaeckel (n 7) 193, 44.
73 David Freestone and Ellen Hey, 'Implementing the Precautionary Principle: Challenges and Opportunities' in David Freestone and Ellen Hey (eds), *The Precautionary Principle and International Law: The Challenge of Implementation* (Kluwer Law International, 1996) 264.
74 This assessment is performed at the national level.
75 Jaeckel (n 7) 44.
76 Freestone and Hey (n 73) 259.
77 De Sadeleer (n 20) 202–211.
78 Peel (n 34) 149, 158–159; Elizabeth Fisher, 'Precaution, Law and Principles of Good Administration' (2005) 52 *Water Science and Technology* 19. But compare Jaeckel (n 7) 44–46; Stephen M Gardiner, 'A Core Precautionary Principle' (2006) 14(1) *The Journal of Political Philosophy* 33, 42.

Focusing on this dimension of implementation of precaution is particularly relevant considering that WTO states face 'real challenges' when defending the adoption of precautionary measures before WTO judicial bodies, even in the context of biotechnology.[79] The analysis in Part III of the book gives reasons against that.

One part of this challenge is the tendency to perceive cases involving precautionary measures as 'false negatives'. Despite the increasing judicial acceptance of precaution, a study conducted in 2013 by the European Environment Agency (EEA) on 88 international cases underlines a judicial trend of international courts to overlook warnings about the harmfulness of some products or activities to human health or the environment.[80] In almost all cases, requests for adopting precautionary measures have been rejected by decision-makers who considered the issue at hand to be a 'false positive'. False positives are cases in which regulatory authorities suspect that an activity poses a risk and act upon this suspected risk by implementing measures based on precaution, but these later turn out to be unnecessary.[81] However, the EEA study concludes by showing that 'only four cases fulfilled the definition of a regulatory false positive'.[82] This means that almost all cases were false negatives, meaning that early warnings existed, but no precautionary actions were taken. Thus, the EEA Report invites consideration of the following lesson:

> [F]ear of false positives is misplaced and should not be a rationale for avoiding precautionary actions where warranted. False positives are few and far between as compared to false negatives and carefully designed precautionary actions can stimulate innovation, even if the risk turns out not to be real or as serious as initially feared.[83]

In line with other international courts, WTO judicial bodies acknowledge the possibility for member states to adopt precautionary measures;[84] nonetheless, its application is repeatedly rejected in WTO courtrooms.[85] In light of the findings stemming from the EEA study, it is legitimate to ponder whether WTO biotechnology legal disputes, in which all requests for adopting precautionary measures

79 Shaw and Schwartz (n 6) 11 (emphasis added).

80 Simultaneously, however, the importance of adopting a precautionary policy to prevent harm to human health and environmental degradation has constantly been discussed. This is clearly a *contradictio in terminis*. See European Environment Agency, *Late Lessons from Early Warnings: Science, Precaution, Innovation*, Report No 1 (2013).

81 Ibid 17–18.

82 Ibid 25 (emphasis added).

83 Ibid 17.

84 See, e.g., AB report, *EC – Hormones* [124]; Panel report, *Australia – Salmon* [5.6] (*Australia – Salmon*).

85 For example, in *Japan – Apples*, the AB concluded that 'the Panel failed to take into account the "precautionary principle", or the caution emphasized by the Panel's experts, in arriving at its conclusion on the likelihood of completion of the pathway': AB report, *Japan – Apples* [218]. See also Panel report, *Korea – Radionuclides*.

were rejected, are false positive or false negative cases. Considering that biotechnology can have short-term and long-term effects, answering this question might become possible over the next decade or so.[86]

What has become clear is that the judicial capacity to assess precautionary requests plays a central role in implementing precaution, especially in the context of the WTO where precaution is (mis)perceived as a tool against the development and innovation that can be achieved by trading new technologies. Nevertheless, few studies discuss the judicial implementation of precaution.[87] This study contributes to filling this gap by focusing on the judicial implementation of precaution under the WTO. To this end, the following section outlines how precaution finds application within WTO law.

4.3 Applicability of precaution under the WTO

The precautionary principle is not specifically mentioned in WTO agreements. Nevertheless, it can be considered encompassed under WTO law on the basis of three grounds: (1) gateways provisions in the context of the *SPS* and *GATT Agreements*, (2) its close relation with the WTO goal of sustainable development and (3) its recognition in several MEAs. Each is discussed in detail in the following sections.

4.3.1 Gateway provisions to precaution in WTO law

4.3.1.1 Gateway to precaution in the SPS Agreement

According to the *SPS Agreement*, WTO states can limit free trade by adopting sanitary and phytosanitary (SPS) measures, which encompass – though are not limited to – biosafety measures.[88] As a general rule, the *SPS Agreement* establishes that SPS measures cannot be maintained 'without sufficient scientific evidence'.[89] At first glance, the strong reliance on scientific knowledge does not seem to leave space for the application of the precautionary principle. Nonetheless, Article 5.7, the sixth paragraph of the preamble and Articles 3.3 and 5.2 are key provisions acting as gateways for precaution to enter the realm of the *SPS Agreement*. They are discussed in the following sections.

4.3.1.1.1 ARTICLE 5.7

Article 5.7 is the key gateway provision in the *SPS Agreement*. It allows the adoption of SPS measures, including biosafety measures, when there is insufficient

86 As Section 1.2 highlights, it is estimated that an accurate assessment of the effects stemming from the alteration of biological process of living beings requires a decade or longer.

87 Fisher, Jones and Schomberg (n 71) 1.

88 See *Glossary of Terms*.

89 *SPS Agreement* art 2 [2].

scientific evidence. The AB and panels have expressly acknowledged that 'the precautionary principle . . . finds reflection in Article 5.7 of the SPS Agreement'[90] and that member states are 'entitled' to take precautionary measures under the *SPS Agreement*.[91]

However, biosafety measures can be adopted only in light of Article 5.7 if member states adopt such measures (1) 'in respect of a situation where relevant scientific information is insufficient'; (2) 'on the basis of available pertinent information'; (3) '[by] seek[ing] to obtain the additional information necessary for a more objective assessment of risk'; and (4) '[by] review[ing] . . . accordingly within a reasonable period of time [that] has to be established on a case-by-case basis'.[92] These four requirements are of a cumulative nature, meaning that if one of them is not satisfied, the measure adopted is inconsistent with Article 5.7.[93]

Thus, the question is whether these cumulative requirements allow precaution to find room in the scope of Article 5.7. In this respect, although the third and fourth requirements are not commonly associated with the precautionary principle, these conditions 'determine consistency'[94] and, even more importantly, '[they] are in accordance with the precautionary principle as [generally] described . . . and as such, the SPS Agreement can be said to incorporate a precautionary element into the WTO'.[95] Indeed, some scholars regard Article 5.7 as 'a sui generis application [of the precautionary principle] in trade law'.[96]

The first requirement under Article 5.7 (i.e., 'insufficiency of scientific evidence') is particularly reminiscent of the precautionary principle. Importantly, the AB clarifies that this first requirement does not cover circumstances characterised by scientific uncertainty:

> The application of Article 5.7 is triggered not by the existence of scientific uncertainty, but rather by the insufficiency of scientific evidence. The text of Article 5.7 is clear: it refers to 'cases where relevant scientific evidence is insufficient', not to 'scientific uncertainty'. The two concepts are not interchangeable.[97]

90 AB report, *EC – Hormones* [124]. Also in AB report, *Japan – Apples*, the AB concluded that 'the Panel failed to take into account the "precautionary principle", or the caution emphasized by the Panel's experts, in arriving at its conclusion on the likelihood of completion of the pathway' [218].

91 Panel report, *Australia – Salmon* [5.6].
See also, *EC – Biotech* (n 18) [7.2983].

92 AB report, *Japan – Agricultural Products II* [89]–[93]. It is interesting to observe that a similar provision is enshrined in art 757.4 of the *North American Free Trade Agreement* art 757 [4].

93 See AB report, *Japan – Agricultural Products II* [89]; Panel report, *EC – Biotech* [7.2973].

94 Segger and Gehring (n 47) 306. See also, Ilona Cheyne, 'Gateways to the Precautionary Principle in WTO Law' (2007) 19(2) *Journal of Environmental Law* 155, 159.

95 Segger and Gehring (n 47) 306.

96 Cheyne (n 94) 159.

97 AB report, *Japan – Apples* [184].

The AB's interpretation may, at first glance, appear to be an attempt to distinguish Article 5.7 from the precautionary principle. However, the AB's interpretation may indeed be viewed as a particular interpretation of the precautionary principle that rests on insufficient evidence. Although most formulations of the precautionary principle in international law refer to scientific uncertainty, there are examples emphasising the importance of adopting precautionary actions even in contexts of insufficient scientific evidence. For instance, the *COMM(2000)* establishes:

> Whether or not to invoke the Precautionary Principle is a decision exercised where scientific information is ***insufficient***, inconclusive, or uncertain.[98]

Another example is provided by the *Ministerial Declaration of the Seventh Trilateral Government Conference on the Protection of the Wadden Sea*, which 'call[s] upon the North Sea ministers to apply the Precautionary Principle . . . by giving nature the benefit of the doubt ***in cases where*** little or ***insufficient data is available***'.[99] Also, the *Convention on the Conservation and Management of Highly Migratory Fish Stocks in the Western and Central Pacific Ocean* points out the need for keeping precautionary measures 'until there are sufficient data to allow assessment of the impact of the fisheries on the longterm sustainability of the stocks'.[100] Accordingly, it stresses the importance of adopting precautionary measures in contexts of insufficient scientific evidence.

WTO law, therefore, provides a further example of precaution applying to contexts of scientifically insufficient evidence. However, as stressed in Section 4.2.1, precaution does not *depend on*, albeit it can apply *in spite of*, the presence of uncertain and/or insufficient scientific evidence. In other words, the trigger for precaution is not uncertainty but the risk of harm. Thus, the consideration of insufficiency of relevant scientific evidence as a *requirement* to trigger Article 5.7 and, accordingly, the precautionary principle should be reconsidered. Nevertheless, the analysis of the judicial interpretation of precaution in WTO biotechnology cases highlights that a less strict and more precaution-oriented judicial interpretation of Article 5.7 can still allow such a provision to act as a gateway to precaution.[101]

To conclude, leading scholars broadly concur that '[WTO] Members are permitted to establish trade barriers based on the precautionary principle'[102] not least because this principle has been explicitly recognised by WTO judicial bodies

98 *COMM(2000)* 7 (emphasis added).

99 *Ministerial Declaration of the Seventh Trilateral Government Conference on the Protection of the Wadden Sea* (emphasis added).

100 *Convention on the Conservation and Management of Highly Migratory Fish Stocks in the Western and Central Pacific Ocean* art 6 [5].

101 See Chapter 8.

102 Grant E Isaac, 'Sanitary and Phytosanitary Issues' in William A Kerr and James D Gaisford (eds), *Handbook on International Trade Policy* (Edward Elgar, 2007) 383.

in the context of the *SPS Agreement*.[103] After all, the panel in *EC – Biotech* reminded us that 'Article 5.7 of the SPS Agreement is *of course* one expression of the precautionary principle'.[104]

4.3.1.1.2 THE SIXTH PARAGRAPH OF THE PREAMBLE AND ARTICLES 3.3 AND 5.2

The AB acknowledges that the sixth paragraph of the preamble and Article 3.3 of the *SPS Agreement* reflect the precautionary principle, provided that certain conditions are met, such as the scientific justification of biosafety measures that must be based on a 'risk assessment appropriate to the circumstances'.[105] The AB clarifies that 'the principle has not been written into the SPS Agreement as a ground for justifying SPS measures that are otherwise inconsistent with the obligations of Members set out in particular provisions of that Agreement'.[106] In other words, the principle cannot be invoked as a justification for non-compliance with the provisions of the *SPS Agreement*.

Despite the invitation to harmonise their policies with international standards, the sixth paragraph of the preamble of the *SPS Agreement* points out that WTO states are not required 'to change their appropriate level of protection of human, animal or plant life or health'.[107] Accordingly, states may choose to base their ALOP on a precautionary policy. However, Article 5 clarifies that in determining their ALOP, members must 'take into account the objective of minimizing negative trade effects'[108] and 'avoid arbitrary or unjustifiable distinctions in the levels it considers to be appropriate in different situations, if such distinctions result in discrimination or a disguised restriction on international trade'.[109] Put differently, the sixth paragraph of

103 AB report, *EC – Hormones* [124]. See Fiona Macmillan, *WTO and the Environment* (Sweet & Maxwell, 2001); Segger and Gehring (n 47); Diahanna L Post, 'The Precautionary Principle and Risk Assessment in International Food Safety: How the World Trade Organization Influences Standards' (2006) 26(5) *Risk Analysis* 1259; John Paterson, 'Sustainable Development, Sustainable Decisions and the Precautionary Principle' (2007) 42(3) *Natural Hazards* 515; Cheyne (n 94); Niu Huei-Chih, 'Can Article 5.7 of the WTO SPS Agreement Be a Model for the Precautionary Principle?' (2007) 4(4) *SCRIPT-ed* 367, www.law.ed.ac.uk/ahrc/script-ed/vol4-4/huei-chih.asp; Nico Schrijver, *The Evolution of Sustainable Development in International Law: Inception, Meaning and Status* (Martinus Nijhoff, 2008); John Bernetich, 'Sovereignty and Regulation of Environmental Risk under the Precaution Principle in WTO Law' (2011) 35 *Vermont Law Review* 717; Ansari and Wartini (n 60); Abdul Haseeb Ansari, 'Article Information: GATT/WTO and MEAs: Resolving the Competing Paradigm' (2007) 6(2) *Journal of International Trade Law and Policy* 2; Markus Gehring and Alexandre Genest, 'Disputes on Sustainable Development in the WTO Regime' in Claire Cordonier Segger et al. (eds), *Sustainable Development Principles in the Decisions of International Courts and Tribunals: 1992–2012* (Routledge, 2015) 357.

104 Panel report, *EC – Biotech* [4.523] (emphasis altered).

105 AB report, *EC – Hormones* [124]. This acknowledgement is also contained in Panel report, *EC – Biotech* [4.523].

106 AB report, *EC – Hormones* [124].

107 Ibid preamble [6].

108 Ibid art 5.4.

109 Ibid art 5.5.

the preamble permits member states to establish a precautionary ALOP as long as it does not impose unjustified and arbitrary constraints on free trade.

Importantly, these conditions should not be viewed as hindering effective operationalisation of the precautionary principle. This is because the precautionary principle should be interpreted as a balancing and dynamic criterion supporting the implementation of biosafety measures which are effective in achieving their goal and, at the same time, non-arbitrary and proportional to the competing interest in trading biotechnology.[110] In light of this, the sixth paragraph of the preamble of the *SPS Agreement* can be interpreted as a gateway to provision.

Article 3.3 allows WTO members to adopt SPS measures that exceed international standards and guidelines, provided such higher level can be (1) scientifically justified or (2) determined in accordance with the conditions enshrined in paragraphs 1–8 of Article 5.[111] This means that member states have two options to base SPS measures on a standard higher than the international one(s). One option is to scientifically justify such a higher standard.[112]

Alternatively, the higher level can be determined in accordance with conditions enshrined in Article 5 requiring, in the first paragraph, to base national measures on risk assessments 'as appropriate to the circumstances' by considering also 'risk assessment techniques developed by the relevant international organizations'.[113] To comply with Article 5.1, risk assessments must be carried out by taking account of available scientific evidence[114] and a number of other factors listed in Article 5.2 – including relevant Process and Production Methods (PPMs) representing a fundamental element in assessing the 'likeness' between conventional and biotechnology products, as the discussion below of precaution in the context of the GATT Agreement highlights. Noteworthy, there is no reason to consider the list of factors under Article 5.2 as a closed.[115] As such, precaution might be a further factor falling under Article 5.2 and taken into account in a risk assessment. This aspect is particularly interesting considering that other jurisdictions consider the precautionary principle as an element to be essentially assessed by decision-makers in the phase of risk management, which follows the preliminary phase of risk assessment.[116]

At this point, it is necessary to take a step back and clarify that risk assessment is the first phase of risk analysis (or risk governance).[117] It is located mainly in the scientific domain and defined 'as a tool of gaining knowledge about risks'.[118]

110 Section 4.4.1 discusses such interpretation of precaution in great detail.
111 *SPS Agreement* art 3 [3].
112 Ibid note No 2.
113 Ibid art 5 [1].
114 Ibid art 5 [2].
115 AB report, *EC – Hormones* [187].
116 See, e.g., *COMM(2000)* 2(4).
117 The general framework of risk analysis (or risk governance) is composed of three phases: risk assessment, risk management and risk communication.
118 Ortwin Renn et al., 'Risks' in Paul Pechan et al. (eds), *Safe or Not Safe: Deciding What Risks to Accept in Our Environment and Food* (Springer, 2011) 1, 13. See also, Anne Ingeborg Myhr and Terje Traavik, 'The Precautionary Principle: Scientific Uncertainty and Omitted Research in the Context of GMO Use and Release' (2002) 15(1) *Journal of Agricultural*

Some proponents of biotechnology argue to apply the precautionary principle at either the risk assessment or risk management stage,[119] while others claim that the principle should only be applied in the risk assessment stage,[120] which informs the judicial deliberations in the risk management phase. Considering precaution in the first, informative phase of risk assessment becomes decisive. This strengthens the consideration of precaution as a factor that can fall under Article 5.2 and that can be considered in assessing biotechnology risks. Nevertheless, the analysis in Chapter 7 of the judicial examination of risk assessment in biotechnology cases shows that panels tend to adopt a restrictive notion of risk assessment, which prevents effective operationalisation of the precautionary principle.[121]

To conclude, the precautionary principle finds room into the scope of the sixth paragraph of the preamble of the *SPS Agreement* allowing member states to establish their own ALOP – that, accordingly, can be precautionary – provided that the interest in trade liberalisation is not unjustifiably constrained. Moreover, although some scholars disagree with approaching Article 3.3 as a gateway provision to precaution, arguing that it 'leaves little room for application of the precautionary principle',[122] the analysis in this section shows that such provision along with Article 5.2 can accommodate the precautionary principle under the *SPS Agreement.* After all, the AB has often pointed out that the 'right of a Member to establish its own level of sanitary protection [that, accordingly, can also be precautionary] under Article 3.3 of the SPS Agreements is an autonomous right and not an "exception" from a "general Obligation" under Article 3.1'.[123]

4.3.1.2 *Gateway to precaution in the* GATT Agreement

4.3.1.2.1 ARTICLE III.4

The consideration of Article III.4 as a gateway provision to precaution stems from its judicial interpretation. This provision embodies the WTO principle of *the*

---

and Environmental Ethics 73, 74; Didier Bourguignon, 'The Precautionary Principle – Definitions, Applications and Governance' (Research Paper No 573.876, European Parliament Think Tank, 2015) <>www.europarl.europa.eu/thinktank>.

119 Marchant and Mossman L. (n 64) 13.

120 Anne Ingeborg Myhr and Terje Traavik, 'The Precautionary Principle Applied to Deliberate Release of Genetically Modified Organisms (GMOs)' (1999) 11(2) *Microbial Ecology in Health and Disease* 65, 73. See also, Chauncey Starr, 'The Precautionary Principle Versus Risk Analysis' (2003) 23 *Risk Analysis* 1, 3; Peter M Chapman, 'Does The Precautionary Principle Have A Role in Ecological Risk Assessment?' (1999) 5(5) *Human and Ecological Risk Assessment: An International Journal* 885.

121 As the AB notes in *US/Canada – Hormones Continued Suspension*, the panels' *trend* to interpret risk assessment restrictively stems from an improper attempt 'to re-establish the rigid distinction between "risk assessment" and "risk management" that the Appellate Body had [already] rejected in [*EC – Hormones*]': AB report, *US/Canada – Hormones Continued Suspension* [542].

122 Akawat Laowonsiri, 'Application of the Precautionary Principle in the SPS Agreement' (2010) 14 *Max Planck UNYB* 565, 601.

123 AB report, *EC – Hormones* [172].

national treatment obligation, which requires member states to treat imported products (or services) no less favourable than ***like national products*** (or like services).[124] Thus, if a member state takes precautionary measures concerning a national product, it can also adopt precautionary measures in relation to international ***like*** products. The judicial interpretation of the central concept of ***likeness*** is consequently relevant, as it answers the question of whether the precautionary principle can be applied when deciding whether products are ***like***.[125] It is also important to note that judicial decisions concerning like products are significant in the biotechnology context, as products produced conventionally or with biotechnology techniques can sometimes be regarded as 'like products', though their difference lies in PPMs of goods.[126]

EC – Asbestos represents a central case for the judicial interpretation of 'likeness' as the AB, by referring to the Report of the Working Party on *Border Tax Adjustments*, identified four general criteria that will turn out to be fundamental for interpreting precaution in the context of Article III.4. The AB clarifies that in analysing the ***likeness*** between products, decision-makers must consider four criteria:

1. the properties, nature and quality of the products;
2. the end-uses of the products;
3. consumers' tastes and habits – more comprehensively termed consumers' perceptions and behaviour – in respect of the products; and
4. the tariff classification of the products.[127]

In light of these criteria, ***all*** evidence must be weighed 'in making an ***overall*** determination of whether the products at issue could be characterised as "like" '.[128] In developing these criteria, the AB distanced itself from the panel's pure economic interpretation of ***like products***,[129] which prevented precaution from find-

124 The ***principle of the national treatment obligation*** and the ***principle of most favoured nation (MFN) treatment obligation***, enshrined in art I.1 of the *GATT Agreement*, embody the ***principle of non-discrimination***, which is a *core* principle of the *GATT Agreement*. In regard to ***MFN treatment obligation***, *see* Jakkrit Kuanpoth, 'The Most Favoured Nation Treatment Principle' in Indira Carr, Shawkat Alam and Md Jahid Hossain Bhuiyan (eds), ***International Trade Law and the WTO*** (The Federation Press, 2013) 101. The significance of the MNF principle is also emphasised in WTO case law. See, e.g., AB report, *US – Section 211 Appropriations Act* [297].

125 Cheyne (n 94) 167.

126 As the name suggests, PPMs refer to 'process and production methods' of a particular good. See Andreas R Ziegler and David Sifonios, 'The Assessment of Environmental Risks and the Regulation of Process and Production Methods (PPMs) in International Trade Law' in Mónika Ambrus, Rosemary Rayfuse and Wouter Werner (eds), ***Risk and the Regulation of Uncertainty in International Law*** (Oxford University Press, 2017) 219.

127 AB report, *EC – Asbestos* [101].

128 Ibid [109] (emphasis in original).

129 The same economic approach of the provision was taken in the previous AB report, ***Japan – Alcoholic Beverages II***. See also the criteria adopted to determine 'likeness' in art I.1 GATT 1994 in Panel report, ***Canada/Japan – Tariff on Imports;*** Panel report, ***Spain – Coffee***

ing room in the scope of this provision and raised a number of concerns on the consequences of approaching the concept of *like products* from a purely economic perspective.[130]

The AB acknowledges that 'consumers' tastes and habits . . . are very likely to be shaped by the health risks associated with a product which is known to be highly carcinogenic'.[131] This, as Cheyne notes, 'would have obvious implications where consumers assessed products on environmental grounds, including a precautionary approach to environmental risks'.[132] In other words, by recognising that risks to human health could affect the consumers' perceptions and behaviour, the AB leaves room for possible precautionary decisions by consumers towards biotechnology – which are routinely sprayed with glyphosate, a pesticide recently classified by the IARC as 'probably carcinogenic to humans'.[133]

Moreover, the AB observes that physical properties of different products range greatly.[134] Accordingly, related threats to human health can also range from lower to higher levels of harm,[135] and the standard of evidence required to support the harmfulness of different products can be more or less stringent:

> There will be few situations where the evidence on the 'likeness' of products will lend itself to 'clear results'. In many cases, the evidence will give conflicting indications, possibly within each of the four criteria.[136]

The AB's reasoning implicitly acknowledges that in most cases concerning the assessment of *likeness*, the lack of 'clear results' requires lowering the scientific threshold to support, for example, the protection of human health of consumers. This echoes the capacity of the precautionary principle to lower the evidentiary threshold to implement protective measures. Moreover, in line with the rationale

---

[4.5]–[4.9]–[4.10]; AB report *Canada – Certain Measures Affecting the Automotive Industry* [80]–[81]–[85]. In relation to the interpretation of the MFN in art II.1 GATS and art I.1 GATT 1994, see especially the analysis in Panel Report, *Canada – Certain Measures Affecting the Automotive Industry* [10.261]–[10.262], [10.40]–[10.48]. An extensive analysis of the different criteria adopted to interpret art I.1 GATT 1994 and art II.1 GATS in WTO case law is conducted in Lothar Ehring, 'De Facto Discrimination in World Trade Law: National and Most Favored-Nation Treatment – or Equal Treatment?' (2002) 3(5) *Journal of World Trade* 921.

130 Most importantly, the economic approach of likeness does not fit the nature of biotechnology cases. See Peter Van de Bossche, *The Law and Policy of the World Trade Organization: Text, Cases and Materials* (Cambridge University Press, 2005) 316.; Kuanpoth (n 124) 107; Ziegler and Sifonios (n 126) 222.

131 AB report, *EC – Asbestos* [122].

132 Cheyne (n 94) 167.

133 International Agency for Research on Cancer and World Health Organization, *Evaluation of Five Organophosphate Insecticides and Herbicides* (IARC/WHO, 20 March 2015) vol 112, www.iarc.fr/en/media-centre/iarcnews/pdf/MonographVolume112.pdf.

134 AB report, *EC – Asbestos* [92].

135 Cheyne (n 94) 167.

136 AB report, *EC – Asbestos* [120].

of the precautionary principle, the AB imposes the burden of proof on the party claiming that there was no danger in adopting asbestos fibres, rather than placing it on the party asking for action to be taken.[137]

Even more noteworthy, the AB highlights that the four criteria developed in *EC – Asbestos* for determining *likeness* 'are neither a treaty-mandated nor a closed list of criteria that will determine the legal characterization of products'.[138] Accordingly, there are no reasons to leave out the consideration of the precautionary principle as a relevant standard,[139] especially in biotechnology cases in which human health and the environment are potentially threatened.

Finally, the developed criteria are particularly relevant in determining the *likeness* between conventional and biotechnology products because they refer to 'properties, nature and quality of the products' and thereby encompass PPMs.[140] The importance of PPMs lies in the fact that when foodstuffs are produced abroad, recipient states can prevent and address health and environmental impacts only by requiring that foreign producers comply with established PPM standards.[141] Despite their relevance, there is ongoing debate on the possibility to prohibit PPMs under the WTO framework, arguably because they carry potential limits to trade.[142]

To conclude, WTO judicial bodies' interpretation of *like products* in the context of Article III.4 has moved towards a greater awareness of the complexity surrounding the assessment of likeness of products, complexity that cannot be reduced to a mere economic evaluation. This fostered the development of four criteria to assess the likeness of products. In assessing the likeness between biotechnology and conventional products, WTO judicial bodies are required to refer to *at least* the four criteria developed by the AB in *EC – Asbestos* and, in light of the first one (i.e., the properties, nature and quality of the products), also to PPMs.[143] Thus, the broad judicial interpretation of *likeness* allows Article III.4 to act as a gateway to precaution. It should not be surprising that the interpretation of precaution in the text of such provision stems from the development of WTO jurisprudence. Indeed, 'WTO law can and does develop incrementally through the findings of the dispute settlement mechanism'.[144]

137 Ibid [148].
138 Ibid [102].
139 Cheyne (n 94) 167.
140 Instead, a pure economic interpretation of *likeness* did not consider PPMs.
141 Ziegler and Sifonios (n 126) 219.
142 Ibid. See also Jagdish Bhagwati, *In Defense of Globalisation* (Oxford University Press, 2004); John H Jackson, 'World, Trade Rules and Environmental Policies: Congruence or Conflict?' (1992) 49(4) *Washington & Lee Law Review* 1227; GATT Secretariat, 'International Trade 90–91' (WTO, vol 1, 1992).
143 Importantly, the judicial assessment must be conducted on a case-by-case basis. See Julia Ya Qin, 'Defining Nondiscrimination under the Law of the World Trade Organization' (2005) 23 *Boston University International Law Journal* 215, 241. It must be observed that the term *like products* is also used in art XIX of *GATT 1994*.
144 Gehring and Segger (n 60) 47.

Bearing this in mind, the following discussion highlights how a thorough analysis of some reasoning given by WTO judicial bodies in relation to Article XX(b) and (g) allow identifying these two general exceptions as further gateways to precaution in WTO law.

4.3.1.2.2 ARTICLE XX(B), (G)

Although Article XX(b) and (g) do not reference the precautionary principle as such, WTO case law has with time demonstrated a precautionary reading of these provisions.[145]

In regard to the exception under Article XX(b), quoted above, over the years WTO judicial bodies have adopted a less rigid interpretation of the 'necessary' parameter that, in the panel's view, refers to measures 'apt to contribute materially to the realization of the declared objective'.[146] This invites the argument that precautionary measures to protect human, animal or plant life or health fall within the scope of Article XX(b), not least because they can 'contribute materially to' handling adverse effects on human, animal or plant life or health posed by trading biotechnology. This means that precautionary measures can be assessed by WTO judicial bodies as 'necessary' when they contribute to realising the stated objective[147] or, where they are 'designed to permit . . . the protection of human health, as well as the conservation of exhaustible natural resources'.[148] Article XX(b), therefore, has the potential to be a gateway provision allowing the introduction of a precautionary policy into the context of the *GATT Agreement*.

Similarly, paragraph (g) of Article XX considers measures 'relating to' the conservation of exhaustible natural resources as 'exception[s] to trade rules', and can act as a further gateway.[149] This appears evident in *US – Shrimp*, in which the AB opened the interpretation of Article XX(g) by ruling that wild animals can be regarded as exhaustible natural resources within the scope of Article XX(g).[150] The evolutionary interpretation of 'exhaustible natural resources', which leaves open the possibility to encompass environmental matters in the scope of Article XX(g), was adopted by reference to modern environmental policies.

> [This] reflects a precautionary approach to the conservation of resources by including all natural resources, living and non-living. It allows the

145 Cheyne (n 94) 162. Section 2.4.1.2 provides an in-depth analysis of art XX(b) and (g) of the *GATT Agreement*.
146 Panel report, *China – Raw Materials* [VII.518].
147 Ibid [VII.518].
148 AB report, *US – Gasoline* 30.
149 However, such measures must be made effective in conjunction with restrictions on domestic production or consumption.
150 AB report, *US – Shrimp* [127]–[131].

> protection of non-endangered species and therefore helps Members to avoid situations of near-extinction or vulnerability to sudden catastrophic events.[151]

Also, in its evolutionary interpretation of this provision, the AB explicitly refers to modern environmental concerns.[152] In doing so, the AB argues that decisions relating to environmental matters need to refer to states' practices outside the WTO. This approach to treaty interpretation has clear normative implications for the application of the precautionary principle under the WTO:

> [I]t is arguable that the reasoning in *US – Shrimp* had the practical effect of applying the precautionary principle to the uncertain implications of allowing species to become extinct.[153]

Nonetheless, it has been noted that 'it is uncertain how the provision might be applied in different circumstances'.[154] In this respect, the intrinsic flexibility of the precautionary principle permits this provision to apply in various contexts.[155]

Additionally, the AB's reasoning in *US – Shrimp* invites consideration of the preamble of the *WTO Agreement* as a further gateway provision. Indeed, by observing that the WTO objective to achieve 'the optimal use of the world's resources in accordance with the objective of sustainable development . . . *reflects* the intentions of negotiators of the *WTO Agreement*',[156] the AB emphasises that this agreement 'must add colour, texture and shading to our interpretation of the . . . GATT 1994'.[157] In other words, the preamble of the *WTO Agreement*, which lists the WTO goals, can be seen as a further gateway provision since '[i]t accommodates the principle by locating the meaning of justifiability in State practice outside the WTO and in the light of sustainable development and contemporary environmental concerns'.[158] After all, the AB's interpretation of Article XX(g) in *US – Gasoline* enables member states 'to choose what type of risk it wishes to respond to or the level of protection it wishes to enjoy'.[159] Accordingly, nothing prevents WTO members from not taking high risks or, to put it differently, to err on the side of caution.

151 Cheyne (n 94) 165.
152 AB report, *US – Shrimp* [129]–[131].
153 Cheyne (n 94) 164.
154 Ibid.
155 Scholars agree that the intrinsic flexibility of precaution, which allows it to encompass different circumstances, is consistent with its status of legal principle. See Jaeckel (n 7) 27; Fisher, Jones and Schomberg (n 71) 5; Freestone (n 59) 136.
156 AB report, *US – Shrimp* [153] (emphasis added).
157 Ibid [153].
158 Cheyne (n 94) 166. Importantly, WTO judicial bodies' references to state practice; norms and principles outside WTO law represent an additional ground to argue that precaution is implicitly acknowledged under the WTO.
159 Ibid 165.

For all these reasons, the precautionary principle finds room in the scope of Articles XX(b) and XX(g) of the *GATT Agreement* and, arguably, also in the preamble of the *WTO Agreement*.[160]

To conclude on the analysis of WTO gateway provisions with Schrijver's words:

> in spite of the reluctance of WTO dispute-settlement bodies in making so far any findings on the status of the precautionary principle under general international law, there is still room for the application of the principle through various gateway provisions of the WTO agreements'.[161]

4.3.2 Precaution as a key means to achieve the WTO goal of sustainable development

Sustainable development is one of the WTO goals listed in the preamble of the *WTO Agreement*.[162] The 2030 Agenda for Sustainable Development recognises the 'significant role' of trade in promoting sustainable development and emphasises the key part that the WTO might play in achieving the Sustainable Development Goals (SDGs) set out in the 2030 Agenda.[163]

As Harding and Fisher observe, the relationship between the precautionary principle and sustainable development 'ha[s] always been very close'.[164] More specifically, the precautionary principle represents a key element of sustainable development. Therefore, this section argues that effective achievement of the WTO goal of sustainable development requires the adoption of a precautionary approach.

Already in 1990, the *Bergen Declaration* and the *Bangkok Declaration* noted that '[i]n order to achieve sustainable development, policies must be based on the precautionary principle'.[165] With the *1992 United Nations Conference on Environment and Development* (UNCED), the concept of precaution 'achieved broad international recognition as one of the underlying principles of sustainable development'.[166] Since then, a number of international documents have underlined the close linkage between precaution and sustainable development. *Agenda 21*, for instance, highlights that to integrate management and sustainable development of coastal areas and the marine environment under their national

160 See Cheyne (n 94) 165.
161 Schrijver (n 103) 195 nn 374.
162 WTO Agreement preamble.
163 WTO, 'The WTO and the Sustainable Development Goals' *WTO* (Web Page), www.wto.org/english/thewto_e/coher_e/sdgs_e/sdgs_e.htm.
164 Ronnie Harding and Elizabeth Fisher, 'Introducing the Precautionary Principle' in Ronnie Harding and Elizabeth Fisher (eds), *Perspectives on the Precautionary Principle* (The Federation Press, 1999) 2, 4.
165 *Bergen Ministerial Declaration on Sustainable Development in the ECE Region* annex I [7]; *Bangkok Declaration* annex 2 [19].
166 Peel (n 34) 16.

jurisdiction, 'it is necessary' inter alia to '[a]pply preventive and precautionary approaches'.[167] More recently, the *New Delhi Declaration* strongly emphasises that '[a] precautionary approach is central to sustainable development'.[168] Among others, the *Johannesburg Plan of Implementation*[169] and the *Rio+20* outcome document[170] stress the key role of the precautionary principle in achieving effective sustainable development.[171]

Even at the national level, there are tribunals and courts, such as the State Administrative Tribunal of Western Australia and the Supreme Court of Western Australia, which have held that 'the precautionary principle is a consideration of relevance to the assessment of sustainable use and development of land'.[172]

The close relationship between the precautionary principle and sustainable development also finds broad support among scholars. In 1999, Freestone underlined that 'precaution occupies a central place in any realistic strategy for the achievement of sustainable development, and particularly sustainable use of the planet's natural resources'.[173] 'It is clear', Schrijver observes, 'that the precaution-

167 *Agenda 21*[17.5]. For more insights on sustainability after Rio Declaration, see especially Jamie Benidickson et al. (eds), *Environmental Law and Sustainability after Rio* (Edward Elgar, 2011).

168 *New Delhi Declaration* [4.1]. See Nico Schrijver, 'Advancements in the Principles of International Law on Sustainable Development' in Marie-Claire Cordonier Segger and CG Weeramantry (eds), *Sustainable Development Principles in the Decisions of International Courts and Tribunals 1992–2012* (Routledge, 2017) 99, 101.

169 *Plan of Implementation of the World Summit on Sustainable Development*, A/CONF.199/20 (4 September 2002) [23], [109](f) ('*Johannesburg Plan of Implementation*').

170 *Brundtland Report* [158].

171 See also *Earth Charter* preamble; Organization for Economic Co-operation and Development, *'Policies to Enhance Sustainable Development' OECD* (Web Page, 2001) 8, www.oecd.org/greengrowth/1869800.pdf.

172 *Wattleup Road Development Co Pty Ltd v State Administrative Tribunal (No 2)* [2016] WASC 279 [53]. See also Justice Brian J Preston, 'The Judicial Development of the Precautionary Principle' *Queensland Government Environmental Management of Fire-fighting Foam Policy Implementation Seminar* (21 February 2017), www.lec.justice.nsw.gov.au/Documents/Speeches%20and%20Papers/PrestonCJ/Justice%20Brian%20J%20Preston%20SC%20Keynote%20Address%20-%20Precautionary%20Principle%20%20delivered%2021.02.17.pdf.

173 Freestone (n 59) 135. See also Timothy O'Riordan and Andrew Jordan, 'Precautionary Principle in Contemporary Environmental Politics' (1995) 4 *Environmental Values* 91, 200; Frank B Cross, 'Paradoxical Perils of the Precautionary Principle' (1996) 53(3) *Washington and Lee Law Review* 851, 854; Afshin A-Khavari and Donald R Rothwell, 'The ICJ and the Danube Dam Case: A Missed Opportunity for International Environmental Law?' (1998) 22 *Melbourne University Law Review* 507, 527–529; Joel A Tickner and Carolyn Raffensperger, 'The Precautionary Principle: A Framework for Sustainable Business Decision-Making' (1998) 5(4) *Environmental Policy* 75, 79–81; Harding and Fisher (n 164) 4–6; Paul Stein, 'Are Decision-Makers Too Cautious with the Precautionary Principle?' (2000) 17 *Environmental Planning and Law Journal* 3, 7; McKinney and Hill (n 64) 77–78, 86; Claudia Saladin, 'Precautionary Principle in International Law' (2000) 6(3) *Journal International Journal of Occupational and Environmental Health* 270; Daniel Dobos, 'The Necessity of Precaution: The Future of Ecological Necessity and the

ary principle and environmental impact assessment, for the time being, concern virtually exclusively the environmental component of sustainable development'.[174] Turnquest and Forte go further by pointing out that '[t]he emergence of the precautionary principle within international environmental law is a salient development for sustainable development and environmental protection'.[175] As Trouwborst stresses, already during the negotiations for the 1997 *Watercourses Convention*, 'several states even expressed the opinion that a mere reference to sustainable development automatically entailed the applicability of the precautionary principle within the framework of the agreement'.[176]

Further, the close relation between sustainable development and the precautionary principle can also be inferred from the fact that a core feature of precaution (i.e., the taking of protective measures at an early stage) is equally important to implementing sustainable development. In 1992, Norton invited us to consider the precautionary principle as *the* means to protect sustainability from its feared ineffectiveness.[177]

Therefore, it becomes evident that the precautionary principle and the WTO goal of sustainable development closely relate to each other. In setting the goal to achieve sustainable development, WTO law cannot disregard the close link between sustainability and precaution, including in relation to biosafety. In fact, considering that sustainable development is a means to protect the right and

---

Precautionary Principle' (2002) 13 *Fordham Environmental Law Journal* 375, 394; Katie Steele, 'The Precautionary Principle: A New Approach to Public Decision-Making?' (2006) 5(1) *Law, Probability and Risk* 19, 20–28; Paterson (n 103) 515–526. See also *Gabčíkovo-Nagymaros Project (Hungary v Slovakia)* (Judge Weeramantry).

174 Schrijver (n 108) 196. See also Aggarin Viriyo, 'Principle of Sustainable Development in International Environmental Law' *Sustainable Development in International Environmental Law* (2012) 1, 13.

175 Danielle Turnquest Moulto and Stephanie Forte, 'Sustainable Development Principles in the Caribbean Court of Justice' in Marie-Claire Coronier Segger and HE Judge CG Weeramantry (eds), *Sustainable Development Principles in the Decisions of International Courts and Tribunals 1992–2012* (Routledge, 2017) 680, 681. See also Rosie Cooney, *The Precautionary Principle in Biodiversity Conservation and Natural Resource Management: An Issues Paper for Policy-Makers, Researchers and Practitioners* (IUCN, 2004) 1–2; Stephen Dovers and Robin Connor, 'Institutional and Policy Change for Sustainability' in Benjamin J Richardson and Stepan Wood (eds), *Environmental Law for Sustainability* (Hart Publishing, 2006) 21, 46; Claudia Som, Lorenz M Hilty and Andreas R Köhler, 'The Precautionary Principle as a Framework for a Sustainable Information Society' (2009) 85(SUPPL. 3) *Journal of Business Ethics* 493, 503; Benjamin J Richardson and Jona Razzaque, 'Public Participation in Environmental Decision-Making' in J Richardson and Stepan Wood (eds), *Environmental Law for Sustainability* (Hart Publishing, 2006) 165, 166.

176 Trouwborst (n 15) 34.

177 Bryan Norton, 'Sustainability, Human Welfare and Ecosystem Health' (1992) 1 *Environmental Values* 97. See also, Som, Hilty and Köhler (n 175) 498–499; Rodrigo Lozano, 'A Holistic Perspective on Corporate Sustainability Drivers' (2015) 22(1) *Corporate Social Responsibility and Environmental Management* 32; Laurence Boisson de Chazournes and Makane Moïse Mbengue, 'The Principles of Precaution and Sustainability' in *Elgar Encyclopedia of International Economic Law* (Edward Elgar, 2017) 621.

collective good of human health and the environment, WTO decision-makers should consider the precautionary principle when balancing trade and biosafety interests.

To conclude the discussion with Trouwborst's words:

> The close ties between the precautionary principle and the concept of sustainable development represent such an uncontentious issue that they need not be discussed in any more detail at this point. For present purposes, it suffices to note the existence of this linkage and keep it in mind in the further course of this study.[178]

4.3.3 Multilateral environmental agreements and the WTO: further implications for precaution in WTO law

The discussion of the precautionary principle in the context of the WTO is 'intrinsically linked to the debate on the relationship between MEAs and WTO rules'.[179] As mentioned earlier in the chapter, in the *Doha Declaration*,[180] WTO states agreed to negotiate 'the relationship between existing WTO rules and specific trade obligations set out in . . . MEAs'.[181] So far, the WTO has never been faced with a formal dispute between MEAs and WTO rules. Nevertheless, there are concerns about potential conflicts, not least because of the expressed reluctance of the United States to join several new MEAs affecting trade interests, including the *Cartagena Protocol on Biosafety* and the *Stockholm Convention on Persistent Organic Pollutants*.[182]

To date, over 250 MEAs concerning the relation between trade and environmental matters are in force. They include agreements,[183] conventions[184] and

178 Trouwborst (n 15) 35.

179 Nathalie Bernasconi-Osterwalder et al., *Environment and Trade – A Guide to WTO Jurisprudence* (Earthscan, 2006) 266.

180 *Ministerial Declaration*, WTO Doc WT/MIN(01)/DEC/1 (20 November 2001) adopted on 14 November 2001.

181 Ibid [31](i).

182 See also Caroline Fehl, *Living with a Reluctant Hegemon: Explaining European Responses to US Unilateralism* (Oxford University Press, 2012); Aditi Mathur and Siddharth Dang, 'Multilateral Environmental Agreements versus World Trade Organization System: A Comprehensive Study' (2009) 1(3) *American Journal of Economics and Business Administration* 219.

183 See, e.g., *Agreement on Port State Measures to Prevent, Deter and Eliminate Illegal, Unreported and Unregulated Fishing* and *International Tropical Timber Agreement*. A recent revision on MEAs was prepared in 2017 by the Committee on Trade and Environment in consultation with MEA secretariats. See Note by the Secretariat, *Matrix on Trade-Related Measures Pursuant to Selected Multilateral Environmental Agreements*, WTO Doc WT/CTE/W/160/Rev.8 TN/TE/S/5/Rev.6 (9 October 2017).

184 See, e.g., *Convention on International Trade in Endangered Species of Wild Fauna and Flora (CITES)*; *CCAMLR*; *ICCAT*; *IPPC*; *CBD*; *the Vienna Convention on Substances that Deplete the Ozone Layer*; *UNFCCC*; *Basel Convention*; *Rotterdam Convention*; *Stockholm*

protocols,[185] many of which refer to the precautionary principle. The fact that WTO states are bound by a plethora of MEAs and the obligations contained therein should affect states' conduct in general, including in its trade relations as well as its conduct within the WTO. This means that the obligations enshrined in the MEAs requiring states to prevent harm to human health and/or environmental harm, in light of the precautionary principle, have normative implications for the application of this principle under the WTO. As highlighted by the AB in *US – Gasoline*, WTO agreements cannot be read 'in clinical isolation from public international law'.[186] The WTO is an intergovernmental organisation and, as such, is governed by international law, albeit not being a party to MEAs itself.

Further, as provided by Article 31(3)(c) of the *Vienna Convention on the Law of Treaties* ('*VCLT*'), 'any relevant rules of international law applicable in the relations between the parties' shall be taken into account in treaty interpretation.[187] As such, states' obligations under MEAs, including the obligation to apply the precautionary principle, can affect the interpretation of WTO agreements.

To conclude, the analysis demonstrates that the precautionary principle can apply under WTO law on the basis of three grounds, namely through (1) gateways provisions in the context of the *SPS* and *GATT Agreements*, (2) its close relation with the WTO goal of sustainable development and (3) its acknowledgement in a number of MEAs. In light of these findings, effective operationalisation of precaution in the context of biotechnology would be judicious considering its potential to aid WTO judicial bodies to address the epistemic issues posed by the international trade in biotechnology. Section 4.4 discusses how precaution can be implemented in the context of the WTO to guide decision-makers in addressing the epistemic challenges surrounding the international trade in biotechnology.

4.4 Implementing precaution in the context of biotechnology under the WTO

This section analyses how the precautionary principle could be implemented under the WTO to aid decision-makers in dealing with the uncertainties surrounding the international trade in biotechnology and to break potential stalemate cases. In so doing, it provides a blueprint against which the analysis of biotechnology cases in Part III of this study is conducted. In approaching this task, one must

Convention. These conventions are listed as MEAs by the 2017 *Matrix on Trade-Related Measures Pursuant to Selected Multilateral Environmental Agreements* (n 183).

185 Some include the *Nagoya Protocol*, the *Cartagena Protocol on Biosafety*, the *Montreal Protocol* and the *Kyoto Protocol*. In 2017, the Committee on Trade and Environment, in consultation with MEA secretariats, updated the information on these MEAs. See *Matrix on Trade-Related Measures Pursuant to Selected Multilateral Environmental Agreements* (n 183).

186 AB report, *US – Gasoline* 16–17.

187 *VCLT* art 31(3)(c). Importantly, the AB has engaged with practices outside WTO law by referring to art 31(3)(c) of the *VCLT*. See, e.g., AB report, *US – Shrimp* [48].

bear in mind that the application of precaution is 'context-dependent'.[188] Accordingly, the present section is informed by the analysis of the WTO's normative framework carried out in Chapter 2.

The aim of this section is twofold. First, it highlights that interpreting the precautionary principle as a balancing and dynamic criterion would support the implementation of effective biosafety measures that do not impose undue or arbitrary constraints on free trade in biotechnology. However, success of this implementation depends on precautionary measures (biosafety measures adopted in light of the precautionary principle) complying with five criteria which are discussed in this section. Second, this section demonstrates that implementing precautionary measures by reversing the burden of proof can, in some circumstances, ensure that precaution can work effectively in biotechnology contexts and break stalemates.

4.4.1 Precaution as a balancing and dynamic criterion to address the epistemic issues in the context of biotechnology

This section argues that precaution should be interpreted in the context of biotechnology as a balancing and dynamic criterion. Success of this interpretation, though, depends on precautionary measures being applied in light of five criteria: (1) effectiveness, (2) proportionality, (3) non-discrimination/consistency, (4) consideration of costs and benefits and (5) re-examination in light of new scientific development.

In light of the first four criteria, member states are required to design precautionary measures that are effective (the first criterion) in achieving the pursued goal (i.e., protection of human health and/or the environment) and based on an up-to-date analysis of costs and benefits relating to the implementation of such measures (the fourth criterion) – analysis that can either demonstrate the need for being precautionary or the (mostly economic) risks of implementing precautionary measures. Simultaneously, precautionary measures should also not be disproportionate (the second criterion) or impose discriminatory or arbitrary constraints on free trade (the third criterion). In other words, adopting biosafety measures in light of the precautionary principle under the WTO requires member states to balance the interests in ensuring biosafety and trading biotechnology. This makes the precautionary principle a *balancing criterion* that, as claimed in this section, must be interpreted in the Alexian sense of the word, meaning that precaution itself is subject to judicial optimisation and balancing with the other principles/interests at stake.

In addition, the last criterion, requiring member states to re-examine precautionary measures in light of new scientific development, aids to interpret the precautionary principle as a *dynamic* (as opposed to *static*) tool. This is because asking member states to re-examine the adopted precautionary measures prevents the precautionary principle from becoming a static or rhetoric tool. Precautionary measures must keep pace with scientific development.

188 Peel (n 34) 6.

Only by adhering to these five criteria is the implementation of biosafety measures in light of the precautionary principle de facto possible under the WTO and, as such, feasible, meaning realistically achievable in this context. Put differently, precaution should be adopted under the WTO as a balancing criterion in the Alexian's meaning of the word. As explained previously, in Alexy's view, any judicial balance 'consists in nothing else than optimization relative to competing principles'[189] that, unlike rules, can be satisfied to varying degrees.[190]

The following analysis of the five mentioned criteria aids to better understand the suggested interpretation of precaution as a balancing and dynamic tool.

4.4.1.1 Effectiveness

It is widely acknowledged that '[a]ny precautionary measure must first and foremost be effective, meaning it has to be capable of achieving the desired level of protection'.[191] This emerges clearly in the *Baltic Sea Declaration*, the signatories of which state their 'firm intention' to:

> [A]pply the precautionary principle, i.e. *to take effective action* to avoid potentially damaging impacts of substances that are persistent, toxic and liable to bioaccumulate even where there is a lack of full scientific certainty to prove a causal link between emissions and effects.[192]

Assessing the effectiveness of a measure requires, first, the determination of the ALOP.[193] Under the WTO, this is acknowledged as a 'right' of WTO states, which can choose to establish a more or less precautionary ALOP. This depends on the values ascribed by states to the prevention of damage to human health and/or the environment.

4.4.1.2 Proportionality

Precautionary measures must also be proportionate to the objective/desired level of protection and risk at hand.[194] In other words, in pursuing non-trade-related

189 Robert Alexy, *A Theory of Constitutional Rights* (J Rivers trans, Oxford University Press, 2002) 47–48 [trans of *Theorie Der Grundrechte* (first published 1985)]; Robert Alexy, 'Balancing, Constitutional Review, and Representation' (2005) 3(4) *International Journal of Constitutional Law* 572, 573.

190 The discussion in Section 3.6.3 emphasises the importance of considering the precautionary principle as a factor to be considered in balancing competing interests by means of Alexy's 'weight formula'.

191 Jaeckel (n 7) 39 (emphasis added). See *COMM(2000)* 17.

192 *Baltic Sea Declaration* (emphasis added).

193 Jaeckel (n 7) 40.

194 Ibid 41; Simon Marr, *The Precautionary Principle in the Law of the Sea: Modern Decision-Making in International Law* (Martinus Nijhoff, 2003) 35–37; Trouwborst (n 15) 147–156. Further, assessing proportionality requires considering both short- and long-term

domestic policy objectives – such as biosafety – precautionary measures should not be more (trade) restrictive than necessary. This criterion is particularly relevant in the context of the WTO, where biosafety measures cannot be implemented in a manner which would constitute a means of 'arbitrary or unjustifiable discrimination between countries where the same conditions prevail or a disguised restriction on international trade'.[195] In this respect, the AB has developed the so-called necessity test that aids WTO judicial bodies to decide whether the contested measure is necessary or, put differently, the least restrictive option.[196]

It is noteworthy that both the proportionality and effectiveness criteria depend on the reversibility or irreversibility of the potential harm.[197] For example, while the impacts of overfishing can, in most cases, be reversed by reducing the scale of modern fisheries, the adverse effects caused by chemical pollution can be irreversible.[198] Trading biotechnology can have both reversible and irreversible impacts on human health and the environment.[199] Therefore, the judicial analysis of precautionary measures in the context of biotechnology requires a case-by-case approach that should be supported by a well-structured proportionality analysis.

4.4.1.3 Non-discrimination and consistency

Biosafety measures under the WTO must also be non-discriminatory in their application and consistent with the measures already adopted in similar circumstances or using similar approaches.[200] The principle of non-discrimination is, in fact, a pillar of WTO law.[201]

Non-discrimination and consistency of precautionary measures are also promoted at the European level[202] as providing 'a degree of certainty and planning reliability for stakeholders'.[203]

---

effects. In this respect, 'Ten or twenty years' is the parameter adopted by the European Commission to define 'long-term effects': *COMM(2000)* 18.

195 WTO Agreement chapeau. As the analysis of proportionality in the previous chapter underlines, qualifiers such as 'appropriate', 'necessary', 'no more restrictive than necessary' and 'reasonable' highlight that proportionality is encompassed under the WTO.

196 See Section 2.4.1.2. The implementation of measures not more (trade) restrictive than necessary aligns with the intention of member states that agreed on establishing the WTO on 'substantial reduction of tariffs and other barriers to trade': *WTO Agreement* preamble.

197 Jaeckel (n 7) 41–43.

198 Ibid 41–42.

199 See Section 1.2.2.

200 See chapeau art XX.

201 See *General Agreement on Tariffs and Trade 1994* annex 1A, arts I.1 and III; *General Agreement on Trade in Services* annex 1B, arts II and XVII; *TRIPs Agreement*, annex 1C, arts 3 and 4.

202 Under the European framework, precautionary measures 'should not be discriminatory in their application . . . [but rather] consistent with the measures already adopted in similar circumstances or using similar approaches': *COMM(2000)* 17.

203 Jaeckel (n 7) 40.

4.4.1.4 Costs and benefits

A plethora of international instruments define precaution by referring to cost-effectiveness, directly[204] or indirectly by adopting the formulation of the precautionary principle enshrined in the *Rio Declaration*, which emphasises the need to adopt 'cost-effective measures'.[205] As suggested by the *European COMM(2000)*, the examination of costs and benefits can perform '[a] comparison . . . between the most likely positive or negative consequences of the envisaged action and those of inaction . . . both in the long- and short-term'.[206]

Performing a cost-benefit analysis might support precautionary requests in the context of biotechnology under the WTO by strengthening the reasonableness of these requests to facilitate their justification in restricting trade. This is because cost-benefit analysis might show that inactions would be unreasonable and cost more than inactions. This would, accordingly, substantiate requests for taking biosafety measures in light of the precautionary principle in a context where the adoption of safeguarding measures is *the exception to the rule* of facilitating free trade.[207]

However, the cost-benefit analysis can also go the other way and demonstrate economic loss from restricting trade, while not showing clear benefits because the risks are uncertain. This validates the fact that by adhering to this criterion, biosafety measures adopted in light of the precautionary principle must also consider their impact on the other interest (i.e., free trade in biotechnology). This, in turn, supports the interpretation of the precautionary principle as a balancing criterion guiding WTO decision-makers in handling the compting requests in the context of biotechnology.

4.4.1.5 Re-examination in light of scientific development

WTO law requires member states to re-examine precautionary measures in light of the development of scientific knowledge. Although this criterion is not universally required, it is a condition set by WTO law for biosafety measures in contexts of scientific uncertainty. This emerges from Article 5.7 of the *SPS Agreement*, which enables WTO states to implement precautionary measures if member states (1) 'seek to [inter alia] obtain the additional information necessary for a more objective [scientific] assessment of risk' and (2) 'review the sanitary or phytosanitary measure accordingly within a reasonable period of time'.[208]

204 See, e.g., *UNFCCC* art 3; *Protocol to the 1979 Convention on Long-Range Transboundary Air Pollution on Further Reduction of Sulphur Emissions* preamble; *Energy Charter Treaty* art 19(1); *Convention to Ban the Importation into Forum Island Countries of Hazardous and Radioactive Wastes and to Control the Transboundary Movement and Management of Hazardous Wastes within the South Pacific Region* arts 1 and 13(1).

205 Among others, the CPB refers to the formulation of the principle as enshrined in Principle 15 of the *Rio Declaration*.

206 *COMM(2000)* 18.

207 Section 2.4.1.2 explains that the *GATT Agreement* enables the adoption of safeguarding measures by means of the 'General Exceptions' under article XX.

208 *SPS Agreement* art 5.7.

Moreover, a re-examination of precautionary measures is in fact part and parcel of the precautionary principle. It reflects the deep relationship between precaution and scientific considerations, in particular a thorough assessment of scientific knowledge including any remaining uncertainties.[209] Unsurprisingly, a re-examination of precautionary measures in light of the development of scientific knowledge is required not only by WTO law but also by other international legal instruments[210]

Further, the re-examination of precautionary measures in light of scientific development can overcome the criticism that the precautionary principle represents a limit to scientific development. Simultaneously, it addresses the 'concern about the ability of law to keep pace with new scientific developments'.[211]

New scientific knowledge may lead to precautionary measures being disproportionate and therefore need adjusting. For example, if new scientific findings lower, or on the contrary increase, the level of uncertainty surrounding the environmental or health effects of contested products, the precautionary measures in force banning the international trade of these products might no longer be proportionate. Accordingly, the precautionary measures in force should be re-examined and arguably replaced with less or more restrictive alternatives, depending on the results of new scientific research along with the examination of both benefits and costs of actions and inactions. In other words, the 'provisional' nature of precautionary measures, as reflected in the *SPS Agreement*,[212] refers to the measures in force, which must be re-examined in light of the scientific development, rather than to precaution itself. Precaution, indeed, must be applied *despite* scientific uncertainty and/or insufficient scientific evidence, and not *because of* it.[213]

In sum, to be operationalised under the WTO, biosafety measures triggered under the precautionary principle should be:

1. *effective*, meaning capable of achieving the desired level of protection;
2. *proportionate* to the objective/desired level of protection and risk at hand and, therefore, the least trade-restrictive measure in pursuing non-trade-related domestic policy objectives;
3. *non-discriminatory* and *consistent*, meaning not applied 'in a manner which would constitute a means of arbitrary or unjustifiable discrimination between countries where the same conditions prevail or a disguised restriction on international trade';[214]
4. supported by a *cost-benefit analysis* of actions and inactions; and

209 Jaeckel (n 7) 36. See also *COMM(2000)* 12; De Sadeleer (n 20) 174–180.
210 See, e.g., *COMM(2000)* 17. *New Delhi Declaration* [4.4].
211 Gary E Marchant, 'The Growing Gap Between Emerging Technologies and the Law' in Gary E Marchant, Braden R Allenby and Joseph R Herkert (eds), *The Growing Gap Between Emerging Technologies and Legal-Ethical Oversight* (Springer, 2011) 19, 26.
212 See *COMM(2000)* and the *SPS Agreement* art 5.7.
213 Trouwborst (n 15) 95.
214 *GATT Agreement* art XX chapeau.

5. *keeping pace with the development of science* and, accordingly, re-examined from time to time in light of the development of scientific knowledge.

Precautionary measures complying with these requirements show the capacity of the precautionary pirinciple to act as a *balancing and dynamic criterion*, which can aid WTO decision-makers to address the epistemic issues surrounding the international trade in biotechnology. This is because precautionary measures designed in light of these criteria attempt to find a point of equilibrium between biosafety and free trade.[215]

What is more, by interpreting the precautionary principle as a balancing and dynamic criterion, it is possible to overcome the following common criticism of precaution:

> Precaution expresses only one side of the risk versus benefit argument. . . . Precaution proclaims, 'look before you leap', an attitude only to be applauded. But desirable innovations can be blocked by an excess of precaution. There is a need for a principle that expresses the complementary aphorism, 'nothing ventured, nothing gained'.[216]

Precaution itself is, however, subject to judicial balancing. This is because adopting biosafety measures in light of the precautionary principle might in some circumstances not lead to the protection of human health and the environment. The 2015 Colombian case on the large-scale use of glyphosate to eradicate illegal coca crops represents a good example in this regard.[217] In a nutshell, for two decades the Colombian government has used glyphosate to eradicate coca crops. When in 2015, the International Agency for Research on Cancer (IARC) classified the glyphosate as 'probably carcinogenic',[218] President Santos suspended aerial spraying of this chemical on illegal crops as a precautionary measure. As Chapter 1 highlights, there was (and still is) contrasting scientific evidence on the harmfulness of glyphosate.[219] This means that, despite the lack of certain scientific evidence on the harmfulness of glyphosate, the Colombian government took precautionary actions to protect human health and the environment.

215 Chapter 8 discusses the level of (un)certainty that should suffice the operationalisation of precautionary measures in the context of biotechnology.

216 Weiss (n 33) 2.

217 Alvaro Javier Idrovo and Laura A Rodríguez-Villamizar, 'Moving Back in Policy Banning Glyphosate Use in Colombia' (2018) 392(10154) *The Lancet* 1194; Adriana Camacho and Daniel Mejía, 'The Health Consequences of Aerial Spraying Illicit Crops: The Case of Colombia' (2017) 54 *Journal of Health Economics* 147. See also Julia Symmes Cobb, 'Colombia Court Upholds Conditions for Restarting Aerial Coca Fumigation' *Reuters* (Online, 19 July 2019), www.reuters.com/article/us-colombia-politics/colombia-court-upholds-conditions-for-restarting-aerial-coca-fumigation-idUSKCN1UE01Q.

218 See IARC and WHO (n 133).

219 See Section 1.2.

After the Colombian government's decision to prohibit the use of this chemical, the number of hectares of illegal coca hit record levels in 2017.[220] This created cartels, raised a legal dispute with the United States and, more noteworthy, adversely affected the national economy and the environment, as drug cartels began a massive process of deforestation for using the land to plant coca. Thus, considering the magnitude of the coca problem, in 2018 the new President Duque asked the Colombian Constitutional Court to permit the re-introduction of glyphosate. As a result, in 2019 the highest court allowed again the Colombian government to re-use glyphosate to eradicate coca crops under strict conditions.[221]

The 2015 Colombian case shows that decision-makers must balance the implementation of biosafety measures in light of the precautionary principle with the other interests at stake. This demonstrates that precaution itself is a principle in the Alexian sense of the word, meaning a principle that WTO decision-makers should optimise and balance with the competing interest of free trade.[222]

To conclude, interpreting the precautionary principle as a balancing and dynamic criterion supports the implementation of biosafety measures under the WTO that are assessed as effective, proportional, non-discriminatory/consistent, supported by a cost-benefit analysis and re-examined occasionally in light of the development of scientific knowledge. By adhering to these five criteria, the adopted precautionary measures would be effective without, however, imposing undue, disproportionate or arbitrary limits to free trade in biotechnology. This can guide WTO judicial bodies in dealing with the epistemic issues surrounding the international trade in biotechnology.

Interpreting precaution as a dynamic criterion is also relevant for operationalising the precautionary principle by means of procedural measures, such as reversing the burden of proof, as discussed in detail in Section 4.4.2.

4.4.2 Precaution and the reversal of the burden of proof to break stalemate cases

In introducing the dimensions of implementing precaution, Section 4.2.3 anticipates that the precautionary principle can be employed through procedural measures, including reversing the burden of proof. The burden of proof exists in administrative and judicial contexts. Nevertheless, this analysis focuses only on the latter, as the implementation of precaution in administrative contexts is beyond the scope of the present study.

220 'Colombia Cocaine Production Acreage at "Record Level"' *BBC* (Online, 20 September 2018), www.bbc.com/news/world-latin-america-45578492.

221 Andrés Bermúdez Liévano, 'Colombia Will Spray Chinese Glyphosate to Control Coca' *Diálogo Chino* (Online, 1 August 2019), https://dialogochino.net/en/agriculture/29391-colombia-will-spray-chinese-glyphosate-to-control-coca/.

222 See Section 3.6.3.

As noted previously,[223] procedural means are merely one way to implement the precautionary principle. In discussing the application of precaution by reversing the burden of proof, the present study neither infers that implementing the precautionary principle is reduced to procedural measures nor assumes that this is *the* most suitable means to operationalise such principle in any context. Rather, bearing in mind that the application of precaution is context-dependent, the present section aspires to highlight that reversing the burden of proof might be necessary to ensure effective implementation of precautionary measures in some circumstances created by trading biotechnology.

Commentators agree on the fact that 'determining what standard of proof should be [adopted] or who bears the burden of proof of risk, are questions of immense practical importance'.[224] The precautionary principle can affect both the allocation of the onus of proof as well as the determination of the standard of proof. Each of these aspects is discussed respectively.

1. *Precaution and reversal of the burden of proof*: The commonly known general rule of evidence, which is also termed 'traditional burden of proof',[225] requires the party who initiates a procedure alleging something (the applicant) to prove what they allege. Once the applicant has complied with his *burden of production*, the onus shifts to the respondent, who can submit evidence disproving the facts alleged by the applicant. Importantly, unlike the burden of production, which moves back and forth between the parties, the *burden of persuasion*, aiming to 'persuade' the judge that the allegations made are true, rests with the applicant.

Within the WTO, the rules establishing who holds the burden of proof change in the context of different WTO agreements. For example, in disputes concerning the application of the general health and environmental exceptions under Article XX of the *GATT Agreement*, the burden of proof rests with the party invoking these exceptions.[226] 'Whether this will be appropriate in all circumstances calls for careful consideration'.[227] In the context of the *SPS Agreement*, the burden of proof lies with the WTO state seeking to challenge biosafety measures. As Foster commented:

> [I]t is a strength of the design and jurisprudence of [this agreement] that the burden of proof lies with a WTO member seeking to challenge risk-response

223 See Section 4.2.3.

224 Birnie, Boyle and Redgwell (n 20) 154. See also Caroline E Foster, *Science and the Precautionary Principle in International Courts and Tribunals – Expert Evidence, Burden of Proof, and Finality* (Cambridge University Press, 2011) 276.

225 *Ei incumbit probatie qui dicit, non qui negat* is a Latin expression literally meaning 'the burden of proof lies with who declares, not who denies'.

226 Similarly, the party requiring the implementation of measures protecting the environment in light of art XIV of the *GATS Agreement* bears the onus of proof. See *General Agreement on Trade in Services* art XIV.

227 Foster (n 224) 264.

measures. This is in alignment with the result that would be produced through a reversal of the burden of proof to accommodate the precautionary principle in meritorious cases under Article XX [of the GATT].[228]

The challenge with applying the traditional burden of proof is that it can lead to inequitable outcomes or render the precautionary principle ineffective,[229] as explained in the following paragraph. Key examples are *Pulp Mills*[230] and *Gabčíkovo–Nagymaros Project*[231] cases. In both cases brought to the attention of the ICJ, the judicial application of the traditional burden of proof was the driving force preventing effective implementation of precautionary measures.

Nonetheless, whether precaution warrants a reversal of the burden of proof remains a thorny, and not uncontroversial, question. The precautionary principle does not *automatically* reverse the burden of proof.[232] However, although reversing the burden of proof is not a requirement under the precautionary principle, it may play a central role in specific circumstances posed by trading biotechnology. Consider a case in which, for example, a local community is protesting against the large-scale cultivation of GM crops requiring daily aerial spraying of pesticides, which can affect the health of residents in that area. Even when the precautionary principle is applied, the community is required to prove threats of significant harm to human health. As Jaeckel notes, in this scenario, a lack of resources and expertise in the local community along with remaining scientific uncertainty may prevent effective application of the precautionary principle.[233] From a different perspective, Cameron observes that '[s]ince the burden of proof should rest with the party seeking to change the status quo, then that party seeking to maintain a less-polluted state ("the state before alteration by human activity") should not . . . be obliged to carry, the burden of proof'.[234] This means that parties asking for the implementation of precautionary measures to ensure biosafety from risks posed by the international trade of biotechnology should not bear the burden of proof.

Nevertheless, considering that the precautionary principle applies to a wealth of cases, reversing the burden of proof might lead to inequalities and non-effective measures in other circumstances. For instance, as Cooney observes, 'asking indigenous or local communities to demonstrate that their use of non-wood

228 Ibid 37.

229 Jaeckel (n 7) 55.

230 *Pulp Mills*. See Monika Ambrus, 'The Precautionary Principle and a Fair Allocation of the Burden of Proof in International Environmental Law' (2012) 21(3) *Review of European Community and International Environmental Law* 259, 260.

231 *Gabčíkovo–Nagymaros Project (Hungary-Slovakia)* [40].

232 Trouwborst (n 15) 222–224; Jaeckel (n 7) 54–57. Instead, Myhr described the shift in the burden of proof as a 'component' of the precautionary principle: Anne Ingeborg Myhr, 'The Precautionary Principle in GMO Regulations' in Terje Traavic and Lim Li Ching (eds), *Biosafety First* (Tapir Academic Press, 2007) 457, 458.

233 Jaeckel (n 7) 55.

234 James Cameron, 'The Precautionary Principle: Core Meaning, Constitutional Framework and Procedures for Implementation' in Ronnie Harding and Elizabeth Fisher (eds), *Perspectives on the Precautionary Principle* (The Federation Press, 1999) 29, 47.

forest products, sea turtle eggs or pasture was not causing any harm would be tantamount to ending the livelihood activities of substantial proportions of the world's rural poor'.[235] This substantiates what has already been claimed in relation to the interpretation of the precautionary principle as a balancing and dynamic criterion: Precaution is a principle in the Alexian sense of the word, meaning that it is subject to optimisation and balancing with the other principles/interests at stake.

Establishing when to reverse the burden of proof is not straightforward. In this respect, an examination of the rationale behind a reversal of the burden of proof[236] can be helpful. As Scobbie emphasises, the reversed allocation of the burden of proof originates from the idea of 'normative fairness' or 'distributive justice',[237] and it has been codified in international treaties[238] and several EU directives.[239] For example, in circumstances in which human activity, such as the international trade in biotechnology, can endanger human health and/or the environment, the *Cartagena Protocol Biosafety* and the *Convention on International Trade in Endangered Species of Wild Fauna and Flora* (CITES) place the burden of proof on the party supporting potentially dangerous activities. This, according to Zander, has become a common state practice.[240] In the EU, for instance, member states agreed on requiring a 'prior approval' before introducing potentially dangerous activities and products, including biotech products, onto the European market.[241] Those wishing to obtain prior approval must provide the other states with evidence that the product in question will not cause harm: 'This is one way of applying the precautionary

235 Cooney (n 20) 234.

236 The reversal of the burden of proof is also termed 'special' allocation of the burden of proof. See Ambrus (n 126).

237 Iain Scobbie, 'Tom Franck's Fairness' (2002) 13(4) *European Journal of International Law* 909; Ambrus (n 230) 260.

238 See, e.g., the *CPB*, *CITES*, *North Sea Declarations* and all the other treaties mentioned in Trouwborst (n 3) 201–212. The *Rio Declaration* is silent on such points because it vaguely requires 'an appropriate placement': *Rio Declaration* Principle 15.

239 See especially *Council Directive 97/80/EC of 15 December 1997 on the Burden of Proof in Cases of Discrimination Based on Sex* [1998] OJ L14, art 4; *Council Directive 2000/43/EC of 29 June 2000 Implementing the Principle of Equal Treatment between Persons Irrespective of Racial or Ethnic Origin* [2000] OJ L180, art 8; *Council Directive 2000/78/EC of 27 November 2000 Establishing a General Framework for Equal Treatment in Employment and Occupation* [2000] OJ L303; *Council Directive 2004/113/EC of 13 December 2004 Implementing the Principle of Equal Treatment between Men and Women in the Access to and Supply of Goods and Services* [2004] OJ L373.

240 Zander (n 15) 97–98, 130–135, 169–171, 224–226, 284–286. See also Trouwborst (n 3) 213–219.

241 See *Directive 2001/18/EC of the European Parliament and of the Council of 12 March 2001 on the Deliberate Release into the Environment of Genetically Modified Organisms and Repealing Council Directive 90/220/EEC* [2001] OJ L 106/1; *Directive (EU) 2015/412 of the European Parliament and of the Council of 11 March 2015 Amending Directive 2001/18/EC as Regards the Possibility for the Member States to Restrict or Prohibit the Cultivation of Genetically Modified Organisms (GMOs) in Their Territory* [2001] OJ L 68/1.

principle, by shifting responsibility for producing scientific evidence' on the party requiring the introduction of biotech products into the European market.[242]

'Normative rules such as the P[recautionary] P[rinciple]', Ambrus clarifies, 'can be regarded as fair when they ensure "distributive justice" an appropriate or proper allocation of burdens and benefits [is] secured by the rules themselves'.[243] Reversing the burden of proof in trading biotechnology and, more generally, potentially harmful products might be appropriate, as it can ensure a distributive justice in contexts in which WTO states wishing to adopt biosafety measures face notable difficulties in justifying precautionary measures. This is particularly relevant considering that the judicial allocation of the burden of proof to establish a prima facie case on the party requiring the adoption of biosafety measures is a major hurdle for implementing the precautionary principle in the context of the WTO.[244]

Many scholars agree that reversing the traditional burden of proof can be a key means to provide substantive implementation of precautionary measures.[245] Indeed, it can solve situations in which the judicial balance between competing interests results in a stalemate. In this case, decision-makers might shift the onus on the party challenging the implementation of biosafety measures, thereby breaking the stalemate and, as a consequence, reducing the epistemic discretion of decision-makers.

2. *Precaution and the standard of proof*: Unlike the question of whether precaution warrants a reversal of the burden of proof, the capacity of the precautionary principle to affect the standard of proof is not debated.[246] As Judge Weeramantry asserted:

> The law cannot function in protection of the environment unless a legal principle is evolved to meet this evidentiary difficulty, and environmental law has responded with what has come to be described as the precautionary principle.[247]

242 *COMM(2000)* 20.

243 Ambrus (n 230) 260 quoting Scobbie (n 237).

244 See Chapter 6.

245 Freestone and Hey (n 73) 249; Ambrus (n 230); Timothy O'Riordan and James Cameron, 'The History and Contemporary Significance of the Precautionary Principle' in Timothy O'Riordan and James Cameron (eds), *Interpreting the Precautionary Principle* (Earthscan, 1994) 12; Gehring and Segger (n 60); Jonathan B Wiener and Michael D Rogers, 'Comparing Precaution in the United States and Europe' (2002) 5(4) *Journal of Risk Research* 317; Margo Brett Baender, 'Pesticides and Precaution: The Bamako Convention as a Model for an International Convention on Pesticides Regulation' (1991) 24(1) *New York University Journal of Legislation and Public Policy* 557; Foster (n 224).

246 Jaeckel (n 7) 55.

247 *Nuclear Tests (New Zealand v France) (Judgment)* [1995] ICJ Rep 1995 (Judge Weeramantry), 342 quoted in Ambrus (n 126) 266.

The fact that precaution applies even in uncertain circumstances, where no conclusive evidence is available, lowers the evidentiary threshold required to trigger biosafety or other precautionary measures.[248] In other words, the precautionary principle lowers the standard of proof as neither side is required to provide clear and convincing evidence of a product (or a project). By affecting the standard of proof, the precautionary principle can, accordingly, break stalemate cases and reduce the epistemic discretion of decision-makers.

The challenge lies in understanding what standard of proof or level of (un)certainty suffices to implement precaution. There is no general answer to this question, especially because the application of precaution must take account of the specific circumstances of each case. As such, in discussing the implementation of the precautionary principle in WTO biotechnology cases, Chapter 8 sheds light on the standard(s) of proof and level of (un)certainty that might allow precaution to apply to the field of biotechnology. For the purpose of the present section, it is important only to stress that regardless of who bears the *burden*, precaution does affect the *standard* of proof by lowering the evidentiary threshold.

4.5 Conclusion

This chapter demonstrates that the precautionary principle is internationally recognised as a tool supporting timely actions to address environmental and human health threats even where scientific uncertainties remain. Nonetheless, its increasing judicial acceptance does not echo practical judicial adoptions of the principle, possibly because of an unjustified fear of 'false positive' cases.

This chapter demonstrates that precaution has migrated across different jurisdictions, including WTO law. It underlines that in spite of the lack of WTO agreements referring explicitly to the precautionary principle, it is encompassed under WTO law on the basis of three grounds, namely through (1) gateways provisions in the context of the *SPS* and *GATT Agreements*, (2) its close relation with the WTO goal of sustainable development and (3) its inclusion in several MEAs.

As applicable, the precautionary principle should be effectively implemented under the WTO, as it can aid WTO decision-makers to address the epistemic issues surrounding the international trade in biotechnology. This study focuses on the judicial implementation of precaution, as it is there that member states have faced real challenges in adopting precautionary measures. In doing so, this study suggests two possible interpretations of precaution that might guide WTO decision-makers to address the epistemic challenges surrounding the international trade in biotechnology.

First, this study shows that to be operationalised under the WTO, biosafety measures triggered in light of the precautionary principle should be (1) effective, (2) proportional, (3) non-discriminatory/consistent, (4) supported by a cost-benefit analysis of actions and inactions; and (5) re-examined from time to time in

248 Trouwborst (n 4) 192.

light of new scientific knowledge. The first four criteria underline the capacity of the precautionary principle to act as a balancing criterion, supporting the adoption of effective biosafety measures that, nonetheless, do not overlook the competing interest of trading biotechnology. Simultaneously, the last criterion shows the dynamic, rather than static, nature of the precautionary principle. Thus, this study argues that interpreting precaution as a balancing and dynamic criterion can guide WTO decision-makers in addressing the epistemic challenges raised by the international trade in biotechnology. This also means that, in fostering a solution to handle scientific uncertainties, the precautionary principle becomes a valid means to address, to some extent, the lack of reliability of empirical assumptions concerning the impact of trading biotechnology to biosafety: *In dubio pro biosafety*.

Second, although reversing the onus of proof is not a general requirement of the precautionary principle, this chapter argues that a reversal can be an important means of implementing the precautionary principle in the context of biotechnology. Indeed, by reversing the burden of proof and lowering the standard of proof, the precautionary principle can support the implementation of effective and equitable measures, break stalemate cases and, accordingly, reduce the epistemic discretion of WTO decision-makers.

The precautionary principle is, accordingly, a valid means to guide WTO decision-makers in addressing the epistemic issues stemming from the still-high level of scientific uncertainty surrounding biotechnology and stalemate situations. Nevertheless, regardless of whether it is interpreted as a balancing and dynamic criterion or as a procedural tool, this chapter shows that the precautionary principle itself is subject to judicial balancing. In other words, precaution should be considered a principle in the Alexian sense of the word, meaning that it is subject to optimisation and balancing with the other principles/interests at stake. This aligns with the findings in Chapter 3 suggesting consideration of the precautionary principle as a factor to be taken into account by WTO decision-makers in balancing competing interests.

So far, the analysis in this book has discussed the normative, judicial, and epistemic issues in balancing free trade and biosafety (see Chapter 2) and presented proportionality analysis and the precautionary principle as legal tools to address such challenges (see Chapters 3 and 4). It now turns to examine how the judicial balance between free trade and biosafety is performed in practice, and how precaution is applied by WTO judicial bodies in biotechnology cases.

Part III

Analysis of WTO biotechnology legal disputes

5 Introduction to and key reasons for a critical analysis of WTO biotechnology legal disputes

5.1 Introduction

The 1998 *EC – Hormones*, 2006 *EC – Biotech*, and 2008 *US/Canada – Hormones Continued Suspension* cases are the only WTO legal disputes concerning trade in biotech products. This Part III of the book analyses these cases to investigate whether, and if so how, the judicial balance between trade and non-trade values in the context of biotechnology has been performed *despite* the challenges identified in previous chapters. These challenges are an implicit prima facie pre-eminence of free trade under the WTO, the normative antinomies between WTO law and other international law regimes, judicial challenges and the epistemic issues surrounding the international trade in biotech products. In analysing the aformentioned three cases, this study illustrates an absense of a reasoned balance between trade and non-trade values as well as numerous difficulties WTO member states encounter when attempting to ensure biosafety by applying the precautionary principle.

This chapter introduces the three case studies and offers a critical analysis to identify the most problematic aspects of the three final judgments. These three cases were selected because they are, to date, the only WTO cases concerning biotechnology. *EC – Biotech* concerns the international trade in potentially harmful GMOs. At first glance, it might appear as though the other two cases, *EC – Hormones* and *US/Canada – Hormones Continued Suspension* (i.e., the *Hormones* cases), do not concern biotechnology. However, both cases regard international trade in meat and meat products injected with synthetic hormones for growth purposes, which in turn are genetically engineered using modern biotechnology.[1] In fact, according to the US National Research Council, the adoption of the synthetic hormones contested in both cases is one of the most contentious uses of biotechnology in animal agriculture.[2] Further, all three cases pertain to international trade in products entailing man-made risks to

1 US National Research Council, *Animal Biotechnology Science-Based Concerns* (National Academies Press, 2002).
2 Ibid 21.

DOI: 10.4324/9781003325741-8

human, animal or plant health and/or the environment caused by the use of biotechnology. The products contested in these three cases are all characterised by a high level of scientific uncertainty regarding their effects on biosafety. Unsurprisingly, the precautionary principle was invoked to support biosafety requests in each case.

This chapter outlines the background to, and related findings of, each case in turn. Section 5.2 deals with *EC – Hormones*, Section 5.3 with *US/Canada – Hormones Continued Suspension*, and Section 5.4 with *EC – Biotech*. Section 5.5 identifies the key judicial issues, which are then further analysed in the following chapters. Section 5.6 draws final conclusions.

5.2 1998 *EC – Hormones*

5.2.1 Case background

The *EC – Hormones* dispute arose out of the adoption of three European (European Communities [EC]) directives[3] banning from the European market meat and meat products derived from cattle to which three natural and three synthetic hormones had been added 'as growth factors'.[4] Importantly, 'there is a fundamental distinction between added hormones (natural and synthetic) and naturally-occurring hormones in meat and other food'.[5] More specifically, risks created by hormones used for growth promotion are 'man-made risks' that must be distinguished from 'naturally-occurring risks' arising from the presence of hormones in, for instance, milk and some vegetables.[6]

According to the EC, the man-made risks caused by hormones used for growth promotion were seriously threatening the health and safety of the European population. Several scientific studies supported this concern.[7] Among other

3 AB report, *EC – Hormones* [2]. The three EC directives at issue are *Council Directive 81/602/EEC of 31 July 1981 Concerning the Prohibition of Certain Substances Having a Hormonal Action and of Any Substances Having a Thyrostatic Action* [1981] OJ L 222/32; *Council Directive 88/146/EEC of 7 March 1988 on Trade in Animals Treated with Certain Substances Having a Hormonal Action and Their Meat, as Referred to in Article 7 of Directive 88/146/EEC* [1988] OJ L 70/16; *Council Directive 88/299/EEC of 17 May 1988 on Trade in Animals Treated with Certain Substances Having a Hormonal Action and Their Meat, as Referred to in Article 7 of Directive 88/146/EEC* [1988] OJ L 128/36.

4 *Council Directive 88/299/EEC* art 2.3. See also Alessandra Guida, 'The 2017 Fidenato Case and the 2015 Directive: The Curious Case of GMOs in Europe' (2020) *Review of European, Comparative and International Environmental Law* 1, 4–5.

5 AB report, *EC – Hormones* [221].

6 Ibid [32].

7 The *1982 Report of the EC Scientific Veterinary Committee, Scientific Committee for Animal Nutrition and the Scientific Committee for Food on the Basis of the Report of the Scientific Group on Anabolic Agents in Animal Production* (*'The 1982 Lamming Report'*); the *1983 Symposium on Anabolics in Animal Production of the Office International des epizooties* (OIE) (*1983 OIE Symposium*); *1987 Monographs of the International Agency for Research on Cancer on the Evaluation of Carcinogenic Risks to Humans, Supplement 7308* (*1987 IARC Monographs*); *1988 and*

concerns, the EC asserted that the carcinogenic effects of hormones on humans (and animals) had been extensively documented by the International Agency for Research on Cancer (IARC).[8] Nevertheless, the EC (along with the European Parliament) was aware that scientific information regarding meat from animals treated with growth-promoting hormones was 'far from complete and that considerable doubt therefore exists about the desirability of their use and of their effect on human health'.[9]

Facing such serious risks and uncertainties, the EC's ban of meat and meat products with these hormones aimed to establish a precautionary level of protection of human health in the context of the *SPS Agreement*. It is worth noting that '[t]he SPS Agreement applies only to man-made risks'.[10]

The European ban of six added hormones affected farmers in the United States and Canada, who used them for faster growth in cattle to decrease costs and improve yields. Both states argued that the European ban was unjustified since the scientific reports supporting their claim highlight that '[h]ormones generally pose no cancer risk where exposure is to levels below those required for detectable hormonal activity'.[11] The United States added that the European measures could not be justified because the EC had submitted no evidence to support its measures on health grounds.[12]

Thus, the United States and Canada complained before a panel – comprising Thomas Cottier, Peter Palecka and Jun Yokota – about the consistency of the European ban with several provisions under the *SPS Agreement*. Such complaints were addressed in two panel reports issued in August 1997, which found that the EC's ban was inconsistent with WTO law.

The reports were appealed before the AB by the EC, United States and Canada. All contested, for different reasons, the panel's decision and approach, as discussed in Section 5.2.2. The appeal resulted in a recommendation that the EC bring the measures found inconsistent with the *SPS Agreement* into conformity with the obligations of the EC under this agreement.[13] After the report was issued, the United

---

1989 JECFA Reports; *1995 European Communities Scientific Conference on Growth Promotion in Meat Production*; European Parliament, Committee on the Environment, Public Health and Consumer Protection, Report on *The USA's Refusal to Comply with Community Legislation on Slaughterhouses and Hormones and the Consequences of this Refusal*, EP 128 381/B, 7 February 1989 (*Collins Report*); articles and opinions by individual scientists relevant to the use of hormones (three articles in *Science*, one in *International Journal of Health Service*, one report in *The Veterinary Record* and separate scientific opinions of H Adlercreutz, E Cavalieri, SS Epstein, JG Liehr, M Metzler, Perez-Comas and A Pinter, all of whom were part of the EC delegation at joint meeting with experts): Panel report, *EC – Hormones* [8.108].

8 Panel report, *EC – Hormones* [4.129].
9 Ibid [4.21] (emphasis added).
10 AB report, *EC – Hormones* [32].
11 Panel report, *EC – Hormones* [4.132].
12 Ibid [3.3].
13 AB report, *EC – Hormones* [255].

States and Canada suspended concessions to the EC until the latter implemented the recommendations and rulings issued by the Dispute Settlement Body (DSB).[14]

5.2.2 Key findings

In *EC – Hormones*, the panel established that the EC's ban on meat and meat products with synthetic hormones was *inconsistent* with WTO law. The AB supported such a decision only partially because it upheld some of the panel's findings and reversed others.

The AB upheld the Panel's interpretation of the European measure as inconsistent with Article 5.1 of the SPS Agreement requiring WTO states to base SPS measures on a risk assessment 'appropriate to the circumstances'.[15] Both the panel and AB clarify that risk assessments can be considered as based on appropriate risk assessments where there is an objective relationship between an SPS measure and the supporting risk assessment.[16] The AB adds that the European scientific reports 'do not rationally support the EC import prohibition'.[17] It specified that these reports 'do not appear to be sufficiently specific to the case at hand'.[18] The panel's conclusion on the incompatibility of the European measure with Article 5.1 of the *SPS Agreement* was, accordingly, justified.[19] The AB establishes that the panel properly performed an *objective assessment of the matter* in light of the standard of review under Article 11 of the *DSU*.[20]

The judicial focus on the *objective relationship* between SPS measures and risk assessment, *rational support* and *sufficiently specific* evidence, overlooks the fact that the context of biotechnology was (and still is) characterised by scientific uncertainty about the effects of the contested products to biosafety. As such, judicial demand for highly specialised risk assessments justifying the implementation of SPS measures might represent a hurdle for effective implementation of these measures in the context of biotechnology. In view of this, how WTO judicial bodies revise risk assessments and, more specifically, what is considered an *appropriate* assessment of risk and an *objective assessment of the matter* in the sense of Article 11 of the *DSU*, warrants further investigation.[21]

The AB also upheld the panel's rejection of the European request to apply the precautionary principle. This is because the panel and AB agreed that 'this principle would not override the explicit wording of Articles 5.1 and 5.2'.[22] Put

14 Panel report, *US/Canada – Hormones Continued Suspension* [4.123].
15 AB report, *EC – Hormones* [253(j)].
16 Ibid [189].
17 Ibid [197].
18 Ibid [200].
19 Ibid [200].
20 Ibid [253(e)].
21 See Section 5.5.
22 AB report, *EC – Hormones* [120]. In this case, the EC did not invoke the precautionary principle because based on the gateway provision of art 5.7 of the *SPS Agreement*. See Section 4.3.1.1.

differently, member states can establish a precautionary management of risk if it aligns with WTO law. However, considering the judicial demand for highly specialised risk assessments supporting SPS measures along with the scientific emphasis under the *SPS Agreement*, adopting a precautionary management of risk becomes difficult for member states. This seems to be confirmed by the fact that all precautionary measures adopted in *EC – Hormones*, *US/Canada – Hormones Continued Suspension* and *EC – Biotech* were assessed as noncompliant with WTO law. Accordingly, it is important to explore whether the judicial interpretation of precautionary measures aligns with the proactive rationale of the precautionary principle.[23]

Finally, in analysing the different levels of protection set by the EC in respect of the hormones in dispute, the AB agreed with the panel that the established levels were unjustifiable and, to some extent, arbitrary.[24] Consequently, *the AB upheld the panel's decision that the European measures are not consistent with Article 5.5* of the *SPS Agreement*.[25] Discussing this judicial finding in further detail, throughout the following chapters, is particularly relevant because it can show whether WTO judicial bodies performed a proportionality analysis to establish whether the contested measures were arbitrary and unjustifiable.

Conversely, *the AB reversed the panel's decision of allocating the burden of proof on the EC*, namely on the responding party, which required the application of precautionary measures, *to establish a prima facie case*.[26] According to the panel, asking the party requiring the adoption of precautionary measures to bear the burden of proof can be inferred from Article 3.2 of the *SPS Agreement*, which establishes a presumption of consistency with such an agreement for measures that conform to international standards, guidelines and recommendations.[27] As the AB noted:

> From this presumption, the Panel extracts a reverse inference that if a measure does not conform to international standards, the Member imposing such a measure must bear the burden of proof in any complaint of inconsistency with a provision of the SPS Agreement.[28]

In the AB's view, the panel's conclusion lacked logic and, accordingly, was reversed.[29] In light of this, performing a comparative analysis of the judicial

23 See Section 5.5.

24 In taking such a decision, the AB also considers the different levels of protection set by the EC in respect of carbadox and olaquindox, which are anti-microbiological agents mixed with feed given to piglets.

25 AB report, *EC – Hormones* [246].

26 Ibid [97]–[108]. The panel described this issue as 'of particular importance' in the context of the *SPS Agreement*: [97].

27 Ibid [101].

28 Ibid [101] (emphasis altered).

29 Ibid [102].

reasoning on the allocation of the burden of proof to establish a prima facie case in all biotechnology cases can aid understanding of whether the panel's decision in *EC – Hormones* (to allocate the burden of proof on the party requiring the implementation of precautionary measures) stemmed from a debatable inference or, rather, from the implicit prima facie pre-eminence of free trade under the WTO.[30]

To conclude, the WTO decision in *EC – Hormones* provides a catalyst for discussion of five key aspects:

1. the judicial examination of the appropriateness of risk assessments supporting the competing requests in the context of biotechnology,
2. the meaning and appropriateness of the standard of review under Article 11 of the *DSU*, which panels employ to examine the biotechnology matter,
3. the judicial evaluation of requests for adopting biosafety measures in light of the precautionary principle,
4. the judicial evaluation of whether the contested measures are arbitrary and unjustifiable and the potential judicial performance of a proportionality analysis to this end,
5. the judicial reasoning behind the allocation of the burden of proof to establish a prima facie case.

Section 5.5 outlines how this study develops these aspects in greater detail, while Section 5.3 presents the background to and key findings of *US/Canada – Hormones Continued Suspension*, which is a legal dispute that arose from *EC – Hormones*.

5.3 2008 *US/Canada – Hormones Continued Suspension*

5.3.1 Case background

EC – Hormones led to another WTO dispute a decade later. The 2008 *US – Hormones Continued Suspension*[31] and *Canada – Hormones Continued Suspension*[32] disputes (2008 *US/Canada – Hormones Continued Suspension*) arose from the EC's complaints regarding the suspension of concessions established by the United States and Canada in *EC – Hormones*.[33] More specifically, after the DSB's

30 See Section 5.5.

31 Panel report, *US/Canada – Hormones Continued Suspension*.

32 Panel report, *Canada – Continued Suspensions*.

33 Trade sanctions against the party that has failed to bring its measures in line with WTO obligations are called 'suspending concessions or other obligations under the covered agreements' (*DSU* art 22.2). Tariff reduction commitments that member states agreed upon in multilateral trade negotiations are an example of concessions. See 'The Process – Stages in a Typical WTO Dispute Settlement Case' *WTO* (Web Page), www.wto.org/english/tratop_e/dispu_e/disp_settlement_cbt_e/c6s10p1_e.htm.

pronouncement in *EC – Hormones*, the EC conducted 17 scientific studies to evaluate risks to human health posed by the six hormones discussed in such a case.[34] Based on those scientific assessments of risks, the EC's Scientific Committee on Veterinary Measures relating to Public Health (SCVPH) issued a first scientific opinion in 1999 (i.e., the '1999 Opinion'), followed by two scientific reviews (i.e., the '2000 Opinion' and the '2002 Opinion'). All three opinions ('the SCVPH Opinions') confirmed that, although '[t]he data available did not . . . allow a quantitative estimate of the risk', it was possible to establish the following:

> In the case of oestradiol-17β, there was a substantial body of recent evidence suggesting that it had to be considered as a complete carcinogen, as it exerted both tumour initiating and tumour promoting effects.
>
> For the other five hormones at issue, [and more generally] [f]or all six hormones [at stake], endocrine, developmental, immunological, neurobiological, immunotoxic, genotoxic and carcinogenic effects could be envisaged. Of the various susceptible risk groups, prepubertal children was the group of greatest concern.[35]

In light of these findings, the EC adopted Directive 2003/74/EC ('the 2003 Directive'), which established:

1. 'the *permanent prohibition* of the placing on the market of meat and meat products from animals treated with oestradiol-17β for growth-promotion purposes'[36]
2. 'the *provisional prohibition*' of the other five hormones (i.e., testosterone, progesterone, trenbolone acetate, zeranol and MGA) discussed in *EC – Hormones*. This provisional ban 'should apply while the Community seeks more complete scientific information from any source, which could shed light and clarify the gaps in the present state of knowledge of these substances'.[37]

Thus, after notifying the DSB of the adoption of the 2003 Directive and the conduction of risk assessments in the SCVPH Opinions, the EC claimed that the DSB's recommendations and rulings in the original *EC – Hormones* dispute were fully implemented. Consequently, US and Canadian suspensions of concessions

34 AB report, *US/Canada – Hormones Continued Suspension* [10].

35 Panel report, *US/Canada – Hormones Continued Suspension* [7.391]; *Canada – Continued Suspension* (n 32) [7.388].

36 AB report, *US/Canada – Hormones Continued Suspension* [11] (emphasis added); *Directive 2003/74/EC of the European Parliament and of the Council of 22 September 2003 Amending Council Directive 96/22/EC Concerning the Prohibition on the Use in Stockfarming of Certain Substances having a Hormonal or Thyrostatic Action and of Beta-Agonists* [2003] OJ L 262/17, preamble [7] (*The 2003 Directive*).

37 *The 2003 Directive*, preamble [10] (emphasis added).

were no longer justified.[38] Conversely, the United States and Canada argued that the adoption of the 2003 Directive and the three scientific risk assessments emerging from the SCVPH Opinions were not sufficient to justify either the permanent European ban or the provisional prohibition under the *SPS Agreement*.

The lack of an agreement between the parties led a panel – established in 2005 and comprising Tae-yul Cho, William Ehlers and Claudia Orozco – to issue two reports ('the panel's reports') in March 2008. These reports found that both the permanent and provisional European bans were not in line with WTO law.[39]

Since the EC, US and Canada contested almost all findings and legal interpretations given by the panel, in October 2008, the legal dispute was brought before the AB that issued two reports ('the AB's reports'), in which nearly all panel findings were reversed for the reasons explained in Section 5.3.2.[40]

The so-called 'Hormones war',[41] which began with 1998 *EC – Hormones*, 'remains a standoff with Europe continuing to pay over $100 m[illion] in compensation for refusing to abide by a WTO ruling'.[42] This is because while the EC and Canada reached a mutually agreed solution in September 2017,[43] no agreement between the EC and US has been reached until now.

5.3.2 Key findings

The panel and AB discussed a range of issues and provisions in this case. Addressing all of these would exceed the scope of this study and be of little relevance. Thus, this study concentrates on the following findings by the AB.

First, *the panel erred in allocating the burden of proof on the complainant requiring the implementation of precautionary measures*. This aspect is worthy of attention because, as discussed in Chapter 4, the allocation of the burden of proof is a thorny question in the context of biotechnology, especially if the party invoked the precautionary principle that, as discussed, can in some circumstances reverse the burden of proof. What is particularly interesting is that the AB has 'several . . .

38 AB report, *US/Canada – Hormones Continued Suspension* [12].

39 The panel also established that the United States and Canada 'failed to rebut [the] presumption' according to which the EC failed to make a prima facie case: Panel report, *US/Canada – Hormones Continued Suspension* [7.269], [8.1].

40 AB report, *US/Canada – Hormones Continued Suspension*; AB report, *Canada – Continued Suspension*.

41 'Hormones war' is an expression commonly adopted by scholars to refer to the two *Hormones*: *EC – Hormones* and *US/Canada – Hormones Continued Suspension*. See, e.g., Md Adil, 'Dispute Settlement Activity Under WTO : Problems and Perspectives' (2017) 7(4) *IUP Law Review* 35, 41–42.

42 Ibid.

43 *European Communities – Measures Concerning Meat and Meat Products (Hormones) – Notification of a Mutually Agreed Solution*, WTO Doc WT/DS48/27, G/L/91/Add.1 G/SPS/W/71/Add.1, G/TBT/D/7/Add.1 G/AG/W/26/Add.1 (3 October 2017).

concerns with the panel's analysis' concerning the burden of proof (and not only).[44] This is discussed in detail in Chapter 6.

Second, the panel infringed the 'due process rights' of the EC. Due process 'guarantees that the proceedings are conducted with fairness and impartiality'.[45] According to the AB, the institutional affiliation of two experts appointed by the panel compromised the independence and impartiality of panellists. Thus, *the AB found that the panel failed to comply with its duties to 'make an objective assessment of the matter' in the sense of Article 11 of the* DSU and to ensure fairness and impartiality in the decision-making process.[46]

Analysing the AB's reasoning on the panel's adoption of the standard of review under Article 11 of the *DSU* can shine light on the appropriateness of such a standard when applied to biotechnology cases. This analysis is particularly relevant considering that the indication under Article 11 of the *DSU* to perform an *objective assessment of the matter* does not provide panels with substantial guidelines to address the complexity surrounding the international trade in biotech products. Accordingly, an in-depth discussion of the current standard of review under Article 11 of the *DSU* can show whether it is suitable to review biotechnology legal disputes.[47]

Third, in the AB's view, *the panel erred in considering that the* permanent *import ban* relating to oestradiol-17ß *was not 'based on' a risk assessment 'appropriate to the circumstances'*, as required by Article 5.1 of the *SPS Agreement*. As anticipated in relation to the analysis of *EC – Hormones*, the judicial review of risk assessments represents a chief reason the panels appointed in all three biotechnology cases rejected the implementation of biosafety measures. This AB's conclusion confirms the importance of discussing such a thorny aspect in detail.[48]

Finally, according to the AB, *the panel also erred in establishing that the* provisional *import ban* relating to the other five hormones *did not meet the requirements of Article 5.7* of the *SPS Agreement* and, as such, *could not be justified in light of the precautionary principle.* More specifically, the AB explains that the panel misinterpreted the first requirement of Article 5.7 of the *SPS Agreement* (i.e., *insufficiency* of scientific evidence) and drew the wrong inference that the existence of international standards concerning the five hormones entails the existence of *sufficient* scientific evidence.

Despite this finding, the AB does not authorise the implementation of the European precautionary measures. This is because the AB decided not to comment on that particular point. In fact, the AB made findings only on some points raised by the panel. As is commonplace in the WTO dispute settlement system, the AB makes findings only on points that are based on either undisputed facts or

44 AB report, *US/Canada – Hormones Continued Suspension* [581].

45 Ibid [433].

46 Ibid [736(b)].

47 See Section 5.5.

48 Chapter 7 provides this analysis.

at least sufficient factual findings in the panel report.[49] In the present case, the AB criticised 'the numerous flaws' in the Panel's analysis of Articles 5.1 and 5.7 of the *SPS Agreement* and 'the highly contested nature of the facts'[50] and concluded that it was unable to make a legal finding based on those facts. This raises an interesting point, namely that the complexity surrounding biotech products can prevent the AB from reaching legal findings.[51] Such complexity is already acknowledged in 2006 *EC – Biotech*.[52]

To conclude, a critical analysis of the panel's examination of risk assessments in the sense of Article 5.1 of the *SPS Agreement* and the European request to adopt precautionary risk management under Article 5.7 of the *SPS Agreement* can aid understanding of why neither biosafety measures nor, in turn, the precautionary principle have ever been implemented in the context of biotechnology. Additionally, a thorough discussion of the judicial findings in relation to the allocation of the burden of proof and the judicial adoption of the standard of review under Article 11 of the *DSU* adds further insights in this regard.

5.4 2006 *EC – Biotech*

5.4.1 Case background

EC – Biotech arose in between the 1998 and 2008 *Hormones* disputes.[53] Specifically, between May and August 2003, the United States, Canada and Argentina (the complaining parties) requested consultations with the EC in relation to protective measures taken by six European member states prohibiting or restricting the marketing of biotech products.[54] Specifically, (1) Austria and France prohibited the 'placing on the market' of some biotech products, (2) Luxembourg prohibited the 'use and sale', (3) Germany 'suspend[ed] the approval and the placing on the market' of the biotech corn Bt-176, (4) Italy suspended the 'commercialization and use' of four of the biotech products and (5) Greece prohibited the importation

49 *Dispute Settlement Understanding* art 17 [6]. See also United Nations Conference on Trade and Development, 'Dispute Settlement – World Trade Organization 3.3 Appellate Review' UNCTAD/EDM/Misc.232/Add.17 (2003), 14.

50 AB report, *US/Canada – Hormones Continued Suspension* [736(c-vi)]–[736(d-vi)], [620], [734].

51 See Cinnamon Carlarne, 'From the USA with Love: Sharing Home-Grown Hormones, GMOs, and Clones with a Reluctant Europe' (2007) 37 *Environmental Law* 301, 308.

52 Robert Howse and Henrik Horn, 'European Communities – Measures Affecting the Approval and Marketing of Biotech Products' (2009) 8(1) *World Trade Review* 49.

53 Alessandra Guida, 'DS291, DS292, DS293: European Communities – Measures Affecting the Approval and Marketing of Biotech Products (EC – Biotech)' in Panagiotis Delimatsis and Leonie Reins (eds), *Trade and Environmental Law Elgar Encyclopedia of Environmental Law Series – Volume XI* (Edward Elgar, 2021).

54 Panel report, *EC – Biotech*. As the panel clarifies, ' "[b]iotech products" in this dispute refers to plant cultivars that have been developed through recombinant deoxyribonucleic acid ("recombinant DNA") technology" ': [2.2].

of the biotech Agrevo oilseed rape.[55] The states claimed that these measures were apt to ensure biosafety in light of the uncertainties remaining about biotechnology and the results of national risk assessments showing potentially adverse effects posed by biotech products to human health and the environment. Conversely, the complaining parties considered the EC's human health and environmental concerns groundless, not least because such products had been already assessed and approved by the scientific committee of the European Communities (i.e., EFSA).[56]

Since the parties failed to reach a mutually agreed resolution, in August 2003, a panel comprising Christian Häberli, Mohan Kumar and Akio Shimizu was established to decide whether the protective measures applicable by the EC were consistent with WTO law. The panel rejected the European claim and required the EC to bring the protective measures into conformity with its obligations under the *SPS Agreement*. The panel's report, as Howse and Horn pointedly note, not only had to 'take a stand on the limits of science, or technocratic regulatory controls, to protect against objective risk, but in this regard faced more complex issues than ever addressed before by an adjudicating body'.[57]

Despite the panel handing down a finding in 2006, the dispute itself has not been resolved as of this writing. Whereas the EC reached a mutually agreed solution with Canada[58] and Argentina[59] in 2020, no solution has been reached between the EC and the United States.[60] It is not possible to predict how this case on GMOs will be resolved. Nonetheless, it seems likely, in the view of Moore and Winham, that:

> A WTO case would play into the hands of European environmental organizations, consumer groups and politicians who portray the US as the world's fast-food superpower trying to force an unwelcome technology down European throats. It also would be a setback for European scientists and leaders working for a more reasoned public debate over biotechnology.[61]

55 Ibid [4.153].

56 Ibid [4.530]–[4.531].

57 Howse and Horn (n 52).

58 *European Communities – Measures Affecting the Approval and Marketing of Biotech Products – Notification of a Mutually Agreed Solution*, WTO Doc WT/DS292/40 G/L/628/Add.1 G/SPS/GEN/398/Add.1 G/AG/GEN/61/Add.1 G/TBT/D/29/Add.1 (17 July 2009).

59 *European Communities – Measures Affecting the Approval and Marketing of Biotech Products – Notification of a Mutually Agreed Solution*, WTO Doc WT/DS293/41 G/L/629/Add.1 G/SPS/GEN/399/Add.1 G/AG/GEN/62/Add.1 G/TBT/D/30/Add.1 (23 March 2010).

60 *European Communities – Measures Affecting the Approval and Marking of Biotech Products – Status Report by the European Communities – Addendum*, WT/DS291/37/Add.150 (12 February 2021).

61 Julia A Moore and Gilbert Winham, 'Let's Not Escalate the "Frankenfood" War' (*The Christian Science Monitor*, 20 December 2002) quoted in Gilbert R Winham, 'The GMO Panel: Applications of WTO Law to Trade in Agricultural Biotech Products' (2009) 31(3) *Journal of European Integration* 409, 425.

Regardless of how the *EC – Biotech* legal dispute will end, the panel's analysis of this case highlights several relevant key findings, as discussed in the following section.

5.4.2 Key findings

In *EC – Biotech*, the panel found that the European measures amounted to a de facto *moratorium* on the relevant biotech products. This led to delay in the approval procedure of biotech products, contrary to annex C(1)(a) of the *SPS Agreement*, which requires processes to assess SPS measures to be 'undertaken and completed without undue delay and in no less favourable manner for imported products than for like domestic products'.[62]

In this case, the panel drafted a 1,087-page report (annexes excluded), a length that, as Winham commented, is 'consistent with the enormity of the issue of agricultural biotechnology in international economic relations'.[63] The panel discussed a range of WTO provisions in this case. However, the panel's analysis of Articles 5.1 and 5.7 of the *SPS Agreement* is at the core of the dispute and, accordingly, of the present study.[64] The panel made the following findings.

The EC acted inconsistently with Article 5.1 of the *SPS Agreement*, because the protective measures were not 'based on' risk assessments, nor were the national assessments of risk 'appropriate to the circumstances'.[65] Nonetheless, the panel argued that the European measures could still be in line with WTO law if assessed as compliant with Article 5.7 of the *SPS Agreement*, which permits member states to adopt SPS measures in contexts with insufficient scientific evidence. However, the panel found that all European measures were also inconsistent with Article 5.7, since they were not triggered in a context (i.e., biotechnology) characterised by *insufficient* scientific evidence, which represents the first requirement to invoke Article 5.7.[66] Consequently, *the panel rejected the European request to apply the precautionary principle, as reflected in Article 5.7.*

Rejecting the European adoption of precautionary measures as not adopted in a context in which there is insufficient scientific evidence contradicts the rationale of the precautionary principle. As discussed in Chapter 4, precaution applies

62 *SPS Agreement* C(1)(a).

63 Winham (n 61) 410.

64 Ilona Cheyne, 'Life after the Biotech Products Dispute' (2008) *Environmental Law Review* 52, 56. See also Denise Prévost, 'Opening Pandora's Box: The Panel's Findings in the EC-Biotech Products Dispute' (2007) 34(1) *Legal Issues of Economic Integration* 67; Andrew Thomison, 'A New and Controversial Mandate for the SPS Agreement: The WTO Panel's Interim Report in the E.C.-Biotech Dispute' (2007) 32 *Columbia Journal of Environmental Law* 287; Christiane R Conrad, 'The EC – Biotech Dispute and Applicability of the SPS Agreement: Are the Panel's Findings Built on Shaky Ground?' (2007) 6(2) *World Trade Review* 233.

65 By implication, the European measures were deemed inconsistent with art 2.2 of the *SPS Agreement* that must be always read in conjunction with art 5.1.

66 *EC – Biotech* (n 54) [7.3234]–[7.3235].

despite uncertain or insufficient scientific evidence. A critical analysis of WTO biotechnology judgments requires, as such, an in-depth understanding of the judicial interpretation of the relationship between the precautionary principle and scientific knowledge surrounding the risks posed by international trade in biotech products.

Further, according to the panel, the chosen (precautionary) level of protection (ALOP) is not relevant in determining whether scientific evidence is sufficient to assess risks.[67] Similarly, in *US/Canada – Hormones Continued Suspension*, the panel found that the EC wrongly considered the chosen ALOP as relevant in determining whether scientific evidence is sufficient to assess risks posed by the five hormones. However, in that case, the AB disagreed with the panel's outcome.[68]

The AB's observation in *US/Canada – Hormones Continued Suspension* raises doubts about the panel's finding on the ALOP in *EC – Biotech*. More specifically, the panels' reasoning on sufficiency and insufficiency of evidence in relation to the establishment of a precautionary ALOP beg the questions of what is considered sufficient evidence and whether the uncertainty surrounding the international trade in biotech products affects the consideration of a body of evidence as sufficient to assess the existence and magnitude of a risk. These, accordingly, must become further topics of investigation.[69]

Finally, in *EC – Biotech*, the panel added that when a party alleges that a triggered SPS measure does not align with Articles 5.1 or 5.7 of the *SPS Agreement*, *the burden of proof to establish a prima facie case lies on the complaining party*. Conversely, in *EC – Hormones*, the panel allocated the burden of proof on the responding party, requiring the application of precautionary measures. Consequently, a legitimate question might be: What is the logic behind the judicial allocation of the burden of proof? As Section 5.5 stresses, a thorough analysis of the judicial allocation of the burden of proof to establish a prima facie case can clarify this aspect.

Therefore, a critical examination of the *EC – Biotech* judgment needs to focus on the same hurdles emerging from the *Hormones* cases: (1) the judicial examination of risk assessments supporting the competing requests of trading biotech products and ensuring biosafety, (2) the contested request to adopt precautionary measures and (3) the judicial allocation of the burden of proof to establish a prima facie case.

To conclude, the three WTO biotechnology judgments produced several complex aspects that warrant an in-depth critical discussion. This study narrows the analytical focus to four of these, for the reasons set out in Section 5.5.

67 Ibid [7.3238].

68 AB report, *US/Canada – Hormones Continued Suspension* [736(d)].

69 Chapter 8 develops these aspects in detail.

5.5 Analytical focus of the case studies

The picture emerging from the background, legal issues and final decisions relating to the three WTO biotechnology cases highlights two key aspects. First, despite WTO dispute settlement bodies handing down decisions in all three cases, the underlying legal disputes remain ongoing. Indeed, the 1998 *EC – Hormones* case led to the 2008 *US – Hormones Continued Suspension* and *Canada – Hormones Continued Suspension* disputes, after which no agreement between the EC and US has been reached. Similarly, in 2006 *EC – Biotech*, no solution has been reached between the EC and US. Second, the lack of a final dispute resolution highlights that the international trade in biotech products is a topical and still unresolved issue under the WTO.

Given that all national requests for implementing biosafety measures were rejected, there appear to be hurdles that prevent implementation of the precautionary principle under the WTO.[70] The key challenge lies in understanding the reasons behind the judicial trend of supporting free trade in contexts in which uncertainties on risks posed by trading biotech products remain. The answer might be found in the 'substantial discretion' of panels to:

1. 'decide which evidence [they] choos[e] to utilize in making findings',[71]
2. determine 'the *credibility and weight* properly to be ascribed to (that is, the appreciation of) a given piece of evidence',[72]
3. decide whether experts disclosing information likely to affect or give rise to justifiable doubts as to their independence or impartiality should be consulted.[73]

However, as the discussed cases are 'centered on issues that potentially alte[r] the rights and obligations of WTO members, [they] should not have been confined to the single discretion of WTO judicial bodies'.[74] This is particularly pertinent considering the existence of an implicit bias towards free trade under the WTO.[75]

Further, it would be simplistic to reduce the complexity of *why biosafety measures and the precautionary principle have never been applied in biotechnology cases* to the lack of defined boundaries of the panels' discretion. Simultaneously, a satisfactory answer to this question can hardly be found in the explanations provided by WTO judicial bodies. This is because the judicial justifications for rejecting the implementation of biosafety measures and the precautionary principle are

70 Adil (n 41).
71 AB report, *EC – Hormones* [135].
72 Ibid [132].
73 AB report, *US/Canada – Hormones Continued Suspension*.
74 Adil (n 41) 41–42.
75 See Section 2.5.

scant. More specifically, WTO judicial bodies give only two reasons when explaining the missed adoption of biosafety measures and precaution in the context of biotechnology:

1. The precautionary principle does not *override* the WTO requirements set out in Articles 5.1 and 5.2 of the *SPS Agreement*,[76] meaning that member states can require the implementation of biosafety measures in light of the precautionary principle only by aligning such measures with the scientific requirements in the sense of these Articles.
2. Biosafety measures cannot apply in light of the precautionary principle if these measures are adopted in a context in which 'sufficient' scientific evidence exists.

These justifications do not elucidate if the rejection of biosafety measures is the result of a reasoned judicial balance or, rather, a consequence of the trade bias under the WTO. Finding an answer to this question requires examining the judicial argumentation provided for four crucial aspects of the biotechnology judgments: (1) the judicial allocation of the burden of proof to establish a prima facie case in contexts in which uncertainties remain, (2) the standard of review applied by panels to examine the competing requests in the context of biotechnology, (3) the judicial review of risk assessments in light of Article 5.1 of the *SPS Agreement* and (4) the judicial examination of requests to adopt a precautionary management of risks posed by trading biotech products in light of Article 5.7 of the *SPS Agreement*. An in-depth analysis of each of them is developed in Chapters 6–8. The following pages offer a brief outline of each of these issues.

1. The *judicial allocation of the burden of proof to establish a prima facie case in contexts in which uncertainties remain* represents the first crucial aspect to investigate, not least because panels adopted different positions in this regard. In *EC – Hormones*, the panel allocated the burden of proof on the *responding party*, which required the application of precautionary measures. Conversely, in *US/Canada – Hormones Continued Suspension*, the panel placed the burden of proof on the *complainant*, requiring the implementation of precautionary measures. In *EC – Biotech*, the panel allocated the burden of proof on the *complainants*, which in this case was the party against the implementation of precautionary measures triggered by the respondent.[77]

76 Specifically, the AB clarifies that 'this principle would not override the explicit wording of Articles 5.1 and 5.2': AB report, *EC – Hormones* [120].

77 In *EC – Biotech*, the judicial interpretation of art 5.7 of the *SPS Agreement* as a qualified right led the panel to establish that in cases in which a complaining party alleges that an *SPS* measure is inconsistent with art 5.1, the burden of proof is on the complaining party, which must establish a prima facie case of inconsistency with both arts 5.1 and 5.7 of the *SPS Agreement*.

The different judicial positions taken and the divergent justifications provided by WTO judicial bodies on the allocation of the burden of proof to establish a prima facie case can undermine legal certainty. Simultaneously, effective operationalisation of biosafety measures in light of the precautionary principle might be hindered. This is because it can be difficult to prove that precautionary measures adopted in the (scientifically uncertain) context of biotechnology meet the science-centric requirements set out in the WTO regulatory framework.

Thus, Chapter 6 provides an extensive analysis of the judicial allocation of the burden of proof to establish a prima facie case in scenarios involving scientific uncertainties. The analysis of this issue becomes even more interesting considering WTO 'rules on the requirements for establishing a prima facie case are less developed than the allocation of the burden of the proof'.[78] Considering that, Chapter 6 also attempts to develop a concept of prima facie case that might assist WTO decision-makers facing cases characterised by scientific uncertainty.

2. For over a decade (from 1998 *EC – Hormones* to 2008 *US/Canada – Hormones Continued Suspension*), WTO judicial bodies have assessed all biosafety measures and requests to implement precaution in the context of biotechnology as not in line with WTO law. *The standard of review applied by panels in reviewing national requests* becomes, accordingly, a further aspect to explore.

Article 11 of the *DSU* establishes that panels are required to examine WTO legal disputes through an *objective assessment of the matter*. This means that performing an objective assessment of the matter is the standard of review employed by panels to examine biotechnology cases. Its adoption, however, might represent a major hurdle to implementing biosafety measures and the precautionary principle. This standard does not provide substantive guidance for panels examining the competing requests in the complex context of biotechnology.

So far, neither WTO law nor WTO jurisprudence have clarified what constitutes an *objective* assessment. Arguably, the term 'objective' under Article 11 of the *DSU* might have two meanings. First, it might suggest the need for panels to perform a *non-subjective perception* of the matter. In other words, judicial assessments should reflect the true (non-subjective) nature of facts and circumstances surrounding the matter. In this case, the standard under Article 11 of the *DSU* would be inappropriate for use in biotechnology cases because a true/rational/objective nature of the biotechnology matter cannot yet be established. Indeed, the scientific uncertainties surrounding the adverse effects of such products to biosafety would prevent its determination. Clearly, any conclusion on the effects

78 Ho Cheol Kim, 'Burden of Proof and the Prima Facie Case: The Evolving History and Its Applications in the WTO Jurisprudence' (2007) 6(3) *Richmond Journal of Global Law & Business* 245, 258.

of these products reflects the interpretation of data given by scientists. Put differently, the fact that scientific data can be interpreted in different ways prevents the establishment of one objective truth.

Second, 'objective' might imply the need for panels to perform an *unbiased* assessment of the matter. However, deciding with an unbiased approach represents a tacit modus operandi of any decision-maker and, as such, it should not be considered a standard of review guiding panels' decisions. In contrast, a standard of review aims to provide decision-makers with substantial guidelines. Article 11 of the *DSU* does not provide any.

Thus, both possible interpretations of *objective assessment of the matter* show the unsuitability of this standard of review in guiding the judicial examination of biotechnology legal disputes. Therefore, Chapter 6 investigates the judicial application of the current standard of review under Article 11 of the *DSU* to the three biotechnology legal disputes to discuss its suitability to guide panels' analysis of scenarios involving scientific uncertainties brought by the international trade in biotech products.

The judicial allocation of the burden of proof to establish a prima facie case and the judicial application of the current standard of review – both discussed in Chapter 6 – represent preliminary issues that need to be explored before discussing the following two substantial hurdles for effective implementation of biosafety measures and the precautionary principle in the context of biotechnology under the WTO.

3. The third point of analysis regards *how WTO judicial bodies have assessed precautionary measures on biosafety in contexts in which they deemed that sufficient scientific evidence exists* and, accordingly, the contested measures had to comply with Article 5.1 of the *SPS Agreement* requiring member states to base their protective measures on a *risk assessment 'appropriate to the circumstances'*.[79]

In all three cases, the dispute settlement bodies interpreted the risk assessments as *not* appropriate to the circumstances and used this as a central reason for rejecting requests to implement biosafety measures. This raises the question: What makes a risk assessment *appropriate to the circumstances*? Exploring such a question is particularly interesting considering that a science-centric risk assessment aligning with WTO law may not be suitable in the context of biotechnology, in which there is still a high degree of scientific uncertainty on the effects of trading

79 *SPS Agreement* art 5.1. The term 'biosafety measures' does not match the broader term of protective measures referring to *all* measures to protect human health and/or the environment from *any* human activity. Instead, in line with the definition provided by the *Cartagena Protocol on Biosafety*, 'biosafety measures' refers only to measures adopted to protect human health and/or the environment from harm posed by the international trade in biotech products. See *Glossary of Terms*.

biotech products on biosafety. After all, evaluation of these products cannot, and should not, be reduced to a scientific matter.[80]

Therefore, Chapter 7 addresses this complex question through a thorough analysis of how WTO judicial bodies reviewed the appropriateness of risk assessments in the three biotechnology legal cases. In so doing, it examines, with particular attention, the role of science and scientific experts advising panels that discuss complex and scientifically uncertain circumstances, such as those surrounding biotechnology legal disputes. The analysis then provides potential suggestions about what *should* make a risk assessment *appropriate* to the scientifically uncertain circumstances of biotechnology, and who *should* be considered an *expert* in the current technology era.

4. The fourth and final point of analysis concerns *how WTO judicial bodies have assessed precautionary measures on biosafety in contexts in which states have argued that insufficient scientific evidence exists* regarding the harmfulness or harmlessness of trade in biotechnology. WTO judicial bodies were requested to assess the compliance of precautionary measures on biosafety with Article 5.7 of the *SPS Agreement*. Article 5.7 permits member states to adopt SPS measures in light of the precautionary principle, which is reflected in this provision, even in contexts in which there is insufficient scientific evidence.

Chapter 8 examines why precautionary measures in the sense of Article 5.7 have been rejected in all WTO biotechnology cases thus far. In approaching this investigation, it offers a *scale of legal evidence and scientific (un)certainties* that might guide WTO judicial bodies in setting the sufficient precautionary evidentiary threshold(s) to adopt protective measures in scientifically uncertain contexts.

5.6 Conclusion

This chapter shows that neither biosafety measures nor the precautionary principle has been operationalised in the WTO cases concerning international trade in biotech products. This implies that requests to enhance free trade in biotech products have always been fostered over requests to ensure biosafety. Arguably, this might be viewed as the result of an implicit prima facie pre-eminence of free trade, not only under the WTO normative framework but also in WTO jurisprudence.

The substantial discretion of panels in assessing legal disputes can only partially explain why biosafety measures were rejected in all three cases. Understanding the three biotechnology judgments requires an extensive discussion of four problematic aspects at the heart of each case: (1) the judicial allocation of the burden of proof to establish a prima facie case; (2) the standard of review applied by

80 Caroline E Foster, *Science and the Precautionary Principle in International Courts and Tribunals – Expert Evidence, Burden of Proof, and Finality* (Cambridge University Press, 2011) 177.

panels; (3) the judicial review of risk assessments supporting biosafety measures in contexts in which there is sufficient scientific evidence; and (4) the judicial review of precautionary management of uncertain risks that member states failed to establish in the three cases, despite their right to establish a precautionary ALOP and the possibility to invoke the precautionary principle in light of Article 5.7 of the *SPS Agreement*.

The first two issues are both developed in Chapter 6, while Chapter 7 addresses the judicial review of risk assessments. Chapter 8 explores the judicial examination of a precautionary management of risk. The final picture emerging from the case analysis indicates whether WTO judicial bodies achieved a balance between the competing requests in the context of biotechnology by design or, rather, by chance.

6 Allocation of the burden of proof to establish a prima facie case and standard of review to examine biotechnology matters

Preliminary issues in the WTO jurisprudence on biotechnology

6.1 Introduction

While the previous chapter identifies the four main issues emerging from the judicial reasoning in *EC – Hormones*, *US/Canada – Hormones Continued Suspension* and *EC – Biotech*, this chapter focuses on the discussion of the two preliminary issues relating to the judicial allocation of the burden of proof to establish a prima facie case and the panels' application of the standard of review to examine biotechnology cases.

In regard to the first issue, it must be observed that '[t]he [WTO] rules on the requirements for establishing a *prima facie* case are less developed than the allocation of the burden of the proof'.[1] This chapter contributes to filling this gap because it aims, in its first part, to critically examine the concept of prima facie case under the WTO, and at the same time it discusses the judicial allocation of the burden of proof to establish such a case and, more generally, to adopt biosafety measures in the context of biotechnology.

There are three main reasons for performing this investigation. First, WTO biotechnology cases highlight the judicial adoption of a 'disturbingly ambiguous and potentially misleading'[2] concept of prima facie case that, as such, deserves to be discussed and arguably refined, not least because it might prevent member states from commencing biotechnology legal disputes. Second, WTO judicial bodies adopt varying requirements for establishing a prima facie case without clarifying which one applies to biotechnology. Third, it is unclear who, in the view of WTO judicial bodies, bears the burden of proof to establish a prima facie case and, more generally, to adopt biosafety measures when scientific uncertainties remain. Casting light on this third aspect is, in turn, another necessary step to understand how effective adoption of biosafety measures can be achieved under the WTO.

1 Ho Cheol Kim, 'Burden of Proof and the Prima Facie Case: The Evolving History and Its Applications in the WTO Jurisprudence' (2007) 6(3) *Richmond Journal of Global Law & Business* 245, 258.

2 John J Barcelo III, 'Burden of Proof, Prima Facie Case and Presumption in WTO Dispute Settlement' (2009) 42(1) *Cornell International Law Journal* 23, 26.

DOI: 10.4324/9781003325741-9

Section 6.2 addresses these controversial aspects with the main purpose of discussing whether the judicial decisions relating to the establishment of a prima facie case and the allocation of the burden of proof allow or, on the contrary, hinder effective operationalisation of biosafety measures in the scientifically uncertain context of biotechnology. In doing so, Section 6.2.1 analyses the concept of prima facie case under the WTO and discusses the judicial requirements for establishing a prima facie case. Section 6.2.2 follows with a thorough examination of the judicial allocation of the burden of proof to establish a prima facie case and to adopt biosafety measures in the three biotechnology cases. Section 6.2.3 suggests how the judicial decisions on the establishment of a prima facie case and allocation of the burden of proof can be improved to fit the scientifically uncertain circumstances surrounding the international trade in biotechnology.

Section 6.3 discusses the other preliminary issue in WTO jurisprudence on biotechnology, which is the panels' adoption of the standard of review under Article 11 of the *DSU* to examine biotechnology matters. As Chapter 5 anticipates, the panels' adoption of an *objective assessment of the matter* as standard to examine biotechnology legal disputes might not ensure a proper judicial revision of biotechnology cases, especially because it does not provide substantial guidelines to panels examining the complex matters behind the biotechnology disputes.

Thus, the analysis in this second part of the chapter explores in detail the suitability of the standard of review under Article 11 of the *DSU* to examine biotechnology legal disputes. In doing so, Section 6.3.1 clarifies how Article 11 has become a general standard applied by panels to review various matters in the WTO agreements. This is particularly interesting considering that WTO law does not set any general standard of review. Section 6.3.2 critically discusses the suitability of an *objective assessment of the matter* to review the three biotechnology legal cases. Section 6.3.3 builds on the findings emerging from the previous two sections and suggests the judicial application of a new standard of review to examine biotechnology matters. Finally, Section 6.4 reflects on both the preliminary issues discussed in this chapter.

6.2 Prima facie case and allocation of the burden of proof in WTO jurisprudence on biotechnology

6.2.1 Establishing a prima facie case under the WTO

A prima facie case is described as 'one in which the evidence in favour of a party is sufficient to call from his opponent'.[3] Against this general understanding of a prima facie case, in *EC – Hormones* the AB explains the following:

> [A] prima facie case is one which, in the absence of *effective refutation* by the defending party, *requires* a panel, *as a matter of law*, to rule in favour of the complaining party presenting the *prima facie* case.[4]

3 LB Curzon, *A Dictionary of Law* (Macdonald & Evans, 2nd ed, 1983) 288. A prima facie case literally means *at first appearance*. It is also commonly defined in civil law systems as *fumus boni juris*, literally meaning *smoke of a good right*.

4 AB report, *EC – Hormones* [104] (emphasis added).

This language has been described as 'impossible to square'.[5] It is unclear if the focus of panels in verifying the existence of a prima facie case is an effective refutation by the defending party or, rather, the sufficiency of the complainant's evidence to establish a prima facie case. In the AB's words, a prima facie case 'seems to be a decisive case, one that is overwhelming and that will yield a claimant victory as a matter of law unless "effectively refuted" '.[6] The AB's explanation of a prima facie case seems to twist the main purpose of a prima facie case, which is aiding panels to understand if there is a sufficient and adequate (or appropriate) body of evidence 'to render reasonable a conclusion in favor of the [asserted] allegation'.[7]

Even more noteworthy, in the biotechnology cases neither the AB nor panels provide clear guidelines on what constitutes a sufficient and adequate body of evidence, how much evidence establishes a prima facie case, or how much evidence is needed for establishing an effective refutation. More generally, WTO jurisprudence provides only scattered indications on the establishment of a prima facie case. Specifically, WTO judicial decision makers have required different levels of evidence for establishing a prima facie case. Nevertheless, there are no clear guidelines on what circumstances require more or less demanding levels of evidence. For example, in 2002 *Canada – Dairy*, the AB claims that 'Member[s] must make out a prima facie case by presenting *sufficient evidence* to raise a presumption in favour of its claim'.[8] This raises the question of what constitutes sufficient evidence. The AB was silent on this matter. Nevertheless, in 2004 *US – Oil Country Tubular Goods Sunset Reviews*, it explains that the obligation to make a prima facie case 'may be satisfied in certain cases simply by submitting the text of the measure or, particularly where the text may be unclear, with *supporting materials*'.[9] Does this mean that 'sufficient evidence' equates 'supporting materials'? Again, the AB did not elucidate this aspect. Rather, in 2005 *US – Gambling*, it only remarks that a '*prima facie* case must be based on "evidence *and* legal argument" put forward by the complaining party in relation to each of the elements of the claim'.[10] While no one would disagree with that, it does not shed light on the aforementioned questions.

More interestingly, in 2007 *Chile – Price Band System*, the AB refers to an evidentiary requirement generally deemed as less demanding than sufficiency: It claims that both evidence and legal argument must be '*adequate*' to establish a prima facie case.[11] Although sufficiency is commonly considered more stringent than adequacy,[12] in the view of WTO judicial bodies, these concepts seem to

5 Barcelo III (n 2) 40.
6 Ibid.
7 Georg Nils Herlitz, 'The Meaning of the Term "Prima Facie" ' (1994) 55 *Louisiana Law Review* 391, 392, 395.
8 AB report, *Canada – Dairy* [66] (emphasis added).
9 AB report, *US – Oil Country Tubular Goods Sunset Reviews* [263] (emphasis added).
10 AB report, *US – Gambling* [138]–[140] (emphasis in original).
11 AB report, *Chile – Price Band System* (art 21.5 *Argentina*) [134]–[136] (emphasis added).
12 See, e.g., Trischa Mann and Audrey Blunden, *Australian Law Dictionary* (Oxford University Press, 2010).

Table 6.1 Summary of WTO judicial bodies' degrees of requirements concerning evidence to establish a prima facie case

	A prima facie case is established by . . .
The least demanding evidentiary level	*. . . submitting **evidence and legal argument** in relation to each of the elements of the claim* (the 2005 *US – Gambling* case)
The intermediate evidentiary level	*. . . submitting the text of the measure or, particularly where the text may be unclear, with **supporting materials*** (the 2004 *US – Oil Country Tubular Goods Sunset Reviews* case) *. . . submitting **adequate evidence** and legal argument in relation to each of the elements of the claim* (the 2007 *Chile–Price Band System* case)
The most demanding evidentiary level	*. . . presenting **sufficient evidence** to raise a presumption* (the 2002 *Canada – Dairy (Article 21.5 – New Zealand and US II* case)

match.[13] This is because in the view of panels and the AB, a body of scientific evidence is *sufficient* when it 'does . . . allow, in quantitative or qualitative terms, the performance of an *adequate* assessment of risks as required under Article 5.1 and as defined in Annex A to the SPS Agreement'.[14] Accordingly, pursuant to WTO judicial bodies, the *sufficiency of scientific evidence* can be inferred from the *adequacy of the assessment of risk* that, to be so, must comply with the scientific requirements of Article 5.1 and the definition of risk assessment under annex A of the *SPS Agreement*. These provisions provide strict and scientific requirements that, as Chapter 7 elucidates, reflect the dominant rule of science under the *SPS Agreement*, which is unsuitable for the scientifically uncertain nature of biotechnology matters.[15] Considering that, in identifying a need for refining the concept of prima facie case under the WTO, Section 6.2.3 anticipates what scientific evidence *should* be considered sufficient and adequate in the context of biotechnology.

To conclude, over the years the AB has referred to varying requirements for establishing a prima facie case, which Table 6.1 orders from the least to the most demanding.

The judicial adoption of varying degrees of evidentiary requirements raises the question of which one is appropriate to establish a prima facie case in the context of biotechnology: The most demanding? The least or, rather, an intermediate level? Arguably, there is no general answer to this question. This seems to be

13 AB report, *Japan – Apples* [179] (emphasis added); AB report, *Japan – Agricultural Products II* [73]–[74]). This explanation of 'sufficiency' is inferred from the AB's clarification of what can be defined 'insufficiency' in the context of art 5.7 of the *SPS Agreement*.

14 AB report, *Japan – Apples* [179] (emphasis added); AB report, *Japan – Agricultural Products II* [73]–[74].

15 Chapter 7 discusses art 5.1 and annex A of the *SPS Agreement* in detail.

confirmed by the AB in 1997 *US – Wool Shirts and Blouses*, in which it clarifies that how much and precisely what kind of evidence is required by panels to establish a prima facie case 'will necessarily vary from measure to measure, provision to provision and case to case'.[16] Moreover, panels are vested with 'ample and extensive discretionary authority to determine *when* it needs information to resolve a dispute and *what* information it needs'.[17] While it is reasonable that the type of information and evidence required can vary from case to case, the lack of boundaries to the panels' discretion is problematic, if only because the absence of clear rules in this regard might entail arbitrariness.

Further, in discussing the establishment of a prima facie case under the WTO, neither the AB nor panels mention that any discussion on biotechnology is ridden with *scientific uncertainty*. This raises the further question of whether judicial examinations take account of the impact that the uncertainties surrounding the international trade in biotechnology might have on an effective establishment of a prima facie case. As we saw earlier, regardless of whether the competing requests in the biotechnology cases are supported by a *sufficient* or *insufficient* body of evidence, *uncertainty* is a constant. As such, WTO judicial bodies should consider the central factor of uncertainty and, at the same time, perform a preliminary evaluation of whether there is sufficient or insufficient scientific evidence in the case at stake.

Before suggesting a more structured judicial approach to the judicial examination of a prima facie case in Section 6.2.3, the next section critically discusses the judicial allocation of the burden of proof to establish a prima facie case and, more generally, to adopt biosafety measures in the three biotechnology cases.

6.2.2 *Allocation of the burden of proof to establish a prima facie case and adopt biosafety measures*

A comparative analysis of the three biotechnology cases shows how the judicial allocation of the burden of proof to establish a prima facie case and justify biosafety measures under the WTO raises further concerns for the reasons discussed in this section. In 1998 *EC – Hormones*, the panel put the burden of proof on the European Communities (EC), which sought to apply biosafety measures.[18] The AB reversed it, not because in its view the adoption of European precautionary measure requires a reversed burden of proof, but simply because the general evidentiary rule requires parties that initiate proceedings (in this case, the United States and Canada) to prove what they allege (in this case a violation of the *SPS Agreement*).[19]

16 AB report, *US – Wool Shirts and Blouses* 323–325. This point is remarked upon in AB report, *US – Carbon Steel* [156]–[157]; AB report, *Japan – Apples* [159]; AB report, *Chile – Price Band System* [134]–[136].

17 AB report, *Canada – Aircraft* [192] (emphasis added).

18 AB report, *EC – Hormones* [99]. See also AB report, *US – Wool Shirts and Blouses* 14.

19 AB report, *EC – Hormones* [106].

By placing the burden of proof on the EC, the panel unfairly relieved the complainants of their ordinary obligation to present evidence to establish a prima facie case. This is because 'in WTO dispute settlement, as in most legal systems and international tribunals, the burden of proof rests on the party that asserts the affirmative of a claim or defence'.[20] In other words, as a general rule, the claimant is called to prove that the submitted legal dispute is worthy of judicial examination. This, in turn, means that the claimant is called to establish a prima facie case. In this respect, the AB, which seems to agree with that, reverses the panel's decision of allocating the burden of proof on the respondent (i.e., the EC) and argues:

> The initial burden lies on the complaining party, which must establish a *prima facie* case of inconsistency with a particular provision of the SPS Agreement on the part of the defending party, or more precisely, of its SPS measure or measures complained about. When that *prima facie* case is made, the burden of proof moves to the defending party, which must in turn counter or refute the claimed inconsistency.[21]

Besides remarking the general rule that the initial burden lies on the complainant(s), this reasoning does not add much. Nonetheless, it carries three important implications. First, in the AB's view this evidentiary rule applies 'in any adversarial proceedings',[22] and the judicial allocation of the burden of proof to establish a prima facie case does not distinguish cases with *sufficient* and *insufficient* scientific evidence. This distinction is, however, key. Indeed, in contexts with insufficient scientific evidence, it is unreasonable to allocate the burden to establish a prima facie case to a party that, otherwise, should prove the non-sufficiency of a body of evidence, which is hardly possible.

Second, by stating that this evidentiary rule applies in any adversarial proceedings, the AB overlooked a key distinction: Cases with *sufficient* and *adequate* (or appropriate) scientific evidence should not equate cases with *sufficient*, and possibly adequate, but *uncertain* scientific evidence. Instead, cases surrounded by scientific uncertainty, such as biotechnology ones, should be managed with specific evidentiary schemes, which would ideally consider that the lack of reliable empirical premises affects gathering sufficient, adequate and non-contradictory evidence to establish a prima facie case or, more generally, to adopt biosafety measures.

Third, the AB's final statement that '[w]hen [a] *prima facie* case is made, the burden of proof moves to the defending party'[23] can be misleading for future

20 AB report, *Chile – Price Band System* (art 21.5 *Argentina*) [134]–[136] (emphasis added).
21 AB report, *EC – Hormones* [98].
22 Ibid.
23 Ibid.

panels, which might require 'too much from a respondent'.[24] As Barcelo observes, 'the AB equates a claimant presenting a prima facie case with raising a rebuttable presumption in the claimant's favour'.[25] However, this seems to conflict with the reasoning given by the AB in *Canada – Dairy (Article 21.5 – New Zealand and US II)*, according to which, 'under the usual allocation of the burden of proof, a responding Member's measure will be treated as WTO-consistent, until sufficient evidence is presented to prove the contrary'.[26] Also, the presumption in the claimant's favour along with the lack of a precise indication of which burden of proof shifts (i.e., the burden of persuasion or the burden of production), might suggest that a responding party bears the burden of persuasion, rather than the burden of production. To remind us, the allocation of the burden of proof has two meanings.[27] The *burden of production* requires parties to present evidence to decision-makers to substantiate their arguments. Conversely, the *burden of persuasion*, as the term suggests, aims to 'persuade' the decision-maker that the allegations made are true. While the former moves back and forth between parties, the latter normally rests on the complaining party without shifting during the proceedings.[28] Nevertheless, the AB's reasoning in *EC – Hormones* might lead panels to claim that the burden of persuasion rests also on a responding party that in this case attempted to adopt biosafety measures.[29]

In this view, the judicial reasoning on the allocation of the burden might be a hurdle not only for the establishment of a prima facie case but, more generally, for effective adoption of biosafety measures – regardless of whether the party requiring the implementation of these measures is the respondent, as in *EC – Hormones*, or the claimant, as in *US/Canada – Hormones Continued Suspension*.

In *US/Canada – Hormones Continued Suspension*, the EC (the complainant) attempted to justify a provisional ban of meat and meat products from animals treated with five hormones[30] under Article 5.7 of the *SPS Agreement*, which allows WTO states to adopt safeguarding measures in contexts without sufficient

24 Barcelo III (n 2) 42.

25 Ibid 26.

26 AB report, *Canada – Dairy* [66].

27 See Section 4.4.2.

28 See especially Monika Ambrus, 'The Precautionary Principle and a Fair Allocation of the Burden of Proof in International Environmental Law' (2012) 21(3) *Review of European Community and International Environmental Law* 259.

29 This is, however, not the only potentially misleading statement of the AB that, in explaining the standard under art 11 *DSU*, asserted that 'the standard [of review applicable under the SPS Agreement] is . . . the "objective assessment of the *facts*"': *EC – Hormones* (n 4) [117] (emphasis added). To be precise, *DSU* art 11 refers to an *objective assessment of the* matter *before it, including an objective assessment of the facts of the case.* The AB's reference to 'facts' might suggest that panels are not called to review legal issues and scientific evidence in addition to the facts. This is because facts do not match with evidence.

30 The contested five hormones are testosterone, progesterone, trenbolone acetate, zeranol and MGA.

scientific evidence. Insufficiency of scientific evidence is, indeed, a requirement to adopt SPS measures under this provision. The panel established the following:

> Since, in that context, the European Communit[y] argues that the relevant scientific evidence is insufficient, we consider that it is for the European Community to identify the issues for which such evidence is insufficient.[31]

However, this is not precisely what the panel asked the EC to prove. Indeed, the EC identified the issues at stake. Nevertheless, the panel rejected the request for adopting biosafety measures as the EC did not prove the *insufficiency of scientific evidence* regarding the effects of the contested hormones.[32] However, how can a party prove the non-sufficiency of a body of evidence? Also, the fact that a party is required to prove the insufficiency of scientific evidence to justify the adoption of biosafety measures in light of Article 5.7 of the *SPS Agreement* is against the rationale of the precautionary principle, which finds reflection in this provision[33] and applies despite uncertain or insufficient scientific evidence.[34]

Similarly to *US/Canada – Hormones Continued Suspension*, the panel in *EC – Biotech* allocated the burden of proof on the complainants (i.e., the United States, Canada and Argentina) that in this case were the party challenging the implementation of precautionary measures triggered by the respondent. While the complainants were required to establish a prima facie case, the responding party (i.e., the EC) was required to prove that its biosafety measures 'were adopted in respect of situations where relevant scientific evidence was insufficient'.[35] Unsurprisingly, in commenting on the panel's decision in the 2006 *EC – Biotech* case, Poli observes that '[t]he burden of proof for a party hoping to rely on Art. 5(7) is very high; eventually, it could amount to a *probatio diabolica* that makes the right contained in Art. 5(7) not to base SPS measures on a completed risk assessment practically unavailable to the importing WTO Member'.[36]

The AB chooses to distance itself from the approach adopted by panels in *EC – Biotech* and *US/Canada – Hormones Continues Suspension* in relation to the allocation of the burden of proof to justify precautionary measures on biosafety.[37]

31 Panel report, *US/Canada – Hormones Continued Suspension* [7.652]; Panel report, *Canada – Continued Suspension* [7.629].

32 The panel established that the United States and Canada 'failed to rebut [the] presumption', thus, the EC failed to make a prima facie case. Panel report, *US/Canada – Hormones Continued Suspension* [7.269], [8.1].

33 See Section 4.3.1.1.

34 See Sections 4.2 and 4.4.

35 Panel report, *EC – Biotech* [7.2944].

36 Sara Poli, 'The EC's Implementation of the WTO Ruling in the Biotech Dispute' (2007) 32(5) *European Law Review* 705, 721.

37 In *EC – Hormones*, the party requesting the adoption of precautionary measures did not evoke art 5.7 of the *SPS Agreement.* This is, arguably, the reason we do not have any judicial reasoning on the need for member states to prove the *insufficiency* of scientific evidence that, as previously mentioned, is a requirement of this provision.

Indeed, in *US/Canada – Hormones Continued Suspension*, the AB describes the panel's approach as 'too inflexible'.[38] More specifically, the AB claims that the panel erred in allocating the burden of proof on the EC and, even more interestingly, it describes such allocation as 'a function of the following considerations':[39]

> First, what is the nature of the cause of action that is framed . . . Second, the practical question as to which party may be expected to be in a position to prove a particular issue. Third, consideration must be given to the requirements of procedural fairness.[40]

The AB's reference to 'the nature of the cause of action', 'practical questions' and 'procedural fairness' is noteworthy for at least two reasons. First, by considering the fact that *the nature of the cause of actions* in the context of biotechnology stems from a national need to ensure biosafety and the debate on *practical questions* surrounding the adverse effects of trading biotechnology to biosafety is still ridden with scientific uncertainty, the party requiring the adoption of precautionary measures would *not* bear a *probatio diabolica*.

Second, the importance of procedural fairness is particularly significant as the analysis of the precautionary principle in Chapter 4 shows that effective operationalisation of precaution in the context of biotechnology requires stakeholders to remember that the burden of proof originates from the idea of normative fairness or distributive justice.[41] Thus, the AB in *US/Canada – Hormones Continued Suspension* seems to take some steps towards a potentially feasible adoption of precautionary measures on biosafety. This is because the AB's acknowledgement that the onus must be allocated in light of, inter alia, practical questions and procedural fairness echoes – or at least does not prevent member states from – potentially successful implementations of the precautionary principle by means of procedural measures, such as reversing the burden of proof. At the same time, it prevents the allocation of a *probatio diabolica* on the party requesting the implementation of biosafety measures in contexts of insufficient scientific evidence.

Nevertheless, as already mentioned, the AB and panels do not specify whether, and if so how, the *uncertainties* surrounding the international trade in biotechnology affect the establishment of a prima facie case and, more generally, the adoption of biosafety measures in such a context. One might argue that cases of scientific uncertainty can fall under the scope of Article 5.7 of the *SPS Agreement*, which covers cases of insufficient scientific evidence. However, this assumption would be wrong because panels and the AB agreed that the concept of *insufficiency* of scientific evidence is not interchangeable

38 AB report, *US/Canada – Hormones Continued Suspension* [705].
39 Ibid [361].
40 Ibid.
41 Iain Scobbie, 'Tom Franck's Fairness' (2002) 13(4) *European Journal of International Law* 909, 910; Ambrus (n 28) 260.

with scientific uncertainty.[42] It is explained that the latter can be identified 'where reputable scientists agree that further research needs to be carried out on a particular question, or their disagreement on issues germane to a dispute makes it clear this is so'.[43] Instead, scientific evidence is considered insufficient if the body of available scientific evidence does not allow the performance of a quantitatively or qualitatively appropriate assessment of risk, meaning a risk assessment complying with the scientific requirements under Article 5.1 and the definition of risk assessment in annex A to the *SPS Agreement.*[44] Chapter 8 discusses the implications stemming from the rigid judicial distinction between *insufficient* and *uncertain* scientific evidence. For the present investigation, it is sufficient to keep in mind that panels and the AB overlook the remaining uncertainties in the context of biotechnology. This invites the argument that in the view of WTO judicial bodies, the presence of uncertainties in the context of biotechnology does not affect the establishment of a prima facie case or the allocation of the burden of proof to adopt biosafety measures in the context of biotechnology.

To conclude, in examining the establishment of a prima facie case, and in allocating the burden of proof to establish this case as well as to adopt biosafety measures in the context of biotechnology, WTO judicial bodies' approach is lacking on many levels. For example, the question of what to do if the empirical premises at stake are unreliable (i.e., in cases of sufficient but uncertain or insufficient scientific evidence) does not find an answer in WTO jurisprudence.[45]

This considered, Section 6.2.3 suggests how the judicial establishment of a prima facie case and allocation of the burden of proof can be improved to fit the scientifically uncertain circumstances surrounding the international trade in biotechnology.

6.2.3 Suggestions for improvements

In light of the findings identified, this section suggests the following two-step process for improving the judicial examination of the establishment of a prima facie case and relating allocation of the burden of proof in the context of biotechnology.

42 See, e.g., AB report, *Japan – Apples* (n 13) [184]; Panel report, *EC – Biotech* [7.1525].

43 Caroline E Foster, *Science and the Precautionary Principle in International Courts and Tribunals – Expert Evidence, Burden of Proof, and Finality* (Cambridge University Press, 2011) 11; Brian Wynne, 'Uncertainty and Environmental Learning – Reconceiving Science and Policy in the Preventive Paradigm' (1992) 2(2) *Global Environmental Change* 111–127.

44 AB report, *Korea – Radionuclides* [5.106]; AB report, *Japan – Apples* [179]. See also AB report, *Australia – Apples* [238]–[239]; AB report, *Canada – Continued Suspension* [677].

45 This is because WTO judicial bodies do not treat cases with sufficient, adequate and certain scientific evidence differently from circumstances of sufficient but uncertain or insufficient scientific evidence.

As the first step, ***WTO decision-makers should allocate the traditional burden of proof*** (which requires the party who initiates a legal dispute to prove what the party alleges) ***on the applicant***. This means that the responding party should not bear the onus to establish a prima facie case as in *EC – Hormones*.

As a general rule, the establishment of a prima facie case under the WTO requires the complainant, who carries the initial burden of production, to submit ***sufficient*** and ***adequate*** (or appropriate) evidence aiming at showing the panel either the inconsistency of the contested health and/or environmental measure with WTO law (as in *EC – Biotech*), or that trade sanctions imposed by other states (to protect health and/or the environment) are unjustified under the WTO (as, for example, the suspensions of concessions applied by the United States and Canada in *US/Canada – Hormones Continued Suspension*).

Defining what makes a body of evidence ***sufficient*** and ***appropriate*** becomes central. To remind us, the aforementioned analysis shows that in the view of panels and the AB, a body of scientific evidence is ***sufficient*** when the related assessment of risk is considered adequate. To be ***adequate*** (or appropriate), decision-makers must evaluate this assessment as complying with the scientific requirements of Article 5.1 and the definition of risk assessment under annex A of the *SPS Agreement*. However, because any discussion on biotechnology is ridden with scientific uncertainty, the judicial focus on scientific opinions does not accommodate the nature of this technology. In examining the judicial revision of risk assessments supporting the competing requests in the biotechnology cases, the analysis in the next chapter provides a thorough discussion of what *is* and what *should* make an assessment of risk ***appropriate*** to the context of biotechnology. For the purposes of the present investigation, it is sufficient to anticipate that facing scientifically uncertain circumstances, such as in the context of biotechnology, panels should assess the *sufficiency* of evidence in quantitative ***and*** qualitative terms by taking account of both majority and minority scientific opinions.[46] Also, panels should deem a body of evidence as ***adequate*** – or, as required by Article 5.1 of the *SPS Agreement*, ***appropriate to the circumstances*** – when it stems from conducting a ***risk assessment that considered scientific and holistic data***, such as physical and social impacts of biotechnology.

This considered, the appointed panel should then proceed to the second step: Assessing ***whether there is sufficient and adequate or, instead, insufficient scientific evidence to establish a prima facie case.*** In the first scenario, decision-makers establish that the case at stake is characterised by ***sufficient, adequate and certain (meaning non-antithetical) evidence***, which potentially allows the applicant to prove the submitted claim or presumption and, in turn, to successfully establish a prima facie case.

If WTO decision-makers evaluate the evidence submitted by the claimant as sufficient, adequate and non-contradictory to establish a fact or raise a presumption, then the burden of production shifts to the responding party, which

46 See Section 7.3.

is required to counter or refute the claimed inconsistency.[47] Importantly, the responding party is not asked to 'persuade' the fact-finder that the complainant's allegations are false. Indeed, the purpose of allocating the burden of proof is described by the AB as 'a claim to *be proven* by the complaining party, or as *a defence* to be established by the responding party'.[48] The responding party is not called to *prove*, but to substantiate a *defence*, not least because the burden of persuasion does not lie on it. Thus, the responding party should produce sufficient and adequate evidence in response to the complainant's statements. Finally, the panel will evaluate both the competing requests and relating evidence to rule its final decision establishing which one prevails.

If, on the contrary, WTO decision-makers evaluate the evidence supporting the claimant's request(s) as *not* sufficient and adequate to establish a fact or raise a presumption – in spite of the fact that sufficient and adequate evidence could have been found in the context of reference – the claimant will lose, and the legal dispute will not be discussed further.

In the second scenario, decision-makers establish that in the case at stake there is a *sufficient* (and arguably also adequate) *but uncertain* or, alternatively, *insufficient* body of scientific evidence. In either case, the empirical premises would be unreliable as they are characterised by uncertainty.

Facing these circumstances, we should progress from the discourse of establishing a prima facie case[49] to address the most pertinent question: *What alternative scheme should decision-makers consider when there is sufficient but uncertain or insufficient scientific evidence in the case at stake?* Put differently, how should decision-makers proceed when facing cases in which the empirical assumptions are unreliable?

The answer might lie in adopting the three factors that WTO decision-makers should take into account to enhance Alexy's theory of balancing and perform a well-structured proportionality analysis in the context of biotechnology, which are the precautionary principle, the *pro homine* principle and the reliability of evidence.[50]

In suggesting erring on the side of biosafety in the face of uncertainties, *the precautionary principle* is a valuable tool guiding decision-makers to address the unreliability of empirical premises stemming from the uncertainties surrounding the international trade in biotechnology. The adoption of this principle can, in fact, reduce the epistemic discretion of decision-makers,[51] as it does affect the standard of proof by lowering the evidentiary requirements; and it can reverse, in some circumstances, the burden of proof.[52] Accordingly, the judicial adop-

47 AB report, *EC – Hormones* [98].
48 AB report, *EC – Tariff Preferences* [98] (emphasis added).
49 This is because the discussion on the establishment of a prima facie case raises the issue of the sufficiency and adequacy of evidence, which is not part of this second scenario.
50 See Section 3.6.
51 See Section 3.6.3.
52 See Section 4.4.2.

tion of this legal tool would provide a solution to cases in which the presence of contradictory (as uncertain) scientific evidence undermines the reliability of the empirical premises at stake.

The suggested operationalisation of the precautionary principle to address the unreliability of empirical premises would be a coherent consequence of WTO judicial bodies' adoption of the *pro homine* principle. The WTO decision-makers' application of the *pro homine principle* to the context of biotechnology would lead decision-makers to ascribe a prima facie priority to the protection of human health from, in our case, risks posed by trading biotechnology. This would, in turn, suggest a possible judicial approach to the unreliability of empirical premises. Considering and enhancing the *reliability of evidence* represent a further means to address cases of unreliability of empirical assumptions, if only because submitting more reliable evidence entails less dubious rulings.[53]

To conclude, by taking the suggested steps, WTO decision-makers might reduce the possibilities of allocating an unfair onus to establish a prima facie case and to adopt biosafety measures in the context of biotechnology, in which the body of evidence supporting the requests at stake might be sufficient and adequate or insufficient but surely uncertain. The judicial consideration of the precautionary principle, the *pro homine* principle and the reliability of evidence can be valid means to address cases, such as the biotechnology ones, where there is unreliability of empirical premises. Therefore, the suggestions provided in this section allow overcoming, or at least mitigating, the discussed issues caused by the questionable judicial examination of the establishment of a prima facie case, and the allocation of the burden of proof to establish this case and to adopt biosafety measures.

The second part of this chapter turns to the following discussion of the other preliminary issue emerging from the biotechnology rulings, which is the panels' application of the standard of review under Article 11 of the *DSU* to examine the biotechnology legal disputes.

6.3 Standard of review to examine WTO biotechnology cases

In the three biotechnology cases, the appointed panels established that all biosafety measures were not in line with WTO law and, consequently, the requests for their adoption were rejected. This raises the question of whether the adopted standard of review, according to which panels must perform an 'objective assessment of the matter',[54] might affect a successful implementation of biosafety measures in the context of biotechnology.

This section discusses whether the standard of review under Article 11 of the *DSU* is appropriate to examine the complex and scientifically uncertain matters surrounding the international trade in biotechnology.

53 Section 3.6.2 offers a number of suggestions for enhancing the reliability of evidence.

54 *Dispute Settlement Understanding* art 11.

6.3.1 Standard of review and WTO law

As Bohanes and Lockhart explain, a standard of review can be described as 'the degree of deference or discretion that the court accords to legislator or regulator' or the 'degree of intrusiveness or invasiveness into the legislator's or regulator's decision-making process'.[55] Conventionally, a standard of review can range from a *de novo* to a *total deferential* standard. The former allows decision-makers 'to verify whether the determination by the national authority was "correct" both factually and procedurally'.[56] The latter restricts the judicial revision to procedural aspects. There are also less or more deferential standards between these two extremes.[57]

At this point, it is important to clarify that WTO law does not set any explicit standard of review to be adopted by panels.[58] Indeed, no WTO agreement indicates the standard that panels must apply in their contexts. The *Anti-Dumping Agreement* is the only exception because its Article 17.6(i) refers explicitly to a deferential standard:

> Under a 'deference' standard, a panel . . . should not seek to redo the investigation conducted by the national authority but instead examine whether the 'procedure' required by the relevant WTO rules had been followed.[59]

Facing the lack of indications of what standard of review should be applied by panels in the context of all the other WTO agreements, the AB in 1998 *EC – Hormones* attempts to fill this shortfall by clarifying that neither the *de novo* nor the *total deference* standards are applicable under the WTO.[60] Rather, panels must perform an *objective assessment of the matter*, as enshrined under Article 11 of the *DSU*, which must be considered the applicable standard of review in the context of the WTO agreements (except for the Anti-Dumping Agreement).[61]

Since then, the standard of review under Article 11 has become a point of reference for panels and it is considered 'a rule that elucidates the required level of scrutiny'.[62] Nevertheless, it has been observed that the different matters covered

55 Jan Bohanes and Nicolas Lockhart, 'Standard of Review in WTO Law' in Daniel Bethlehem et al. (eds), *The Oxford Handbook of International Trade Law* (Oxford University Press, 2009) 378, 379.

56 AB report, *EC – Hormones* [111].

57 Peter L Strauss, Todd D Rakoff and Cynthia R Farina, *Administrative Law: Cases and Comments* (Foundation Press, 2003) 902; Lukasz Gruszczynski, 'Standard of Review of Health and Environmental Regulations by WTO Panels' in G van Calster and D Prévost (eds), *Research Handbook on Environment, Health and the WTO* (Edward Elgar Publishing, 2013) 731, 733.

58 Gruszczynski (n 57) 734.

59 AB report, *EC – Hormones* [111].

60 Ibid [117].

61 Ibid.

62 Gruszczynski (n 57) 735.

by the WTO agreements might arguably require the adoption of different standards of review.[63] Even more noteworthy is that there is ground for questioning the appropriateness of the standard of review under Article 11 of the *DSU* to examine health and environment-related matters in trade contexts for the reasons discussed in the following section.

6.3.2 *(Un)suitability of the standard of review adopted by panels to examine biotechnology legal disputes*

The AB's indication for panels to consider an *objective assessment of the matter* as standard of review had a 'direct impact'[64] on the final rulings in *EC – Hormones, EC – Biotech* and *US/Canada – Hormones Continued Suspension*. The reasons are manifold.

First, *the definition* of the standard of review under Article 11 of the *DSU* is extremely vague. In stating that 'a panel should make an objective assessment of the matter before it, including an objective assessment of the facts of the case and the applicability of and conformity with the relevant covered assessment',[65] Article 11 of the *DSU does not elucidate what makes 'objective' an assessment of the matter.*

The AB attempts to fill this shortfall by pointing out that the 'deliberate disregard of, or refusal to consider evidence submitted to a panel' along with the 'wilful distortion or misrepresentation of [such] evidence' are incompatible with the carrying out of an *objective assessment of the matter*.[66] This is, however, a negative definition of the current standard of review that does not clarify what makes *objective* an assessment of the matter.[67]

Also, terms like 'deliberate' or 'wilful' highlight the AB's emphasis on *the good faith of the panel* that, accordingly, seems to be key to establish whether an *objective assessment of the matter* was performed. This emerged clearly in *EC – Hormones*, in which the EC claims that the panel 'wrongly interpreted' and 'manifestly distorted' key scientific statements issued by some experts appointed by the panel.[68] The AB acknowledges that the panel '[made a] mistake . . . in interpreting Dr Lucier's statement',[69] 'interpreted the view of Dr André' incorrectly'[70] and 'did not in fact represent the opinions of its experts accurately'.[71] Nev-

63 Ehlermann Claus-Dieter and Nicolas Lockhart, 'Standard of Review in WTO Law' (2004) 7(3) *Journal of International Economic Law* 491, 503–521; Gruszczynski (n 57) 736.

64 Gruszczynski (n 57) 731.

65 *Dispute Settlement Understanding* art 11.

66 AB report, *EC – Hormones* [133].

67 Moreover, in providing further details on *how* the panel had to proceed to assess the matter 'objectively', the AB asserted that '[t]he Panel cannot realistically refer to all statements made by the experts': Ibid [138]. This is an additional negative assertion that does not explain what the panel is required to refer to in practice.

68 Ibid [110].

69 Ibid [138].

70 Ibid [139].

71 Ibid [144].

ertheless, it argues that '"[d]isregard" and "distortion" and "misinterpretation" of the evidence . . . imply not simply an error of judgment in the appreciation of evidence but rather an egregious error that calls into question the good faith of a panel'.[72] It adds that the panel's mistakes '[do] not constitute a *deliberate* disregard of evidence or *gross* negligence amounting to bad faith'.[73] This means that what counts to establish whether an *objective assessment of the matter* was performed is that the panel did not misinterpret evidence *on purpose*.[74] From this perspective, the AB concludes that the panel in *EC – Hormones* conducted an objective assessment of facts, though 'it sometimes misinterpreted some of the evidence before it'.[75]

This AB's approach begs the question: How can the panel's purpose be established? By examining the intentions of the members of the panel? This is hardly possible. Further, the reference to the good faith of panels makes it difficult to prove the judicial performance of a *non-objective assessment of the matter*. In *EC – Hormones*, for instance, the EC could succeed in its claim that the panel's exclusion of some evidence was against law by demonstrating that the panel exceeded its discretion and, *as such*, made its findings with gross negligence amounting to bad faith.[76] Clearly, the onus allocated on states willing to demonstrate that the panel exceeded its discretion is incredibly demanding. Also, there is no reason to assume that WTO judicial bodies would favour the request of one state over those of another[77] – though there are theories challenging the impartiality of WTO judicial bodies as a result of their political (more so than legal) role that inevitably affects their decisions.[78]

Interestingly, in *US/Canada – Hormones Continued Suspension*, the AB establishes that the panel did not perform an *objective assessment of the matter*. It observes that the panel sought to determine 'what the correct scientific conclusions are'[79] and became, for such a reason, 'the jury on the correct science . . . by picking and choosing between conflicting and contradictory opinions of the experts in an arbitrary manner'.[80] The AB notes that this happened in 2006 *EC – Biotech*, in which the panel's review of scientific evidence was described as 'rather aggressive' and 'intrusive'.[81] This is because rather than establishing whether the EC reasonably supported its conclusion by relying on the submitted evidence,

72 Ibid [133].
73 Ibid [133] (emphasis in original).
74 Ibid [133].
75 Ibid [253](e).
76 By referring to [138] of its report in *EC – Hormones*, the Appellate Body mentioned this aspect in AB report, *Canada – Wheat Exports and Grain Imports* [186].
77 Andrew T Guzman, 'Determining the Appropriate Standard of Review in WTO Disputes' (2009) 42(1) *Cornell International Law Journal* 45.
78 Ibid.
79 AB report, *US/Canada – Hormones Continued Suspension* [585].
80 Ibid.
81 Gruszczynski (n 57) 739.

the panel 'adopted the role of final arbiter'[82] through an arbitrary disregard of evidence supporting the implementation of the European biosafety ban.

Considering this, the AB in *US/Canada – Hormones Continued Suspension* suggests the following three steps that panels should take to conduct an objective assessment of whether contested biosafety measures comply with WTO law:[83]

> [Step 1] *identifying* the scientific basis and evidence relied upon in the risk assessment;
> [Step 2] *verifying* that the scientific evidence comes from respected and qualified sources; and
> [Step 3] *determining* whether the reasoning articulated by the European Communities on the basis of the scientific evidence is objective and coherent.[84]

A substantive analysis of the panel's report shows, however, that the panel arguably took all these steps in *US/Canada – Hormones Continued Suspension*:

> Step 1: Six scientific experts were consulted by the panel 'in order to obtain a more complete picture both of mainstream scientific opinion and of any divergent views'.[85] As such, the panel *identified* the scientific basis and evidence relied upon in the risk assessment.
> Step 2: The panel appointed only highly qualified scientists. The AB indeed acknowledges that 'Drs. Boisseau and Boobis are qualified and knowledgeable – and thus experts'.[86] In other words, the panel *verified* that the scientific evidence came from respected and qualified sources.
> Step 3: By relying on scientific opinions issued by respected and qualified sources, the panel *determined* that the EC's SPS measure was not objective and coherent.

Considering that all steps outlined by the AB seem to be taken by the panel in this case, it is unclear why the AB concluded that an *objective assessment of the matter* was not performed in the sense of Article 11 of the *DSU*.

The AB's indications are, accordingly, insufficient, especially in relation to the panel's duty to verify that scientific evidence comes from respected and qualified sources (the second step). This suggestion ignored that 'respected and qualified sources' are not necessarily reliable, if a conflict of interest exists. The scientific opinions issued by Boisseau and Boobis are respected and qualified, but they are arguably not reliable because of their affiliation with the Joint

82 Ibid 739–740.

83 Specifically, in this case, the panel was required to establish the compliance of the *SPS* measures with art 5.1 of the *SPS Agreement*.

84 AB report, *US/Canada – Hormones Continued Suspension* [590].

85 Panel report, *US/Canada – Hormones Continued Suspension* [7.418].

86 AB report, *US/Canada – Hormones Continued Suspension* [459].

FAO/WHO Expert Committee on Food Additives (JECFA) – i.e., the very committee that drafted a report that served as evidence in this case and stands in conflict with some of the other evidence Boisseau and Boobis were asked to evaluate.[87]

Second, the *scope* of the standard under Article 11 of the *DSU* is *not sufficiently narrow* to steer panels' examination of matters brought to their attention. Put differently, the indication of performing an *objective assessment of the matter does not provide guidelines to panels:*

> [T]h[e] broad formulation [under Article 11 DSU] does not assist in defining an operable standard of review because any assessment of the facts, whether highly deferential, marginally deferential, or not deferential at all, can be 'objective'.[88]

Clearly, issuing objective decisions should be a tacit modus operandi of any decision-maker. Indeed, scholars observe that under the WTO, the reference to *objective* does not seem to concern a standard of review but rather a *guarantee* of due process rights, such as fairness, impartiality and neutrality of a panel in assessing the submitted evidence.[89] To some extent, this was also acknowledged by the AB, which in *EC – Hormones* claims:

> The duty to make an objective assessment of the facts is, among other things, an *obligation* to consider the evidence presented to a panel and to make factual findings on the basis of that evidence.[90]

This reading of the standard under Article 11 of the *DSU* as a guarantee of due process rights in the context of the WTO confirms its unsuitability in guiding panels' revision of biotechnology matters. Moreover, without any substantive indication about how to review the complexity surrounding the international trade in biotechnology, the performance of an improper judicial decision is plausible. After all, this is what happened, according to the EC, in *EC – Hormones* and, in the view of the AB in *US/Canada – Hormones Continued Suspension*, as discussed earlier.

87 Although international scientific standards would, arguably, considerably improve the coherence between scientific studies, the AB neither specifies which standards nor provides any concrete reference to their existence. AB report, See *US/Canada – Hormones Continued Suspension* [591]. Section 3.6.2 suggests normative improvements that can considerably reduce the likelihood that panels will select non-impartial experts whose consultation can jeopardise, as in this case, the fairness of proceedings.

88 Bohanes and Lockhart (n 55) 389.

89 Gruszczynski (n 57) 735; Matthias Oesch, 'Standards of Review in WTO Dispute Resolution' (2003) 6(3) *Journal of International Economic Law* 635, 638; Guzman (n 77) 50.

90 AB report, *EC – Hormones* [133] (emphasis added).

Third, the lack of substantive guidelines entails the *lack of indications of what degree of deference or discretion is accorded to WTO states.* This is a serious gap under the WTO, especially because, as the AB reminded us in *EC – Hormones*, panels have *a substantial margin of discretion* 'to decide which evidence it chooses to utilize in making findings'[91] and to determine 'the credibility and weight properly to be ascribed to (that is, the appreciation of) a given piece of evidence'.[92]

In light of this, a pertinent question might be the following: What are the limits to panels' discretion in reviewing biotechnology matters by means of the standard of review under Article 11 of the *DSU*? The AB missed the opportunity to clarify this key aspect in *EC – Hormones*.[93] Nevertheless, it is worth noting that in *Korea – Alcoholic Beverage*, the AB clarifies:

> A panel's discretion as trier of facts is not, of course, unlimited. That *discretion* is always *subject to*, and is circumscribed by, among other things, the panel's duty to render an *objective assessment of the matter* before it, [as discussed] [i]n *European Communities – Hormones*.[94]

In other words, as long as the judicial assessment of the matter is objective, panels can discretionally choose the evidence to adopt in making findings as well as determine credibility and weight to be ascribed to a given piece of evidence. This, in turn, means that panels' duty of conducting an *objective assessment of the matter* is seen as a limit to the panellists' discretion. This confirms that Article 11 of the *DSU* should guarantee due process rights, rather than being approached as a standard of review.

To conclude, in deciding upon biosafety requests, according to the AB, panels must conduct an *objective assessment of the matter* in the sense of Article 11 of the *DSU*. This means, as the AB explains, that panellists must not *disregard*, *distort* or *misinterpret* evidence *purposively*. As long as the assessment of the matter is objective, which arguably means *unbiased*, panels have a substantial margin of discretion in selecting evidence, making findings and determining the credibility and weight to ascribe to evidence. Consequently, it is hard to call panels out for having performed a *non-objective assessment of the matter*.

As scholars have observed, the standard under Article 11 of the *DSU* is ambiguous and unsuitable to examine environment and health-related disputes.[95]

91 Ibid [135].
92 Ibid [132].
93 Gruszczynski (n 57) 735.
94 AB report, *Korea – Alcoholic Beverages* [162] (emphasis added). See also AB report, *Canada – Wheat Exports and Grain Imports* [186].
95 Gruszczynski (n 57) 731; Wybe Th Douma, 'The WTO and Climate Change' in Daniel A. Farber and Marjan Peeters (eds), *Elgar Encyclopedia of Environmental Law* (Edward Elgar Publishing, 2015) 298, 302.

Indeed, it does not clarify what makes *objective* an assessment of the matter. Also, it neither provides substantial guidelines to panels nor indicates the degree of deference accorded to WTO states.

As broadly acknowledged, the standard of review can be described as 'one of the mechanisms attempting to strike an appropriate balance between the autonomy of WTO Members and the need for uniform and effective enforcement of WTO law'.[96] This means that the standard under Article 11 of the *DSU* would properly accomplish its function if its adoption would guide decision-makers to strike an appropriate balance between the autonomy of WTO members to adopt the invoked (precautionary) level of protection and the need for uniform and effective enforcement of WTO law.[97] However, the vague indication to perform an *objective assessment of the matter* does not seem to accomplish this fundamental function. Rather, it might aid to guarantee the due process rights under the WTO. An example of the unsuitability of the standard under Article 11 of the *DSU* to guide panels in striking such a balance is provided by the final ruling in *EC – Hormones*, where the EC 'was held to have breached the *SPS Agreement* notwithstanding that it was not shown that the ban had the effect of restricting international trade'.[98] This, according to Macmillan, is one of the most interesting aspects of this case.[99] We can infer that without adopting a standard of review guiding the judicial balance between trade and non-trade values, panels' decisions might result in a rejection of biosafety measures evaluated as 'really designed to protect its population from the risk of cancer',[100] not 'arbitrary, unjustifiable' or 'resulting in discrimination or a disguised restriction'.[101] In other words, final rulings *guided* by the standard under Article 11 of the *DSU* can unfairly deny the adoption of measures that aim at ensuring biosafety and, importantly, are proportional to the competing interest in trading biotechnology. This, in turn, means that the standard of performing an *objective assessment of the matter* does not support – or at least, it does not facilitate – the judicial performance of a well-structured proportionality analysis in the context of biotechnology.

In light of these findings, Section 6.3.3 suggests the judicial adoption of a 'multilevel deference' standard of review, which might provide sufficient guidelines to panels examining legal disputes on the international trade in biotechnology.

96 Bohanes and Lockhart (n 55) 381. After all, the AB acknowledges that '[t]he standard of review appropriately applicable . . . under the SPS Agreement, of course, must reflect the balance established in that Agreement between the jurisdictional competences conceded by Members to the WTO and the jurisdictional competences retained by the Members themselves': AB report, *EC – Hormones* [115].

97 This crucial function of a standard of review is also recognised by the AB in AB report, *EC – Hormones* [115].

98 Fiona Macmillan, *WTO and the Environment* (Sweet & Maxwell, 2001) 140.

99 Ibid.

100 AB report, *EC – Hormones* [245].

101 Ibid [246], [253](m).

6.3.3 Suggestions for improvements

As the previous two sections highlight, a suitable standard of review should be sophisticated enough to guide the judicial balance between trade rules and domestic policies on human health and/or environmental protection:

> On the one hand, it is important that trading rules be applied to all states in a consistent and even handed way. Doing so encourages trade and discourages the adoption of costly protectionist measures. On the other hand, the AB and panels must respect domestic preferences and priorities.[102]

This balance is particularly challenging considering that WTO judicial bodies must guarantee member states' right to autonomously set their own ALOP. 'In this case', Bohanes and Lockhart observe, 'the appropriateness of the level of health [and environmental] protection is completely removed from the ambit of review by a WTO panel'.[103] The standard of review under Article 11 of the *DSU* does not indicate, however, the degree of deference accorded to WTO states.

In light of this, the EC in *EC – Hormones* suggests the judicial application of the *de novo* or *total deference* standards.[104] The AB, however, clarifies that neither of these standards is a valid alternative to the *objective assessment of the matter* under Article 11 of the *DSU*. In regard to the *de novo* standard, it explains that panels explicitly rejected the idea of examining cases *ex novo*, meaning from a new perspective, since 'they are in any case poorly suited to engage in such review'.[105] It adds that the *total deference* standard under Article 17.6 of the *Anti-Dumping Agreement* cannot be considered a general standard to be applied by panels, not least because it 'could not ensure an "objective assessment" '.[106] This seems to imply that Article 17.6 of the *Anti-Dumping Agreement* is in tension with Article 11 of the *DSU*. There are, however, no reasons for assuming that a *total deference* standard would necessarily lack objectivity, which is confirmed by the following reasoning of the AB in *US – Hot Rolled*:

> Article 17.6(i) requires panels to make an 'assessment of the facts'. The language of this phrase reflects closely the obligation imposed on panels under Article 11 of the DSU to make an 'objective assessment of the facts' . . . [I]t is inconceivable that Article 17.6(i) should require anything other than

102 Guzman (n 77).

103 Bohanes and Lockhart (n 55) 380. *Dispute Settlement Understanding* art 3.2 establishes that 'the dispute settlement system of the WTO . . . serves to preserve the rights and obligations of Members'.

104 As Section 6.3.1 explains, the *de novo* standard allows panels to review factual and procedural aspects of the case while the *total deference* standard requires the judicial examination of only procedural aspects.

105 AB report, *EC – Hormones* (n 4) [117].

106 Ibid.

> that panels make an objective 'assessment of the facts of the matter'. In this respect, we see no 'conflict' between Article 17.6(i) of the Anti-Dumping Agreement and Article 11 of the DSU.[107]

Bringing this abstract discussion back to the question of what standard of review would guide panels in performing an appropriate examination of biotechnology legal disputes, there are at least two additional reasons for considering both the *total deference* and the *de novo* as not suitable standards for the examination of biotechnology matters. First, even if the deference to states would not hinder an *objective assessment of the matter*, '[s]electing an appropriate standard of review involves a balancing of the advantages of neutrality against those of state sovereignty'.[108] Accordingly, the standard of deference under Article 17.6 of the *Anti-Dumping Agreement* is not appropriate considering that total deference to states loses the advantage of neutrality. The *de novo* standard could guarantee neutrality to judgments. However, by reviewing factual, legal and procedural issues, WTO judicial bodies 'would greatly undermine the authority of states to determine their own policies, including in areas long thought to be under domestic control such as health policy, environmental regulation . . . standards'.[109] This is the reason why even the *de novo* standard does not represent a valid alternative to Article 11 of the *DSU*.

Therefore, none of the standards of review suggested by the EC can properly guide WTO judicial bodies in balancing trade obligations and domestic policies in the context of biotechnology.

At this point, one might wonder if it is possible to suggest the judicial application of a new standard of review that fits the context of the international trade of biotechnology. The answer is affirmative. Applying a new standard of review under the WTO is, indeed, feasible considering that WTO law does not set any general standard to be adopted by panels in examining legal matters in the context of the WTO agreements (except for the *Anti-Dumping Agreement*). This leaves room for decision-makers to apply a new standard of review. Also, the reason leading the AB to avoid stipulating positive, affirmative obligations of panels, in conducting an *objective assessment of the matter*, arguably lies in the fact that '[it] does not wish to set out a generic standard that might limit its flexibility to consider each case on its merits'.[110] After all, the AB 'has, in practice, significant flexibility in determining the appropriate standard of review'.[111] However, this flexibility leads to a high degree of unpredictability for WTO states. In view of all this, adopting a new standard of review is desirable to enhance transparency – considering the discussed unsuitability of Article 11 of the *DSU* – and it is feasible under the WTO.

107 AB report, *United States – Anti-Dumping Measures on Certain Hot-Rolled Steel Products from Japan*, WTO Doc WT/DS184/AB/R (24 July 2001) [55] ('*US – Hot Rolled Steel*').
108 Guzman (n 77).
109 Ibid.
110 Bohanes and Lockhart (n 55) 424.
111 Guzman (n 77).

The following analysis shows how a ***multilevel degree of deference*** standard of review might accomplish its function better than Article 11 of the *DSU*.[112] Adopting a ***partial deferential*** standard would, in fact, provide substantial guidelines to panels' examining the competing requests in the context of biotechnology. It suggests three steps of judicial review, which highlight different levels of deference to member states, as explained here.

The first step concerns the ***panel's review of national requests for establishing a precautionary risk management***. To remind us, the management of risk occurs at the national level.[113] As such, facing national concerns caused by potentially adverse impacts of trading biotechnology to human health and/or the environment, the panel should acknowledge the states' right to establish their own ALOP, which might be ***precautionary***:

> In these circumstances, the concept of standard of review describes the *absence* of any power to review and highlights the exclusive, non-reviewable competence of a governmental authority to take certain decisions.[114]

Accordingly, the lack of judicial interference implies total deference to states in this first step of review. After all, the panel in *EC – Hormones* acknowledged that member states are 'entitled under the SPS Agreement to take a precautionary approach . . . [even if the contested risks are highlighted by a small or minority] part of the available scientific evidence'.[115]

The second step regards the panel's review of risk assessments justifying – or, on the contrary, challenging – the adoption of biosafety measures in the context of the *SPS Agreement*. In light of Article 5.1 of the *SPS Agreement*, WTO states must ensure that their SPS measures, including biosafety measures, must be based on risk assessments 'appropriate to the circumstances of the risks to human, animal or plant life or health'.[116] In reviewing the appropriateness of risk assessments, the appointed panel should take account of two key aspects. First, the international trade in biotechnology lacks scientific certainty. This is an unchallenged circumstance to take account of in examining the matter. Second, a national risk assessment conducted in a scientifically uncertain field can hardly be ***appropriate***

112 The suggestion to adopt a multilevel degree of deference as standard of review is reminiscent of the so-called theory or test of 'calibrated proportionality', which is widely adopted by Australian courts. See Rosalind Dixon, 'Calibrated Proportionality' (2020) 48(1) *Federal Law Review* 92; Carlos Bernal, 'The Migration of Proportionality to Australia' (2020) 48(2) *Federal Law Review* 288; Caroline Henckels, 'Proportionality and the Separation of Powers in Constitutional Review: Examining the Role of Judicial Deference' (2017) 45 *Federal Law Review* 181; Dan Meagher, 'The Brennan Conception of the Implied Freedom: Theory, Proportionality and Deference' (2011) 30(1) *University of Queensland Law Journal* 119.

113 *SPS Agreement* art 2.1.

114 Bohanes and Lockhart (n 55) 380 (emphasis in original).

115 Panel report, *EC-Hormones* [4.27].

116 *SPS Agreement* art 5.1.

if it relies solely on scientific data. Rather, an appropriate assessment of risks also adopts holistic data, which take account of physical and social impacts of biotechnology.[117] Unsurprisingly, the European legislator has introduced the new Article 26-b to the Directive 2001/18/EC – disciplining the introduction of GMOs into the European market – relying on *Ganzheitliche Gesichtspunkte* (i.e., 'holistic factors'): '[H]olistic, trans-scientific aspects that bridge risk assessment and risk management, to justify [national] bans [to GMOs]'.[118]

As the analysis in the next chapter discusses in detail, the importance of conducting a holistic, and not only scientific, assessment of risks lies in the fact that the evaluation of biotechnology cannot be reduced to a scientific matter. In *EC – Hormones*, the scientific experts selected by the panel repeatedly emphasised that some questions raised by panellists '[were] not related to a scientific expertise' and, as such, could not be replied to by scientists.[119]

Considering that, in this second stage, the appointed panel should revise the appropriateness of risk assessment(s) in the context of biotechnology by bearing in mind the importance of encompassing both scientific and holistic data relating to the contested biotech products. But *what is* a panel specifically required to do to examine the appropriateness of risk assessment(s)? Considering that member states must base their biosafety measures on appropriate risk assessments in the sense of Article 5.1 of the *SPS Agreement*,[120] Christoforou points out that '[t]he task of the panel is to decide whether a contested measure is based on a[n appropriate] risk assessment, not whether the scientific theory upon which the conclusions of the risk assessment are based is scientifically correct and acceptable'.[121] In doing so, the panel provides 'a positive solution to the dispute' in the sense of Article 3.7 of the *DSU*.[122]

This means that the deference to member states is only partial. Panels are, in fact, called to review if member states base the contested biosafety measures on risk assessments adopting a scientific *and* a holistic approach to be assessed 'appropriate to the circumstances'[123] in the context of biotechnology. Moreover, panels should also examine whether the party claiming the safety of the contested biotech products and, accordingly, challenging the adoption of biosafety measures, supports its claim by carrying out risk assessments appropriate to the circumstances, meaning encompassing scientific and holistic data. This is,

117 See especially Apolline Roger, 'In the Public Interest? A Comparative Analysis of Norway and EU GMO Regulations' (2015) 24(3) *Review of European, Comparative and International Environmental Law* 264.

118 Miranda Geelhoed, 'Divided in Diversity: Reforming the EU's GMO Regime' (2016) 18 *Cambridge Yearbook of European Legal Studies* 20.

119 Panel report, *EC – Hormones* [6.189]–[6.203]–[6.234].

120 *SPS Agreement* art 5.1.

121 Theofanis Christoforou, 'Settlement of Science-Based Trade Disputes in the WTO: A Critical Review of the Developing Case Law in the Face of Scientific Uncertainty' (2000) 8(3) *New York University Environmental Law Journal* 622, 636.

122 Ibid; *Dispute Settlement Understanding* art 3.7.

123 *SPS Agreement* art 5.1.

however, not imposed by the *SPS Agreement*, as discussed in the next chapter, which casts light on *how* panels should proceed in reviewing the appropriateness of risk assessments.

The purpose of the third and final phase is to *review the proportionality of the contested biosafety measures* in relation to the competing request for trading biotechnology. In doing so, the appointed panel should review whether the contested biosafety measure:

1. complies with Article 2.2 of the *SPS Agreement*, which requires the application of biosafety measures 'only to the extent necessary' to reach their purpose. This allows to understand if there are alternative measures which are less trade restrictive but equally capable of keeping the ALOP established by the state involved while avoiding protectionism
2. is implemented without creating 'discrimination or a disguised restriction on international trade' or 'arbitrary or unjustifiable distinctions in the levels it considers to be appropriate in different situations' by pursuing Article 5.5 of the *SPS Agreement.*

In other words, the appointed panel should examine whether the biosafety measure at stake is *proportional* to the competing interest of enhancing free trade in biotechnology. This means that in this third stage, the panel should perform a well-structured proportionality analysis in light of the discussion in Chapter 3. There is no deference to member states in this third level of review.

To conclude, the standard of review is a mechanism guiding panels in balancing the autonomy of WTO states and the need for consistent and effective enforcement of WTO law.[124] The developed *multilevel degree of deference* standard of review, which Table 6.2 summarises, suits the scientifically uncertain nature of biotechnology, as it does not reduce the judicial review to an examination of scientific aspects surrounding biotechnology. Indeed, in applying the standard of review, the purpose of panels is neither a judgment on the scientific material nor a political opinion on national decisions to manage risk through a precautionary approach.

Even more noteworthy, its three levels of deference would guide panels in striking an appropriate balance between the autonomy of WTO states to establish a precautionary ALOP and the need for consistent and effective enforcement of WTO law. Obviously, WTO judicial bodies must address any review with an objective, in the meaning of *unbiased*, assessment of the matter, which should be conceived not as a standard of review, but rather as a tacit *modus operandi* of any decision-maker.

By following the proposed review process by means of the *multilevel degree of deference* standard of review, the WTO can avoid posing a threat to national

124 Bohanes and Lockhart (n 55) 381.

Table 6.2 *Multilevel degree of deference* as new standard of review to be applied by panels when examining biotechnology cases

WTO panels' steps of review	*What WTO panels should review*	*How WTO panels should review the matter*	*Level of deference to WTO states*
Step 1: *Risk Management*	The national right to adopt a precautionary approach when facing uncertain risks posed by the international trade in biotech products falls outside the scope of review of WTO Panels		Total deference to WTO states
Step 2: *Risk Assessment*	– Whether biosafety measures are 'based on' a national risk assessment considered 'appropriate to the circumstances' (art 5.1 of the *SPS Agreement*) and, as such, encompassing scientific *and* holistic data – Whether requests challenging the adoption of biosafety measures support the safety of biotech product(s) by means of a risk assessment encompassing scientific *and* holistic data	In the sense of Article 3.7 of the DSU requiring 'a positive solution to the dispute'	Partial deference to WTO states. Panels are not asked to judge if national data are scientifically acceptable
Step 3: *Proportionality of Biosafety Measures*	Whether biosafety measures are proportional to the competing interest of free trade, meaning that they are applied: – 'only to the extent necessary' to reach their purpose (art 2.2 of the *SPS Agreement*) – without creating 'discrimination or a disguised restriction on international trade' (art 5.5 of the *SPS Agreement*) – without creating 'arbitrary or unjustifiable distinctions in the levels it considers to be appropriate in different situations' (art 5.5 of the *SPS Agreement*)	By performing a well-structured proportionality analysis, which allows WTO panels to determine whether the contested measure is (1) suitable, (2) necessary, and (3) proportional to the competing interest of free trade	No deference to WTO States

sovereignty, and arguably even to biosafety that member states hardly can ensure in trade contexts.

6.4 Conclusion

This chapter emphasises a need for significant improvements in relation to both the allocation of the burden of proof to establish a prima facie case and the adoption of an *objective assessment* as standard of review to examine biotechnology cases. The analysis in the first part of this chapter shows an ambiguous judicial description of a prima facie case, which aims to aid panels in understanding if there is a sufficient and adequate (or appropriate) body of evidence to reach a conclusion in favour of the asserted allegation. The AB seems, however, to twist the main purpose of this case by considering the prima facie case as a decisive case. The analysis also shows the judicial adoption of several degrees of requirements concerning evidence to establish a prima facie case and the lack of indication of whether, and if so how, scientific uncertainties affect the establishment of this case. Additionally, it emerges that the judicial allocation of the burden of proof might be a hurdle not only for the establishment of a prima facie case but, more generally, for effective adoption of biosafety measures. The reasons, as discussed, are manifold, such as (1) the lack of a judicial distinction between the allocation of the burden of proof in cases of *sufficient* and *insufficient* scientific evidence; (2) cases with *sufficient* and *adequate* (or appropriate) scientific evidence should not equate cases of *sufficient*, and arguably adequate, but *uncertain* scientific evidence; (3) AB's deceptive statements that might lead future panels to impose a high demand on evidence or even a *probatio diabolica* on a respondent.

The analysis in the second part of this chapter on the judicial application of the standard of review to examine biotechnology cases uncovers further concerns. It underlines that facing the lack of a general standard established by WTO law, the AB in *EC – Hormones* suggests the consideration of an *objective assessment of the matter* as a standard of review to be applied by panels in all WTO agreements (except for the *Anti-Dumping Agreement*). Since then, panels have reviewed all WTO matters by means of Article 11 of the *DSU*. Nevertheless, this study shows that the application of an *objective assessment of the matter* as a standard of review does not suit the scientifically uncertain and complex nature of biotechnology cases. This standard, in fact, does not provide guidelines to panels that, consequently, examine the biotechnology cases by adopting their substantial discretion. This can be highly problematic, especially because the absence of clear rules in this regard might entail arbitrariness.

The lack of judicial attention towards remaining uncertainties and the lack of a different judicial approach between cases of sufficient and insufficient scientific evidence emerge as common findings from the discussion of both the preliminary issues discussed in this chapter. Consequently, the concept of prima facie case has been refined and a new standard of review has been suggested to guide panels in dealing with biotechnology cases, where the *quantitatively sufficient* but *qualitatively insufficient* body of *uncertain* scientific evidence on biotechnology makes unreliable the empirical premises in question.

The suggestions offered in this chapter highlight how WTO decision-makers might reduce the possibility of allocating an unfair onus to establish a prima facie case and to adopt biosafety measures in the context of biotechnology, in which the body of evidence supporting the requests at stake might be sufficient and adequate or insufficient but surely uncertain. Specifically, this study points out that the judicial consideration of the precautionary principle, the *pro homine* principle and the reliability of evidence can be valid means to address cases, such as the biotechnology ones, in which the unreliability of empirical premises can make difficult for member states to establish a prima facie case and for decision-makers to evaluate the establishment of this case.

Further, this chapter develops a *multilevel degree of deference* standard of review, which can provide substantial guidance to support a proper examination of the uncertain and complex biotechnology matters. Through its three main steps, the developed standard provides substantial indications about the deferential levels that panels should apply in revising biotechnology cases. This supports a proper balance between the autonomy of member states to adopt a precautionary ALOP and the need for consistent and effective enforcement of WTO law, which is the main function that a standard should accomplish. Moreover, this facilitates (or at least aligns with) the discussed judicial need to perform a well-structured proportionality analysis in the context of biotechnology. Indeed, the adoption of a suitable standard of review and the performance of a well-structured proportionality analysis both support a judicial balance by *design*, rather than by *chance*, meaning depending on the discretion of the appointed panel.

Therefore, future judicial adoptions of the revised model concerning the allocation of the burden of proof to establish a prima facie case and the new standard of review might represent important steps towards effective implementation of biosafety measures in light of the precautionary principle that, nonetheless, can still be strongly undermined by the two *substantial* issues in WTO jurisprudence on biotechnology, which are the judicial examination of biosafety measures and relating risk assessments in contexts of (quantitatively) sufficient scientific evidence and the judicial examination of biosafety measures in contexts of (qualitatively) insufficient scientific evidence. WTO biotechnology cases embody both these circumstances, which are, respectively, discussed in Chapters 7 and 8.

7 Adopting precautionary measures on biosafety in contexts of sufficient scientific evidence

7.1 Introduction

As general rule, WTO law requires member states to ensure that the implementation of biosafety measures does not impose arbitrary, discriminatory or unnecessary constraints on the competing interest in trading biotechnology.[1] Member states must also consider the specific requirements of the WTO agreements invoked to implement biosafety measures in trade contexts.

In all three biotechnology cases, one thorny question is whether the contested biosafety measures met the requirements of the *SPS Agreement*, which is, in fact, the main focus of the judicial analysis. Under the *SPS Agreement*, WTO states can apply biosafety measures if they meet the criteria of Articles 2.2 and 5.1 that, according to both panels and the AB, must be read in conjunction.[2] This means that biosafety measures must (1) rely on 'risk assessments *appropriate to the circumstances*',[3] (2) be based on '*scientific principles*',[4] and (3) 'not maintained without *sufficient* scientific evidence'.[5] If there is insufficient scientific evidence to support biosafety measures, WTO states may still be able to argue for provisional precautionary measures on biosafety under Article 5.7, which is discussed in Chapter 8. Interestingly, in the three biotechnology cases, the EC claims that biosafety measures, which aimed at implementing a precautionary approach to address the potentially adverse impacts of international trade in biotechnology, can be adopted in cases of sufficient as well as insufficient scientific evidence.

This chapter analyses how WTO judicial bodies have assessed precautionary measures on biosafety in contexts where they deemed that sufficient scientific

1 *GATT Agreement* chapeau, art XX; *SPS Agreement* art 2.3; *TBT Agreement* preamble. See Sections 2.4.1.1 and 2.4.1.2.

2 AB report, *EC – Hormones* [253-(n)].

3 *SPS Agreement* art 5.1 (emphasis added). These measures must also be in line with international standards or, alternatively, with specific requirements established under the *SPS Agreement*.

4 Ibid art 2.2 (emphasis added).

5 Ibid (emphasis added).

DOI: 10.4324/9781003325741-10

evidence exists. Chapter 8 does the same for instances in which states have argued that insufficient scientific evidence exists regarding the harmfulness or harmlessness of trade in biotechnology. The analysis emerging from both these chapters can then show whether, and if so how, WTO judicial bodies have performed a proportionality analysis between the competing requests for free trade in biotechnology and biosafety in both circumstances of sufficiency and insufficiency of scientific evidence. This investigation also casts light on the judicial interpretation and potential application of the precautionary principle, which the EC invoked in all three biotechnology cases.

In discussing the judicial examination of precautionary measures on biosafety in contexts of sufficient scientific evidence, this chapter develops two main arguments. First, it shows that the WTO law requirements of *sufficiency* of scientific evidence and *appropriateness* of risk assessments are unsuitable to fit the scientifically uncertain nature of biotechnology cases. Second, the way WTO judicial bodies interpreted these criteria narrows the scope of the related provisions (i.e., Articles 2.2 and 5.1) even further and, at the same time, underlines the judicial overlooking of the still-high degree of scientific uncertainties surrounding biotechnology. This, in turn, impairs effective implementation of precautionary measures on biosafety in the context of those biotechnology cases in which there is a sufficient body of evidence in quantitative terms but significant scientific uncertainty remains nonetheless.

As Chapter 1 highlights, the scientific literature includes numerous studies supporting both the safety and the harmfulness of biotechnology. As such, it can be the case that quantitatively sufficient evidence exists on both sides of the argument. Nevertheless, the evidence may be qualitatively insufficient to inform final legal decisions on the effects posed by the international trade of these products.[6] As such, this chapter analyses how WTO judicial bodies have examined precautionary measures on biosafety in contexts where sufficient, though uncertain, scientific evidence exists.

The chapter suggests how risk assessments should be conducted to be deemed as *appropriate* to the scientifically uncertain circumstances surrounding the international trade of biotechnology, and who should advise the panels on the reliability of opposing and uncertain risk assessments in the context of biotechnology.

The chapter develops as follows. Section 7.2 provides a critical analysis of the criteria that WTO law requires member states to meet to align biosafety measures with Articles 2.2 and 5.1 of the *SPS Agreement*. Section 7.3 discusses the judicial interpretation of these requirements in WTO jurisprudence on biotechnology. Building on the emerging findings, Section 7.4 underlines a need for improvements and, in so doing, offers suggestions that might allow effective adoption of precautionary measures on biosafety in contexts of sufficient but uncertain scientific evidence. Section 7.5 outlines final conclusions.

6 This is because antithetical scientific opinions make the empirical assumptions supporting the competing requests unreliable.

7.2 Appropriate risk assessment in the context of sufficient evidence: critical analysis of the criteria under Articles 2.2 and 5.1 of the *SPS Agreement*

The *SPS Agreement* 'reflects [the WTO] faith in science'.[7] Sanitary and phytosanitary measures, which include biosafety measures,[8] must be 'scientific[ally] justif[ied]',[9] especially if they are not based on international standards established by recognised international expert bodies.[10]

In line with this, Article 2.2 of the *SPS Agreement* requires member states to base their biosafety measures 'on *scientific principles*'[11] and 'not maintain [them] without *sufficient* scientific evidence'.[12]

7.2.1 'Scientific principles' under Article 2.2

As neither the *SPS Agreement* nor WTO judicial bodies have clarified the term *scientific principles*, Gruszczynski implies the following:

> The ordinary meaning of the word 'principle' denotes a general rule or law, which shows how a particular theory is put into practice. Thus, the requirement to base an SPS measure on scientific principles may be understood as requiring a certain *scientific quality* from both scientific evidence and risk assessment.[13]

From this perspective, biosafety measures applicable under the *SPS Agreement* should be based on qualitatively reliable scientific evidence and risk assessments. However, considering that WTO law does not elucidate this requirement, it might be wiser to interpret *scientific principles* as the result of the scientific ethos of the *SPS Agreement*, which requires member states to scientifically justify their biosafety measures. Regardless of the interpretation ascribed to this criterion of Article 2.2, the emphasis on science does not accommodate the nature of cases

7 Jacqueline Peel, *Science and Risk Regulation in International Law* (Cambridge, 2010) 171. See also Jacqueline Peel, 'A GMO by Any Other Name . . . Might Be an SPS Risk!: Implications of Expanding the Scope of the WTO Sanitary and Phytosanitary Measures Agreement' (2007) 17(5) *European Journal of International Law* 1009.

8 See *SPS* measures under *Glossary of Terms.*

9 *SPS Agreement* art 3.3.

10 The Codex Alimentarius (Codex), International Plant Protection Convention (IPPC) and World Organisation for Animal Health (OIE) are the relevant standard-setting bodies under the WTO.

11 *SPS Agreement* art 2.2 (emphasis added).

12 Ibid (emphasis added). In this respect, see especially, Alessandra Guida, 'Are WTO Decision-makers Regulating Technological Risks or Are Technological Risks Steering WTO Biotechnology Legal Decisions?' (2021) *Risk Analysis* 1, 4.

13 Lukasz Gruszczynski, 'Science in the Process of Risk Regulation under the WTO Agreement on Sanitary and Phytosanitary Measures' (2006) 7(4) *German Law Journal* 371 (emphasis added).

involving scientific uncertainty, such as biotechnology disputes. Indeed, requiring a scientific justification where scientific evidence is uncertain might be highly demanding for member states.

7.2.2 *'Sufficiency of scientific evidence' under Article 2.2*

The requirement of sufficient scientific evidence under Article 2.2 is arguably intended to prevent arbitrary or unjustifiably discriminatory implementation of biosafety measures. However, the lack of WTO law's explanation of what makes scientific evidence *sufficient* leaves us wondering whether Article 2.2 refers to sufficiency in both quantitative and qualitative terms and whether the precautionary measures invoked in all three biotechnology cases are permitted in such contexts.

Remarkably, in *EC – Hormones* the AB acknowledges that a panel that is required to determine whether sufficient scientific evidence occurs, 'may, of course and should, bear in mind that responsible, representative governments commonly act from the perspective of prudence and precaution where risks are irreversible'.[14] This means, as Gruszczynski notes, that 'the AB implanted into the concept of sufficiency a certain *margin of precaution* . . . (at least in all cases in which risk is irreversible)'.[15] In *US/Canada – Hormones Continued Suspension*, the AB goes even further by stating that *the chosen ALOP*, that in this case is precautionary, *is not disconnected from* 'the determination of whether scientific evidence is sufficient to assess the existence and magnitude of a risk',[16] even though the '[t]he determination as to whether available scientific evidence is sufficient to perform a risk assessment must remain, in essence, a rigorous and objective process'.[17]

The analysis in Section 7.3 casts light on whether WTO judicial bodies' evaluation of biosafety measures aiming at preventing potentially irreversible risks to human health and/or the environment, considers the relation between sufficiency of scientific evidence and precaution.

Further, in *Japan – Apples*, and previously in *Japan – Agricultural Products II*, the AB clarifies that a body of scientific evidence is *sufficient* in the sense of Article 2.2 when it 'does . . . allow, in quantitative or qualitative terms, the performance of an *adequate assessment of risks* as required under Article 5.1 and as defined in Annex A of the *SPS Agreement*'.[18] This means that scientific evidence under Article 2.2 can be evaluated as sufficient in quantitative *or* qualitative terms, arguably depending on the circumstances of each case. Also, it emerges that the evaluation of sufficient scientific evidence is inferred from the fact that adequate risk

14 AB report, *EC – Hormones* [124].
15 Gruszczynski (n 13) 375 (emphasis added).
16 AB report, *US/Canada – Hormones Continued Suspension*.
17 AB report, *US/Canada – Hormones Continued Suspension* [686].
18 AB report, *Japan – Apple* [179] (emphasis added); AB report, *Japan – Agricultural Products II* [73]–[74]. This explanation of 'sufficiency' is inferred from the AB's clarification of what can be defined 'insufficiency' in the context of art 5.7 of the *SPS Agreement*.

assessments cannot be performed without sufficient scientific evidence.[19] In other words, *if* a risk assessment is considered ***adequate*** in the sense of Article 5.1, which requires member states to base biosafety measures on risk assessments 'appropriate to the circumstances',[20] and annex A(4), which provides a definition of risk assessment,[21] ***then*** the scientific evidence at stake will be sufficient.

At this point, it must be investigated what defines a risk assessment as adequate or appropriate in the sense of Article 5.1 and annex A(4).

7.2.3 'Appropriateness of risk assessments' in the sense of Article 5.1 and Annex A(4)

The *SPS Agreement* remains silent also in defining ***appropriateness*** of risk assessment under Article 5.1. In line with WTO law, the panel in *EC – Biotech* was 'not convinced that we should attach much significance to . . . the term "adequate" [or 'appropriate', as it] may have been intended as nothing more than a reference to the definition [of risk assessment] in Annex A(4)',[22] according to which:

> The evaluation of the ***likelihood*** of entry, establishment or spread of a pest or disease within the territory of an importing Member according to the sanitary or phytosanitary measures which might be applied, and of the associated potential biological and economic consequences [pest and disease risk], or
>
> (ii) the evaluation of the ***potential*** for adverse effects on human or animal health arising from the presence of additives, contaminants, toxins or disease-causing organisms in food, beverages or feedstuffs [food-borne risks].[23]

In defining risk assessment, the annex adopts different levels of likelihood: National assessments of risk must show the 'likelihood' of risk (i.e., probability)[24] in case of pest and disease and the 'potential' of risk (i.e., possibility)[25] in cases of food-borne risks.[26] However, it has been noted that '[a]s both types of risk may relate to the life and health of humans and animals, it seems that there are no compelling reasons for differentiating between those two situations'.[27]

19 We can assume that the term 'adequate' adopted by the AB is an alternative way to explain the 'appropriateness' of risk assessment required by art 5.1 of the *SPS Agreement*, which requires member states to conduct 'risk assessment as appropriate to the circumstances'.
20 *SPS Agreement* art 5.1.
21 Ibid annex A(4).
22 Panel report, *EC – Biotech* [7.3235].
23 *SPS Agreement* annex A(4).
24 Gruszczynski (n 13) 381–382. In *Australia – Salmon*, the AB equated likelihood with probability.
25 Ibid 382. In AB report, *EC – Hormones*, the AB claims that the ordinary meaning of 'potential' refers to 'possibility' [184].
26 Gruszczynski (n 13) 381.
27 Ibid 382.

Further, Article 5.1 also is not a model of clarity. This provision specifies that member states willing to implement biosafety measures must perform appropriate risk assessments justifying the adoption of such measures. There is, however, no mention of how the party challenging the employment of these measures should perform the assessment of the biotechnology risks at stake. This is highly controversial. There is, in fact, no reason for exempting the party supporting the safety of the contested biotech product(s) from carrying out a risk assessment *appropriate to the circumstances* in the sense of Article 5.1. Accordingly, the requirement of performing appropriate risk assessments under Article 5.1 seems to echo the implicit prima facie pre-eminence of free trade under the WTO.[28]

Naturally, this lack of guidance about the definition of appropriateness of risk assessments might be interpreted as a serious gap under the WTO normative framework. Alternatively, it might be seen as a means to 'provid[e] *some flexibility for Members*'.[29] This second interpretation is not unreasonable considering that it aligns with the judicial acknowledgement that facts of real cases can be more or less appropriate to the circumstances:

> WTO rules are not so rigid or so inflexible as not to leave room for reasoned judgements in confronting the endless and ever-changing ebb and flow of real facts in real cases in the real world.[30]

In the view of WTO judicial bodies, the appropriateness of risk assessment can, in fact, change according to the *flow of the facts* of the case and *the time* in which it has been conducted.[31] Also, appropriate risk assessments can be shaped by adopting the *view of the majority* or even *divergent and minority* of the relevant scientific community,[32] 'especially where the risk involved is life-threatening in character and is perceived to constitute a clear and imminent threat to public health and safety',[33] such as in the biotechnology cases.[34] In line with this flexibility arguably granted by WTO law to member states to perform risk assessments appropriate to the circumstances, Button observes:

> [T]he Appellate Body has been careful not to tie the SPS system to any particular model of risk assessment. Rather, the Appellate Body has been

28 See Section 2.5.

29 Panel report, *US – Animals* [7.323] (emphasis added); AB report, *EC – Hormones* [129]; Panel report, *Australia – Salmon* [8.57]; AB report, *Australia – Salmon* [130]; AB report, *US/Canada – Hormones Continued Suspension* [562]; AB report, *Australia – Apples* [237], [244].

30 AB report, *Japan – Alcoholic Beverages II* 34. This was recalled by the panel in Panel report, *US – Animals* [7.342].

31 Panel report, *EC – Biotech* [7.3031]. See also AB report, *Australia – Apples* [7.323].

32 AB report, *EC – Hormones* [194]; AB report, *US/Canada – Hormones Continued Suspension* [529], [535]. See also AB report, *Canada – Continued Suspension* [677].

33 AB report, *EC – Hormones* [194]. See also AB report, *Canada – Continued Suspension* [677].

34 This aspect was recalled in AB report, *Korea – Radionuclides* [5.106].

> concerned to stress that *its main focus* will be to see that *governments are responding to real, identified* and *evaluated risks* and are not engaging in knee-jerk reactions to purely hypothetical risks'.[35]

Section 7.3 shows whether panels and the AB adopted a 'flexible' approach to the interpretation of Article 5.1 in the biotechnology cases.

Although no specific model of appropriate risk assessment emerges from the WTO jurisprudence, from the judicial explanation of sufficient scientific evidence in the sense of Article 2.2 it is possible to infer that a *risk assessment might be adequate if it encompasses quantitatively or qualitatively sufficient scientific evidence.* However, this is not true in the context of biotechnology, where *quantitatively* sufficient scientific evidence on the effects of biotechnology does not necessarily shape risk assessments 'appropriate to the circumstances' in question. The uncertainties surrounding biotechnology make the *quality* and reliability of scientific evidence key factors to be considered in assessing biotechnology risks.

Further, a cross-analysis of a number of WTO rulings reveals that appropriate risk assessments show the existence of a *rational or objective relationship* between the biosafety measures at stake and available scientific evidence[36] that must be *determined on a case-by-case basis.*[37] Nevertheless, in the AB's view, a '"clear *disproportion*" generally implies that a "rational or objective relationship" does not exist between the measure and the relevant scientific evidence'.[38] In other words, 'examining the rationality of the relationship *involves a kind of proportionality test*'.[39] After all, designing biosafety measures that are proportional to the interest in free trade is a general WTO rule applying to all protective measures.[40] In light of this, Section 7.3 shows whether the judicial case-by-case examination of appropriateness of risk assessments is performed through proportionality.

To conclude, this section elucidates the requirements of Article 2.2 (i.e., biosafety measures must be based on scientific principles and cannot be maintained without sufficient evidence) and Article 5.1 (i.e., biosafety measures must be based on an appropriate risk assessment). As Figure 7.1 illustrates, these two provisions must be read in conjunction because they inform each other.[41]

35 Catherine Button, *The Power to Protect: Trade, Health and Uncertainty in the WTO* (Hart Publishing, 2004) 66 (emphasis added).

36 AB report, *Japan – Apples* [162]. See also Panel report, *Japan – Apples* [8.103], [8.180], [8.198]; AB report, *Japan – Agricultural Products II* [84].

37 AB report, *Japan – Agricultural Products II* [84]; Panel report, *Japan – Apples* [8.103].

38 AB report, *Japan – Apples* [163] (emphasis added).

39 Gruszczynski (n 13) 375 (emphasis added). This should not be surprising if it is considered that, as the 2017 report of the Thematic Session of the TBT Committee on 'Risk Assessment' underlines, the principle of proportionality and the precautionary principle are 'risk assessment features in the EU's regulatory process': Moderator's Report, *Thematic Session of the WTO TBT Committee on Risk Assessment*, WTO Doc G/TBT/GEN/226 (19 June 2017) [1] (emphasis added).

40 See *GATT Agreement* chapeau, art XX; *SPS Agreement* art 2.3; *TBT Agreement* preamble.

41 AB report, *EC – Hormones* [253](n).

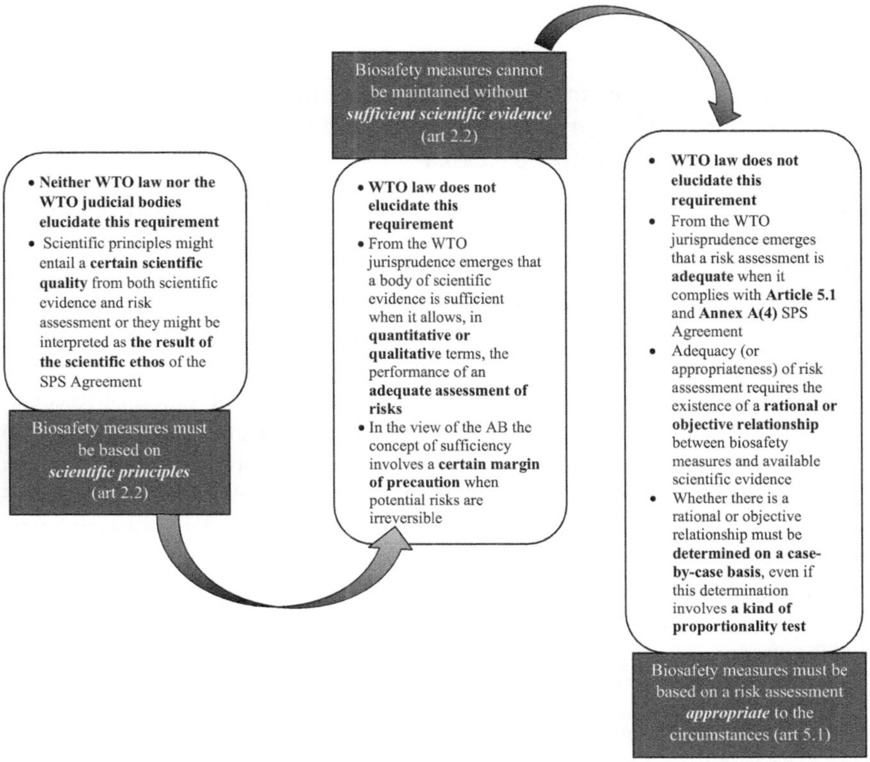

Figure 7.1 Scientific principles, sufficient scientific evidence and appropriateness of risk assessments under WTO law

From the joint analysis of the requirements of Articles 2.2 and 5.1, two main findings emerge. First, WTO law does not elucidate what *scientific principles* are, what scientific evidence can be considered *sufficient*, and what makes a risk assessment *appropriate to the circumstances*. This might be seen as either a significant gap under the WTO normative framework or as a way to provide member states with greater flexibility in performing appropriate risk assessments. Second, the evident scientific ethos of the *SPS Agreement* along with the judicial explanation of Articles 2.2 and 5.1 highlight that the requirements of these two provisions do not necessarily suit the scientifically uncertain nature of biotechnology.

Bearing these outcomes in mind, Section 7.3 discusses the judicial interpretation of the requirements of Articles 2.2 and 5.1 in WTO biotechnology cases, in which WTO judicial bodies were called to evaluate the appropriateness of risk assessments in the context of sufficient evidence. In doing so, it sheds light on whether WTO judicial bodies provide member states with flexibility in performing their risk assessments. It also shows whether the scientific ethos of the *SPS Agreement* hinders effective implementation of biosafety measures in contexts with sufficient, though uncertain, scientific evidence surrounding the international trade in biotechnology.

7.3 Judicial interpretation of sufficiency of scientific evidence and appropriateness of risk assessment in WTO biotechnology cases

In all three biotechnology cases, the EC claims that the submitted risk assessments complied with Article 5.1 and, accordingly, Article 2.2 and annex A(4) of the *SPS Agreement*. In discussing the WTO judicial bodies' decisions on such compliance, this section aims at showing four controversial aspects of the judicial reasoning. First, the strict judicial interpretation of appropriateness of risk assessments and sufficiency of scientific evidence do not fit the uncertain nature of biotech disputes. Second, panels adopt a quantitative interpretation of risks and scientific evidence at stake. This is despite the fact that a qualitative approach to risks and evidence is key to enhancing the reliability of empirical premises, which is affected by the still-high level of uncertainty. Third, panels arbitrarily select evidence. In other words, they rely on evidence by some experts without saying why they dismiss the evidence by other experts. Fourth, the dominant scientific ethos under the *SPS Agreement* seems to lead WTO judicial bodies to not accomplish their role as gatekeeper. Each of these points is respectively developed in the following three sections.

7.3.1 Judicial interpretations of appropriateness of risk assessments and sufficiency of scientific evidence do not fit the uncertain nature of biotech disputes

Facing the lack of specific indications under the *SPS Agreement* about the meaning and scope of Articles 2.2 and 5.1 and annex A(4), WTO judicial bodies adopt a quite demanding interpretation of risk assessments and scientific evidence supporting biosafety requests in the three biotechnology cases.

This clearly emerged in *EC – Hormones*, in which the panel acknowledged that the EC 'had demonstrated the existence of a risk assessment carried out in accordance with Article 5 of the SPS Agreement'.[42] Nevertheless, according to the panel, all examined scientific reports showed that the use of hormones for growth-promotion purposes is safe if good practice is followed.[43] The AB upholds this finding and underlines that the scientific material adopted by the EC to support its ban was relevant but *not sufficiently specific* to the case at hand.[44] It adds that Article 5.1 of the *SPS Agreement* requires member states to *sufficiently*

42 AB report, *EC – Hormones* [196].

43 Ibid. The panel report also stressed that there was 'no discernible health risk in the use of the [contested products]': Panel report, *EC – Hormones* [4.36].

44 AB report, *EC – Hormones* [200].

support or *reasonably warrant* their measures. Consequently, the EC's ban was inconsistent with this provision.[45]

Similarly, the panel in *EC – Biotech* recalled the AB's reasoning in *EC – Hormones* and claimed that the risk assessments must *sufficiently warrant* or *reasonably support* the biosafety measure at issue.[46] It also adds that the risk assessments supporting the biosafety measures at stake were not appropriate in the sense of Article 5.1 because they did not comply with the definition of risk assessment under annex A(4).

These judicial interpretations of risk assessment and sufficiency of scientific evidence appear quite rigid. As Cheyne observes, 'the Panel was overly strict in its interpretation of what constituted a risk assessment and particularly when dealing with scientific evidence and opinion which questions or throws doubts on the findings of previous risk assessments'.[47] Further, as Franken and Burchardi add, panels do not provide any guidance on the minimum requirements for performing a risk assessment in the sense of annex A(4).[48]

In *EC – Hormones* and *EC – Biotech*, the required level of sufficiency to be shown in the assessments of risk complying with Article 5.1 arguably refers to Article 2.2, according to which WTO states cannot maintain biosafety measures without *sufficient* scientific evidence[49] – except as provided for in paragraph 7 of Article 5. Within the context of biotechnology, where scientific uncertainties carry numerous doubts on the reliability of evidence at stake, it is reasonable to state that the sufficiency of evidence should be assessed in quantitative *and* qualitative terms by taking account of both majority and minority scientific opinions.[50] Nevertheless, WTO judicial bodies seem to focus only on the quantity of studies on biotechnology. The fact that the numerous uncertainties in the context of biotechnology affect the sufficiency of evidence in qualitative terms is ignored. This is proven by the judicial request for specialised risk assessments adopting sufficiently specific scientific material: These assessments of risk can hardly be conducted considering the still-high degree of scientific uncertainty on the effects of biotechnology.

In this view, WTO judicial bodies seem to underestimate the importance of providing guidance to address cases characterised by scientific uncertainties. For instance, in *Australia – Apples*, the AB claims that '[a] degree of scientific uncertainty does not justify a departure from the requirements of Articles 5.1 and 5.2'.[51]

45 Ibid [208].

46 Panel report, *EC – Biotech* [7.3028].

47 Ilona Cheyne, 'Life after the Biotech Products Dispute' (2008) *Environmental Law Review* 52, 63.

48 Lorenz Franken and Jan-Erik Burchardi, 'Beyond Biosafety – An Analysis of the EC – Biotech Panel Report' (2007) 62(1) *Aussenwirtschaft* 77.

49 Art 5.1 must be read in conjunction with art 2.2. In *EC – Hormones*, the ruled inconsistency of the European ban with art 5.1 makes useless, according to WTO judicial bodies, any further discussion on its consistency with art 2.2 of the *SPS Agreement*.

50 See the analysis in Section 7.4.

51 AB report, *Australia – Apples* [244].

In *EC – Hormones*, it specifies that 'the uncertainty that theoretically always remains since science can *never* provide *absolute* certainty that a given substance will not *ever* have adverse health effects . . . is not the kind of risk which, under Article 5.1, is to be assessed'.[52] This statement is partially inaccurate and lacking. Although risks necessarily entail uncertainty, it should be observed that uncertainty is not 'a kind of risk'. Rather, in Wynne's view, *risk* represents a 'kind of uncertainty'.[53] Also, the indication of the level of uncertainty that WTO states should consider in conducting their assessment of risk is missing. Accordingly, what degree of uncertainty enables WTO states to adopt biosafety measures is blurry at best.

In this view, the judicial interpretation of the requirements under Articles 2.2 and 5.1 in *EC – Hormones* and *EC – Biotech* does not accommodate the scientifically uncertain nature of biotechnology. As Neugebauer underlines, this judicial approach 'may entail more stringent requirements than those textually supported by the SPS Agreement'.[54] Similarly, Cheyne emphasises that the '[panel's] approach to evidence that is used to cast doubt on the validity of a previous risk assessment is rather harsh'.[55]

The panel in *EC – Biotech* 'seems to have inadvertently opened', according to Prévost, 'a Pandora's Box of negative consequences for the balance between trade and health'.[56] Evidence of this can be found in the fact that in *US/Canada – Hormones Continues Suspension*, the panel adopted, according to the AB, 'the same "restrictive notion of risk assessment" that the Appellate Body found to be erroneous in *EC – Hormones*'.[57]

Importantly, the AB's approach to risk assessment does not actually seem to be less rigid than the one adopted by the panel. The AB describes, in fact, the performance of an appropriate risk assessment as 'a rigorous investigative and fact-finding process'[58] that must compulsorily precede any panel's review of SPS measures.[59] 'With this focus on detailed and context-specific risk assessments', Button notes,

52 AB report, *EC – Hormones* [186] (emphasis in original).

53 According to Wynne, there are four kinds of uncertainty, which are *risk*, *uncertainty*, *ignorance* and *indeterminacy*. See Brian Wynne, 'Uncertainty and Environmental Learning – Reconceiving Science and Policy in the Preventive Paradigm' (1992) 2(2) *Global Environmental Change* 111, 114. See also Andy Stirling, 'Science, Precaution, and the Politics of Technological Risk: Converging Implications in Evolutionary and Social Scientific Perspectives' (2008) 1128 *Annals of the New York Academy of Sciences* 95, 99.

54 Regine Neugebauer, 'Fine-Tuning WTO Jurisprudence and the SPS Agreement: Lessons from the Beef Hormone Case' (2000) 31(1) *Law & Policy in International Business* 1255, 1266.

55 Cheyne (n 47) 60. Specifically, Cheyne's comment refers to the panel's analysis in *EC – Biotech*.

56 Denise Prévost, 'Opening Pandora's Box: The Panel's Findings in the EC – Biotech Products Dispute' (2007) 34(1) *Legal Issues of Economic Integration* 67, 101.

57 See AB report, *US/Canada – Hormones Continued Suspension* [542]; Panel report, *US/Canada – Hormones Continued Suspension* [7.579]; Panel report, *Canada – Continued Suspensions* [7.549].

58 AB report, *Canada – Continued Suspension* [288]; AB report, *US – Softwood Lumber VI (Article 21.5 – Canada* [35]–[36].

59 AB report, *Canada – Continued Suspension* [288]; AB report, *US – Softwood Lumber VI (Article 21.5 – Canada)* [35]–[36].

'the Appellate Body's emphasis is clearly on positive evidence of harm'.[60] However, requiring positive evidence of harm ignores the EC's choice of adopting (in all biotechnology cases) a precautionary approach to *prevent* the claimed risks.

To conclude, in light of WTO judicial bodies' desire for highly specialised and comprehensive risk assessments along with a rigid judicial interpretation of the requirements under Articles 2.2 and 5.1 and annex A(4), one comes to doubt the broadly acknowledged claim that the WTO's take on risk assessment 'provid[es] some flexibility for Members'.[61] As a consequence, Gruszczynski and Sykes point out that the strict judicial approach to risk assessments and scientific evidence may undermine the right of member states to establish their ALOP, which can be precautionary.[62] To remind us, the requests for implementing a higher (i.e., precautionary) ALOP in *EC – Hormones*, *EC – Biotech* and *US/Canada – Hormones Continued Suspension* were all rejected by WTO judicial bodies as considered, inter alia, not sufficiently justified.

7.3.2 Panels' quantitative interpretation of biotechnology risks

The judicial quantitative interpretation of biotechnology risks and scientific evidence represents a further aspect that might prevent effective implementation of biosafety measures in the context of biotechnology, where there is sufficient but uncertain evidence.

A key example can be found in *EC – Biotech*, where the panel establishes that all risk assessments supporting the European biosafety measures could not be considered appropriate in the sense of Article 5.1 since they did not 'indicate relative *probability* of the potential risks [the EC] identifies', as instead required by annex A(4) of the *SPS Agreement* defining risk assessment.[63] Then it adds that all European risk assessments showed *possibilities* of risks without, however, highlighting the *potential or likelihood* of such risks occurring.[64]

To remind us, annex A(4) highlights that a risk assessment should show (1) the *likelihood* of risk (i.e., probability) in case of pest and disease,[65] and (2) the

60 Button (n 35) 66.

61 Panel report, *US – Animals* [7.323]; AB report, *EC – Hormones* [129]; Panel report, *Australia – Salmon* [8.57]; AB report, *Australia – Salmon* [124]–[130]; AB report, *US/Canada – Hormones Continued Suspension* [562]; AB report, *Australia – Apples* [237], [244]; AB report, *Japan – Alcoholic Beverages II* 34. See Jeffrey Atik, 'Science and International Regulatory Convergence' (1996) 17(1) *Northwestern Journal of International Law & Business* 736, 745; Button (n 35) 67.

62 Gruszczynski (n 13) 385; Alan O Sykes, 'Domestic Regulation, Sovereignty and Scientific Evidence Requirements: A Pessimistic View' (2002) 3 *Chicago Journal of International Law* 353, 364–365.

63 Panel report, *EC – Biotech* [7.3044]. The panel repeated this quotation, referring to Austrian measures for all the other measures in question.

64 Ibid [7.3147]. Although this statement refers to the German scientific document, it was repeated for all European risk assessments submitted in this case.

65 This was also confirmed by the AB that equated likelihood to probability in AB report, *Australia – Salmon*.

potential of risk (i.e., possibility) in cases of food-borne risks.[66] In *EC – Biotech* the panel's reference to *probability* as an alternative of *potential* does not consider that annex A(4) makes a distinction between them.[67] Also, it ignores what was argued by the AB in the previous *EC – Hormones* case:

> The Panel's use of 'probability' as an alternative term for 'potential' creates a significant concern. . .. 'Probability' implies a higher degree or a threshold of potentiality or possibility. It thus appears that here the Panel introduces a *quantitative* dimension to the notion of risk.[68]

One could argue that the adoption of a *quantitative interpretation of risk* is not surprising, if only because risk is commonly described as the product of the following formula:[69]

$$\text{Risk} = \text{gravity} \times \text{probability of harm}$$

Nevertheless, a quantitative dimension of risk cannot grasp the complexity surrounding the adverse effects posed by trading biotechnology that, rather, should be addressed through a qualitative approach to risk.[70] Indeed, this quantitative formula does not leave room for the consideration of the emerging social function of risk.[71] As Thayyil notes, a deep understanding of risk in the regulation of technology can be achieved only by examining 'what are broadly categorized as sociological conceptualizations of risk'.[72] To do so, risks surrounding the international trade in biotechnology should be approached in quantitative and qualitative terms.

66 *SPS Agreement* annex A(4).

67 The panel defined *potential* as 'the possibility of something happening . . . in the future': Panel report, *EC – Biotech* [7.3184].

68 AB report, *EC – Hormones* [184] (emphasis added).

69 Arie Trouwborst, *Precautionary Rights and Duties of States* (Martinus Nijhoff, 2006) 26–29. For further insights on the quantitative interpretation of risk, see Ortwin Renn et al., 'Risks' in Paul Pechan et al. (eds), *Safe or Not Safe: Deciding What Risks to Accept in Our Environment and Food* (Springer, 2011) 1, 3; Catherine Althaus, *Calculating Political Risk* (UNSW Press, 2008) 20–23.

70 In this respect, see *EC – Biotech* [7.3027].

71 See Steve Rayner, 'Cultural Theory and Risk Analysis' in S Krimsky and D Goldin (eds), *Social Theories of Risk* (Praeger Pub, 1992) 53, 83–116; Scott Lash, 'Risk Culture' in B Adam, U Beck and J Van Loon (eds), *The Risk Society and Beyond: Critical Issues for Social Theory* (SAGE, 2000) 47; Alan Scott, 'Risk Society or Angst Society: Two Views of Risk, Consciousness and Community' in B Adam, U Beck and J Van Loon (eds), *The Risk Society and Beyond: Critical Issues for Social Theory* (SAGE, 2000) 33; Mary Douglas and Aaron Wildavsky, *Risk and Culture: An Essay on the Selection of Technological and Environmental Dangers* (University of California Press, 1982).

72 Naveen Thayyil, *Biotechnology Regulation and GMOs – Law, Technology and Public Contestations in Europe* (Edward Elgar, 2014) 64.

Interestingly, the AB distances itself from the panels' quantitative approach to risk and, in doing so, emphasises the following:

> It is essential to bear in mind that the risk that is to be evaluated in a risk assessment under Article 5.1 is not only risk ascertainable in a science laboratory . . . but also . . . the actual potential for adverse effects on human health in the real world where people live and work and die.[73]

This is in line with the argument that the analysis of biotechnology risks must be qualitative – rather than only quantitative.

Despite the AB's disagreement about the panel's quantitative approach to risk in the 1998 *EC – Hormones* case, the panels adopt the same interpretation of risk in the 2006 *EC-Biotech* and in the 2008 *US/Canada – Hormones Continued Suspension* disputes. In the AB's view, this trend stems from an improper attempt 'to re-establish the rigid distinction between "risk assessment" and "risk management" that the Appellate Body had [already] rejected in [*EC – Hormones*]'.[74] What is more, the AB claims that the judicial adoption of a quantitative interpretation of biotechnology risks can likely lead panels to err in their interpretation and application of Article 5.1, as it did in *US/Canada – Hormones Continued Suspension*.[75] Two observations can be made here.

First, the panels' decisions to declare all risk assessments in the three biotechnology cases as inadequate are, arguably, debatable. The panels' adoption of a quantitative interpretation of biotechnology risks might have led panellists to err in their interpretation of risk assessments, as warned by the AB.

Second, one may also question the panel's decision in *EC – Hormones* to consider the biosafety measures at stake as not complying with Article 3.3 of the *SPS Agreement because of* the established inconsistency of these measures with Article 5.1. To remind us, Article 3.3 allows WTO states to introduce SPS measures which result in a higher level of biosafety protection than would be achieved by measures based on the relevant international standards if:

- there is a scientific justification (condition No 1), *or*
- the SPS measures comply with provisions of paragraphs 1 through 8 of Article 5. (condition No 2).[76]

In other words, biosafety measures not in line with the scientific requirements of, inter alia, Article 2.2 (i.e., scientific justification) or not complying with Article 5, cannot reflect an ALOP higher than the one that would be achieved by relying on international standards.

73 AB report, *EC – Hormones* [187].
74 AB report, *US/Canada – Hormones Continued Suspension* [542].
75 Ibid [555].
76 *SPS Agreement* art 3.3.

However, WTO judicial bodies do not apply this literal interpretation of Article 3.3 in *EC – Hormones*. Indeed, even if the biosafety measures in questions were assessed as not complying with Article 5.1 (condition No 2 of Article 3.3), the EC could have been allowed to adopt a higher ALOP if its biosafety measures were scientifically justified (condition No 1 of Article 3.3). And, arguably, they were: Although supported only by a part of the scientific community, the European requests for adopting biosafety measures were scientifically supported by experts' opinions claiming a number of risks posed by the contested biotech products. Nevertheless, the AB followed a curious interpretation of Article 3.3: While this provision lists two alternative conditions (i.e., 'or') under which a biosafety measure can be imposed, the AB maintained that both conditions of Article 3.3 have to be met.[77] Consequently, the EC's request for establishing a precautionary ALOP was rejected as not aligning with WTO law.

This (forced) judicial interpretation of Article 3.3 reaffirms the *science-based approach* taken by WTO judicial bodies in the biotechnology cases, which is not in line with the scientifically uncertain nature of biotechnology, nor with the *precautionary approach*. Indeed, on occasion it parts with ordinary rules of legal interpretation.

To conclude, panels fall short of the AB's recommendations for not adopting (1) a *quantitative* interpretation of risk that, unlike a qualitative approach, cannot fully capture the complexity surrounding biotechnology, (2) a distinction between risk assessments and risk management, and (3) *probability* of risk as an alternative for *potential*, because the former implies a higher evidentiary threshold making the performance of an appropriate assessment of risk in the sense of Article 5.1 quite difficult for member states.

As a consequence of this judicial approach to biotechnology risks, which does not accommodate scientific uncertainty, the WTO member states could not enjoy their right of establishing a precautionary level of protection. Such a level of protection is not an exception from a general obligation to trade, as was claimed by the panel in *EC – Hormones*. Rather, it is an autonomous right of member states.[78] WTO law defers, in fact, the management of risk to WTO states.[79] This is one of the reasons behind the suggestion for applying a 'multilevel degree of deference' standard of review recommending total deference of risk management to the national level.[80] As stressed by Cheyne commenting on a WTO biotechnology case:

> The specific outcome of [*EC – Biotech*] was easily portrayed as illegitimate interference with national sovereignty, legitimate concerns about human health and environmental protection, and the right of consumers to make their own choices.[81]

77 AB report, *EC – Hormones* (n 2) [175]–[176].
78 Ibid [172].
79 *SPS Agreement* art 3.3.
80 See Section 6.3.3.
81 Cheyne (n 47) 64.

In the same view, Poli emphasises how '[b]ringing safeguard measures in line with Art. 5(1) or (7) is a sticky wicket and represents the most important implementation challenge for the EC'.[82] In other words, the biotechnology legal rulings hinder member states from accomplishing their numerous international obligations to safeguard human health and the environment.[83] For example, Prévost observes that the panel's interpretation of Article 31.3(c) *VCLT* in *EC – Biotech* represents a step backwards from the progressive approach of the AB in *US – Gasoline* and *US – Shrimp*.[84] This is because while the AB emphasises that WTO law is not to be read 'in clinical isolation from public international law',[85] in *EC – Biotech* the panel claims that according to Article 31.3(c) *VCLT*, only those rules of international law 'applicable in the relations between the parties', meaning *all* WTO members, are to be considered.[86] This led the panel to not take account of the international obligations invoked by the EC in relation to the *CBD* and the *Cartagena Protocol on Biosafety*, which are not ratified by Argentina, Canada and the United States (i.e., the complainants). 'The narrow view of the Panel regarding the role of other international law in the interpretation of WTO agreements is lamentable',[87] not least because it could have promoted the coherence of the international law system by following the progressive approach of the AB in *US – Gasoline* and *US – Shrimp*.[88] In other words, as Henckels highlights, the panel in *EC – Biotech* lost the opportunity 'to situate its judgment within the broader realm of public international law and to demonstrate an awareness of the interconnectedness of international instruments'.[89]

7.3.3 Panel's arbitrary selection of evidence

Another problematic aspect regarding the judicial examination of biosafety measures in the context of sufficient, but uncertain, scientific evidence regards the arbitrary selection of evidence. In other words, WTO decision-makers rely on evidence by some experts without saying why they dismiss the evidence by other

82 Sara Poli, 'The EC's Implementation of the WTO Ruling in the Biotech Dispute' (2007) 32(5) *European Law Review* 705, 721.

83 Section 2.6 discusses WTO member states' international obligations to safeguard human health and the environment in greater detail.

84 Prévost (n 56) 89.

85 AB report, *US – Gasoline* 16–17.

86 AB report, *EC – Biotech* [7.68].

87 Prévost (n 56) 92–93.

88 For greater insight into the different views expressed in doctrine as to the panel's interpretation of 31.3(c) *VCLT* in *EC – Biotech*, see Franken and Burchardi (n 48) 80–83; Gabrielle Marceau, 'Conflicts of Norms and Conflicts of Jurisdictions The Relationship between the WTO Agreement and MEAs and Other Treaties' (2001) 36(6) *Journal of World Trade* 1081; Joost Pauwelyn, 'The Role of Public International Law in the WTO: How Far Can We Go?' (2001) 95(3) *American Journal of International Law* 535.

89 Caroline Henckels, 'GMOs in the WTO: A Critique of the Panel's Legal Reasoning in EC-Biotech' (2006) 7 *Melbourne Journal of International Law* 278.

experts. The judicial analysis in *US/Canada – Hormones Continued Suspension* provides manifold examples in this regard.

For instance, in this case both the 1999 and 2002 scientific opinions supporting the European ban to the contested products showed genotoxicity of oestradiol-17β, which is one of the contested hormones. The examination of these scientific opinions 'should have been', according to the AB, 'the focus of the Panel's analysis, yet they are not mentioned in the Panel's analysis. The Panel does not give any reasons why it did not consider them relevant'.[90] Similarly, the scientific opinions provided by Dr Cogliano and Dr Guttenplan, both supporting the EC's ban by stressing potential adverse effects on human health of the same hormone (i.e., oestradiol-17β), are rejected by the panel without any sort of explanation.[91]

It is also interesting to note that the panel in *US/Canada – Hormones Continued Suspension* automatically ascribes more weight to the testimony of experts endorsing the view of the majority of the relevant scientific community.[92] However, already in the 1998 *EC-Hormones* case, and more recently in the 2019 *Korea – Radionuclides* case, the AB clarifies that also divergent and minority scientific opinions coming from qualified and respected sources can support biosafety measures.[93] Accordingly, the panel in *US/Canada – Hormones Continued Suspension* was required to explain the reasons behind its choice of preferring the majority views over the minority ones.[94]

In light of this, in *US/Canada – Hormones Continued Suspension* the panel became, as the AB notes, 'the jury on the correct science . . . by picking and choosing between conflicting and contradictory opinions of the experts in an arbitrary manner'.[95] As a consequence, the AB concludes that the panel erred in law, exceeded its authority and failed to conduct an objective assessment of whether the European risk assessment satisfied Article 5.1 and annex A of the *SPS Agreement*.[96] This means that the lack of boundaries to the substantial discretion given to panels can entail arbitrariness that, consequently, affects the reliability of final legal decisions.

Further, it emerges that, facing opposing scientific opinions, the panellists decided to arbitrarily, though coherently, rely only on scientific opinions supporting the safety of biotechnology. Put differently, in contexts of sufficient but uncertain and opposing scientific evidence, the panel *erred on the side of trade*. This, in turn, echoes the bias towards free trade in WTO law as well as WTO

90 AB report, *US/Canada – Hormones Continued Suspension* [610].

91 Ibid annex D [145], [613].

92 Ibid [597].

93 AB report, *EC – Hormones* [194]; AB report, *Canada – Continued Suspension* [677]; AB report, *US/Canada – Hormones Continued Suspension* [677]; AB report, *Korea – Radionuclides* [5.106].

94 AB report, *US/Canada – Hormones Continued Suspension* [613].

95 Ibid [585].

96 Ibid [615]–[616].

jurisprudence on biotechnology. This adds a further piece to the final picture of why biosafety measures adopted to address biotechnology risks have never been applied in contexts of sufficient scientific evidence.

7.3.4 WTO judicial bodies and their role as gatekeeper in examining scientific evidence and risk assessments

Another problematic factor that can be observed in the judicial examination of biosafety measures is that WTO judicial bodies do not seem to fulfil their gatekeeper role. As Foster underlines, 'court[s] must sift out the scientific issues, assess the quality and reliability of the evidence relevant to each issue and seek to reach findings accurately reflecting the state of current scientific knowledge'.[97] Nevertheless, WTO judicial bodies tend to defer the final decisions on the appropriateness of scientific evidence and risk assessments to experts. While there is merit in involving subject experts in court cases, the risk is for those experts to heavily influence the final decision or to take on a role as gatekeeper, even though 'it is not the experts who must make a final decision'.[98]

This issue emerges in *US/Canada – Hormones Continued Suspension*, where the AB highlights that 'a significant portion of the Panel's reasoning *consists of* summaries of the responses of the experts'.[99] However, experts' opinions should only *inform* panels' decisions.

More specifically, the panel's final decision on the appropriateness of scientific evidence and risk assessments supporting the biosafety measures at stake is conducted through a sort of survey of experts' opinions aiming at checking whether the majority of experts agreed with the conclusions drawn in the European risk assessment.[100] For example, the panel attempts to determine whether there was a general acceptance that oestradiol-17β was a genotoxic *in vivo* or that its genotoxic mechanism caused cancer.[101] The panel is not, however, a scientific body entitled (or trained) to establish this aspect. As Christoforou asserts, '[t]he task of the panel is to decide whether a contested measure is based on a[n appropriate] risk assessment, not whether the scientific theory upon which the conclusions of the risk assessment are based is scientifically correct and acceptable'.[102] This is because, as a number of scholars emphasise, panellists are laypersons lacking in

97 Caroline E Foster, *Science and the Precautionary Principle in International Courts and Tribunals – Expert Evidence, Burden of Proof, and Finality* (Cambridge University Press, 2011) 80.

98 Andrew T Guzman, 'Food Fears: Health and Safety at the WTO' (2004) 45(1) *Virginia Journal of International Law* 1, 23; Theofanis Christoforou, 'Settlement of Science-Based Trade Disputes in the WTO: A Critical Review of the Developing Case Law in the Face of Scientific Uncertainty' (2000) 8(3) *New York University Environmental Law Journal* 622, 629–634.

99 AB report, *US/Canada – Hormones Continued Suspension* [598] (emphasis added).

100 Ibid.

101 Ibid [610]; [607]–[609].

102 Christoforou (n 98) 636.

scientific knowledge and, as such, are 'not qualified to judge the plausibility of the competing parties' scientific views'.[103] Moreover, Guzman adds that WTO judicial bodies 'lack the resources to carry out their own investigation in anything more than a cursory way'.[104] After all, the panel itself admits that panellists 'are in any case poorly suited to engage in such review'.[105] For this reason, Eliason suggests the following:

> What we need are legal experts who are knowledgeable enough about science to recognize the uncertainty and hypothetical qualities that make up the very essence of scientific research. These legal experts should not judge the scientific evidence, but rather should apply their scientific knowledge to avoid misunderstandings of scientific procedures when applying legal standards.[106]

Having decision-makers struggling with a full comprehension of scientific matters is, however, not unique to the WTO.[107]

While WTO judicial bodies are ill-equipped to engage in a scientific review of member's evidence concerning biotechnology, Guzman observes that national governments 'have greater capacity and more time to undertake the evaluation of information'.[108] Panels should, in fact, examine only the appropriateness of the submitted scientific evidence and risk assessments, without investigating on the general acceptance of the scientific material brought to their attention.

In conclusion, the judicial analysis of scientific evidence and risk assessments in *US/Canada – Hormones Continued Suspension* shows that panels' role of gatekeeper is not always duly performed. The panel focused on the acceptance of the submitted evidence into the scientific community and deferred the review of both scientific evidence and risk assessments to experts.[109] This undermines the final

103 Ibid 635. See also Vern R Walker, 'Keeping the WTO from Becoming the "World Trans-Science Organization": Scientific Uncertainty, Science Policy, and Factfinding in the Growth Hormones Dispute' (1998) 31(2) *Cornell International Law Journal* 251, 319; Robert Howse, 'Democracy, Science, and Free Trade: Risk Regulation on Trial at the World Trade Organization' (2000) 98(7) *Michigan Law Review* 2329; Andrew T Guzman, 'Determining the Appropriate Standard of Review in WTO Disputes' (2009) 42(1) *Cornell International Law Journal* 45.

104 Guzman (n 98) 23.

105 AB report, *EC – Hormones* [117]; AB report, *US/Canada – Hormones Continued Suspension* [602].

106 Antonia Eliason, 'Science versus Law in WTO Jurisprudence: The (Mis)Interpretation of the Scientific Process and the (In)Sufficiency of Scientific Evidence in EC-Biotech' (2009) 41 *New York University Journal of International Law & Policy* 341, 401.

107 Xuexia Liao, 'Evaluation of Scientific Evidence by International Courts and Tribunals in the Continental Shelf Delimitation Cases' (2017) 48(2) *Ocean Development and International Law* 136, 139; John E Noyes, 'Judicial and Arbitral Proceedings and the Outer Limits of the Continental Shelf' (2009) 42 *Vanderbilt Journal of Transnational Law* 1211, 1251–1252.

108 Guzman (n 103).

109 It seems that panellists found it difficult to distinguish their role from that of experts, as noted by the AB, which described the panel's analogy between its role and the role of experts as 'unfortunate': *US/Canada – Hormones Continued Suspension* (n 16) [595].

legal decision and jeopardises a reasoned judicial balance between the competing interests in trading biotechnology and ensuring biosafety.[110]

In summary, this section explores four problematic aspects regarding the judicial examination of biosafety measures in the context of sufficient, but uncertain, scientific evidence.

First, *the strict judicial interpretations* of appropriateness of risk assessments and sufficiency of scientific evidence *do not fit the scientifically uncertain nature of biotechnology*. For this reason, member states could not enjoy their right of establishing a precautionary ALOP and did not have flexibility in conducting appropriate risk assessments aligning with Articles 2.2 and 5.1 and annex A(4) of the *SPS Agreement*. This is against the fact that establishing a precautionary ALOP is an autonomous right of member states.[111] This also does not align with the broad acknowledgement that WTO rules are flexible so as to leave room for member states to perform risk assessments appropriate to the circumstances.[112]

Second, the panel focused on a *quantitative interpretation of biotechnology risks*, neither of which leaves room for precautionary actions nor accommodates uncertainty. Also, it interfered with the national sovereignty to manage risks related to biotechnology and hinders member states from accomplishing their numerous international obligations to safeguard human health and the environment.[113]

Third, *the panel* in *US/Canada – Hormones Continued Suspension arbitrarily selected evidence*, which consequently affected the reliability of the final legal decision. Also, it shows that in contexts of sufficient but uncertain and opposing scientific evidence, the panel erred on the side of trade. This underlines a prima facie pre-eminence of free trade also in the WTO jurisprudence on biotechnology.

Finally, *WTO judicial bodies do not seem to properly accomplish their role of gatekeeper* because they tend to defer the final decisions on the appropriateness of scientific evidence and risk assessments to experts. This, accordingly, undermines final legal decisions and jeopardises a reasoned judicial balance between the competing interests in trading biotechnology and ensuring biosafety.

These observations allow the conclusion that the scientific complexities surrounding the international trade in biotechnology perhaps 'require rethinking of the wisdom of using, in the text of SPS, "science" as an arbiter in trade disputes concerning food safety'.[114] As Peel notes:

> Narrowly focused science-based approaches to risk regulation, which have emerged in dominant international governance institutions such as the

110 In this respect, see the suggestions offered in Sections 3.6.2 and 7.4.

111 AB report, *EC – Hormones* [172].

112 Panel report, *US – Animals* [7.323]. See also AB report, *EC – Hormones* [129]; Panel report, *Australia – Salmon* [8.57]; AB report, *Australia – Salmon* [130]; AB report, *US/Canada – Hormones Continued Suspension* [562]; AB report, *Australia – Apples* [237], [244].

113 See Section 2.6.

114 Robert Howse and Henrik Horn, 'European Communities – Measures Affecting the Approval and Marketing of Biotech Products' (2009) 8(1) *World Trade Review* 49.

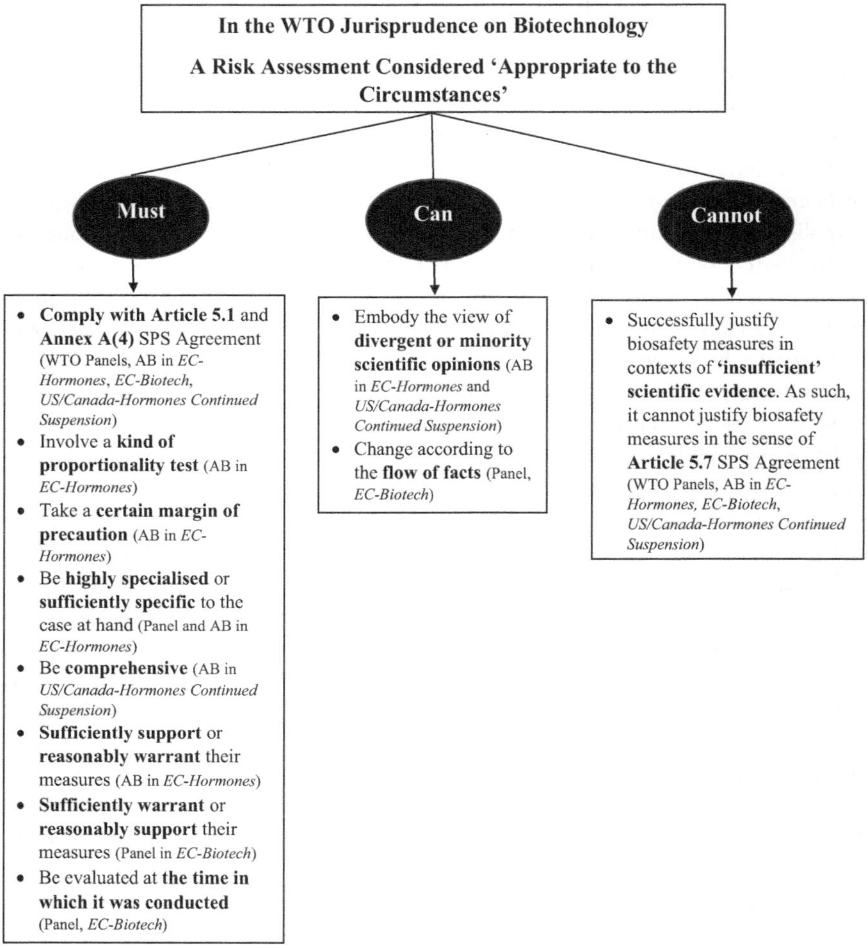

Figure 7.2 'Appropriateness' of risk assessment in the WTO jurisprudence on biotechnology

WTO, threaten such efforts by perpetuating a myth that complex risk questions can be reduced to matters of science.[115]

Additionally, by focusing on the existence of a considerable body of literature on the topic of biotechnology, WTO judicial bodies appear to be blind to the remaining scientific uncertainties that exist and affect the quality and reliability

115 Peel (n 7) 11. See also Silvio O Funtowicz and Jerome R Ravets, 'Three Types of Risk Assessment and the Emergence of Post-Normal Science' in Krimsky Sheldon and Dominic Golding (eds), *Social Theories of Risk* (Praeger Pub, 1992) 251, 253.

of scientific evidence and risk assessments. This clearly emerges from the analysis conducted in this chapter, which shows a judicial focus on the scientific justification of biosafety measures[116] that must be maintained with sufficient scientific evidence[117] and based on risk assessments that, in the view of panels and the AB, can be considered 'appropriate to the circumstances'[118] if complying with a number of scientific and strict requirements that Figure 7.2 summarises.

In light of this, Section 7.4 suggests potential improvements for performing judicial examinations of risk assessments that fit circumstances of sufficient but uncertain scientific evidence.

7.4 Suggestions for improvements

As Chapter 1 establishes, there is considerable evidence for both sides of the argument regarding the harmfulness or harmlessness of biotechnology.[119] As a consequence, WTO judicial bodies consider the field of biotechnology characterised by a *sufficient* body of scientific evidence. However, having sufficiency in quantitative terms does not necessarily entail the existence of qualitatively sufficient scientific evidence. In fact, the presence of opposing scientific opinions can prevent scientists from providing a specific and comprehensive estimation of risks. Accordingly, the challenge lies in the fact that the scientific uncertainties around biotechnology inevitably affect the level of confidence in risk assessments and, as such, the quality and reliability of evidence brought to the attention of WTO decision-makers.[120]

In light of these factors, this section discusses what should make *appropriate* a risk assessment in the scientifically sufficient but uncertain context of biotechnology (Section 7.4.1) and who should be considered an expert and, as such, inform panellists on the effects posed by the international trade in biotechnology to biosafety (see Section 7.4.2).

7.4.1 *What should make* appropriate *a risk assessment in the scientifically uncertain context of biotechnology?*

A risk assessment encompassing only scientific data should not be considered appropriate to the circumstances surrounding the international trade in biotechnology, if only because of the still-high degree of remaining scientific uncertainty about this technology. Consequently, this study suggests considering *appropriate* those assessments of biotechnology risks supplementing the uncertain scientific

116 *SPS Agreement* art 2.2.
117 Ibid.
118 Ibid art 5.1.
119 See Section 1.2.
120 Panels in Panel report, *EC – Biotech* [7.3065] and Panel report, *Canada – Hormones Continued Suspension* [7.611] acknowledged that scientific uncertainty can affect the level of confidence in risk assessments.

evidence in question with inferences, multiple and positive correlations and holistic data. The following sub-sections elaborate on this argument.

7.4.1.1 Inferences *along with* multiple and positive correlations *to supplement uncertain scientific evidence and to shape risk assessments appropriate to biotechnology circumstances*

The panel in *US/Canada – Hormones Continued Suspension* underlined that it is for member states 'to provide *convincing evidence*'[121] justifying their request for restricting free trade of the contested biotech products. This judicial request for positive evidence of harm prevents member states from adopting biosafety measures in contexts of sufficient but uncertain (or insufficient) scientific evidence.[122]

The *causal link* between biotechnology and harm to human health and/or the environment represents an evidentiary requirement that is hard to prove, not least because of scientific uncertainties and the long-term nature of adverse effects to biosafety posed by trading biotechnology.[123] Also, it is against the proactive rationale of the precautionary principle that, to remind us, was invoked to support the biosafety measures in all three biotechnology cases. What is more, in *US/Canada – Hormones Continued Suspension* the EC underlines that conclusive evidence on the adverse effects of the contested hormones to human health, 'might require scientific testing on humans', which would be 'totally unethical' and would imply 'to do the impossible'.[124]

'In the world of regulatory risk assessment', Jasanoff argues, 'causation generally is viewed as a linear and mechanistic phenomenon' against the complexity of the real world that hardly can be addressed by means of 'linear and mechanistic' approaches.[125] Indeed, requiring convincing evidence and, as such, the proof of a causal link between biosafety measures and scientific evidence showing adverse effects of biotechnology is unsuitable. Against this background, taking account of inferences and positive correlations to establish the appropriateness of risk assessments in contexts of sufficient but uncertain scientific evidence might mitigate the WTO judicial bodies' emphasis on positive evidence of harm for the following reasons.

Inference can be described as 'a probable conclusion, not based on deduction, but loose usage, experience or statistical correlation. Inference does not absolutely establish a premise but constitutes a *demonstration of probability*'.[126]

121 Panel report, *US/Canada – Hormones Continued Suspension* [6.61] (emphasis added).

122 Chapter 8 discusses how the judicial request for convincing evidence prevents member states from adopting precautionary measures in contexts of insufficient scientific evidence.

123 For a critique of the judicial request for a causal link, see Ulrich Beck, *Risk Society – Towards a New Modernity* (Mark Ritter trans, SAGE Publications, 1992) 1 [translation of: *Risikogesellschaft: Auf dem Weg in eine andere Moderne* (first published 1986)] 63.

124 Panel report, *US/Canada – Hormones Continued Suspension* [258].

125 Sheila Jasanoff, 'The Songlines of Risk' (1999) 8(2) *Environmental Values* 135, 141.

126 Allen J Moses, 'Daubert, Pain, Evidence and Inference in Treating TMD' (1997) 64(4) *Defense Counsel Journal* 613, 614 (emphasis added).

This means that inferences can aid decision-makers to interpret probabilities, which is particularly relevant in the context of biotechnology considering that the panels' interpretation of probability of risks in *EC – Hormones*, *EC – Biotech*, and *US/Canada – Hormones Continued Suspension* has been harshly criticised by the AB.[127] Inferences should be, however, consolidated by correlations.[128]

Correlation is generally defined as 'a statistical measure that indicates the extent to which two or more variables fluctuate together'.[129] As is well known, correlation does not imply causation. For example, even if a study relates an increased body-mass index (BMI) with an increased risk of developing cancer, it would be erroneous to conclude that BMI *causes* cancer.[130] Tufte adds that other potential variables should be taken into account by means of *statistical tests*.[131] After all, decision-makers in Japan have already forsaken the idea of convincing evidence and rigorous proof of causality in environmental matters by considering 'a causal connection if statistical correlations can be established between pollution levels and certain diseases'.[132]

Moreover, it must be clarified that the assumption according to which *A causes B* merely because *A correlates with B* is a logical fallacy,[133] though 'sometimes people commit the opposite fallacy – dismissing correlation entirely, as if it does not imply causation. This would dismiss a large swath of important scientific evidence'.[134] Interestingly, one of the most debated questions of the previous decades – 'Is tobacco harmful to human health?' – demonstrates that policy-makers can commit this opposite fallacy – rather than the logical one. Indeed, when in 1964 the US Surgeon General published a report arguing that cigarette smoking causes lung cancer,[135] tobacco companies and 'some of the world's most

127 AB report, *EC – Hormones* [184].

128 Nancy Pennington and Ried Hastie, 'A Cognitive Theory of Juror Decision Making: The Story Model' (1991) 13 *Cardoso Law Review* 519, 534.

129 Margaret Rouse, 'Correlation' *WhatIs.com* (Web Page, November 2016), http://whatis.techtarget.com/definition/correlation.

130 Andrew G Renehan et al., 'Body-Mass Index and Incidence of Cancer: A Systematic Review and Meta-Analysis of Prospective Observational Studies' (2008) 9612(371) *Lancet* 569.

131 Edward R Tufte, *The Cognitive Style of PowerPoint: Pitching Out Corrupts Within* (Graphics Press, 2nd ed, 2006); John Aldrich, 'Correlations Genuine and Spurious in Pearson and Yule' (1995) 10(4) *Statistical Science* 364.

132 Beck (n 123) 63–4 (emphasis altered).

133 Steven Novella, 'Evidence in Medicine: Correlation and Causation' (2009) *Science-Based Medicine* 1.

134 Ibid 3.

135 Michael Nielsen, 'If Correlation Doesn't Imply Causation, Then What Does?' *Michael Nielsen, DDI – Data-Driven Intelligence* (Blog Post, 23 January 2012), 7 <>www.michael-nielsen.org/ddi/if-correlation-doesnt-imply-causation-then-what-does/>. See also US Department of Health, Education and Welfare, *Smoking and Health – Report of the Advisory Committee to the Surgeon General of the Public Health Service* (Washington DC, 1964 Public Health Service Publication No 1103).

prominent statisticians'[136] rejected the report's assertions since they considered it was 'based primarily on correlations between cigarette smoking and lung cancer'.[137] More specifically, it was argued that the potential existence of an unknown factor could be the cause of lung cancer *and* people's desire to smoke (i.e., nicotine craving). This would have implied that even if correlated, 'the decision to smoke or not smoke would have no impact on whether you got lung cancer'.[138] On the contrary, the correlations highlighted in the report have been proven true, though only years later.

This example invites Novella to argue that, although a simple correlation cannot be considered enough to reach a conclusion of causation, '*multiple correlations all triangulating on the conclusion* that smoking causes lung cancer, combined with biological plausibility, does'.[139] In the same view, Kaye and Freedman highlight that '[t]wo variables are *positively correlated* when their values tend to go up or down together'.[140]

To bring this discussion back to the topic at hand, inferences along with multiple and positive correlations should supplement uncertain scientific evidence to shape appropriate risk assessments in the context of biotechnology, in which, importantly, multiple examples of inferences and correlations can be found. For instance, scientific experts consulted for the 2015 *Declaration of the 3rd National Congress of Physicians in the Crops – Sprayed Town* adopted statistical assessments conducted over several years to demonstrate the existence of *positive correlations* between the increasing number of cancer patients and the growing number of GM crops in the living areas of these patients.[141] The Declaration adopts geographic maps to illustrate that the Cordoba and Santa Fe areas where GM crops resistant to glyphosate are cultivated coincide precisely with the areas in which cancer mortality is increasing.[142]

Therefore, *positive correlations* by means of statistical data led scientific experts to *infer* that GM crops contribute to cause cancer. To refer back to Kaye and Freedman, this inference is based on a correlation showing that the two variables at stake are positively correlated (i.e., positive correlation) as their values tend to go up together.[143] However, as Novella states, a single correlation cannot be considered enough to reach a conclusion of causation. For this reason, the

136 Nielsen (n 135) 7. See also Judea Pearl, *Causality: Models, Reasoning, and Inference* (Cambridge University Press, 2000).

137 Nielsen (n 135) 7.

138 Ibid.

139 Novella (n 133) 3 (emphasis added).

140 David H Kaye and David A Freedman, 'Statistical Proof' in David L Faigman et al. (eds), *Science in the Law – Standards, Statistics and Research Issues* (West Group, 2002) 150, 200 (emphasis added).

141 *Declaration of the 3rd National Congress of Physicians in the Crop-Sprayed Towns* (Presidents Medardo Avila-Vazquez and Miryam Gorban) 2016 IJHNFM: International Journal of Human Nutrition and Functional Medicine (26 November 2015).

142 Ibid.

143 Kaye and Freedman (n 140) 200.

positive correlation drawn in the 2015 Declaration should not be taken in isolation. Rather, to reach a conclusion of causation, it must be read together with other (i.e., multiple) positive correlations, all triangulating on the conclusion that biotech products can, in this case, cause cancer. The result stemming from the following two American trials might represent those 'other' positive correlations.

When in 2016 the WHO's IARC classified glyphosate as 'probable carcinogen', Mr Hardeman, a US farmer, sued the biotech multinational Monsanto before the San Francisco Federal Court as he claims that the mist from the spray of Monsanto's Roundup[144] frequently fell on his body and, as such, caused his lymphoma.[145]

Hardeman's attorneys presented animal studies showing a *positive correlation* between a long-term exposition to the product and cancer. Such studies highlight that the values of exposure to that herbicide and risks of lymphomas increase together. Accordingly, Hardeman's defence *inferred* that the risk of lymphomas increases the more a person uses Roundup.

Conversely, Monsanto denied the existence of a causal link between lymphoma and the use of Roundup and pointed to the common nature of Mr Hardeman's lymphoma.

The judgment sided with Mr Hardeman and established that it was more than 50% likely that the use of Roundup caused Mr Hardeman's cancer. In spite of the lack of proof of the causal linkage, the jury declared that Monsanto's herbicide was a substantial factor in causing Mr Hardeman's cancer.

This case aligns with the previous case brought to the attention of a California jury by the groundskeeper Mr Johnson who, after having sprayed Monsanto's Roundup and *Ranger Pro* herbicides for years, was diagnosed with a lymphoma.[146] Despite the disease, he kept spraying the herbicides, not least because after a pesticide certification course, he was told that *Ranger Pro* was 'safe enough to drink'.[147]

Like the Hardeman case, scientific experts hired by Mr Johnson's attorneys showed *positive correlations* between these herbicides and risks of getting cancer.

144 The multinational Monsanto describes Roundup as 'the flagship of Monsanto's agricultural chemicals business': Monsanto, 'Roundup' *Monsanto* (Web Page), www.monsantoglobal.com/global/au/products/Pages/roundup.aspx.

145 See Vibha Varshney, 'Glyphosate Use Increased 1500% Since Genetically Modified Crops Were Introduced' *DownToEarth* (Web Page, 26 July 2018) www.downtoearth.org.in/blog/food/glyphosate-use-increased-1500-since-genetically-modified-crops-were-introduced-61241. See also, 'California Jury Finds Roundup Weedkiller to be "Substantial Factor" in Causing Man's Cancer' *Sustainable Pulse* (Online, 19 March 2019), https://sustainablepulse.com/2019/03/19/california-jury-finds-roundup-weedkiller-to-be-substantial-factor-in-causing-mans-cancer/?utm_source=newsletter&utm_medium=email&utm_campaign=breaking_california_jury_finds_roundup_weedkiller_to_be_substantial_factor_in_causing_man_s_cancer&utm_term=2019-03-21#.XMqzBKRS_Tf.

146 Dorothy Atkins, 'Monsanto Owes $289M In Landmark Roundup Cancer Trial' *Law360* (Online, 10 August 2018), www.law360.com/articles/1071336n.

147 Ibid.

Thus, they *inferred* that Monsanto's herbicides caused Mr Johnson's lymphoma and also that Monsanto acted maliciously since it was aware of this health risk 'since at least the 1990s, when studies began showing a *correlation* between the products and the lymphoma'.[148]

In August 2018, the jury found Monsanto responsible for a negligent failure to warn the plaintiff about the risks in using those herbicides, which were considered substantial causes of Johnson's lymphoma.[149]

In short, the *2015 Declaration of the 3rd National Congress of Physicians in the Crops – Sprayed Town* along with the 2018 and 2019 American decisions represent past cases in which the judges/jury relied on the correlation between the use of biotech products and cancer. Also, the American trials provide an example of how *positive correlations* can lead decision-makers to *infer* that there is *causation* between the correlated values at stake. In this respect, it is also interesting to note that in the 2016 *Giovanni Pesce and Others* case, the European Advocate General Bot advises the ECJ to consider 'significant correlations' as sufficient to justify the implementation of precautionary measures aiming at safeguarding olives from potential risks stemming from the spread of a bacterium causing their rapid desiccation.[150] This echoes the capacity of the precautionary principle to lower the evidentiary threshold.

To conclude, inferences along with positive and multiple correlations can (and should) be taken into account in examining whether the assessments of biotechnology risks are appropriate to the circumstances in the sense of Article 5.1. They can, in fact, supplement the lack of qualitatively sufficient evidence and, in some cases, foreshadow causation. Obviously, also the appropriateness of risk assessments supporting the safety (and not only the harmfulness) of biotech products should encompass, if available, inferences and correlations.[151]

As inferences and correlations might stem from a holistic, rather than scientific, approach to biotechnology legal matters, the analysis proceeds by stressing the importance of considering not only scientific but also holistic data in assessing biotechnology risks.

7.4.1.2 Holistic data *to supplement uncertain scientific evidence and to shape risk assessments appropriate to biotechnology circumstances*

The scientific ethos of the *SPS Agreement* finds echo in the panel's consideration of risk assessments as 'scientific examination of data and factual studies [which

148 Ibid. See also Bonnie Eslinger, 'Groundskeeper Accepts Slashed $78M Roundup Award' *Law360* (Online, 31 October 2018), www.law360.com/articles/1097846/groundskeeper-accepts-slashed-78m-roundup-award (emphasis added).

149 The jury ordered Monsanto to pay $289 million for compensatory and punitive damages: Atkins (n 146); Eslinger (n 150).

150 Opinion of Advocate General Bot, *Giovanni Pesce and Others* (Joined Cases C-78/16 and C-79/16) [2016] ECR 340, [116].

151 As of May 2020, there are scientific studies but not inferences or positive and multiple correlations showing a positive impact of biotech products to human health or the environment.

does not involve] social value judgments made by political bodies'.[152] In contrast, scholars observe that risk assessment is not purely scientific, if only because 'political and value-related decisions may frequently enter this process'.[153] Also the AB seems not to reduce risk assessments to a mere scientific examination in labs. Indeed, in *EC-Hormones*, it acknowledges that risk assessments must consider 'not only risk ascertainable in a science laboratory',[154] meaning risks stemming from *experimental studies*, but also 'risk in human societies . . . where people live and work and die'.[155]

The analysis of adverse effects on human health in the real world is conducted through *observational studies*, which monitor how people (and local environments) react to, in our case, the introduction of biotech products into a specific place. From Beck's perspective, the current society is a laboratory in which, however, experiments are carried out '*without* scientific checking, *without* surveys, *without* statistics, *without* correlation analysis, under the condition that the victims are *not* informed – and with an *inverted* burden of proof, if they should happen to detect something'.[156]

In examining the appropriateness of risk assessments in the context of biotechnology, WTO judicial bodies should verify whether data stemming from observational studies have been encompassed – along with the experimental ones – in those assessments. This, in turn, means that national assessments of biotechnology risks should adopt not only a scientific but also a *holistic approach*, which takes into account both physical and social impacts of biotechnology.[157] The inferences and correlations drawn by experts in the *2015 Declaration of the 3rd National Congress of Physicians in the Crops – Sprayed Town* arose out of, for example, observational studies on the effects of biotech to people living a specific area of Cordoba and Santa Fe.

The suggestion of conducting appropriate risk assessments by considering holistic data concerning biotechnology should come as no surprise. The AB in

152 Panel report, *EC – Hormones* [8.94]; AB report, *US/Canada – Hormones Continued Suspension* [527].

153 Gruszczynski (n 13) 379. See also Jacqueline Peel, 'Risk Regulation under the WTO SPS Agreement: Science as an International Normative Yardstick?' (Jean Monnet Working Paper, 2002/4) 66.

154 AB report, *EC – Hormones* [187]; AB report, *US/Canada – Hormones Continued Suspension* [527].

155 Ibid.

156 Beck (n 123) 69 (emphasis in original). Beck's reasoning is not far from the idea published in *Risk Assessment – Report of a Royal Society Study Group*, which in Section 4.1 listed 'five good reasons' to conduct 'observations of experiments on Man': Royal Society, *Risk Assessment: Report of a Royal Society Study Group* (London: Royal Society, 1983) 76–77. Similarly, Schwarcz argues that '[w]e live in a large chemistry lab': Joe Schwarcz, *Is That a Fact? – Frauds, Quacks, and the Real Science of Everyday Life* (ECW Press, 2014) 9.

157 See especially Apolline Roger, 'In the Public Interest? A Comparative Analysis of Norway and EU GMO Regulations' (2015) 24(3) *Review of European, Comparative and International Environmental Law* 264.

EC – Hormones and *US/Canada – Hormones Continued Suspension* notes indeed that national risk assessments supporting biosafety measures take account of socio-cultural factors, such as 'the intense concern of consumers' towards biotech products, the consideration of which entails the adoption of a holistic approach.[158] What is more, Macmillan notes that '[t]he lack of a holistic approach to environmental protection may undermine environmental benefits gained through the liberalisation of trade in environmental services'.[159]

Importantly, the judicial examination of risk assessments employing a holistic approach (along with a scientific one) would also allow WTO judicial bodies not to lose touch with reality. Outside courtrooms and laboratories, there are actions and initiatives all around the world which claim the existence of evident social and physical impact of biotech products to people and/or the environment where such products are imported or cultivated to be exported. For example, in 2017, the civil society initiative International Monsanto Tribunal Advisory Opinion established that the biotech company Monsanto did (and still does) not act in conformity with, inter alia, the right to a healthy environment, the right to health, the right to food and the right to freedom of scientific research.[160] The importance of this decision, though not legally binding, lies in the fact that the judges achieved such a conclusion by examining holistic data provided by the experience of 28 witnesses, who were described by Judge Tulkens as 'experts through their personal history'.[161]

In light of this, the judicial evaluation of the appropriateness of risk assessments in the context of biotechnology should not ignore the importance of encompassing holistic data in addition to scientific ones. This would align with the European regulation of biotech products as the European legislator has already introduced a new Article 26-b to the Directive 2001/18/EC (which restricts the introduction of GMOs into the European market) by relying on *Ganzheitliche Gesichtspunkte* (holistic factors): '[H]olistic, trans-scientific aspects that bridge risk assessment and risk management, to justify [national] bans [to GMOs]'.[162]

158 AB report, *EC – Hormones* [245]; AB report, *US/Canada – Hormones Continued Suspension* [535]. See Peel (n 7) 194–195.

159 Fiona Macmillan, *WTO and the Environment* (Sweet & Maxwell, 2001) 218.

160 'The International Monsanto Tribunal' is 'a unique "Opinion Tribunal" which was convened by civil society to clarify the legal obligations and consequences of some of the activities of the Monsanto Company': International Monsanto Tribunal, 'Chapter 12 'The Legal Opinion?' *Monsanto* (Web Page), www.monsanto-tribunal.org/upload/asset_cache/1016160509.pdf.

161 Judge Tulkens, 'Closing Speech' *Monsanto Tribunal* (Web Page, October 2016), www.monsanto-tribunal.org/. The potential role of witnesses as 'experts' is further discussed in Section 7.4.2.

162 Miranda Geelhoed, 'Divided in Diversity: Reforming the EU's GMO Regime' (2016) 18 *Cambridge Yearbook of European Legal Studies* 20; Alessandra Guida, 'The 2017 Fidenato Case and the 2015 Directive: The Curious Case of GMOs in Europe' (2020) *Review of European, Comparative and International Environmental Law* 1.

Regardless of whether the assessment of biotechnology risks should be reduced to a scientific evaluation of experimental studies, scientists should not be the only experts to be consulted by panels. The question, in turn, is: Who should be considered expert to inform panels about the impacts of these products to biosafety? This aspect is particularly relevant in the context of biotechnology, where '[e]xperts appointed by a panel can significantly influence the decision-making process'.[163] Accordingly, Section 7.4.2 offers some suggestions in this regard.

7.4.2 Who should advise panels on the reliability of opposing and uncertain risk assessments concerning biotechnology?

This section suggests how to mitigate the scientific ethos under the WTO that, unsurprisingly, is also reflected in the panels' process of appointing and consulting with experts in the biotechnology legal disputes.

Thus far, panels have appointed only scientists to support their decisions in the context of biotechnology.[164] However, *the complexity surrounding biotechnology cannot be reduced to a scientific matter*. Accordingly, scientists are, arguably, not the only experts that panels should consult to be advised on the effects posed by biotechnology to biosafety. This seems to be confirmed by the fact that on some occasions, the experts appointed by panels in the biotechnology legal disputes did not answer questions on the effects of biotechnology to human health and/or the environment because these questions were not of a scientific nature. For example, in *EC – Hormones*, Dr Ritter, one of the panel's experts, gave the following answer to the (non-)scientific question raised by the panel:

> The hour is late and I am going to go out on a limb and even though a number of us have consistently said during the day that *we feel uncomfortable* with drawing comparisons, if it would assist the Panel, carbadox is a genotoxic carcinogen.[165]

In the same case, the Chairman asked the panel's experts whether a double dose of hormones, which were allowed for implants in the ear, 'was typical for European situation or is that a phenomenon which is observed world-wide?'[166] Dr André observed that scientists could not answer the non-scientific question raised by the Chairman.[167] Similarly, in *US/Canada – Hormones Continued Suspension*, the US delegate asked whether the panel's experts were aware of evidence proving

163 AB report, *US/Canada – Hormones Continued Suspension* [480].

164 The panel's reference to 'scientific controversies' in Panel report, *EC – Biotech* [4.1008] conveys the idea that scientists are the experts to be consulted in biotechnology cases.

165 Panel report, *EC – Hormones* annex [773] (emphasis added).

166 Ibid annex [170].

167 Specifically, Dr André replied, 'It is not a scientific question . . . [I] can return through the same question, do you think people drive faster than allowed in any country or in another one? It is a problem of respect of regulation, only': Ibid annex [170].

that risks from implants in bovine ears were being processed into the human food supply.[168] Facing such a question, the Chairman gave voice to a deafening silence among panels' experts by explaining that they 'may not be in a position to respond to that question'.[169]

These are only a handful of examples showing that the evaluation of biotechnology cannot be reduced to a scientific matter. As Foster notes, certain issues concerning the impact of biotechnology to human health and/or the environment 'are more social than scientific in character'.[170] This confirms the need for adopting a holistic approach in the context of biotechnology and it, arguably, invites also to take account of social studies regarding biotechnology.

Consulting social experts along with scientists would, in turn, develop the concept of *expert* (of technologies) under the WTO, which seems not to be keeping pace with the fast changes brought by the current technology era in which witnesses of technology effects are taking a key role. When in 2017 the International Monsanto Tribunal was established, the judge Tulkens, in delivering her legal opinion on the effects of some biotech products to human rights, emphasised the capacity of witnesses to fill gaps in the experts' knowledge:

> The experts are not just experts through knowledge, since the witnesses have truly been experts through their personal history. They provide, in this way, key elements to understanding the reality of what happened.[171]

The Tribunal's final judgment, though not legally binding, shows the valuable role that *expert witnesses*, meaning people who become experts through their experience, may have in guiding judicial examination of matters concerning biotechnology.[172] After all, already in 1996, Angell underlined the close relationship between lay people, experts and witnesses.[173] In doing so, she claims that the judicial appointment of expert witnesses would be '[t]he most important reform we could make to raise scientific standards in the courtroom'.[174] Nevertheless, while some scholars observe that historically the role of experts has generally

168 Panel report, *Canada – Continued Suspension* [829].

169 Ibid [834]. See also the answer given by Dr Boisseau in the same report [839].

170 Foster (n 97) 177.

171 Judge Tulkens (n 161).

172 Indeed, the Court's decision establishing that the activities of Monsanto violated several human rights stems from judges' consultation with farmers from Argentina, American scientists, international lawyers, medical toxicologists from Sri Lanka and Germany and academics (v). The judges did not have the chance to hear any testimony from Monsanto because the multinational decided not to be represented in the trial. See International Monsanto Tribunal, 'Chapter 4 – Who are the Witnesses?' (Web Page), https://vimeo.com/273548130.

173 Marcia Angell, *Science on Trial – The Clash of Medical Evidence and the Law in the Breast Implant Case* (WW Norton & Company, 1996) 205.

174 Ibid.

been distinct from the role of witnesses,[175] others argue that only reputable experts recommended by established scientific organisations should be considered 'expert witnesses'.[176] However, by consulting only reputable experts (i.e., experts through their knowledge) decision-makers would not benefit from opinions received by witnesses who had a direct or indirect personal experience with the contested products. For example, by consulting only reputable scientists in the three biotechnology cases, WTO judicial bodies have lost the chance to consider potentially useful testimonies, social and medical evidence given by communities living in areas where the biotech products in question were cultivated for trade purposes.

In line with this suggestion, there is ample literature showing the importance of an extended peer community. For example, it has been observed that 'the Post Normal Science (PNS) literature highlights how science and policymaking interact if values are in conflict, decision stakes are high, and decisions are urgently needed'.[177] 'The goal of PNS is quality, a more robust "science for policy"'.[178] In doing so, PSN shows the relevance of an extended peer community to bring together a broader range of relevant perspectives. Specifically, the PNS community has developed the numeral unit spread assessment pedigree (NUSAP) system, which is 'a more formal way to combine quantitative and qualitative measures of uncertainty that is being used in support of policy making'.[179]

Importantly, a constructive consultation between WTO decision-makers, scientists, non-scientific experts, such as social scientists, and expert witnesses requires panels' composition of an *expert review group*, rather than the appointment of individual experts. To remind us, Section 3.6.2 suggests in this regard an amendment to Article 13 of the *DSU* that currently gives panels the possibility of appointing

175 Foster states that although '[t]he boundary between the expert and the witness has been recognised as fragile', historically the role of experts was distinct from that of witnesses: Foster (n 97) 86.

176 Angell (n 173) 205.

177 Guida (n 12) 10. See also Jerome R Ravetz, *The Roots of Present Day Science; An Essay by J.R. Ravetz. Edited for the Science Foundation Course Team of the Open University by Steven Rose* (The Open University, 1971); Silvio O Funtowicz and Jerome R Ravetz, 'Science for the Post-Normal Age' (1993) 25(7) *Futures* 739; Jerome R Ravetz, 'What Is Post-Normal Science' (1999) 31 *Futures* 647; Silvio O Funtowicz and Jerome R Ravetz, 'Values and Uncertainties' in GH Hadorn et al. (eds), *Handbook of Transdisciplinary Research* (Springer, 2008) 361; J Turnpenny, M Jones and I Lorenzoni, 'Where Now for Post-Normal Science?: A Critical Review of Its Development, Definitions, and Uses' (2011) 36(3) *Science, Technology & Human Values* 287; Roger Strand, 'Post-Normal Science' in Clive L Spash (ed), *Routledge Handbook of Ecological Economics: Nature and Society* (Routledge, 2017); Brian Wynne, 'Uncertainty and Environmental Learning – Reconceiving Science and Policy in the Preventive Paradigm' (1992) 2(2) *Global Environmental Change* 111.

178 Dorothy J Dankel, Nora S VaageJeroen and Jeroen P van der Sluijs, 'Post-Normal Science in Practice' (2017) 91 *Futures* 1, 2.

179 Guida (n 12) 10, citing P Jeroen Van Der Sluijs et al., 'Combining Quantitative and Qualitative Measures of Uncertainty in Model-Based Environmental Assessment: The NUSAP System' (2005) 25(2) *Risk Analysis* 481.

individual experts or experts review group. However, facing biotechnology matters involving highly complex scientific issues and considering the suggestion of consulting scientific along with non-scientific experts, Article 13 of the *DSU* should impose on panels the creation of ***expert review groups*** in biotechnology legal disputes. As Crawford-Brown, Pauwelyn and Smith observe, 'the rationality of scientific risk estimates lies in the dialogue between scientists'.[180] Consequently, panels seeking scientific advice 'should step away from their preference of appointing individual scientists . . . in favor of appointing an advisory experts group or community'.[181]

Also, we have to remind ourselves that the suggestion of appointing non-scientific experts would not be prevented by the participation restriction in expert review groups set out in Appendix 4, paragraph 2 of the *DSU*. This is because Article 13.1 of the *DSU* allows panels 'to seek information and technical advice ***from any individual or body which it deems appropriate***'.[182] The challenge lies in interpreting who should be considered 'appropriate'. In this respect, this study shows that appropriate risk assessments in the context of biotechnology should take account of scientific ***and*** holistic data. By analogy, an individual or institution should be considered 'appropriate' to inform a panel if it can provide (1) scientific data explaining the degree of risk and remaining level of uncertainty concerning adverse effects of biotechnology to human health and the environment, and (2) physical and social (i.e., holistic) data on the impact of these products to biosafety.

To conclude, the creation of an expert review group composed of experts providing scientific and holistic data might build what the author of this book defines as a ***constructive bridge of knowledge*** between WTO decision-makers, scientists, social experts and expert witnesses of the effects posed by biotechnology to biosafety.[183] This would, on the one hand, contribute to untangle the complex relationship between law and science and, on the other hand, mitigate the scientific ethos of risk assessments carried out in the context of the *SPS Agreement*. Further, the suggestion of creating a constructive bridge of knowledge between WTO judicial bodies and experts of biotechnology would contribute to enhance the reliability of evidence brought to the attention of decision-makers. As such, the suggestions provided in this chapter contribute to further refine the application of Alexy's theory of balancing to biotechnology legal disputes that, to remind us, should also encompass the ***reliability of evidence*** representing a key factor to perform a well-structured proportionality analysis of – and, accordingly, a reasoned balance between – the competing interests in the context of biotechnology.[184]

180 Douglas Crawford-Brown, Joost Pauwelyn and Kelly Smith, 'Environmental Risk, Precaution, and Scientific Rationality in the Context of WTO/NAFTA Trade Rules' (2004) 24 *Risk Analysis* 461, 468.

181 Ibid.

182 *Dispute Settlement Understanding* Appendix 4 [4] (emphasis added). See the analysis in Section 3.6.2.

183 Guida (n 12) 10.

184 See Section 3.6.2.

7.5 Conclusion

This chapter highlights the manner in which WTO judicial bodies have assessed biosafety measures in contexts of sufficient, but uncertain, scientific evidence. It emerges that the judicial examinations of scientific evidence and risk assessments supporting biosafety measures in these contexts are clearly a can of worms.

The chapter highlights that, as general rule, biosafety measures must be scientifically justified (Article 2.2), not maintained without sufficient scientific evidence (Article 2.2), based on risk assessments appropriate to the circumstances (Article 5.1) and comply with the definition of risk assessment under annex A(4). WTO law does not elucidate these key requirements, arguably to provide member states with greater flexibility in conducting risk assessments appropriate to the circumstances. This is not, however, what emerges from the analysis of WTO biotechnology legal disputes, in which the decision-makers appear to be blind to the remaining scientific uncertainties that exist and affect the quality and reliability of scientific evidence and risk assessments in the context of biotechnology.

The chapter, indeed, shows that in interpreting the sufficiency of scientific evidence and the appropriateness of risk assessments in *EC – Hormones*, *EC – Biotech*, and *US/Canada – Hormones Continued Suspension*, the decision-makers (1) implemented a strict judicial interpretation of the relevant provisions under the *SPS Agreement* (Articles 2.2 and 5.5, and annex A(4)), (2) adopted a quantitative interpretation of biotechnology risks, (3) selected scientific evidence arbitrarily, and (4) arguably did not duly accomplish their role of gatekeeper. Consequently, member states (1) did not have flexibility in conducting appropriate risk assessments aligning with Articles 2.2 and 5.1 and annex A(4) of the *SPS Agreement*, (2) could not enjoy their right of establishing a precautionary ALOP, and (3) could hardly accomplish their numerous international obligations to safeguard human health and the environment.

As a result, the judicial examination of biosafety measures and relating risk assessments conducted in contexts of sufficient and uncertain scientific evidence undermined the reliability of final legal decisions, interfered with the national sovereignty in managing biotechnology risks, and jeopardised a reasoned judicial balance between free trade and biosafety.

Against this background, this chapter suggests what should make *appropriate* a risk assessment and who should advise WTO decision-makers in the scientifically uncertain context of biotechnology. It underlines that rather than looking for positive evidence of harm and, in doing so, verifying the existence of a causal link, WTO decision-makers should consider biosafety measures as scientifically justified and based on appropriate risk assessments even when supported by inferences and positive and multiple correlations. This is because inferences and correlations can supplement the uncertain scientific evidence at stake and, in some circumstances, entail causation.

The chapter, then, emphasises the importance of considering *appropriate* those risk assessments encompassing not only scientific but also holistic data on the contested biotech products. Holistic data allow, in fact, taking account of physical and social impacts of biotechnology to biosafety, which is necessary to grasp the complexity surrounding this technology and, in turn, to shape appropriate risk assessments.

In this view, the present chapter underlines that biotechnology risk assessments should not be reduced to a scientific evaluation of experimental studies. Accordingly, scientists should not be the only experts consulted by panels examining biotechnology legal disputes. Rather, building a constructive bridge of knowledge between WTO decision-makers, scientists, social experts and expert witnesses would contribute to untangle the complex relationship between law and science, mitigate the scientific ethos of risk assessments carried out in the context of the *SPS Agreement*, and further refine the judicial performance of a well-structured proportionality analysis of – and, accordingly, a reasoned balance between – the competing interests in the context of biotechnology.

Chapter 8 adds a key piece to the picture emerging from this analysis. It critically analyses the judicial examination of national requests for ensuring biosafety from biotechnology risks by pursuing Article 5.7, which permits member states to adopt biosafety measures in contexts of *insufficient* scientific evidence and in light of the precautionary principle.

8 Adopting precautionary measures on biosafety in contexts of insufficient scientific evidence

8.1 Introduction

In all three biotechnology cases, WTO judicial bodies examined whether the contested biosafety measures could be adopted in light of the precautionary principle under the *SPS Agreement*. As Chapter 4 shows, there are several gateway provisions to precaution in the context of this Agreement. Article 5.7 is one of them. This provision permits member states to adopt biosafety measures even in contexts of insufficient scientific evidence, and it was recalled by WTO judicial bodies in *EC – Hormones* and invoked by the EC in *EC – Biotech* and *US/Canada – Hormones Continued Suspension*. Importantly, insufficiency of scientific evidence is a requirement or, as inferred by the panel in *EC – Biotech*, the most relevant condition,[1] to adopt biosafety measure in light of Article 5.7 and, consequently, the precautionary principle.

This chapter analyses the manner in which WTO judicial bodies have assessed precautionary measures on biosafety in contexts where member states have argued that insufficient scientific evidence exists regarding the harmfulness or harmlessness of trade in biotechnology. To remind us, in some cases the evidence available for both sides of the argument may be sufficient in quantitative terms but nevertheless leave significant scientific uncertainties. These remaining uncertainties can render the evidence insufficient in qualitative terms.

This chapter aims to demonstrate that while WTO judicial bodies have expressly acknowledged that Article 5.7 reflects the precautionary principle, their judicial interpretation of this provision is not in line with precaution. The chapter advances suggestions as to how precaution could be effectively applied under Article 5.7 to guide WTO judicial bodies in addressing circumstances in which qualitatively insufficient evidence and, consequently, unreliable empirical premises exist.

The chapter develops as follows. Section 8.2 provides critical reflections on Article 5.7. Section 8.3 offers an in-depth analysis of the judicial interpretation of the role of insufficient evidence in adopting biosafety measures in the context

1 Panel report, *EC – Biotech* [7.2939].

DOI: 10.4324/9781003325741-11

of Article 5.7 and, most importantly, the judicial distinction between the two concepts of scientific insufficiency and uncertainty. Section 8.4 offers suggestions for how precaution could be applied in cases with scientific uncertainty and insufficient qualitative evidence. Section 8.5 draws final conclusions.

8.2 Adopting biosafety measures in cases of insufficient evidence: critical reflections on Article 5.7 of the *SPS Agreement*

Article 5.7 of the *SPS Agreement* represents an exception to the WTO general rule allowing member states to adopt biosafety measures in contexts of sufficient scientific evidence.[2] To remind us, four cumulative requirements must be met to adopt biosafety measures in light of Article 5.7:

1. The relevant scientific evidence in question must be insufficient.
2. Biosafety measures must be adopted on the basis of available pertinent information.
3. Member states invoking this provision to adopt biosafety measures must obtain additional information necessary for a more objective assessment of risk.
4. The adopted biosafety measures must be reviewed within a reasonable period[3] that depends on the circumstances of each case.[4]

Further, panels, the AB and numerous scholars broadly agree on considering Article 5.7 as a gateway to the precautionary principle.[5] Nevertheless, this provision provides a sui generis formulation of precaution in trade contexts, not least because the first, third and fourth requirements are not commonly associated with the precautionary principle,[6] even though they are in accordance with it, as discussed in Chapter 4.[7]

Noteworthy is that a critical reflection on the formulation of Article 5.7 highlights that successful adoption of biosafety measures in light of the precautionary principle might be challenging in the context of this provision, for two main reasons.

First, proving the insufficiency of scientific evidence to meet the first requirement of Article 5.7 is hardly possible and indeed unreasonable, as Chapter 6 highlights. Consequently, the consideration of insufficiency of scientific evidence

2 *SPS Agreement* art 2.2. See Panel report, *EC – Biotech* [7.2973]; AB report, *Japan – Agricultural Products II* [80].

3 *SPS Agreement* art 5.7.

4 AB report, *Japan – Agricultural Products II* [93].

5 See Section 4.3.1.1.

6 Ilona Cheyne, 'Gateways to the Precautionary Principle in WTO Law' (2007) 19(2) *Journal of Environmental Law* 155, 159.

7 See Section 4.3.1.1.

as a *conditio sine qua non* to justify biosafety measures in light of Article 5.7 and, accordingly, the precautionary principle should be reconsidered.

Second, the requirement to perform a *more objective assessment of risks* recalls, to some extent, the standard of review applied by panels to examine biotechnology matters. To remind us, according to the AB, panels must examine legal disputes through an *objective assessment of the matter* in the sense of Article 11 of the *DSU*, which is considered the general standard of review under the WTO.[8] WTO law does not elucidate what makes *objective* a risk assessment or what makes it *more* objective.

Arguably, the term *objective* might have two meanings. It might suggest the need for performing a *non-subjective* assessment of risks. However, any conclusion on the assessment of biotechnology risks reflects the interpretation of data given by scientists. Put differently, the fact that scientific data can be interpreted in different ways prevents the establishment of one objective truth.

Alternatively, *objective* could imply the need for member states to perform an *unbiased* risk assessment. Conducting a risk assessment with an unbiased approach should be, however, an implicit condition – rather than a requirement for adopting biosafety measures in contexts of insufficient scientific evidence.

Therefore, the third requirement of Article 5.7 should also be re-examined or, at least, clarified as to allow effective adoption of biosafety measures by pursuing this provision.

Bearing these observations in mind, Section 8.3 casts light on the judicial interpretation of precautionary measures on biosafety in contexts in which member states argued that insufficient scientific evidence exists regarding the harmfulness or harmlessness of trade in biotechnology and, as such, biosafety measures could be justified in light of Article 5.7 and, consequently, the precautionary principle.

8.3 Judicial interpretation of the role of insufficient evidence in adopting biosafety measures

In the three biotechnology cases, WTO judicial bodies establish that all precautionary measures on biosafety were adopted in contexts of sufficient scientific evidence. Accordingly, those measures did not meet the first requirement of Article 5.7 of the *SPS Agreement*, insufficiency of scientific evidence. This is the main reason, though not the only one, leading WTO decision-makers to conclude that the biosafety measures adopted in the context of biotechnology could not be justified in light of Article 5.7 and, consequently, the precautionary principle.

This section demonstrates that this judicial reasoning is problematic for three reasons.

First, as anticipated, *member states can hardly prove that there is insufficient scientific evidence*. Proving that something does not exist allocates on member states a sort of *probatio diabolica*. This is especially true considering that in the context

8 See Section 6.3.

of biotechnology, member states should, arguably, proof the insufficiency of scientific evidence in ***qualitative*** terms. This is because there is a consistent and, accordingly, quantitatively sufficient literature on biotechnology.[9]

At this point, a reasonable question might be how WTO judicial bodies establish the lack of (qualitatively) insufficient scientific evidence in the biotechnology cases and, consequently, the non-compliance of biosafety measures with Article 5.7.[10] In *EC – Biotech*, the panel ***infers*** sufficiency of scientific evidence from the fact that the risk assessments conducted by the EC scientific committees complied with Article 5.1 and annex (A)[11] that, to remind us, outline strict requirements to perform appropriate risk assessments in contexts of sufficient scientific evidence.[12] The compliance of the European risk assessments with Article 5.1 and annex A(4) exclude, by implication, the alignment of these assessments with Article 5.7. In following this reasoning, the panel failed, according to Eliason, to interpret Article 5.7:

> To the *EC – Biotech* panel, scientific evidence is insufficient if a risk assessment has previously been performed that met the criteria of Article 5.1. Therefore, in cases of GMOs with existing risk assessments, a member's safeguard measure could never be approved under Article 5.7 if it failed to meet the criteria of Article 5.1. This relegates the use of Article 5.7 to the limited circumstances in which no previous risk assessment was possible, an unlikely scenario where novel scientific products requiring extensive characterization and testing prior to commercial release are involved.[13]

Similarly, in *US/Canada – Hormones Continued Suspension*, the panel concluded that sufficient scientific information existed about the hormones in question because of the existence of international standards about the use of hormones in beef production. However, the AB disagrees, arguing that 'the existence of an international standard does not create a legal presumption of sufficiency for purposes of Article 5.7',[14] and, thus, reverses the panel's findings.[15]

In this regard, it is important to take a step back and remind us that the *SPS Agreement* encourages WTO states to harmonise their measures by basing SPS measures on international standards[16] that in the field of biotechnology are gen-

9 See Section 1.2.

10 In *EC – Hormones*, WTO judicial bodies did not discuss the criterion of insufficiency because the EC did not invoke art 5.7 to justify the adoption of precautionary measures.

11 Panel report, *EC – Biotech* [7.3273], [7.3300], [7.3327], [7.3356], [7.3369].

12 See Section 7.2.

13 Antonia Eliason, 'Science Versus Law in WTO Jurisprudence: The (Mis)Interpretation of the Scientific Process and the (In)Sufficiency of Scientific Evidence in EC-Biotech' (2009) 41 *New York University Journal of International Law & Policy* 341, 405.

14 AB report, *US/Canada – Hormones Continued Suspension* [697].

15 Ibid [736(d)].

16 *SPS Agreement* preamble and art 3.

erally set out by the *Codex Alimentarius* (Codex).[17] Importantly, SPS measures conforming to international standards, guidelines or recommendations *are presumed to be consistent* with the *SPS Agreement*.[18] As such, they are deemed as based on sufficient scientific evidence in the sense of Article 2.2 and appropriate risk assessments complying with Article 5.1.[19]

In light of this, some observations are in order. By presuming that the existence of international standards entails that sufficient scientific evidence occurs, 'the mere existence of an international standard would *ipso jure* make it impossible for a Member to adopt measures under Article 5.7 of the SPS Agreement'.[20] This situation is concerning because scientific uncertainty in the context of biotechnology should invite panels to conduct a review of all measures adopted under the WTO, without presuming any compliance with WTO law only because of the adoption of science-based international standards, guidelines or recommendations set out by the Codex. This is because even international standards are unlikely to be based on qualitatively sufficient evidence if the subject matter is characterised by scientific uncertainty.

Further, as Thow et al. highlight, it must be underlined that '[w]hile Codex articulates its standards as a useful "floor" – the basis for potentially more stringent national standards – the WTO language in effect made Codex standards more like a "ceiling"'.[21] The compliance of biosafety measures based on international standards with WTO law is, in fact, assumed, meaning that those measures are not examined at all. This equates, according to Cosbey and Fontanelli, to 'voluntarism under duress'.[22]

Therefore, proving that precautionary measures on biosafety meet the first requirement of Article 5.7, insufficiency of scientific evidence, is hardly possible. Then, the judicial interpretation of this requirement makes the compliance of these measures with Article 5.7 even more difficult.

Second, requiring member states to prove that there is insufficient scientific evidence to comply with the first requirement of Article 5.7 and, consequently, the precautionary principle which is reflected in this provision, underlines a *judicial misinterpretation of this principle*. This is because the precautionary principle

17 Codex is the international agency setting the relating standards of reference.

18 *SPS Agreement* preamble and art 3.2.

19 Chee Yoke Ling and Lim Li Ching, 'Biosafety First' in Terje Traavik and Lim Li Ching (eds), *Biosafety First – Holistic Approaches to Risk and Uncertainty in Genetic Engineering and Genetically Modified Organisms* (Tapir Academic Publishers, 2007) 427, 429–430.

20 AB report, *US/Canada – Hormones Continued Suspension* [691].

21 Anne Marie Thow et al., 'Global Governance of Front-of-Pack Nutrition Labelling: A Qualitative Analysis' (2019) 11(2) *Nutrients* 1, 2.

22 Aaron Cosbey, *A Forced Evolution? The Codex Alimentarius Commission, Scientific Uncertainty and the Precautionary Principle* (IISD, 2002); Filippo Fontanelli, 'ISO and Codex Standards and International Trade Law: What Gets Said Is Not What's Heard' (2011) 60 *International and Compative Law Quarterly* 895; Thow et al. (n 21).

applies not because of insufficient (or uncertain) scientific evidence but in spite of it, as extensively discussed in Chapter 4.[23]

Also, the precautionary principle lowers the evidentiary threshold, while the panel in *US/Canada – Continued Hormones Suspension* seems to raise the bar to adopt precautionary measures in the context of Article 5.7. Given the existence of international standards for meat and meat products from animals treated with the five hormones in question, in the 2008 case the panel claims that the EC could justify a (precautionary) ALOP by basing the contested provisional ban on 'a *critical mass* of new evidence and/or information that calls into question the fundamental precepts of previous knowledge and evidence to make relevant, previously sufficient, evidence now insufficient'.[24] This means that 'if relevant evidence already exists, not any degree of insufficiency will satisfy the [first] criterion under Article 5.7'.[25] Rather, there must be a *critical mass of new evidence and/or information* turning the existent and sufficient scientific evidence into insufficient evidence, which justifies the adoption of precautionary measures under Article 5.7.[26] In other words, when facing requests for adopting a precautionary ALOP in contexts of insufficient scientific evidence, the panel raises (instead of lowers) the evidentiary threshold.

Noteworthy is that the AB describes the panel's approach to Article 5.7 as 'too inflexible'[27] and underlines that it sets a 'too high threshold' of evidence,[28] which is against the proactive rationale of the precautionary principle calling for actions at an earlier stage, even when there is not yet conclusive scientific evidence as to the harmfulness.[29] As Eliason stresses, the fact that the precautionary principle 'carries with it the specter of unfairly protectionist domestic regulations, [it] is in part due to the misinterpretation of the role of scientific evidence in analyzing the validity of such measures [under the WTO]'.[30]

A further thorny aspect revealing a judicial misinterpretation of precaution lies in the fact that in the view of WTO judicial bodies, precautionary measures adopted in the context of Article 5.7 cannot be supported by appropriate risk assessments. As Chapter 7 discusses in detail, in the view of WTO judicial bodies, the appropriateness of risk assessments *depends on* the sufficiency of scientific evidence.[31] Put differently, the existence of insufficient scientific evidence precludes

23 See Section 4.2.

24 Panel report, *US/Canada – Hormones Continued Suspension* [7.648] (emphasis in original).

25 Ibid; Panel report, *Canada – Continued Suspension* [7.626].

26 Panel report, *US/Canada – Hormones Continued Suspension* [7.648]; Panel report, *Canada – Continued Suspension* [7.626].

27 AB report, *US/Canada – Hormones Continued Suspension* [705].

28 Ibid [706]; [736 (d–ii)].

29 Aline L Jaeckel, *The International Seabed Authority and the Precautionary Principle – Balancing Deep Seabed Mineral Mining and Marine Environmental Protection* (Brill Nijhoff, 2017) 29.

30 Eliason (n 13) 406.

31 See Sections 7.2 and 7.3.

member states from performing appropriate risk assessments in the context of Article 5.7:

> *If* the conclusions of the risk assessment are not sufficiently supported by the scientific evidence referred to . . . *then* there cannot be a risk assessment appropriate to the circumstances, within the meaning of Article 5.1.[32]

This is further confirmed in *US/Canada – Hormones Continued Suspension*, where the AB claims that 'Article 5.7 contemplates situations where there is some evidentiary basis indicating the possible existence of a risk, but *not enough to permit the performance of a risk assessment*'.[33]

These judicial interpretations of Article 5.7 convey the idea that biosafety measures triggered in light of the precautionary principle under this provision are either based on inappropriate risk assessments or not based on a risk assessment at all.[34] This, in turn, demonstrates a misunderstanding of the precautionary principle, a careful application of which should, in fact, involve an in-depth risk assessment.[35]

Thus, the judicial approach to the requirement of insufficient scientific evidence under Article 5.7 shows a need for further steps towards a more sophisticated interpretation of the precautionary principle in the context of this provision. This is especially true considering that WTO judicial bodies appear reticent in providing insights on the interpretation and application of this principle in trade contexts. For instance, in *EC – Biotech*, the question of whether biosafety measures could be justified in light of the precautionary principle and the *Cartagena Protocol on Biosafety* under the WTO represents, according to Cheyne, '[o]ne of the most interesting arguments which the Panel did not choose to explore'.[36] Also, in *EC – Hormones*, the EC argues for the application of the precautionary principle by stressing its customary international status – rather than through the gateway provision of Article 5.7. The AB clarifies that the status of the principle was still debated and any judicial position in this regard was 'unnecessary, and probably imprudent'.[37] Nevertheless, taking a position on (at least) the interpretation of the precautionary principle in trade context would have enhanced the scarce jurisprudence on its application under the WTO.

32 Panel report, *Japan – Apples (Article 21.5)* [8.136] (emphasis added). It recalls Panel report, *Australia – Salmon* [8.57].

33 AB report, *US/Canada – Hormones Continued Suspension* [678] (emphasis added).

34 See also AB report, *Korea – Radionuclides* [5.106]; AB report, *Canada – Continued Suspension* [677].

35 Jaeckel (n 29) 36; Nicolas De Sadeleer, *Environmental Principles: From Political Slogans to Legal Rules* (Oxford University Press, 2002) 174–180. See also *COMM(2000)* 12.

36 Ilona Cheyne, 'Life after the Biotech Products Dispute' (2008) *Environmental Law Review* 52, 61.

37 AB report, *EC – Hormones* [123] ('*EC – Hormones*').

Third, the common decision that all precautionary measures on biosafety in the three biotechnology cases were adopted in contexts of sufficient scientific evidence is also based on *the questionable judicial distinction between scientific insufficiency and uncertainty*. It is explained that *scientific uncertainty* occurs when 'reputable scientists agree that further research needs to be carried out on a particular question, or their disagreement on issues germane to a dispute makes it clear this is so'.[38] Instead, 'relevant scientific evidence will be *insufficient*, within the meaning of Article 5.7, if the body of available scientific evidence does not allow for an adequate assessment of risks, as required under Article 5.1 and as defined in Annex A to the SPS Agreement'.[39]

WTO's distinction here is at odds with other international legal instruments. For example, the *Cartagena Protocol on Biosafety* establishes that a '[l]ack of scientific certainty due to insufficient relevant scientific information and knowledge regarding [the living modified organisms] . . . shall not prevent that Party from taking a decision . . . to avoid or minimize such potential adverse effects'.[40] The Protocol explicitly refers to the precautionary principle to avoid or minimise adverse effects of GMOs on biosafety. As such, it underlines how taking precautionary actions might be necessary to address the lack of scientific certainty *due to* insufficient relevant scientific evidence. WTO judicial bodies should, in turn, acknowledge that the concepts of scientific uncertainty and insufficiency are interwoven.

Further, drawing a distinction between scientific uncertainty and insufficient scientific information affects the application of precautionary measures in the context of Article 5.7. Although the analysis in Chapter 4 highlights that this provision may constitute a sui generis application of the principle applying in contexts of insufficient scientific evidence,[41] this does not exclude its employment also in circumstances of scientific uncertainty. In other words, considering that Article 5.7 reflects the precautionary principle, member states should be allowed to invoke this provision in contexts of insufficient as well as uncertain scientific evidence. This is particularly so given that WTO does not expressly regulate cases characterised by scientific uncertainty. To remind us, Article 5.1 of the *SPS Agreement* covers circumstances of *sufficient* scientific evidence, while Article 5.7 relates to situations of *insufficient* scientific evidence that, according to panels and the AB, differ from cases of *scientific uncertainty*. There is no indication of how scientifically uncertain circumstances should be addressed.

38 Caroline E Foster, *Science and the Precautionary Principle in International Courts and Tribunals – Expert Evidence, Burden of Proof, and Finality* (Cambridge University Press, 2011) 11; Brian Wynne, 'Uncertainty and Environmental Learning – Reconceiving Science and Policy in the Preventive Paradigm' (1992) 2(2) *Global Environmental Change* 111–127.

39 AB report, *Korea – Radionuclides* [5.106]; AB report, *Japan – Apples* [238]–[239]; AB report, *Canada – Continued Suspension* [677] (emphasis added).

40 *Cartagena Protocol on Biosafety* arts 10(6) and 11(8).

41 Cheyne (n 6) 159.

It is also worth noting that there is no mention of the judicial distinction between scientific uncertainty and insufficiency in the literature. The reason arguably lies in the fact that one might assume that Article 5.7 referring to scientific insufficiency applies also to cases of scientific uncertainty. This assumption would be wrong. The judicial distinction between scientific insufficiency and uncertainty is, in fact, stressed in several cases.[42] As recent as 2017, the panel in the *Russian – Pigs* case argued that 'insufficiency of scientific evidence does not extend to situations of "scientific uncertainty"'.[43] Similarly, in the 2018 *Korea – Radionuclides* case, the panel rejected Korea's request for banning radioactive food products in light of Article 5.7 chiefly for the same reason.[44]

In light of this, and bearing in mind that the precautionary principle can be interpreted under the WTO normative framework,[45] the employment of this principle should be considered *the* legal means to deal with scientific uncertainties and qualitatively insufficient evidence in the context of biotechnology. This would, accordingly, fill the gap under WTO law that does not cover cases of scientific uncertainty.

To conclude, this section argues that it is problematic to require insufficient scientific evidence in order to justify precautionary measures under Article 5.7. Indeed, it shows a misperception of the precautionary principle at the WTO judicial level. Also, it reveals a gap under the WTO that does not elucidate how to deal with scientifically uncertain cases, and a lacuna in the literature that does not offer contributions on the implications stemming from the questionable judicial distinction between scientific insufficiency and uncertainty.

Against this background, Section 8.4 suggests how precautionary measures on biosafety could apply in the context of biotechnology and, more generally, to cases with scientific uncertainty and qualitatively insufficient scientific evidence.

8.4 Suggestions for improvements

A common question that arises in regard to technology that involves scientific uncertainty and, accordingly, qualitatively insufficient scientific evidence is: What standard of proof and level(s) of uncertainty suffice for adopting biosafety measures? In relation to biotechnology, international law and WTO law do not provide clear guidance.[46] As Weiss forecasts, this 'leaves open to interpretation the very issue that will be crucial in any future dispute hinging on the international law governing trade'.[47]

42 See, e.g., Panel report, *EC – Biotech* [7.1525]; Panel report, *Canada – Continued Suspension* [7.608].
43 Panel report, *Russia – Pigs (EU)* [7.659].
44 Panel report, *Korea – Radionuclides* [7.111].
45 See Section 4.3.
46 See Sections 7.3 and 7.4.
47 Charles Weiss, 'Can There Be Science-Based Precaution?' (2006) 1 *Environmental Research Letters* 1, 5.

The precautionary principle, which can apply to cases of sufficient, insufficient and uncertain scientific evidence, affects the standard of proof by lowering the evidentiary threshold.[48] In light of this, some international treaties, such as the *United Nations Fish Stocks Agreement*, set out specific precautionary standards.[49] What is more, precaution becomes a standard by itself or, as Andorno observes, it may be seen as 'a new legal standard for a technological age'.[50]

However, what remains unclear is the minimum level of evidence allowing precaution to apply. As an analogy, for governments to introduce strict social distancing measures in the face of the COVID-19 epidemic, there had to be some level of evidence that the virus can spread through airborne droplets. While much uncertainty remained about the transmission and infectious potential of the virus at the time these precautionary measures were introduced, there was some evidence to suggest that social distancing would significantly lower the rate of new infections. In the case of biosafety measures, governments equally require a degree of evidence about the harmfulness of particular biotech products to justify restricting trade in the name of biosafety. However, what level of evidence is required remains unclear, which leaves judicial bodies with little guidance as to how to balance trade interests with biosafety concerns.

This section provides suggestions about appropriate standard(s) of proof (or level of legal evidence) and level of uncertainty that might allow precautionary measures to apply in the context of biotechnology. In doing so, it shows that the WTO judicial bodies' standard of proof is too high. In fact, it seems to align with criminal cases, even though trade issues are civil matters. Thus, the present section offers a comparative analysis of the minimum level of legal evidence required by other international courts, international treaties, environmental agencies and domestic regulations to adopt a precautionary approach. Moreover, this analysis refers to a *scale of legal evidence and scientific (un)certainties*, which is developed at the end of this section to guide WTO judicial bodies in balancing free trade and biosafety in cases of scientific uncertainty and qualitatively insufficient scientific evidence.[51]

8.4.1 Standards of proof and the case of biotechnology

The *standard of proof* is described as 'the quantum or amount of evidence required to prove the essential factual propositions constituting the elements of

48 Jaeckel (n 29) 55.

49 *Agreement for the Implementation of the Provisions of the United Nations Convention on the Law of the Sea of 10 December 1982 Relating to the Conservation and Management of Straddling Fish Stocks and Highly Migratory Fish Stocks* art 6(3)(b); ibid 42.

50 Roberto Andorno, 'The Precautionary Principle: A New Legal Standard for a Technological Age' (2004) 1 *Journal of International Biotechnology Law* 11.

51 The precautionary principle is not an absolute principle and, as such, its adoption must be balanced with the other interests at stake.

the actions'.[52] In other words, standards of proof aid to determine what degree of evidence and level of certainty are necessary to prove facts at stake. Standards vary depending on the case, the nature of evidence[53] and the area of law in which they are applied.

A commonly acknowledged difference is between criminal cases, which usually involve a higher standard of proof (e.g., 'beyond reasonable doubt'), and civil cases that generally require a lower standard, such as 'substantial and credible evidence' or 'preponderance of evidence'.[54] More specifically, Judge Anthony P. Calisi explains that in civil cases, the court's task is to decide whether the evidence of one of the parties is *preponderant* to the others.[55]

The most relevant aspect of civil court cases regards the beginning of the trial, where both sides of the scale are equal.[56] On the contrary, at the beginning of a criminal case,

> the scales of justice are already 100 percent in favor of the defendant. By the end of trial, if the prosecution hasn't tipped the scales to 99 percent in their favor, they haven't met their burden of proof beyond a reasonable doubt.[57]

The approach taken by WTO judicial bodies to biotechnology cases seems more akin to criminal law than civil law courts. This is because at the beginning of a biotechnology case, the scales of justice seem already in favour of the party supporting free trade. Indeed, if the party asking for the implementation of biosafety measures has not tipped the scales to a *high percentage* in its favour by the end of the trial, the adoption of biosafety measures is rejected in trade contexts. This WTO judicial bodies' approach is, however, unjustified for three reasons.

First, WTO biotechnology cases are civil matters and, as such, the standard of proof adopted by WTO judicial bodies in these cases should not as high as the one adopted in criminal cases, especially if the precautionary principle is invoked, and consequently, the evidentiary threshold should be lowered.

Second, if anything, the standard of proof usually used for criminal cases could be applied only if the interest receiving higher protection was biosafety, rather than free trade. Indeed, an analogy between biotechnology and criminal matters would have not been surprising given the growing number of international environmental treaties that consider conducts jeopardising health and the

52 Trischa Mann, *Australian Law Dictionary* (Oxford University Press, 2nd ed, 2013) 584.

53 Ibid.

54 Schweizer adds that the main difference between the standards of proof in criminal and civil cases 'lies in the degree of belief (or conviction) required for finding for the party bearing the burden of proof': Mark Schweizer, 'The Civil Standard of Proof – What Is It, Actually?' (2016) 20(3) *The International Journal of Evidence & Proof* 217, 219.

55 See Anthony P Calisi, 'What's the Burden of Proof in Personal Injury Civil Court Cases?' *Injury Claim Coach* (Web Page), www.injuryclaimcoach.com/civil-court-cases.html.

56 Ibid.

57 Ibid.

environment as *crimes*. For instance, the *Basel Convention on the Transboundary Movements of Hazardous Wastes and their Disposal* establishes that illegal shipments of hazardous waste are considered a crime.[58] More interestingly, the 2016 UNEP published *The Rise of Environmental Crime – A Growing Threat to Natural Resources Peace, Development and Security* to outline a growing need to deal with environmental crimes rather than civil law liability for environmental damages.[59] Similarly, in 2017 the Judges of the Advisory International Monsanto Tribunal considered fully justified 'the imposition of *criminal sanctions* for conduct [posed by the biotech multinational Monsanto] resulting in serious environmental harm'.[60] In sum, a WTO judicial bodies' approach akin to criminal cases may have been perceived as an alignment of WTO law with international law if biosafety – rather than free trade – was the interest receiving higher protection.

Third, WTO law is not based on a rationale similar to the one adopted in criminal cases, in which the broadly accepted 'Blackstone Ratio' applies, according to which:

> [A]ll presumptive evidence of felony should be admitted cautiously: for the law holds, that *it is better that ten guilty persons escape, than that one innocent suffer*.[61]

By relying on this ratio(nale), decision-makers in criminal courtrooms assume that *an accused person is considered innocent until they are proven guilty*. This assumption sits behind the decision to tip the scales of justice in favour of the defendant at the beginning of criminal trials.

The WTO judicial bodies' approach to biotechnology cases echoes an implicit prima facie priority of free trade in biotechnology, which is legally groundless for the reasons discussed in Chapter 2. This, in turn, means that when facing uncertainties or doubt, WTO judicial bodies tend to err on the side of trade. In other words:

> *The safety in trading biotechnology is presumed until they are proven dangerous.*

However, this judicial approach does not align with international law attaching primary importance to biosafety.[62] An alignment of WTO law with international

58 International Monsanto Tribunal Advisory Opinion (The Hague, 18 April 2017) 45.

59 Christian Nellemann, *The Rise of Environmental Crime – A Growing Threat to Natural Resources Peace, Development and Security* (United Nations Environment Programme, 2016).

60 International Monsanto Tribunal Advisory Opinion (The Hague, 18 April 2017), 45 (emphasis added).

61 William Blackstone, *Commentaries on the Laws of England: A Facsimile of the First Edition of 1765–1769* (University of Chicago Press, vol 1, book 4, 1979) (emphasis added).

62 See Section 2.6.

law could, in fact, lead to a rationale diametrically opposed to the current one, that is to say:

> *The harmfulness of biotechnology is presumed until they are proven safe.*

This approach would also echo the rationale of the precautionary principle calling for actions at an earlier stage, even when there is still scientific uncertainty on the harmfulness of the contested products. After all, as Van Den Belt and Gremmen emphasise, '[i]t is sometimes stated that adoption of the Precautionary Principle entails the abandonment of the old maxim "innocent until proven guilty" in favor of the new maxim "guilty until proven innocent" '.[63]

Since acceptance of this idea seems unlikely within the WTO, at the very least, the interests of trade and biosafety would need to be considered as equal. To minimise the consequences stemming from the judicial approach to biotechnology cases, WTO decision-makers should align their approach to civil – rather than criminal – cases. This means that at the beginning of a trial concerning the international trade in biotechnology, both sides of the scale should be equal. This would, in turn, require WTO decision-makers to establish whether the evidence of one of the parties is preponderant to the others.

This study argues that *preponderance of evidence* (or *balance of probabilities*) could be the standard of proof to assess requests for implementing biosafety measures in contexts where the body of scientific evidence is sufficient in quantitative and qualitative terms and the precautionary principle is not invoked or does not apply, meaning that one or more of its three components are not met (i.e., *risk* of environmental or human health harm, *uncertainty* about harm to human health and/or the environment, and *action* at an early stage).

However, *preponderance of evidence* should *not* be the standard adopted in cases in which the following circumstances occur:

1. The body of scientific evidence in question is qualitatively insufficient as the high level of scientific uncertainties affects the reliability of the empirical premises at stake.
2. The precautionary principle applies and, accordingly, the evidentiary threshold must be lowered.

Unsurprisingly, these two circumstances occur in all three WTO biotechnology cases. So what should be the standard of proof in cases in which the precautionary principle has been invoked? Put differently, to what extent does or should the precautionary principle affect the evidentiary threshold to prove the safety or the harmfulness of biotechnology? The following sections seek to answer this question.

63 Henk Van Den Belt and Bart Gremmen, 'Between Precautionary Principle and "Sound Science": Distributing the Burdens of Proof' (2002) 15(1) *Journal of Agricultural and Environmental Ethics* 103, 104.

8.4.2 Evidentiary threshold and the precautionary principle in biotechnology cases

The Hon Justice Brian J Preston argues that 'the degree of scientific uncertainty . . . is *inversely proportional* to the degree of potential environmental damage'.[64] He explains the rationale for the inverse relationship between environmental damage and uncertainty about that damage and, in doing so, refers to the adoption of precautionary measures:

> [I]f the potential environmental damage or consequence is greater there should be a lower or more easily crossed threshold for the uncertainty about that potential environmental damage so as to trigger the need to take precautionary measures to prevent that environmental damage. Conversely, if the potential environmental damage or consequence is less serious, there can be a higher threshold for the uncertainty about that potential environmental damage before precautionary measures need to be taken.[65]

In line with this, a recent study of several European cases reveals 'a [judicial] trend toward requiring less evidence of harm where there was a severe threat to human health'.[66]

This approach seems reasonable and logical and can help in discussing what standard of proof may be suitable for legal disputes involving requests for trade in biotechnology *versus* requests for precautionary measures aiming at ensuring biosafety.

At this point, it is important to remind us that, although WTO law does not provide an explicit formulation of the precautionary principle, the AB in *EC – Hormones* emphasises that responsible governments commonly take prudent and precautionary actions to avert 'serious and irreversible risks',[67] such as those to human health and the environment claimed by the EC in all biotechnology cases. By relating precautionary actions and biotechnology to serious and irreversible risks, the AB acknowledges a high potential for human health and environmental damage. In light of the inverse relationship between environmental damage and uncertainty about the considered damage, the threshold of

64 Hon Justice Brian J Preston and Land and Environment Court of New South Wales Chief Judge, 'The Judicial Development of the Precautionary Principle (Seminar Presentation at the Queensland Government Environmental Management of Firefighting Foam Policy, 21 February 2017)' 12 (emphasis added), www.lec.justice.nsw.gov.au/Documents/Speeches%20and%20Papers/PrestonCJ/Justice%20Brian%20J%20Preston%20SC%20Keynote%20Address%20-%20Precautionary%20Principle%20%20delivered%2021.02.17.pdf.

65 Ibid.

66 Kenisha Garnett and David J Parsons, 'Multi-Case Review of the Application of the Precautionary Principle in European Union Law and Case Law' (2017) 37(3) *Risk Analysis* 502, 513.

67 AB report, *EC – Hormones* [124].

uncertainty for triggering precautionary measures should be low. In other words, since biotechnology involves *high* risks to human health and/or the environment, the threshold of uncertainty for triggering precautionary measures under WTO law should be *low*.

Nevertheless, as precaution does not apply for every minor or imaginary threat, a certain threshold of risk –, that is *gravity* times *probability* of harm – must be reached. *Establishing whether this threshold has been met might be particularly challenging for decision-makers examining biotechnology cases.* This is because there is no agreement among scientists on the gravity and probability of biotechnology risks. To remind us, in regard to the *gravity* of harm, there are, for instance, scientific studies claiming that the resistance of genetically engineering crops to certain antibiotics causes serious human health problems,[68] while others state that '[n]o expert panel has ever identified significant risk, associated with the use of A[ntibiotic] R[esistance] M[arker]s'.[69] Similarly, scientists disagree also on the *probability* of occurrence of risks posed by biotechnology. A good example is provided by the occurrence of harm posed by the use of glyphosate on biotech products: In 2015 the IARC classified this pesticide as 'probably carcinogenic to humans'[70] while in 2016 the Food and Agriculture Organization of the UN (FAO) Panel of Experts on Pesticide Residues in Food and the Environment and the WHO concluded that 'glyphosate is unlikely to pose a carcinogenic risk to humans from exposure through the diet'.[71] Consequently, WTO judicial bodies dealing with legal disputes on the international trade in biotechnology face unreliable empirical premises stemming from the uncertainties on the harm posed by these products to biosafety. Consequently, establishing the evidentiary threshold that suffices precaution to apply is very difficult and, arguably, confined to the discretion of the appointed panel.

Against this background, the adoption of a *scale of legal evidence and scientific (un)certainties* suggested in Section 8.4.3 might guide WTO judicial bodies in evaluating the state of knowledge concerning the contested biotech products and, accordingly, to set the precautionary evidentiary threshold on a case-by-case basis.

68 Trudy Netherwood et al., 'Assessing the Survival of Transgenic Plant DNA in the Human Gastrointestinal Tract' (2004) 22 *Nature Biotechnology* 204.

69 DA Goldstein et al., 'Human Safety and Genetically Modified Plants: A Review of Antibiotic Resistance Markers and Future Transformation Selection Technologies' (2005) 99(1) *Journal of Applied Microbiology* 7, 18. See Section 1.2.2.

70 International Agency for Research on Cancer and World Health Organization, *Evaluation of Five Organophosphate Insecticides and Herbicides* (IARC/WHO, 20 March 2015) vol 112, www.iarc.fr/en/media-centre/iarcnews/pdf/MonographVolume112.pdf. See Section 1.2.2.

71 'Biotech Gallery – IARC (International Agency for Research on Cancer): Glyphosate Cancer Determination Challenged by World Consensus' *Genetic Literacy Project* (Web Page, 22 October 2017), https://geneticliteracyproject.org/glp-facts/iarc-international-agency-research-cancer-glyphosate-determination-world-consensus/.

8.4.3 *Suggestions for an appropriate standard of proof to apply precautionary measures in biotechnology cases: the Bayesian* scale of legal evidence and scientific (un)certainties

8.4.3.1 *Meaning and purposes of a scale of legal evidence and scientific (un)certainties*

This study suggests the judicial adoption of a *scale of legal evidence and scientific (un)certainties*, which might be a lighthouse for WTO judicial bodies navigating the complex issues raised by the uncertainties surrounding biotechnology. This is because the scale developed in this section outlines a hierarchy of uncertainties taking account of the probabilities of harm and the related standard(s) of proof to apply in light of the considered level(s) of gravity.

As WTO law and its jurisprudence do not provide insights on how to design such a scale, reviewing literature on the management of uncertainties in other fields is enlightening. Research on the impact of climate change is most illuminating in this regard. Indeed, successive reports by the Intergovernmental Panel on Climate Change (IPCC) have provided 'increasingly formal classifications for subjective and objective information'[72] concerning uncertainties.[73] Specifically, working groups have issued guidelines for assisting policy and legal decision-makers in assessing the state of knowledge on climate change and, at the same time, treating uncertainties relating to climate change in a consistent manner.[74] In approaching this task, the *IPCC Fifth Assessment Report on Consistent Treatment of Uncertainties* (AR5), which is one of the latest reports, expresses 'the certainty in key assessment findings' about the causes of climate change and the impacts of these changes on human and natural systems through 'a *qualitative level of confidence* (from very low to very high) and, when possible, probabilistically with a *quantified likelihood* (from exceptionally unlikely to virtually certain)'.[75]

72 James S Risbey and Milind Kandlikar, 'Expressions of Likelihood and Confidence in the IPCC Uncertainty Assessment Process' (2007) 85(1–2) *Climatic Change* 19.

73 IPCC is the UN body that assesses the science related to climate change; see www.ipcc.ch/.

74 IPCC issued five assessment reports in 1990 (supplemented in 1992), 1995, 2001, 2007 and 2014. As of this writing, the IPCC is in its sixth assessment cycle, in which the IPCC is producing the Sixth Assessment Report (AR6). The first three Working Group contributions were released in August, February, and April 2022. The Synthesis Report will be the last of the AR6 products and is scheduled to be released in late 2022 or early 2023 to inform the 2023 Global Stocktake under the United Nations Framework Convention on Climate Change. More information on the Sixth Assessment Report is available at https://www.ipcc.ch/assessment-report/ar6/.

75 RK Pachauri and LA Meyer (eds), *Climate Change 2014 Synthesis Report Summary for Policymakers. Contribution of Working Groups I, II and III to the Fifth Assessment Report of the Intergovernmental Panel on Climate Change* (IPCC, 2014) 2 (emphasis added), www.ipcc.ch/.

This study suggests adopting the *quantitative* scale of the IPCC Report (hereafter *IPCC scale*) to guide WTO judicial bodies in assessing the still-debated likelihood of harm posed by trading biotechnology to biosafety.[76]

Nevertheless, to be useful in real legal disputes on biotechnology, a quantitative scale expressing the probability of harm must be combined with a *qualitative scale* indicating the standards of proof relating to the quantitative qualifiers. In this view, Weiss complements the IPCC scale with a qualitative scale, taking account of the standards of proof in civil and criminal cases (hereafter *legal scale*).[77] 'The qualitative nature of the proposed scale', Weiss explains, 'should make it more accessible to members of the public that are not accustomed to thinking in quantitative terms'.[78] Importantly, he adds that both the IPCC and the legal scales are *Bayesian scales*, meaning that they express scientists' subjective interpretations of the uncertainties in question.[79] At this point, some reflections are in order.

As the two suggested Bayesian scales (i.e., IPCC and legal scales) are designed by scientists and adopted by policymakers and legal scholars,[80] *it would be wrong to assume that the meaning ascribed to some key concepts by scientific experts matches with policymakers' and legal thinkers' understanding of the same notions.* This is especially true considering the difficulty of panels in interpreting the scientific opinions of the appointed experts:

> The difference between legal speak and science speak may seem at first glance to be slight. In practice, however, a scientist's unwillingness to make unqualified statements may result in a dialogue between the scientist and the lawyer where each speaks at the other with seeming mutual comprehension while in fact neither party is fully aware of the semantic differences that result in different meanings being given to the same phrases in a scientific versus a legal context . . . The gap in the legal understanding of science affects not only the validity of the panels' interpretations of science, but also the logic underlying their legal rationale in applying the SPS Agreement.[81]

76 The IPCC scale for expressing the likelihood of an outcome refers to *virtually certain*, 99–100% *probability*; *very likely*, 90–100%; *likely*, 66–100%; *about as likely as not*, 33–66%; *unlikely*, 0–33%; *very unlikely*, 0–10%; and exceptionally unlikely, 0–1%: Pachauri and Meyer (n 75) 2.

77 Charles Weiss, 'Precaution: The Willingness to Accept Costs to Avert Uncertain Danger' in Kurt Marti et al. (eds), *Coping with Uncertainty: Modeling and Policy Issues* (Springer, 2006) 315, 316.

78 Charles Weiss, 'Communicating Uncertainty in Intelligence and Other Professions' (2007) 21(1) *International Journal of Intelligence and CounterIntelligence* 57, 65.

79 Weiss (n 77) 316. The limits of Bayes's theorem are discussed in Laurence H Tribe, 'Trial by Mathematics: Precision and Ritual in the Legal Process' (1971) 84(6) *Harvard Law Review* 1329.

80 Even Distinguished Professor Charles Weiss, who developed the mentioned legal scale, is a scientist.

81 Eliason (n 13) 353, 345.

The central concept of *evidence*, for example, is used, according to Goodstein,[82] 'much more loosely in science than in law'.[83]

In light of this, the scale proposed in this study and illustrated in Figure 8.1 takes account of the chasm dividing the legal and scientific world. In combining the quantitative IPCC scale[84] and Weiss's qualitative legal scale,[85] it provides a brief explanation of the legal and scientific perception of the different levels of evidence required by decision-makers to meet the indicated standards of proof.[86]

Referring to this scale might aid WTO judicial bodies to assess the state of knowledge concerning biotechnology and, accordingly, to set the precautionary evidentiary threshold on a case-by-case basis. Now the question is where the precautionary evidentiary threshold should fit. There is not a general and certain answer to this question, not least because the application of the precautionary principle is context-dependent and, at the same time, the judicial analysis of the WTO disputes on the international trade in biotechnology must be performed through a case-by-case approach. Nevertheless, the lack of any indication in this regard along with the implicit prima facie pre-eminence of free trade and the substantial discretion of panels might result in questionable rulings or judicial arbitrariness.

For these reasons, the following section discusses what standard(s) of proof and level(s) of (un)certainty WTO judicial bodies might reasonably require of the parties involved in biotechnology legal disputes.

8.4.3.2 Practical relevance of a scale of legal evidence and scientific (un)certainties to apply precautionary measures in the context of biotechnology

In suggesting the level of evidence that might suffice the implementation of precautionary measures in the context of biotechnology, this study takes account of some pronouncements of international courts along with indications provided

82 David Goodstein, 'How Science Works in Committee on Science, Technology, and Law Policy and Global Affairs' in Committee on the Development of the Third Edition of the Reference Manual on Scientific Evidence and Committee on Science-Technology-and Law Policy and Global (ed), *Reference Manual on Scientific Evidence* (National Academies Press, 3rd ed, 2011) 37, 51.

83 Ibid. See also Douglas Crawford-Brown, Joost Pauwelyn and Kelly Smith, 'Environmental Risk, Precaution, and Scientific Rationality in the Context of WTO/NAFTA Trade Rules' (2004) 24 *Risk Analysis* 461, 462; Eliason (n 13) 353.

84 Likelihood scale used in the AR5. See guidance note for lead authors of the *IPCC Fifth Assessment Report on Consistent Treatment of Uncertainties'* (Web Page), https://wg1.ipcc.ch/AR6/documents/AR5_Uncertainty_Guidance_Note.pdf. The AR5 did not adopt the 'high confidence (67–95%)' level, which was considered in the previous *IPCC Fourth Assessment Report on Consistent Treatment of Uncertainties* (AR4). Nevertheless, the scale in Figure 8.1 recalls this level because it has been recently adopted by the Environment Agency (EEA) Report to set a precautionary threshold, as further discussed in this section.

85 The scale based on legal standards of proof is outlined in Charles Weiss, 'Expressing Scientific Uncertainty' (2003) 2 *Law, Probability, and Risk* 25, 37–38; Weiss (n 78) 61; Weiss (n 47) 3.

86 See Weiss (n 85) 36–38.

Bayesian Probability	IPPC Scale	Legal Scale	Levels of Evidence: Legal and Scientific Perspectives	
100%	Virtually certainty (99%-100%)	Virtually certain or Beyond a reasonable doubt (99%-100%)	Virtually certain or Beyond any doubt	Fundamental theory on conclusion from experiment that explains a wide variety of observations (eg, law of gravitation, theory of relativity)
			Beyond a reasonable doubt	Rigorously proven; critical experiment(s) give(s) a clear and unambiguous result (eg, Earth's early atmosphere contained no oxygen; AIDS is caused by HIV)
		Clear and convincing evidence (90%-100%)	Substantially proven; a few details remain to be worked out (eg, dinosaurs went extinct due to a large meteor or comet impact)	
90%	Very likely (90%-100%)	Clear showing (80%-90%)	Very probable (eg, zebra mussels succeed in US because they have no natural predators)	
80%	Likely (66%-100%) or	Substantial and credible evidence (66%-80%)	Probable; evidence points in this direction, but not fully proven (eg, dust mites cause asthma)	
70%	High Confidence (67-95%)	Preponderance of the evidence (50%-66%)	More likely than not. If I have to choose, this seems more likely to be true than untrue (eg, there has been liquid water on the surface of Mars at some time within the past 100 million years)	
60%	About as likely as not			
50%	Or Medium Likelihood (33%-66%)	Clear indication (33%-50%)	Attractive but unproven; evidence is beginning to accumulate in this direction (eg, about half of all stars have at least one planet)	
40%		Probable cause, Reasonable belief (20%-33%)	Plausible hypothesis, supported by some evidence (eg, global warming will lead to the expansion of tropical diseases.	
30%	Unlikely (0%-33%)			
20%		Reasonable indication (10%-20%)	*none*	
10%	Very unlikely (0%-10%)	Reasonable, articulable grounds for suspicion (0%-10%)	Possible, worth researching (eg, synthetic chemicals have caused articulable decrease in human sperm counts)	
0%	Exceptionally unlikely (0%-1%)	No reasonable grounds for suspicion (0%-1%)	No reasonable grounds for suspicion	Unlikely: available evidence is against it, or violates existing paradigms, but not entirely ruled out (eg, cell phones or high voltage power lines cause cancer)
		Impossible (<1%-0%)	Impossible	Against the known laws of physics or other science (eg, perpetual motion machines)

Figure 8.1 Scale of legal evidence and scientific (un)certainties

by domestic regulations in relation to the level of evidence required to trigger precautionary actions.

In 2017, the IACtHR issued an advisory opinion in response to a request by Colombia concerning state obligations around environmental protection in the context of the rights to life and to personal integrity.[87] In emphasising the impor-

87 *Environment and Human Rights (Advisory Opinion)* (Inter-American Court of Human Rights, OC-23/17, 15 November 2017).

tance of implementing precautionary actions to avoid 'serious and irreversible' damage to the environment, the Court states:[88]

> This Court understands that States *must* act in accordance with the precautionary principle, in order to protect the right to life and personal integrity, in cases where there are *plausible indications* that an activity could cause serious and irreversible damage to the environment, *even* in the absence of scientific certainty. Therefore, States *must* act with due caution to prevent possible harm.[89]

Three significant observations stem from the Court's statement. First, precautionary actions are seen as a duty of states (i.e., 'States *must* act with due caution to prevent . . .'). Second, the Court confirms that the absence of scientific certainty is not the trigger for precaution, which applies '*even* in the absence of scientific certainty'. Third, the Court seems to set the evidentiary threshold for precautionary measures at the level of *plausibility*.

The combined *scale of legal evidence and scientific (un)certainties* in Figure 8.1 highlights that the *plausible hypothesis* corresponds to the legal standard of *probable cause, reasonable belief* (20–33%). If applied to the context of biotechnology, member states demanding the adoption of precautionary measures to ensure biosafety should be required to prove there is *reasonable belief* that the claimed harm will occur.

Setting the evidentiary threshold of precaution at the level of *probable cause, reasonable belief* aligns with US administrative law establishing that a court must be convinced that the implementation of protective measures is not 'arbitrary and capricious': 'This corresponds to the well-known legal standard of "*reasonable belief*"'.[90]

Noteworthy is that the reference to 'arbitrary and capricious' in US domestic law mirrors the conditions set out in the chapeau of Article XX of the *GATT Agreement*, according to which the adoption of safeguarding measures in the context of the *GATT*, *SPS*, and *TBT Agreements* is '[s]ubject to the requirement that such measures are not applied in a manner which would constitute a means of *arbitrary or unjustifiable discrimination* between countries where the

88 The IACtHR adopts a weak application of the precautionary principle (i.e., 'serious and irreversible' damages to the environment) as do WTO judicial bodies.

89 The official opinion, available only in Spanish, states:

> [E]sta Corte entiende que, los Estados deben actuar conforme al principio de precaución, a efectos de la protección del derecho a la vida y a la integridad personal, en casos donde haya *indicadores plausibles* que una actividad podría acarrear daños graves e irreversibles al medio ambiente, aún en ausencia de certeza científica. Por tanto, los Estados deben actuar con la debida cautela para prevenir el posible daño.

Medio Ambiente y Derecho Humanos (Opinión Consultiva) (Corte Interamericana de Derechos Humanos, OC-23/17, 15 Noviembre 2017) (emphasis added).

90 Weiss (n 47) 5; Bernard Schwartz, *Administrative Law* (Aspen Publishers, 3rd ed, 1991).

same conditions prevail, or a disguised restriction on international trade'.[91] This strengthens the idea that setting an evidentiary threshold at the standard of *probable cause, reasonable belief* seems *reasonable* even under the WTO.

The suitability of the *probable cause, reasonable belief* standard in relation to precaution seems to be further validated by the Seabed Disputes Chamber within the International Tribunal for the Law of the Sea (ITLOS) that, in providing guidance on the precautionary principle, states the following:

> [T]he precautionary approach is also an integral part of the general obligation of due diligence of sponsoring States . . . This obligation applies in situations where scientific evidence concerning the scope and potential negative impact of the activity in question is insufficient but where there are *plausible indications* of potential risks.[92]

As the suggested *scale of legal evidence and scientific (un)certainties* highlights, a 'plausible hypothesis (indication)' relates to the standard of *probable cause, reasonable belief*. At this point, one must not fail to acknowledge that ITLOS was looking specifically at the international seabed, which is the common heritage of humankind. This allows the court to apply a particularly high standard of precaution.[93]

Despite the notable differences between the application of precaution in relation to the international seabed and in trade contexts, the *probable cause, reasonable belief* standard should still be taken into account under the WTO, if only because the judicial reference to *reasonableness* emerges in the WTO jurisprudence on biotechnology. Specifically, in *US/Canada – Hormones Continued Suspension*, the AB acknowledges that 'a panel reviewing a member's SPS measure under Article 5.1 should seek to determine whether there is any *reasonable scientific basis* for such measures and respect the "important and autonomous right" of Members to set their level of S[anitary and] P[hyto]S[anitary] protection'.[94] Similarly, the AB in *EC – Hormones* and the panel in *EC – Biotech* require that

91 *GATT Agreement* art XX chapeau (emphasis added).

92 *Responsibilities and Obligations of States Sponsoring Persons and Entities with Respect to Activities in the Area* (Advisory Opinion) [131] (emphasis added).

93 Moreover, ITLOS seems to adopt a different standard of proof in 2010's *M/V 'Louisa' Case, in which the applicant is required to show a credible risk* of serious harm to the marine environment and that, under the circumstances, it is appropriate to take measures to prevent such harm: *M/V 'Louisa' Case (Saint Vincent and the Grenadines v Kingdom of Spain) (Provisional Measures)* [13]. As 'a precautionary approach seems to be inherent in the very *notion of provisional measures*', we can infer that ITLOS considered in this case *substantial and credible evidence* as a suitable standard to justify the implementation of precautionary measures. See *Southern Bluefin Tuna Cases (New Zealand v Japan, Australia v Japan)* (Provisional Measures) [9].

94 AB report, *US/Canada – Hormones Continued Suspension* [75] (emphasis added). See also AB report, *EC – Hormones* [172].

risk assessments must ***reasonably support*** biosafety measures to comply with Article 5.1 of the *SPS Agreement*.[95] It has been observed that this language 'clearly implies that a state wishing to impose trade-restrictive measures exceeding international standards must carry out a risk assessment based on scientific evidence sufficient to create a "***reasonable belief***" that such a restriction is warranted':[96]

> A mere hunch (a 'superstition', in the words of the EC [in the *EC – Hormones* case]) is insufficient. This standard of proof [i.e., 'reasonable belief'] ***sets a balance*** between the sovereign right of a sovereign state to set its own health standards and the right of the exporter (and the consumer) to be free of arbitrary restrictions on trade.[97]

In this view, the consideration of ***probable cause, reasonable belief*** (20–33%) as standard of proof allowing precaution to apply 'may have useful application to sticky situations in international trade law, in which exceptions to the international trade regime are justified by a claim of threat to human health or the environment'.[98]

In light of these considerations, and bearing in mind the inverse relationship between environmental damage and uncertainty, the high degree of potential harm posed by the international trade in biotechnology to biosafety – which is also acknowledged by the AB in *EC – Hormones*[99] – might invite WTO judicial bodies to require parties asking for the implementation of precautionary measures to meet the standard of ***probable cause, reasonable belief***. This implies that precautionary measures on biosafety in the context of biotechnology should be substantiated by ***plausible hypothesis supported by some evidence***,[100] which is the scientific level of certainty corresponding to this legal standard of proof (see Figure 8.1).

At the same time, the party challenging the adoption of precautionary measures or requiring the introduction of potentially biotech products should also meet the same standard of proof and scientific level of certainty. After all, the rules on the allocation of the burden of proof originate from the idea of normative fairness or distributive justice.[101] Nevertheless, this is not necessarily true if the protection of human health and the environment from uncertain, though serious and potentially irreversible risks, is prioritised over free trade to offset the implicit prima facie pre-eminence of free trade under the WTO. This would accordingly impose a higher standard of proof on the party requiring the introduction of

95 AB report, *EC – Hormones* [186]; Panel report, *EC – Biotech* [7.3028].
96 Charles Weiss, 'Scientific Uncertainty and Science-Based Precaution' (2003) 3(2) ***International Environmental Agreements: Politics, Law and Economics*** 137, 152 (emphasis added).
97 Ibid (emphasis added).
98 Weiss (n 47) 5; Garnett and Parsons (n 66) 513.
99 AB report, *EC – Hormones* [124].
100 Weiss (n 85) 38.
101 See Section 8.4.3.1.

biotech products. For example, in providing guidance to decision-makers examining the adoption of precautionary measures, the 2013 EEA Report refers to the IPCC scale and establishes the following:

> Using the . . . IPCC sliding scale for assessing the state of knowledge on climate change, . . . we argue that there should at least be a *'high confidence'* (67–95%) in the scientific evidence indicating no harm before a case can reasonably be claimed to be a false positive.[102] ['False positives' are cases in which precautionary measures were taken but later turned out to be unnecessary.]
>
> This is consistent with the strength of evidence often sought in regulatory policy before preventive actions are taken, and with the classification systems of international bodies.[103]

In other words, the EEA Report raises the evidentiary threshold for the party requiring the adoption of potentially harmful products or, arguably, challenging the application of precautionary actions. This party should, in fact, meet the *substantial and credible evidence* (66%–80%) standard of proof. This, in turn, implies that such a request should be supported by a risk assessment showing that there is at least a *high confidence* in the scientific evidence indicating no harm posed by the international trade in biotechnology to biosafety. This approach should not be surprising considering that some domestic regulations ask for even higher levels of proof. For instance, the *US Food Quality Protection Act of 1996* requires parties proposing new projects or interventions to make a '*clear showing* [80%–90%] that their proposal is safe'[104] for people and the environment.

Although it would be reasonable to require both the parties to a dispute to meet the *probable cause, reasonable belief* standard, it must be noted that the WTO judicial request for a higher standard of proof to the party challenging the implementation of precautionary measures – or requiring trade liberalisation of biotech products – would imply the judicial adoption of the *pro homine* principle, which is recommended for the reasons outlined in Chapter 3. To remind us, the WTO judicial consideration of the *pro homine* principle would represent an important step towards a desirable harmonisation between WTO law and international human rights law.[105] At the same time, it would mitigate the prima facie pre-eminence of free trade under the WTO.

102 European Environmental Agency, *Late Lessons from Early Warnings: Science, Precaution, Innovation*, Report No 1 (2013), 17.

103 Ibid 18 (emphasis added).

104 Weiss (n 47) 3 (emphasis added). See US Food and Drug Administration *1996 Food Quality Protection Act*, Title IV, Amendments to the Federal Food, Drug and Cosmetic Act, ss 408(b) 2(a)(ii) and 408(b) 2(C)(ii)(I) and 408(C)(2)(ii), www.fda.gov/opacom/laws/foodqual/fqpa4.htm.

105 See Section 3.6.1.

8.4.4 Complementing the Bayesian scale with frequentist statistics

A final observation regards the judicial consideration of *positive correlations* and *inferences* drawn from observational data highlighting the need or, on the contrary, the lack of necessity for taking precautionary measures. To remind us, the analysis in the previous chapter suggests the adoption of a scientific *and* holistic approach to shape risk assessments *appropriate to the circumstances* in the context of biotechnology.[106] It highlights that experimental studies should be supplemented by observational (or empirical) analyses, which can provide decision-makers with a clearer picture of the adverse effects posed by biotechnology to biosafety.

Against this background, it must be noted that the *scale of legal evidence and scientific (un)certainties* suggested in this chapter is a Bayesian scale.[107] This means that it does not express empirical data through statistics.[108] This is, in fact, the role of the so-called *frequentist probabilities* that are considered opposed to the *subjective probabilities* ascribed by the Bayesian scale:

> [Frequentist statistics] assign objective probabilities, based on experience, to risky events. These assign objective probabilities, based on experience, to risky events. These probabilities are derived from *empirical correlations* between effect and presumed cause, for example from the statistical relationship between auto accidents and miles driven . . . The results of such analyses are often expressed as a *statistical correlation.*[109]

Considering that empirical data, statistical correlations, and inferences are highly relevant in the field of biotechnology – for the reasons discussed in the previous chapter – the judicial establishment of the standard of proof and relating level of (un)certainty to adopt precautionary measures should also take account of the results stemming from frequentists statistics relating to the impact of trading biotechnology to biosafety. After all, Chapter 7 underlines that these data are already taken into account in other fora. For instance, in the *Giovanni Pesce and Others* case, the European Advocate General Bot advises the ECJ to consider '*significant correlations*' as sufficient to justify the implementation of precautionary measures.[110]

To conclude, the case-by-case analysis of biotechnology legal disputes could lead WTO judicial bodies to allow or, on the contrary, reject the implementation of precautionary measures even in light of empirical data, statistical correlations and inferences stemming from frequentist statistics, which should complement the suggested Bayesian scale.

106 See Section 7.4.1.
107 This is because both the IPCC and legal scales are Bayesian scales.
108 Weiss (n 77) 316.
109 Weiss (n 85) 39 (emphasis added).
110 *Opinion of Advocate General Bot, Giovanni Pesce and Others* (Joined Cases C-78/16 and C-79/16) [2016] ECR 340 [116] (emphasis added).

8.5 Conclusion

This chapter casts light on how WTO judicial bodies have assessed precautionary measures on biosafety in contexts in which member states have argued that insufficient scientific evidence exists regarding the harmfulness or harmlessness of trade in biotechnology. In doing so, it conducts an in-depth analysis of Article 5.7 of the *SPS Agreement*, which permits member states to adopt biosafety measures in contexts of insufficient scientific evidence. This analysis reveals that the first and third requirements of this provision – insufficiency of scientific evidence and performance of a more objective risk assessment, respectively – should be reconsidered, or at least elucidated, as they might prevent effective implementation of precautionary measures on biosafety in the context of Article 5.7.

The analysis then focuses on WTO judicial bodies' interpretation of these measures. It emerges that establishing the non-compliance of precautionary measures on biosafety with Article 5.7, because of the lack of proof that insufficient scientific evidence occurs, is highly problematic for three reasons. First, proving the insufficiency of scientific evidence is hardly possible. Second, asking for such a proof reveals a judicial misinterpretation of the precautionary principle, which applies in spite of the lack of sufficient scientific evidence, lowers the evidentiary threshold and should be supported by appropriate risk assessments. Third, the judicial conclusion that the precautionary measures on biosafety are not justified under Article 5.7 is based on a debatable distinction between insufficient and uncertain scientific evidence that overshadows the close link between these two concepts and, at the same time, shows a gap under WTO law – which does not accommodate circumstances of scientific uncertainty – and in the literature – which has a gap on discussions about the consequences stemming from this judicial distinction.

To overcome these challenges, the present chapter offers suggestions for effective operationalisation of precautionary measures on biosafety in contexts of uncertain and qualitatively insufficient scientific evidence. Specifically, it develops a *scale of legal evidence and scientific (un)certainties* that can guide (and reduce arbitrariness of) WTO judicial bodies in establishing the sufficient level of harm and degree of scientific (un)certainty to justify precautionary measures in the context of biotechnology.

Naturally, the judicial balance between the competing requests for free trade and precautionary measures on biosafety must be performed on a case-by-case basis through, ideally, the adoption of a structured proportionality analysis. Precaution is, in fact, not an absolute principle. Nevertheless, the guidance provided by the suggested scale, which combines the quantitative IPCC scale with the qualitative scale offered by Weiss, can reduce the chances for panels to issue arbitrary final rulings. Indeed, the combined scale indicates what levels of evidence might be sufficient to adopt biosafety measures in circumstances where the precautionary principle is invoked and qualitatively insufficient scientific evidence remains.

In light of the emerging findings, it might be reasonable for WTO decision-makers to require the party asking for the implementation of precautionary measures to meet the *probable cause, reasonable belief* (20%–33%) standard of proof, which, in turn, implies to substantiate this request by means of *plausible hypothesis supported by some evidence.*[111] This would echo the inverse relationship between the *high* degree of potential biosafety damage taken into account under the WTO and the *low* level of uncertainty that should, accordingly, suffice the operationalisation of precaution. Also, in line with the findings emerging in Chapter 7, this chapter suggests implementing precaution when significant or positive correlations demonstrate that the claimed outcome is *more than 50% likely.*[112]

Whether the party challenging the adoption of precautionary measures or requiring free trade in biotechnology should meet the same legal and scientific standards asked of the party requiring the adoption of precautionary measures on biosafety (i.e., *probable cause, reasonable belief*), will arguably depend on the trade policy that WTO judicial bodies pursue. An alignment of WTO law with international human rights law might require decision-makers to apply the *pro homine* principle in future biotechnology legal disputes. In this case, the present chapter highlights that the party challenging the adoption of precautionary measures or requiring free trade in biotechnology might be asked to provide *at least substantial and credible evidence* (66%–80%), indicating no harm caused by trading biotechnology to biosafety.

The suggestions offered in this chapter show a structured approach to addressing cases in which the implementation of precautionary measures on biosafety is required in contexts of qualitatively insufficient scientific evidence. In doing so, it contributes to filling a gap in the literature. It also contributes to further enhancing the discussion of how to perform a well-structured proportionality analysis that, as Chapter 3 highlights, WTO judicial bodies should perform in the context of biotechnology by adopting, among others, the precautionary principle and the *pro homine* principle.

111 Weiss (n 85) 38.
112 See Section 7.4.1.

Part IV

Final insights

9 Conclusion

9.1 Introduction

Given the rate of technological advances, international trade in biotechnology will likely remain flourishing in the future. This is especially true considering that biotechnology is viewed as the means to counteract climate-related problems, such as protecting crops from extreme weather events, improving agricultural productivity and securing food production for a growing population.[1] However, it is important to remark that if biotechnology is to contribute to human and environmental welfare, it 'must be considered in the context of sustainable development'.[2]

It is time for the WTO to step up and assume its '*central role*'[3] in achieving the 2030 Agenda for Sustainable Development and the related SDGs. This would require it to, inter alia, translate the proclaimed intention of harmonising trade, environmental and human health policies to legal changes.

WTO judicial bodies have the potential to support sustainable development of international trade in biotechnology by striking a reasoned balance between trade and non-trade interests. This study shows that performing a well-structured proportionality analysis, which should consider the remaining uncertainties surrounding the international trade in biotechnology by means of the precautionary principle, can aid in this regard. However, this study identifies several challenges for WTO states to protect human health and the environment and for WTO judicial bodies to balance trade and non-trade values. Section 9.2.1 recaps these challenges, which were discussed in Parts I and II of this book. This study also demonstrates the main judicial issues in examining the three biotechnology legal disputes: *EC – Hormones*, *US/Canada – Hormones Continued Suspension* and

1 Wakjira Tesfahun, 'Climate Change Mitigation and Adaptation through Biotechnology Approaches: A Review' (2018) 3(1) *Current Investigations in Agriculture and Current Research* 299, 303.

2 Mikael Kurlsson, 'Biosafety Principles for GMOs in the Context of Sustainable Development' (2003) 10(1) *International Journal of Sustainable Development and World Ecology* 15.

3 WTO, 'The WTO and the Sustainable Development Goals' *WTO* (Web Page) (emphasis added), www.wto.org/english/thewto_e/coher_e/sdgs_e/sdgs_e.htm.

DOI: 10.4324/9781003325741-13

EC – Biotech. In this respect, Section 9.2.2 summarises the four main judicial hurdles discussed in detail in Part III of this study.

The conclusions stemming from the analysis and findings of this study to overcome these challenges are offered throughout this study and are summarised in Section 9.3. This summary also emphasises how this study answers its two research questions:

1. How should WTO judicial bodies balance the free trade in biotechnology and biosafety?
2. To what extent can proportionality analysis and the precautionary principle assist WTO judicial bodies to achieve such a balance?

Section 9.4 offers indications for future investigations, while Section 9.5 provides final observations.

9.2 The complexities surrounding the international trade in biotechnology

9.2.1 Epistemic, normative and judicial challenges in ensuring biosafety and balancing trade with non-trade interests under the WTO

International trade in biotechnology entails scientific uncertainty that brings *epistemic issues*. More specifically, when faced with opposing scientific opinions, WTO judicial bodies have epistemic discretion in deciding which of the presented scientific evidence they consider as reliable. Self-evidentially, this is problematic if the relevant decision-makers are not trained in science.

Further, in deciding whether biosafety measures justify trade limitations, panels and the AB rely on the WTO normative framework that 'was not drafted with the full complexity of biotechnology issues in mind'.[4] This study highlights that measures protecting human health and the environment find room in the *GATT*, *SPS* and *TBT Agreements*. However, these are considered exceptions to the substantive obligations to facilitate free trade. Indeed, this study highlights a clear bias towards protecting free trade over non-trade values, such as biosafety. This pre-eminence of free trade under the WTO can be observed in several aspects: (1) a WTO *democratic deficit* in relation to non-trade interests; (2) a range of WTO requirements undermining national sovereignty on health and environmental policies; (3) the lack of WTO provisions specifically designed to ensure the protection of human health and the environment; (4) the lack of sufficient WTO institutional responses and efforts to ensure the protection of human health and the environment; and (5) the lack of a process for challenging trade measures that

4 Arthur E Appleton, 'The Labeling of GMO Products Pursuant to International' (2000) 8(1994) *New York University Environmental Law Journal* 566, 570.

negatively affect human health of individuals as the dispute settlement body is a mechanism between WTO states. However, prioritising trade is not in keeping with the preamble of the *WTO Agreement*, which lists several equal goals, including expanding the production of and trade in goods and services and sustainable development. As this study extensively demonstrates, trade liberalisation is neither the only nor the main WTO objective.[5]

As a direct consequence of the pre-eminence of trade liberalisation, WTO law is characterised by *normative issues*, which entail three main consequences. First, the WTO goal of sustainable development becomes unattainable, as it would require effective integration of economic growth, environmental protection and social development. Second, the bias towards free trade hinders a reasoned judicial balance when trade and non-trade values are in conflict. This is because biosafety is conceived as a justification to limit free trade rather than an objective in its own right. Third, the pre-eminence of trade interests undermines the ability of WTO states to respect their international environmental and/or health obligations. Indeed, measures to protect health or the environment can, simultaneously, be prescribed by international human rights law or international environmental law, and be prohibited (or at least not supported) by the WTO. This underlines *normative antinomies* between WTO law and international human rights law and international environmental law,[6] which are further fuelled by the fragmentation of international law.

In addition to epistemic and normative hurdles, this study reveals *judicial issues* in balancing trade and non-trade interests. Performing a reasoned balance is indeed undermined by the bias towards free trade under the WTO normative framework, the fact that the WTO is considered institutionally not ready for balancing trade and non-trade interests and the lack of an analytical structure under the WTO supporting judicial balance of competing rights or interests.

These epistemic, normative and judicial issues surrounding the international trade in biotechnology must then be added to the controversial aspects emerging from the judicial examination of the three biotechnology legal disputes, as summarised in the following section.

9.2.2 *Controversial aspects in the judicial examination of biotechnology legal disputes*

An in-depth analysis of *EC – Hormones*, *US/Canada – Hormones Continued Suspension* and *EC – Biotech* reveals four barriers making it difficult for member states to ensure biosafety and for WTO judicial bodies to perform a reasoned judicial balance between the competing interests of free trade and biosafety. The *judicial allocation of the burden of proof to establish a prima facie case* in contexts lacking scientific certainty, such as biotechnology, is the first major hurdle

5 See Section 2.3.
6 See Section 2.6.

emerging from the case analysis.[7] This study claims that the judicial allocation of the burden of proof in the three biotechnology cases can be a barrier not only for the establishment of a prima facie case, but more generally for effective adoption of biosafety measures. Indeed, Chapter 6 presents manifold reasons pointing in that direction, such as (1) WTO judicial bodies' consideration of a prima facie case as a decisive case, rather than as a case aiding panels to understand if there is a body of evidence sufficient to achieve a reasonable conclusion in favour of the asserted allegation(s); (2) the lack of a judicial distinction between the allocation of the burden of proof in cases with *sufficient* as compared to *insufficient* scientific evidence; (3) cases with *sufficient* and *adequate* (or appropriate) scientific evidence equate, in the view of WTO judicial bodies, cases of *sufficient* and arguably adequate, but *uncertain* scientific evidence; and (4) AB's deceptive statements that might lead future panels to set a very high bar for evidence or even a *probatio diabolica* on a respondent calling for the adoption of biosafety measures.

The consideration of Article 11 of the *DSU* as a *standard of review* applied by panels to examine legal disputes over biotechnology is the second major issue in the judicial examination of biotechnology cases. Article 11 requires panels to perform an *objective assessment of the matter*. As this study shows, this does not suit the scientifically uncertain and complex nature of biotechnology cases, as it does not provide guidance to WTO panels, leaving them to adopt substantial discretion. This can be highly problematic, if only because it can entail arbitrariness. Clearly, conducting objective, in the sense of unbiased, judicial evaluations of the matters should be an intrinsic feature of any legal decision. Indeed, scholars observe that the reference to *objective* under the WTO does not seem to concern a standard of review but rather a *guarantee* of due process rights, such as fairness, impartiality and neutrality of a panel in assessing the submitted evidence.[8] Thus, this study argues that performing an objective assessment of the matter should not be considered a standard of review but, rather, a tacit judicial modus operandi.

The third barrier pertains to the *judicial assessment of precautionary measures on biosafety in contexts in which WTO judicial bodies deemed that sufficient scientific evidence exists.* In all three WTO biotechnology legal disputes the risk assessments supporting the requests for adopting biosafety measures were evaluated as *not* appropriate to the circumstances. This study argues that WTO judicial bodies overlooked remaining scientific uncertainties affecting the quality and reliability of scientific evidence and risk assessments in the context of biotechnology. Specifically, in evaluating the sufficiency of scientific evidence and the appropriateness of risk assessments in the three cases, WTO decision-makers (1) followed a narrow interpretation of the relevant provisions under the *SPS*

7 WTO panels allocated the burden of proof differently in each biotechnology case, which prevents legal certainty.

8 See Section 6.3.

Agreement (i.e., Articles 2.2 and 5.5, and annex A(4)); (2) adopted a quantitative interpretation of biotechnology risks despite the fact that the complexity surrounding biotechnology can only be grasped through quantitative *and* qualitative analyses; (3) selected scientific evidence in an arbitrary manner; and (4) did not duly accomplish their role of gatekeeper.[9] As a consequence, member states did not have flexibility to conduct appropriate risk assessments aligning with the *SPS Agreement*, could not enjoy their right to establish a precautionary ALOP and hardly accomplished their numerous international obligations to safeguard human health and the environment.

Therefore, this study argues that the judicial examination of precautionary measures on biosafety and relating risk assessments conducted in contexts of sufficient and uncertain scientific evidence undermined the reliability of final legal decisions, interfered with national sovereignty in managing biotechnology risks and jeopardised a reasoned judicial balance between free trade and biosafety – not least because of a prima facie pre-eminence of free trade in WTO jurisprudence on biotechnology.

The last hurdle in examining the three biotechnology cases relates to the *judicial review of precautionary measures on biosafety in contexts in which member states have argued that insufficient scientific evidence exists* regarding the harmfulness or harmlessness of trade in biotechnology. An in-depth analysis of Article 5.7 of the *SPS Agreement* highlights that its requirements to adopt precautionary measures on biosafety 'if there is insufficient scientific evidence' and by ensuring the performance of 'a more objective risk assessment' might hinder effective implementation of precautionary measures.

Further, this study argues that the judicial decision in *EC – Biotech* and *US/Canada – Hormones Continued Suspension*, that the precautionary measures on biosafety did not comply with Article 5.7 because of the lack of proof that insufficient scientific evidence occurs, is highly problematic for three reasons. First, proving insufficiency of scientific evidence is hardly possible. Second, requesting such proof reveals a judicial misinterpretation of the precautionary principle, which is reflected in Article 5.7 and applies despite scientific uncertainties. Indeed, precaution lowers the evidentiary threshold and should be supported by appropriate risk assessments. Third, the claim that the precautionary measures on biosafety are not justified under Article 5.7 is based on a debatable judicial distinction between *insufficient* and *uncertain* scientific evidence. This distinction ignores the close link between these two concepts and unveils a gap in WTO law, namely that WTO law does not sufficiently engage with circumstances of scientific uncertainty. As a result of the judicial interpretation of Article 5.7, precautionary measures on biosafety have never been successfully implemented in the context of that Article.[10]

9 See Section 7.3.
10 See Section 8.3.

In light of these findings, the following section offers some reflections on how to overcome the current challenges. In so doing, it provides an answer to the two research questions investigated in this study.

9.3 Where to from here: suggestions for a way forward

9.3.1 Striking a reasoned balance between trade and non-trade interests: proportionality as a solution for judicial *issues in the context of biotechnology*

This study highlights that performing proportionality analysis in the context of biotechnology under the WTO has compelling justifications. This holds true despite the lack of explicit reference to proportionality in the WTO agreements and the scepticism about the balancing test, which is the third test of proportionality analysis. Conducting a *proportionality analysis*, meaning taking the three tests of suitability, necessity and balancing (or proportionality *stricto sensu*), would allow WTO judicial bodies to *support a reasoned and rational balance between trade and non-trade interests by means of an analytical structure.* This is because, in light of the foundations provided by Alexy's theory of balancing, balancing can be conceived as a rational process, which is supported by a well-defined structure.[11]

Thus, this study recommends the performance of a proportionality analysis to *place the WTO's judicial balance on a structured footing.* This would not only introduce an analytical structure, but also reduce WTO panels' empirical epistemic discretion in stalemate cases and support the WTO goal of sustainable development, which 'seeks balance, and does not favour one or another international regime'.[12]

9.3.2 Overcoming the normative antinomies between WTO law and other international law regimes: proportionality as a solution for normative *issues in the context of biotechnology*

This study highlights that proportionality can also foster a solution to the normative antinomies between WTO law and other international law regimes. *Proportionality is broadly considered a valid approach to 'defragmentation' of international law.* Accordingly, the judicial adoption of this approach might turn the WTO into a forum in which the normative antinomies between WTO law and international law regimes, which are partially caused by the fragmentation of international law, can be, to some extent, resolved.[13]

This is particularly so given the perception of the WTO as a forum in which a process of harmonisation between WTO law and international law is unlikely to

11 See Section 3.4.

12 Cairo Robb, Marie-Claire Cordonier Segger and Caroline Jo, 'Sustainable Development Challenges in International Dispute Settlement' in Marie-Claire Cordonier Segger (ed, with HE Judge and CG Weeramantry), *Sustainable Development Principles in the Decisions of International Courts and Tribunals* (Routledge, 2017) 147, 170.

13 See Sections 3.1 and 3.4.

take place.[14] WTO judicial bodies have the opportunity to counter this perception. The adoption of proportionality to address legal disputes involving trade *versus* non-trade values might help harmonise norms of different legal regimes. This, in turn, would demonstrate the capacity of WTO judicial bodies to contribute to resolving, at least to some extent, the phenomenon of fragmentation of international law.

This contribution towards resolving the fragmentation of international law would be particularly timely for the WTO judiciary, especially for the AB. This is because the Trump administration questioned the role of the WTO judiciary and blocked new appointments to the AB to ignite a crisis of the WTO regime.[15] Fostering a solution to the current fragmentation of international law can, accordingly, show the role, which is far from marginal,[16] that the WTO judiciary might take in the international legal (and political) scenario.

9.3.3 Adopting a proportionality analysis in the context of biotechnology

This study shows that WTO judicial bodies can perform a well-structured proportionality analysis by undertaking five main steps.[17] Having identified free trade and biosafety as the interests to be balanced (the first step), WTO judicial bodies should assign the value of their abstract weight (the second step). The difficulty in determining the abstract weight of these interests lies in the dominant commercial ethos under the WTO, which might arguably lead WTO decision-makers to consider the abstract weight of the interest in trading biotechnology greater than the abstract weight of the interest in ensuring biosafety, despite the fact that no formal hierarchy exists between WTO goals.

In this regard, this study emphasises that the *pro homine* principle might be a valid means to offset the implicit prima facie pre-eminence of free trade under the WTO. Further, because the *pro homine* principle is also a normative conflict-resolution technique, its adoption might further aid in fostering a solution to mitigate the fragmentation of international law.

14 Ronnie RF Yearwood, *The Interaction between World Trade Organisation (WTO) Law and External International Law: The Constrained Openness of WTO Law (a Prologue to a Theory)* (Routledge, 2012) i.

15 Emre Peker, '"The WTO Is in Crisis": Dispute Puts Global Trade Regulator at Risk' *Wall Street Journal* (Online, 9 December 2019), www.wsj.com/articles/the-wto-is-in-crisis-dispute-puts-global-trade-regulator-at-risk-11575889201. Because of this block, the chairman of the WTO's AB, Thomas Graham, resigned on 11 December 2019. As a result, the AB did not have enough members to decide new cases and 'pending appeals would be thrown into legal limbo': Bryce Baschuk, 'WTO Faces Cliff-Edge Crisis Next Week as Mediator Eyes Departure' *Bloomberg* (Online, 12 March 2019), www.bloomberg.com/news/articles/2019-12-02/wto-faces-cliff-edge-crisis-next-week-as-mediator-eyes-departure.

16 Tamar Megiddo, 'Beyond Fragmentation: On International Law's Integrationist Forces' (2019) 44(1) *Yale Journal of International Law* 4, 123; Joel P Trachtman, *The Future of International Law* (Cambridge University Press, 2013) 237.

17 See Sections 3.5 and 3.6.

As a third step, WTO judicial bodies should ascribe the value for the intensity of interference of the interests on a case-by-case basis. In doing so, performing the necessity test (i.e., the second step of proportionality analysis) can guide WTO judicial bodies in determining whether the contested biosafety measure represents the least restrictive and least onerous among equally effective alternatives.[18] Also, performing the suitability test (the first step of proportionality analysis) would aid WTO decision-makers to determine whether the contested biosafety measure is appropriate to achieve the desired and legitimate end, as the AB required in *Korea – Various Measures on Beef*.[19]

Fourth, WTO judicial bodies should ascribe a value to the reliability of empirical premises of the interests in trading biotech products and ensuring biosafety. This is not a simple task considering that the uncertainties surrounding the effects of international trade in biotech products to biosafety prevent stakeholders from assessing the reliability of the empirical assumptions concerning the safety or harmfulness of biotech products.

Thus, to assess whether the justification based on risks to biosafety is grounded on reliable or unreliable empirical premises, this study refines Alexy's theory of balancing by adding the reliability of evidence to the balancing process. Specifically, this study highlights that WTO judicial bodies should examine the reliability of evidence brought to their attention by (1) asking the appointed experts to adopt the same WoE process, (2) thoroughly evaluating the appropriateness of risk assessments, and (3) improving the likelihood of appointing reliable experts through the suggested amendment of Section VI.2 of the *Rules of Conduct*, Article 13 of the *DSU* and Appendix 4, paragraph 2 of the *DSU*.[20]

As a final step, decision-makers could insert the emerging values of the abstract weight, intensity of interference and reliability of empirical premises into Alexy's weight formula to obtain a concrete balancing outcome. If this balance results in a stalemate, the precautionary principle can reverse the burden of proof and place it on the proponent of biotechnology. Further, the precautionary approach affects the standard of proof by lowering the evidentiary threshold. In doing so, *precaution represents a valid means to break a stalemate*.[21] Its adoption, which aligns with the suggestion of adopting the *pro homine* principle, reduces the broad discretion of panels to enhance the impartiality of final rulings.

9.3.4 *Handling scientific uncertainties: precaution as a solution for the* epistemic *issues in the context of biotechnology*

This study shows that WTO decision-makers addressing biotechnology legal disputes did not adopt a structured approach to managing the scientific uncertainties

18 *GATT Agreement* chapeau; *SPS Agreement* art 2.3.
19 AB report, *Korea – Various Measures on Beef* [161].
20 See Section 3.6.2.
21 See Section 4.4.2.

concerning the effects of biotechnology to biosafety. Consequently, they did not address the epistemic issues stemming from these uncertainties.

Against this background, the present study illustrates that the precautionary principle represents a means to overcome the epistemic issues in the context of biotechnology.[22] Although WTO law does not mention the principle *expressis verbis*, it can apply under WTO law on three grounds: (1) gateways provisions in the context of the *SPS* and *GATT Agreements*, (2) its close relation with the WTO goal of sustainable development, and (3) its acknowledgement in a number of multilateral environmental agreements to which WTO member states are parties.[23]

As the principle requires action even when uncertainty remains, its implementation can be key to addressing scientific uncertainties surrounding the international trade in biotechnology: 'Under the precautionary principle, the benefit of any such doubt is to go to the environment. *In dubio pro nature*'.[24] This also means that the adoption of the precautionary principle under the WTO might mitigate the WTO ethos *pro trade* and, simultaneously, foster a solution to the lack of reliability of empirical assumptions concerning the impact of trading biotechnology on biosafety: *In dubio pro biosafety.*

However, this study reveals a judicial reticence of panels and the AB to precaution that, nonetheless, is unjustified. The judicial fear of 'false positives' is misplaced, if only because 'false negatives', meaning that early warnings existed but no precautionary actions were taken, are statistically more likely than 'false positives'.[25]

Even more noteworthy is that this study demonstrates that the interpretation of *precaution as a balancing and dynamic criterion* supporting the implementation of biosafety measures would not impose undue constraints on free trade in biotechnology and, simultaneously, would not hinder technological innovation.[26] Rather, 'carefully designed precautionary actions can stimulate innovation, even if the risk turns out not to be real or as serious as initially feared'.[27] Success of this interpretation, though, depends on designing and implementing precautionary measures on biosafety that are *effective* in achieving the pursued goal of protecting human health and/or the environment; *based on an up-to-date analysis of costs and benefits* relating to the implementation of such measures; *proportionate*, and *not discriminatory* or *arbitrary* towards free trade. In other words, adopting biosafety measures in light of

22 See Sections 4.2 and 4.4.

23 See Section 4.3.

24 Arie Trouwborst, 'The Precautionary Principle in General International Law: Combating the Babylonian Confusion' (2007) 16 *Review of European Community & International Environmental Law* 185, 187.

25 See Section 4.2.3.

26 See Section 4.4.1.

27 European Environment Agency, *Late Lessons from Early Warnings: Science, Precaution, Innovation*, Report No 1 (European Environment Agency, 2013) 17.

the precautionary principle under the WTO requires member states to balance the interests in ensuring biosafety and trading biotechnology. This makes the precautionary principle a ***balancing criterion*** that must be interpreted in the Alexian sense of the word, meaning that precaution itself is subject to judicial optimisation and balancing with other principles/interests. Additionally, precautionary measures on biosafety should be periodically ***re-examined in light of new scientific developments***. This ensures precautionary measures are ***dynamic*** (as opposed to ***static***). Indeed, by asking member states to re-examine these measures from time to time, the precautionary principle does not risk becoming a static or rhetoric tool.

For all these reasons, WTO judicial bodies should support, rather than be reticent towards, the adoption of the precautionary principle to biotechnology cases or, more generally, legal disputes involving scientific uncertainties on the safety or harmfulness of products to human health and/or the environment.[28] After all, this study emphasises the close link between the adoption of the precautionary principle and the WTO goal of sustainable development.

9.3.5 Implementing precaution in the context of biotechnology

Effective adoption of the precautionary principle might be pre-empted by the lack of indication of the standard of proof and level(s) of uncertainty that suffice to adopt precautionary measures on biosafety measures. In exploring this controversial aspect, this study highlights that the standard of proof adopted by WTO judicial bodies to address biotechnology legal disputes is too high – it seems to align with criminal cases.

This judicial approach is unjustified. The WTO could apply the standard of evidence taken in civil cases – *preponderance of evidence* (or *balance of probabilities*) – when the body of scientific evidence is sufficient in quantitative and qualitative terms and the precautionary principle is not invoked or does not apply. However, in all three WTO biotechnology cases, qualitatively insufficient evidence and requests to adopt the precautionary principle occur. Thus, the question arises to which extent the precautionary principle affects (or should affect) the evidentiary threshold to prove the safety or the harmfulness of biotechnology. Since biotechnology involves *high* risks to human health and/or the environment, the threshold of uncertainty for triggering precautionary measures under WTO law should be *low*. This is because of the logic behind the inverse relationship between the degree of scientific uncertainty and the degree of potential environmental or human health damage. Nevertheless, as precaution does not apply for every minor or imaginary threat, a certain threshold of risk – that is, *gravity*

28 As mentioned previously, further reasons for adopting precaution in the context of biotechnology lie in the fact that it can reverse, in some circumstances, the burden of proof, and it lowers the standard of proof to break stalemate cases and, accordingly, reduce the epistemic discretion of WTO decision-makers.

times *probability* of harm – must be reached. Establishing whether this threshold has been met might be particularly challenging for decision-makers examining biotechnology cases, if only because there is no agreement among scientists on the gravity and probability of biotechnology risks.

In this regard, the present study recommends the judicial adoption of a *scale of legal evidence and scientific (un)certainties* to guide WTO judicial bodies' evaluation of the state of knowledge concerning biotechnology and set the precautionary evidentiary threshold on a case-by-case basis.[29] The suggested scale outlines a hierarchy of uncertainties, considering the probabilities of harm and the related standard(s) of proof to apply in light of the considered level(s) of gravity. It combines the quantitative IPCC scale[30] and Weiss's qualitative legal scale.[31] In doing so, it provides a brief explanation of the legal and scientific perception of the different levels of evidence. As Eliason asserted:

> A solution of some sort must be found to the problem of the interpretation of scientific evidence. *EC – Hormones*, *EC – Biotech*, and *US/Canada – Hormones Suspension* are only the beginning of what will be an increasingly complex string of cases requiring in-depth evaluations of cutting-edge scientific technologies.[32]

The proposed scale of legal evidence and scientific (un)certainties offers a solution in this regard.

In exploring where the precautionary evidentiary threshold might fit, this study highlights that setting the evidentiary threshold for precautionary measures at the standard of *probable cause, reasonable belief* seems reasonable even under the WTO, if only because WTO decision-makers considered the criterion of *reasonableness* in all three biotechnology legal disputes.[33] Consequently, precautionary measures on biosafety should be substantiated by *plausible hypothesis supported by some evidence*,[34] which is the scientific level of certainty correspond-

29 See Section 8.4.

30 Likelihood scale used in the AR5. See guidance note for lead authors of the *IPCC Fifth Assessment Report on Consistent Treatment of Uncertainties* (Web Page), https://wg1.ipcc.ch/AR6/documents/AR5_Uncertainty_Guidance_Note.pdf.

31 Charles Weiss, 'Expressing Scientific Uncertainty' (2003) 2 *Law, Probability, and Risk* 25, 37–38; Charles Weiss, 'Communicating Uncertainty in Intelligence and Other Professions' (2007) 21(1) *International Journal of Intelligence and CounterIntelligence* 57, 61; Charles Weiss, 'Can There Be Science-Based Precaution?' (2006) 1 *Environmental Research Letters* 1, 3.

32 Antonia Eliason, 'Science Versus Law in WTO Jurisprudence: The (Mis)Interpretation of the Scientific Process and the (In)Sufficiency of Scientific Evidence in EC-Biotech' (2009) 41 *New York University Journal of International Law & Policy* 341, 400–401 (emphasis in original).

33 AB report, *US/Canada – Hormones Continued Suspension* [75]. See also AB report, *EC – Hormones* [172], [186]; Panel report, *EC – Biotech* [7.3028].

34 Weiss, 'Expressing Scientific Uncertainty' (n 31) 38.

ing to this legal standard of proof (i.e., *probable cause, reasonable belief*).[35] Also, in establishing the precautionary threshold, WTO judicial bodies should consider *positive correlations* and *inferences* stemming from frequentists' statistics relating to the impact of trading biotechnology to biosafety.[36] Indeed, this study underlines the importance of correlations and inferences for conducting *appropriate risk assessments* in the context of biotechnology, as summarised in Section 7.4.1.

To conclude, the developed scale of legal evidence and scientific (un)certainties might support effective implementation of the precautionary principle to tackle the epistemic issues in the context of biotechnology.

9.3.6 Allocating the burden of proof to establish a prima facie case and adopt biosafety measures in the context of biotechnology

This study demonstrates that in examining the establishment of a prima facie case and in allocating the burden of proof to establish this case and adopt biosafety measures in the context of biotechnology, the WTO judicial bodies' approach is lacking on many levels. The analysis on this topic in Section 6.2.3 leads to the following suggestions.

First, the appointed panel should allocate the traditional burden of proof to the applicant that should support its request(s) with *sufficient* and *adequate* (or appropriate) evidence. Facing the numerous unknowns stemming from scientific uncertainties in the context of biotechnology, panels should assess the *sufficiency* of evidence in quantitative *and* qualitative terms by considering both majority and minority scientific opinions.[37] Simultaneously, WTO decision-makers should deem a body of evidence *adequate* – or, as required by Article 5.1 of the *SPS Agreement*, *appropriate to the circumstances* – when it stems from a risk assessment that considered scientific *and* holistic data showing physical and social impacts of biotechnology on biosafety. Indeed, this study emphasises that the assessment of this technology cannot be reduced to a scientific matter.

Second, the appointed panel should assess whether there is sufficient and adequate or, rather, insufficient scientific evidence to establish a prima facie case. At this point, two alternative scenarios may present.

In the first scenario, decision-makers might establish that the case is characterised by sufficient, adequate and certain (meaning non-antithetical) evidence, which allows the applicant to prove the submitted claim or presumption and, in turn, to successfully establish a prima facie case. The parties must, accordingly, submit sufficient and adequate evidence supporting their claims or presumptions.

In the second scenario, decision-makers might find that the case presents sufficient (and arguably also adequate) but uncertain or insufficient scientific evidence. In either case, the empirical premises would be unreliable and characterised by

35 See Section 8.4.3.
36 See Section 7.4.1.
37 See Section 7.3.

uncertainty. In this respect, the present study highlights that the judicial consideration of the precautionary principle, the *pro homine* principle and the reliability of empirical premises might represent valid means to address these circumstances. In sum, the precautionary principle is a valuable tool guiding decision-makers to address the unreliability of empirical premises. It can reduce the epistemic discretion of decision-makers, affect the standard of proof by lowering the evidentiary requirements and reverse, in some circumstances, the burden of proof. Similarly, the application of *the pro homine* principle to the context of biotechnology would lead decision-makers to ascribe a prima facie priority to the protection of human health from risks posed by trading biotechnology. Additionally, considering and enhancing the *reliability of evidence* can help address cases in which the unreliability of empirical premises occurs, if only because more reliable evidence helps shape more reliable risk assessments informing WTO decision-makers about the effects of biotechnology on biosafety.

These suggestions mitigate the issues caused by the questionable judicial establishment of a prima facie case and allocation of the burden of proof to establish this case and to adopt biosafety measures in the context of biotechnology.

9.3.7 Creating a **bridge of knowledge** *between WTO decision-makers and experts of biotechnology*

This study highlights that the creation of an expert review group might support WTO decision-makers. This group should consider scientific and holistic data provided by scientists and social scientists (such as psychologists and sociologists), who are *experts through their knowledge of and expertise in* biotechnology. The group should also include expert witnesses, who, in the words of Judge Tulkens, have 'truly been experts through their personal history'[38] so as to become *experts through their experience* with biotechnology. This could build what can be defined as a *constructive bridge of knowledge* between WTO decision-makers and those with knowledge of, expertise in, and experience with biotechnology. This might also be useful for similar challenges around other new technologies, such as genome editing.[39]

As certain issues concerning the impact of biotechnology on biosafety 'are more social than scientific in character',[40] a *holistic evaluation of biotechnology*

38 Judge Tulkens, 'Closing Speech' *Monsanto Tribunal* (Web Page, October 2016), www.monsanto-tribunal.org/.

39 Robin Fears and Volker ter Meulen, 'Assessing Security Implications of Genome Editing: Emerging Points from an International Workshop' (2018) 6(34) *Frontiers in Bioengineering and Biotechnology* 1. See also Alessandra Guida, 'Are WTO Decisionmakers Regulating Technological Risks or Are Technological Risks Steering WTO Biotechnology Legal Decisions?' (2021) *Risk Analysis* 1; Rim Lassoued et al., 'Risk and Safety Considerations of Genome Edited Crops: Expert Opinion' (2019) 1 *Current Research in Biotechnology* 11.

40 Caroline E Foster, *Science and the Precautionary Principle in International Courts and Tribunals – Expert Evidence, Burden of Proof, and Finality* (Cambridge University Press, 2011) 177.

should supplement the scientific approach adopted under the WTO. Adopting a holistic approach means considering not only laboratory but also observational studies, which might reveal physical and social effects of biotechnology on human health and/or the environment.

In exploring who can potentially provide WTO judicial bodies with holistic data, this study highlights the key role of social scientists and expert witnesses. It also emphasises that the creation of an expert review group composed not only of scientists has several advantages. First, it would facilitate judicial understanding of the complexity surrounding biotechnology, which is not reduced to a scientific matter. Second, it would help untangle the complex relationship between law and science. Third, it would mitigate the scientific ethos under the WTO that, unsurprisingly, is also reflected in panels' process of appointment of only scientific experts. Finally, it would develop the concept of *expert* under the WTO to keep pace with the fast changes brought by current technology, which requires a rethink of who has expertise on the effects posed by biotechnology to biosafety.[41]

9.3.8 *Refining the concept of appropriateness of risk assessments in the context of biotechnology*

In all three biotechnology cases, WTO judicial bodies establishes that the contested precautionary measures on biosafety are not based on *appropriate risk assessments*. This study shows that the reason lies in the questionable judicial revision of risk assessments and the lack of clarification of what constitutes an appropriate risk assessment in contexts lacking certain scientific evidence.[42] In this view, this study identifies that, rather than searching for positive evidence of harm and verifying the existence of a causal linkage, WTO decision-makers could consider biosafety measures based on appropriate risk assessments when these assessments show *inferences* and *positive and multiple correlations*. Inferences and correlations, which might in some circumstances entail causation, can supplement the uncertain scientific evidence in the context of biotechnology. They can also show holistic data on the contested biotech products to aid panels and the AB to grasp the complexities surrounding biotechnology.

9.3.9 *Adopting a* multilevel degree of deference *as a new standard of review to examine biotechnology cases*

This study underlines that the standard of review under Article 11 of the *DSU*, which requires member states to conduct an *objective assessment of the matter*, is not suitable for examining scientifically uncertain scenarios surrounding the international trade in biotechnology, not least because it does not provide substantial

41 See Section 7.4.2.
42 See Section 7.4.1.

guidelines to decision-makers. In exploring a solution and considering that the AB excludes only a '*total* deference' standard, this study demonstrates the advantages of adopting a ***multilevel degree of deference as new standard of review*** to examine biotechnology legal disputes.[43]

This new standard recommends three levels of deference: (1) total deference of the assessment regarding the management of biotechnology risks to WTO states, (2) only partial deference to member states concerning the assessment of these risks, and (3) no deference to WTO states regarding the evaluation of whether the contested biosafety measures are proportional to the competing interest of trading biotechnology.

Through its three levels, the suggested standard provides substantial indications about the deferential levels that panels should apply in revising biotechnology cases. Its adoption can, in turn, support a reasoned balance between the autonomy of member states to adopt a precautionary ALOP and the need for consistent and effective enforcement of WTO law, which is the main function that a standard of review should accomplish. What is more, in providing substantial guidelines to WTO decision-makers, the adoption of the *multilevel degree of deference* standard would facilitate the performance of a well-structured proportionality analysis in the context of biotechnology.

9.4 Future research

Future investigations may build on the findings of this study and shine further light on its underexplored topic. One question for future research is whether there is room under the WTO to design rules that take account of the main principles of *social and environmental justice*, which are intrinsically interconnected.[44] This could contribute to a better alignment between WTO law and international human rights law. This study shows that the WTO aims at facilitating international trade while protecting the environment from adverse impacts caused by trade relations. According to Giuseppe Palmisano, President of the European Committee of Social Rights, 'deterioration of the environment has an undeniable impact on the enjoyment of many social rights'.[45] This is highly relevant considering that the *GATT Agreement* 'includes a few legal loopholes of a nature that

43 See Section 6.3.3.

44 It is sufficient to observe that in 2009, the Human Impact Report highlighted that the social well-being of four billion people was adversely affected by environmental disasters that have been largely caused by human activities. Kofi Annan et al., *Human Impact Report Climate Change – The Anatomy of a Silent Crisis* (Global Humanitarian Forum, 2009).

45 Giuseppe Palmisano, 'Council of Europe, High-level Conference – Environmental Protection and Human Rights' (Online, 27 February 2020), www.coe.int/en/web/european-social-charter/european-committee-of-social-rights/-/asset_publisher/t5SoWyFqMYBR/content/deterioration-of-the-environment-has-an-undeniable-impact-on-the-enjoyment-of-many-social-rights-said-giuseppe-palmisano-at-the-high-level-conference-?_101_INSTANCE_t5SoWyFqMYBR_viewMode=view/>.

could authorize a country to close its market to products manufactured in violation of [fundamental social] rights'.[46] Put differently, international trade of goods that negatively impact the environment (and/or human health) contributes to undermining full enjoyment of social rights. WTO states could conceivably close their markets to those products in light of the *GATT Agreement*. Nevertheless, ensuring international social justice is not as such a goal of the WTO.[47] Future research could explore the potential role of the WTO in relation to the guarantee of social rights.

Another potential topic for future investigations is the emergence of new legal concepts and rights that might affect the distribution of new technologies. For instance, future studies on the concept of *ecocide* might reveal useful insights on the growing awareness of a need to address human health and environmental damage as *crimes*. There are numerous calls for further research on whether, and if so how, the crime of ecocide might (or should) be included in the *Rome Statute* alongside crimes against humanity.[48] This would shed light on the changes and development of the law over the technology era and how these changes might affect the international trade of potentially harmful technology. Similarly, it might be interesting to investigate how the emergence of new rights, such as the *rights of nature*, can affect the regulation of new technology products, which can potentially undermine enjoyment of these rights.

The findings from this study suggest a fractured legal framework for the regulation of the international trade in biotechnology. This invites further interdisciplinary research to better understand the capacity of the law, especially WTO law, to navigate the uncertain and troubled waters of regulating new technologies.

9.5 Final observations

The WTO judicial balance between trade and non-trade interests in the context of biotechnology happens by chance and not by design. This study suggests a number of tools and processes, including a structured proportionality

46 Alain Supiot, 'What International Social Justice in the Twenty-First Century' (Keynote address to the XXI World Congress of the International Society for Labour and Social Security Law, Cape Town, 15–18 September 2015) 14, https://islssl.org/wp-content/uploads/2015/11/Supiot_CapeTown_September_2015_EN.pdf. See also Gabrielle Zoe Marceau and Aline Doussin, 'Le Droit Du Commerce International, Les Droits Fondamentaux et Les Considérations Sociales' (2009) 2(2) *L'Observateur des Nations Unies* 241.

47 Supiot (n 46) 14.

48 Isabella Kaminski, 'Vulnerable Nations Call for Ecocide to Be Recognized As an International Crime' *The Climate Docket* (Online, 6 December 2019), www.climatedocket.com/2019/12/06/ecocide-international-criminal-court-vanuatu/; International Monsanto Tribunal Advisory Opinion (The Hague, 18 April 2017), www.monsanto-tribunal.org/upload/asset_cache/1016160509.pdf; Phil Henderson, 'The Poetics of Settler Fatalism: Responses to Ecocide from within the Anthropocene' (2019) 7(1) *Pivot* 5; Owain Jones, Kate Rigby and Linda Williams, 'Everyday Ecocide, Toxic Dwelling, and the Inability to Mourn' (2020) 12(1) *Environmental Humanities* 388.

analysis and scale of legal evidence to address scientific uncertainties, to improve the WTO's handling of trade disputes involving biotechnology. In doing so, this study reveals several challenges for the WTO dispute settlement system that would need to be addressed to help the WTO balance between free trade and biosafety. These challenges must be understood in the broader context of the WTO and its current crisis.

Indeed, it is well known that the WTO dispute settlement mechanism is facing an 'impasse'[49] and urgently needs 'broader reforms to the WTO system'.[50] Elliot, in 2019, predicted that the WTO is 'set to plunge into the biggest crisis in its 25-year history'.[51] In 2018, McDougall stressed that '[i]f a solution is not found, the already severely compromised dispute settlement system will be rendered dysfunctional by late 2019'.[52] These predictions came true when, in 2019, US President Trump crippled the AB on the grounds it overstepped its bounds. His action was not reversed by the new US President Biden, who said that he would not appoint new members to the AB because the United States continues to have systemic concerns with the functioning of the judicial body as have all previous administrations over the past 16 years.[53] This, in effect, paralysed the WTO's ability to resolve trade disputes between countries.

The solution to the WTO's challenges, McDougall argues, might lie in guiding principles for the dispute settlement bodies:

> Restoration of the dispute settlement function may only be possible as part of a new bargain that updates the balance of rights and obligations . . . and

49 Robert McDougall, 'Impasse in the WTO Dispute Settlement Body: Consequences and Responses' (2018) 11 *ECIPE Policy Brief* 1.

50 Andrew Stoler, 'Crisis in the WTO Appellate Body and the Need for Wider WTO Reform Negotiations' *IIT* (Web Page) 4, https://iit.adelaide.edu.au/system/files/media/documents/201904/IIT%20PB02%20Crisis%20WTO%20Appellate.pdf.

51 Larry Elliot, 'WTO Faces Crisis over Settlement Disputes Unless Trump Backs Off' *The Guardian* (Online, 8 December 2019), www.theguardian.com/world/2019/dec/08/wto-faces-crisis-over-settlement-disputes-unless-trump-backs-off.

52 Robert McDougall, 'Crisis in the WTO: Restoring the WTO Dispute Settlement Function' (Centre for International Governance Innovation [CIGI] Papers No 194, October 2018) 1, www.cigionline.org/sites/default/files/documents/Paper%20no.194.pdf.

53 Bryce Baschuk, 'Biden Picks Up Where Trump Left Off in Hard-Line Stances at WTO' *Bloomberg* (Online, 23 February 2021), www.bloomberg.com/news/articles/2021-02-22/biden-picks-up-where-trump-left-off-in-hard-line-stances-at-wto. As of this writing, the Biden administration strongly supported the appointment of Ngozi Okonjo-Iweala, Nigeria's ex-finance minister, as WTO Director-General. She was frontrunner for the role until the Trump administration wanted another woman, South Korea's Yoo Myung-hee who eventually withdrew her candidacy. If confirmed in the role, Ngozi Okonjo-Iweala would be the first woman and the first African to lead the WTO. BBC News, 'Biden Ends Deadlock over First African and First Woman to Lead WTO' (Online, 5 February 2021), www.bbc.com/news/business-55958682.

> [a]rriving at such an accommodation might be facilitated by consideration of a number of guiding principles by which dispute settlement should operate.[54]

This study proposes to consider proportionality and the precautionary principles as valuable means to balance trade/economic and non-trade/non-economic obligations. This can contribute to a significant reform of the WTO institution. Indeed, this study suggests ways and means through which the WTO dispute settlement mechanism could become more transparent while also accommodating the whole spectrum of interests of its member states, from trade to public health, environmental protection and economic growth. Until now, the WTO has failed to appreciate the interconnectedness of these interests. In fact, as recent as 2019, WTO Director-General Roberto Azevêdo denied any correlation between products that find their way into trade flows, such as biotech products, and agriculture damage or deforestation.[55] As Fournier observes, 'When the head of the . . . WTO says trade does not impact the environment, we should all be worried'.[56]

It would be perilous to ignore risks to health or the environment just because scientific uncertainties around the risks remain. This rings especially true during our current global health crisis. The COVID-19 pandemic clearly demonstrates the importance of taking precautionary actions to reduce further risk to humans, even when uncertainties remain about the transmission and precise effects of the virus. The same argument applies to the risks of trading biotechnology.

The WTO would, thus, be well advised to reconsider the importance of precaution and shift its focus from enabling free trade to supporting *sustainable* trade for living beings and the environment. The suggestions offered in this study can contribute to this aim.

To conclude with a well-known quotation of Christian Lange: 'Technology is a useful servant but a dangerous master'.[57] Finding a point of equilibrium between technological development and biosafety is key to exploiting the incredible advantages offered by new technologies without being exploited by them.

54 McDougall (n 52), 12–13.

55 'Sewing, Azevedo, Malmstrom on Global Trade: Davos Panel' *Bloomberg* (Online, 24 January 2019), www.bloomberg.com/news/videos/2019-01-24/sewing-azevedo-malmstrom-on-global-trade-davos-panel-video. But see Juan Robalino and Luis Diego Herrera, 'Trade and Deforestation: What Have We Found?' *WTO* (Web Page, 2010), www.wto.org/english/res_e/publications_e/wtr10_robalino_herrera_e.htm.

56 Perrine Fournier, 'WTO Chief Is in Denial over Climate Impact of Trade' *Climate Home News* (Online, 30 January 2019), www.climatechangenews.com/2019/01/30/wto-chief-denial-climate-impact-trade/.

57 Hjalmar Branting and Christian Lange, 'Internationalism' *The Nobel Prize* (Web Page, 13 December 1921), www.nobelprize.org/prizes/peace/1921/lange/lecture/.

Index

1947 GATT Agreement 42
1994 GATT Agreement 42
2030 Agenda for Sustainable Development 7

abstract weight, in law of balancing 114, 118–119
African (Banjul) Charter on Human and Peoples' Rights 79
Agenda 21 160–161
Agreement Establishing the World Trade Organization see *WTO Agreement*
Agreement of Safeguards 34
Agreement on Agriculture (AoA) 34–35
agricultural technologies (AgTech) and hunger reduction goals 3–4
Alexy, Robert 36, 100, 109, 113–114
Alexy's theory of balancing structure 113–118, 211; reliability of evidence 298
Alexy's weight formula 121–122
alien species, 81, 83; *see also* invasive alien species (IAS)
allergenicity 12–13
Ambrus, Monika 175
analytical methodology 32–33
Andenas, Mads 97
Angell, Marcia 258
animal and plant health *see SPS Agreement*
animals, wild, as exhaustible natural resources 158–159
antibiotic resistance 13
Anti-Dumping Agreement 213, 220–221
Appellate Body (AB) *see* WTO judicial bodies
appropriateness of risk 236–239
Aristotle 99
Article 5.7 *(SPS Agreement)* 264–271, 295
Article 11 (ICESCR) 294
Article 27.3 *(TRIPs Agreement)* 19–20
Article XX *(GATT Agreement)* 47–56, 105, 119, 158–160
Australia - Apples 237–238
Australian court system 161
Australia - Salmon (1998) 81
Australia - Tobacco Plain Packaging (Indonesia) (2018) 70–71
Ayres, Glyn 50
Azevêdo, Roberto 308

balance of probabilities as standard of proof 275
balancing test 100, 107–110
Baltic Sea Declaration 166
Bangkok Declaration 160
Barak, Aharon 99, 100, 108
Barcelo III, John J. 206
Basel Convention 70, 74, 84, 85–87, 274
Bayesian scale 278–286
Beatty, David 100
Beck, Ulrich 255
Berbera, Hayde Rodarte 123
Bergen Declaration 160
Biden, President Joe 307
biodiversity 17, 80–84
biosafety measures: definition and overview 5; obligation to exchange information 75–76; *SPS Agreement* 150
biotechnology: benefits and risks summarised *22–23*; definition and overview 3–4; and economic development 11–12; and enhanced food production 9–11; ethical and moral dimensions 20–21, 34–35; research, funding sources 127; risks to environment 16–18; risks to human health 12–16; social issues 18–23

biotechnology cases: standard of review 212–226
biotechnology products: economic benefits of 4; likeness with conventional products 153; Process and Production Methods (PPMs) 153; risks of 4–5
Blackstone Ratio 274
Bohanes, Jan 213, 220
Boisseau, Dr. 128, 216
Boobis, Dr. 128, 216
Border Tax Adjustments 155
Brandt Report 65
Brazil - Retreaded Tyres (2007) 51
Brazil - Taxation (2017) 48–49, 51, 55, 61
BRS Conventions 85–87
Brundtland Report 29, 78
burden of argumentation, in law of balancing 117
burden of persuasion 172, 206
burden of production 172, 206
burden of proof: allocation of 210; *EC - Hormones* 185; to establish prima facie case 293–294; and precautionary measures 188–189, 193; reversal of 171–176; suggestions for improvement 209–212
Button, Catherine 233–234, 238–239

Calisi, Judge Anthony P. 273
Cameron, James 173
Canada - Dairy (2002) 202, 206
Cannizzaro, Enzo 98
carcinogens 15, 86, 156, 170–171; glyphosate 277; and glyphosate 253–254; tobacco 251–252; *see also EC - Hormones*
Cartagena Protocol on Biosafety 5, 71–73, 75, 82–83, 163, 174, 243, 270
CETA (Comprehensive Economic and Trade Agreement) 43
Cheyne, Ilona 156, 237, 242, 269
Chile - Price Band System (2007) 202
China - Rare Earths 54
China - Raw Materials (2011) 48, 52, 55, 71
Cho, Tae-yul 188
Christoforou, Theofanis 223, 245–246
climate change 278–280; challenges of 3–4; GM (genetically modified) crops and resilience 10
Codex Alimentarius (Codex) 267
Colombia: and glypohsate/coca court decision 170–171; and obligations for environmental protection 281–282
COMM (2000) 151, 168
Communication on the Precautionary Principle 140–141
competing interests: abstract weight of 119; balancing and proportionality analysis 106; identification of 118
Comprehensive Economic and Trade Agreement (CETA) 43
conceptual methodology 32–33
conflict-resolution techniques 124
conservation, definitions and interpretations 52, 55
Constitution of the World Health Organization 69
constructive bridge of knowledge 260, 303–304
consumers, responsibility to inform 75–76
contamination, environmental 74–75
Convention on Biological Diversity (CBD) 80–81, 82, 83
Convention on International Trade in Endangered Species (CITES) 174
Cooney, Rosie 173–174
correlation 251–253, 286; *see also* multiple correlations
costs and benefits, as criteria for precautionary measures 168
Cottier, Thomas 98, 105, 183
COVID-19 pandemic 7, 8, 272
Crawford-Brown, Douglas 130, 260
credibility of evidence 126; *see also* reliability of evidence in balancing process
crime, environmental damage as 306
CRISPR technology 7

Da Silva, Virgilio Afonso 109
deference: *multilevel degree of deference* 224–226; *total deference* standard 213, 220–222
democratic deficit 59–61
demonstration of probability, inference as 250–251
de novo standard 213, 220–221
De Oliveira Mazzuoli, Valerio 123
De Tavernier, Johan 19
discriminatory measures, arbitrary or unjustifiable 47

Doha Ministerial Declaration 85–86, 163
Dworkin, Ronald 114

Earth Summit (1992) 80
EC - Asbestos (2001) 51, 155, 157
EC - Biotech 23, 35, 60, 82, 139, 152, 232; allocation of burden of proof 204–209; analysis 194–198; background and overview 190–192; establishment of *prima facie* case 201–204; and inference 251; inferred sufficiency of evidence 266; judicial interpretations 236–239; key findings 192–193; *probable cause/reasonable belief* standard 283–284; quantitative interpretation of risk 239–243
EC - Hormones 23, 35, 71, 73, 141, 217; allocation of burden of proof 204–209; analysis 194–198; background and overview 182–184; establishment of *prima facie* case 201–204; holistic data 255; and inference 251; judicial interpretations 236–239; key findings 184–186; precautionary principle 276–277; *probable cause/reasonable belief* standard 283–284; quantitative interpretation of risk 240–242; role of panel 257; sufficiency of evidence 231
ecocide 306
EC - Tariff Preferences 45
effectiveness, as criterion for precautionary measures 166
Ehlers, William 188
Eliason, Antonia 127, 128, 246, 268, 301
Elliott, Larry 307
Elsig, Manfred 124
empirical methodology and legal doctrine 32–33
environmental contamination 74–75
environmental law, international, and WTO law 79–88
environmental rights as human rights 76
environmental risks 16–18
EPA (Environmental Protection Agency) Report (2016) 126
epistemic discretion 131–134, 135
epistemic issues 93, 292–293; and precautionary principle 165–171; precaution as solution 298–300
European Committee of Social Rights 305
European Convention on Human Rights 102, 144
European Court of Human Rights (ECtHR) 102, 123, 144
European Environmental Agency (EEA) Report (2013) 285
expert review groups 259–260; *see also* panels
expert witnesses *see* panels

false negatives and false positives, precautionary principle 148–149
Fisher, Elizabeth 160
fisheries 151
food allergies 12–13
Food and Agricultural Organization (FAO) 9–10
food-labelling regulations 20, 76
food safety *see SPS Agreement*
Forte, Stephanie 162
Foster, Caroline E. 172–173, 245, 258
Fournier, Perrine 308
Freedman, David A. 252
Freestone David 161
free trade, pre-eminence of and bias toward 59–64, 92, 94, 118, 244–245
free trade agreements (FTAs) 43
frequentist probabilities 286
Fukushima Dai-ichi Nuclear Power Plant (FDNPP) 73

Gabčikovo-Nagymaros Project 143, 173
gatekeeper role of WTO judicial bodies 245–249
GATT Agreement (1994) 34, 42; Article XX 47–56, 105, 119, 158–160, 282; precautionary principle 154–160
GE crops *see* GMOs
Gehring, Markus W. 143, 145
General Agreement on Tariffs and Trade (GATT 1947) 42
German Federal Constitutional Court 115, 116
Giovanni Pesce and Others case (2016) 254, 286
glyphosate 13–14, 15, 74–75, 86, 170–171, 253–254, 277
GMOs (genetically modified organisms): definition and overview 3; GE crops and labelling regulations 76;

GM seeds and crops 76; and hunger reduction 9–11; *see also EC - Biotech*
Goodstein, David 280
Gowan Comércio Internacional e Serviços L^da v Ministero della Salute 146
Gremmen, Bart 275
growth factors *see* hormones, synthetic
Gruszczynski, Lukasz 230
Guzman, Andrew T. 246

Häberli, Christian 191
Halle, Mark 63–64
Hammurabi, Code of 101
Hardeman, Mr. (Monsanto lawsuit) 253
Harding, Ronnie 160
Harrison, James 67–68
hazardous wastes 86
health, human, protection of, as WTO goal 44–45
health and environmental safety measures: pre-eminence of free trade 59–64
health risks, causal risks 250–251
herbicides 74–75; herbicide residues 16; herbicide-resistant crops 13–14
Hilf, Meinhard 106
holistic data in risk assessment 223–224, 254–257, 303–304
hormones, synthetic 182–183; *see also EC - Hormones; US/Canada - Hormones Continued Suspension*
Horn, Henrik 127, 191
Howse, Robert 127, 191
human health and the environment, in context of GATT Agreement 47–56
human rights law, international 65–68; health, human, adverse effects, obligations to consider 71–72; precautionary approach, obligations to take 72–73; responsibility to inform consumers 75–76; and right to health 69–76; trading biotechnology, obligations to prevent risks 74–75
hunger: and distribution inequalities 9–10; and GMOs 9–11

ICESCR (International Covenant on Economic, Social and Cultural Rights) 69–70, 78
IHRs (International Health Regulations) 73, 74
India, farmer suicides 19
Indonesia - Chicken (2017) 51, 61
inferences as demonstration of probability 250–251, 286, 304
INOVAR-AUTO program (Brazil) 48–49
institutional dimension of precautionary principle 146–147
intellectual property rights (IPRs) 18–19, 76
intensity of interference, in law of balancing 114–115, 119, 120–121, 125
Inter-American Court of Human Rights (IACtHR) 102, 123, 281–282
Intergovernmental Panel on Climate Change (IPCC) 278–280
International Agency for Research on Cancer (IARC) 15, 170, 183
International Bank for Reconstruction and Development (IBRD) 42
International Court of Justice (ICJ) 103, 123
(ICESCR) International Covenant on Economic, Social and Cultural Rights 66
international environmental law: and WTO law, possible normative antimonies 89–91
International Health Regulations (IHRs) 71
international human rights law: and WTO law, possible normative antimonies 77–78
International Monetary Fund (IMF) 42
International Monsanto Tribunal 258, 274
International Plant Protection Convention (IPPC) 75
International Trade Organization (ITO) 42
International Tribunal for the Law of the Sea (ITLOS) 143–145, 283
invasive alien species (IAS) 17, 80–81
IPCC (Intergovernmental Panel on Climate Change) 278–280

Jaeckel, Aline L. 173
Japan - Agricultural Products II (1999) 82, 231
Japan - Apples (2003) 82, 105, 231
Jasanoff, Sheila 250
Johannesburg Declaration on Sustainable Development (2002) 78

Johannesburg Plan of Implementation 161
Johnson, Mr. (Monsanto lawsuit) 253–254
Joseph, Sarah 60
judicial dimension of precautionary principle 147–148

Kaye, David H. 252
Korea - Alcoholic Beverage 218
Korea - Radionuclides (2018) 73, 244, 271
Korea - Various Measures on Beef (2000) 50, 51, 52, 104, 105, 120, 298
Ksentini, Fatma Zohra 78–79
Kumar, Mohan 191
Kumm, Mattias 28, 100
Kuo, Ming Sung 97
Kurlsson, Mikael 30–31

Lange, Christian 308
law of balancing: in Alexey's structure 114–116; weighing and balancing exercise 50, 104; *see also* proportionality
"least trade restrictive" measures 51–52
legal scale 279–280, 301
Leonelli, Giulia Claudia 16
likeness, central concept of 155–157
Lixinski, Lucas 124
Lockhart, Nicolas 213, 220

Macmillan, Fiona 57, 72, 219, 256
marine habitats 83–84, 87–88
Marrakesh Agreement 42
Mathews, Jud 110
Max Planck Commentaries on World Trade Law 45
McBeth, Adam 68
McDougall, Robert 307–308
Megiddo, Tamar 112
Meléndez-Ortiz, Ricardo 63–64
methodology used in book 32–34
Ministerial Declaration of the Seventh Trilateral Government Conference 151
Mitchell, Andrew D. 50, 106
Mohallem, Freitas 124
Monsanto 19, 253–254, 256; International Monsanto Tribunal 258, 274
Moore, Julia A. 191
multilevel degree of deference 304–305
multiple correlations 250, 252–253, 254, 261, 304

Nagoya Protocol 71, 73, 83
national treatment obligation 154–155
natural resources, exhaustibility of 52, 55–56
"necessary" measures, definitions and interpretations 49–52; and alternative measure 50–51; historical summary 53–54; weighing and balancing exercise 50
necessity test 99–100, 104, 107
Neugebauer, Regine 238
New Delhi Declaration 161
non-discrimination and consistency, as criteria for precautionary measures 167
normative antinomies: potential resolution of 296–297; WTO law and international environmental law 79–88; WTO law and international human rights law 65–68; WTO law and right to health 69–76; WTO law and right to healthy environment 76–79
normative issues 293
normative methodology 34
Norton, Bryan 162
Novella, Steven 252
numeral unit spread assessment pedigree (NUSAP) system 259

objectivity of assessments 214–218, 265
observational studies 255
Okonjo-Iweala, Ngozi 7
Orozco, Claudia 188
Overby, Penny 66

Palecka, Peter 183
Palmisano, Giuseppe 305
panels: composition of in WTO dispute-settlement system 44; and expert witnesses 126–128, 129–130; guidelines given to 196, 213; and margin of discretion 112, 128; and objective assessment 201–202, 204; role of advisors 257–260; and standards of review 214–219
patents 18–19, 76

Pauwelyn, Joost 124, 130, 260
Peel, Jacqueline 247–248
peer review process 130–131
pesticide use 14, 84–88; and cancer 277; pesticide residues and human health 15–16
Petersmann, Ernst-Ulrich 71
plausible hypothesis 282, 283, 284, 288, 301
Poli, Sara 207, 243
positive correlations 252–253, 286, 304
Post Normal Science (PNS) literature 259
precautionary approach: implementation 300–302; obligations to take 72–73; as solution to epistemic issues 298–300
precautionary measures 8; and burden of proof 188–189, 193; obligation to take, under UNFCCC 87–88; and scale of legal evidence 280–285
precautionary principle 26, 27–31, 134–135; background and overview 138–143; and biodiversity 80; burden of proof in stalemate cases 171–176; in context of biotechnology 136–138; criticism of 145–146; as decision-making tool 211–212; epistemic issues in biotechnology 165–171; and evidentiary threshold 276–277; and free trade agreements (FTAs) 43; gateway provisions in WTO law 149–160; *GATT Agreement* as gateway 154–160; migration across jurisdictions 143–146; multilateral environmental agreements 163–164; proportionality analysis 131–134; risk assessment 153–154; and "sufficient" scientific evidence 195; sustainable development goals 160–163; three dimensions 146–149; timely action 142–143; and *total deference* standard 222; and uncertainty 141–142; and WTO requirements 195
preponderance of evidence 300; as standard of proof 275
Preston, Brian J. 276
Prévost, Denise 243
prima facie cases: and burden of proof 204–209, 210–211, 302–303; establishment of 201–204; evidentiary requirements 203–204; and scientific uncertainty 204
probable cause/reasonable belief standard 282–284, 301
probatio diabolica 207–208, 265–266
procedural dimension of precautionary principle 147
Pro Homine (pro personae) principle in balancing process 123–125, 134, 212, 297, 303
proportionality: background and overview 97–99; as criterion for precautionary measures 166–167; migration across jurisdictions 101–103; proportionality balancing 26; in standard of review 224; structure 99–101; under the WTO 104–107
proportionality analysis 28–31; adoption of 297–298; Alexy's theory of balancing structure 113–118; Article XX *(GATT Agreement)* 105; balancing trade and non-trade interests 296; biotechnology scenarios, applied to 118–122; justification for use in WTO cases 103–112; *Pro Homine* principle 123–125; proportionality stricto sensu (balancing test) 107–110; reliability of evidence in balancing process 125–131
protective measures 46–48, 51–52, 94
Pulido, Bernal 100, 108, 116
Pulp Mills case 173

quantitative interpretation of risk 239–243

Ranger Pro herbicide 253
reasoned judicial balance 29, 88, 92, 95, 96, 111, 195, 247, 293, 296
"relating to" parameter, definitions and interpretations 55–56, 62–63
reliability of empirical premises, in law of balancing 115, 120
reliability of evidence 125–131, 134, 303
Report of the Independent Commission on International Development Issues 65
Report of the United Nations Conference on Trade and Development 60–61
"respect, protect and fulfil," obligations to 69–70
Ribeiro, Dilton 123
rights of citizens contrasted with rights of states 70

rights of nature 306
right to a healthy environment 67, 256; and WTO law 76–79
right to development 12, 65–66
right to food 10, 66, 256
right to freedom of scientific research 256
right to health 16, 67, 69–76, 256
Rio Declaration on Environment and Development (1992) 73, 80, 139, 141, 142, 168
Rise of Environmental Crime, The (UNEP) 274
risk assessment 126–127; appropriate 304; and establishment of *prima facie* cases 203; quantitative interpretation 239–243; and social impacts 222–224; threshold of risk 300–301
risk of harm, environmental and human 140–141
Rome Statute 306
Rotterdam Convention 84, 85–87
Roundup (glyphosate) 13–14, 15, 74–75, 86, 170–171, 253–254, 277
Russian - Pigs 271

safeguarding measures 34
scales: of legal evidence 8; qualitative (Weiss) 301; quantitative (IPCC) 301
Schrijver, Nico 160, 161–162
Scientific Committee on Veterinary Measures relating to Public Health 187–188
scientific development, as criteria for precautionary measures 168–169
scientific evidence: and establishment of *prima facie* cases 203–204; insufficiency contrasted with uncertainty 208–209; for protective measures 58; sufficient and appropriate, defining 210; sufficient and insufficient evidence and *prima facie* cases 205
scientific evidence, insufficient 151; Article 5.7 of *SPS Agreement* 264–271; Bayesian scale 278–286; evidentiary threshold and precautionary principle 276–277; judicial interpretation 265–271; and SPS measures 207; standards of proof 272–275
scientific evidence, sufficient 294–295; advisors to panels, role of 257–260; appropriateness, determination of 249–257; "appropriateness" defined 232–236; holistic data 254–257; judicial interpretations 236–239; "principles" defined 230–231; reliability of evidence 260; selection of evidence, arbitrary nature of 243–245; "sufficiency" defined 231–232; WTO judicial bodies' gatekeeper role 245–249
scientific uncertainty 8; contrasted with insufficient scientific evidence 93; precautionary approach, obligations to take 72–73; and precautionary principle 168–169; and re-examination of precautionary measures 168–169
Scobbie, Iain 174
Seabed Disputes Chamber 283
seabed mining 143–144
seed saving 18–19, 76
Segger, Marie-Claire Cordonier 143, 145
Shimizu, Akio 191
Smith, Kelly 130, 260
sociocultural factors *see* holistic data
socio-economic considerations: and precautionary principle 146; and right to health 72; social and environmental justice 305–306; socio-economic justice 18
SPS Agreement 57–59, 73, 93, 133; Article 3.3 152–154; Article 5.7 149–152, 264–271; and man-made risks 183; preamble 152–154; precautionary principle 149–154; proportionality analysis 105; and risk assessments 184; scientific principles, definitions 230–231
SPS (sanitary and phytosanitary) measures 149
stalemate cases 26, 93; breaking 298; burden of proof and precautionary principle 171–176; judicial, breaking 31; precautionary principle to break 131–134
standards of proof 272–275
standards of review 212–226; multilevel degree of deference 304–305; suggested improvements 220–226; suitability of 214–219
Stockholm Convention 84–87, 163
Stockholm Declaration (1972) 78
Stone Sweet, Alec 100, 110

structured judicial balance 29, 88, 92, 95, 96, 111, 195, 247, 293, 296
suicides, Indian farmers 19
suitability test 99, 105, 107
sustainable development 29, 63–64, 66; and precautionary principle 160–163
Sustainable Development Goals (United Nations) 3–4, 7
synthetic hormones *see* hormones, synthetic

Tătar v Romania 144
TBT Agreement 57–59; proportionality analysis 105
Thai - Cigarettes (1990) 49–50, 71
Thayyil, Naveen 240
Theory of Constitutional Rights, A (Alexey) 113–114
Thomas, Gigesh 19
tobacco products 70–71
total deference standard 213, 220–222
trade 23–28; biotech risks, obligations to prevent 74–75; epistemic issues 26; judicial issues 25–26; and non-trade interests, balancing 25, 28, 296; normative issues 24–25; trade measures, process to challenge 63–64
trade liberalisation *see* free trade, pre-eminence of and bias toward
Transatlantic Trade and Investment Partnership (TTIP) 43
Treaty on Plant Genetic Resources 76, 82
triadic scale, German Federal Constitutional Court 115, 116
TRIPs (Trade-Related Aspects of Intellectual Property Rights) Agreement 19–20, 76, 106
Trouwborst, Arie 163
Trump, President Donald 307
TTIP (Transatlantic Trade and Investment Partnership) 43
Tufte, Edward R. 251
Tulkens, Judge 256, 258
Tuna - Dolphin (1991) 50
Tuna - Dolphin II (1994) 50
Turnquest Moulto, Danielle 162

uncertainty: and precautionary principle 141–142; and premise of precautionary principle 30; scientific 26; *see also* scientific uncertainty
UNCLOS (United Nations Convention on the Law of the Sea) 83–84, 85, 87
UNCTAD (United Nations Conference on Trade and Development) 60–61
UN Declaration on the Right to Development (1986) 65–66
United Nations Conference on Environment and Development (UNCED) 160
United Nations Environment Programme (UNEP) 2019 report 8
United Nations Fish Stocks Agreement 272
United Nations Framework Convention on Climate Change (UNFCCC) 10–11, 85, 87–88
United Nations Human Rights Committee (UNHRC) 102
Universal Declaration (1948) 69
US/Canada - Hormones Continued Suspension (2008) 23, 35, 71, 73, 127–130, 238; allocation of burden of proof 204–209; analysis 194–198; arbitrary selection of evidence 244–245; background and overview 186–188; establishment of *prima facie* case 201–204; and inference 251; key findings 188–190; *probable cause/reasonable belief* 283; quantitative interpretation of risk 241; role of panel 257–258; sufficiency of evidence 231, 266, 268–269; WTO in gatekeeper role 246–247
US Food Quality Protection Act (1996) 285
US - Gambling (2005) 202
US - Gasoline (1996) 55, 159, 164, 243
US - Hot Rolled 220
US - Oil Country Tubular Goods Sunset Reviews (2004) 202
US - Restrictions on Imports of Tuna (1991) 61
US - Shrimp (1998) 52, 55, 62, 105, 158–159, 243
US - Wool Shirts and Blouses (1997) 204

values, incommensurable 109
Van Den Belt, Henk 275
Vienna Convention on the Law of Treaties (VCLT) 164
Vienna Declaration on Human Rights and Programme of Action 65

Watercourses Convention (1997) 162
Weeramantry, Judge 175
weighing and balancing exercise 105
weight formula 116–117, 121–122
weight of evidence (WoE) 126
Weiss, Charles 271, 279, 287, 301
WHO Constitution 69–70
Winham, Gilbert 191, 192
Wirth, David A. 81, 87
world hunger *see* hunger
WTO (World Trade Organization): background and overview 5; Committee on Trade and Environment (CTE) 137; dispute-settlement system 43–44; DSB (dispute settlement body) 44; history and role 42–43; judicial and epistemic challenges 88, 92–93; judicial bodies and gatekeeper role 245–249; mandate and agreements 42–43; protection of human health and the environment as goals 44–46
WTO Agreement 5, 24, 159; preamble 44–45; WTO judicial bodies 6–7
WTO (World Trade Organization) law: challenging cases 5–6; gateway provisions to precautionary principle 149–160; and international environmental law 79–88; and international trade law 65–68; lack of definitions 235, 236; multilateral environmental agreements 163–164; and right to a healthy environment 76–79; and right to health 69–76; science-centric requirements and biotech 24; and standard of review 213–214
WTO Rules of Conduct 128–129
Wynne, Brian 238

Yokota, Jun 183

Zander, Joakim 174
Zero Hunger, Sustainable Development Goals 3–4
Zleptnig, Stefan 97